CHERRYPICKERS' GUIDE

TO RARE DIE VARIETIES OF UNITED STATES COINS

Fourth Edition · Volume II

Half Dimes Through Dollars, Gold, and Commemoratives

To Matthew ... Enjoy !

2000-P Sacagawea Dollar,
Enhanced Tail Feathers

Bill Fivaz 9/21/24

Bill Fivaz · J.T. Stanton

foreword by Q. David Bowers

The Cherrypickers' Guide to Rare Die Varieties of United States Coins

© 2006 Whitman Publishing, LLC
3101 Clairmont Road • Suite C • Atlanta GA 30329

The WCG™ grid used throughout this publication is patent pending.

All rights reserved, including duplication of any kind and storage in electronic or visual retrieval systems. Permission is granted for writers to use a reasonable number of brief excerpts and quotations in printed reviews and articles, provided credit is given to the title of the work and the author. Written permission from the publisher is required for other uses of text, illustrations, and other content, including in books and electronic or other media.

Correspondence concerning this book may be directed to the publisher, at the address above.

ISBN: 0794820530 • Printed in China

Disclaimer: Expert opinion should be sought in any significant numismatic purchase. This book is presented as a guide only. No warranty or representation of any kind is made concerning the completeness of the information presented. The authors are professional numismatists who regularly buy, trade, and sometimes hold certain of the items discussed in this book.

Caveat: The price estimates given are subject to variation and differences of opinion. Before making decisions to buy or sell, consult the latest information. Past performance of the rare coin market or any coin or series within that market is not necessarily an indication of future performance, as the future is unknown. Such factors as changing demand, popularity, grading interpretations, strength of the overall coin market, and economic conditions will continue to be influences.

Advertisements within this book: Whitman Publishing, LLC does not endorse, warrant, or guarantee any of the products or services of its advertisers. All warranties and guarantees are the sole responsibility of the advertiser.

The Official RED BOOK® Series includes:

A Guide Book of Morgan Silver Dollars; A Guide Book of Double Eagle Gold Coins; A Guide Book of United States Type Coins; A Guide Book of Modern United States Proof Coin Sets; A Guide Book of Shield and Liberty Head Nickels; A Guide Book of Buffalo and Jefferson Nickels; A Guide Book of Flying Eagle and Indian Head Cents; A Guide Book of Washington and State Quarters; A Guide Book of United States Commemorative Coins; A Guide Book of Barber Silver Coins; and *A Guide Book of Liberty Seated Coins.*

For a complete catalog of numismatic reference books, supplies, and storage products, visit Whitman Publishing online at **www.whitmanbooks.com.**

About the covers: On the front cover, the die varieties pictured are, from top to bottom, the extremely rare 1970-D Doubled Die Obverse Washington quarter; the interesting 1909-S Repunched Mintmark Saint-Gaudens double eagle; the very rare 1876 Large/Small Date Liberty Seated half dollar; the well-known 1901-S Misplaced Mintmark Liberty Head half eagle; the very strong 1968-D Doubled Die Reverse Washington quarter; and the 1944-D Liberty Walking half dollar with hand-engraved initials. The back cover shows the 1862 Doubled Die Obverse gold dollar; the Proof 1952 "Superbird" Franklin half dollar; and the 1885-CC "Dash Under Second Eight" Morgan dollar (VAM 4). The cover coin is the 1888-O "Scarface" Morgan dollar, a dramatic double die, courtesy of Dr. Michael S. Fey.

Front cover still life by Brent Cook Photography.

WCG™ • OCG™

Protect The Value Of Your Coins

PCI Inc.® will certify and encapsulate your coins to protect them from damage and wear and enhance their marketability

It is easy to submit your coins directly to PCI for grading and certification. If you are submitting one coin or thousands, no submission kits to buy or special clubs to join.

If you do not have internet access, simply call 1-800-277-COIN (2646) and request a submission form. If you have internet access, it is as easy as www.pcicoins.com and download the form; or, if you like, we have an active form you can fill out on the computer, then print it out.

✔ With PCI you get your coins back FAST! Our standard service is 5 business days* and we return ship by FED-EX 2 day.
*U.S. coins valued up to $999

✔ PCI will not "body bag" damaged or cleaned coins. They will be graded and certified in our exclusive RED LABEL holder noting the reason for the special label.

✔ PCI offers special label designations, or attributions, from specialty references like the Cherry Pickers Guide, Overton Book of Bust Half Varieties, Vam Numbers for Morgan Dollars, Bolender Numbers for Bust Dollars, etc.

✔ PCI has the ability to offer special custom PEDIGREE labeling up to 19 characters, including blank spaces. Example: JONES COLLECTION=16 characters.

Visit the PCI website at www.pcicoins.com for pricing on our various services, submission information, to register for e-mail and website specials or contest, and to purchase collecting supplies and reference books.

P.O. Box 486 • Rossville, GA 30741 • Toll-Free: 1-800-277-2646 (277-COIN)
FED-EX/UPS: 115 Howard Street • Rossville, GA 30741

NGC VarietyPlus®

Accurate Variety Attribution

Recognized value in NGC grading and encapsulation.

- **Cherrypicker** varieties
- **Red Book** varieties
- 8TF & 7/8TF Morgans by **VAM** numbers
- TOP 100 & HOT 50 Morgans by **VAM** numbers
- TOP 50 Peace Dollars by **VAM** numbers
- Half cents by **Cohen** numbers
- Large cents by **Sheldon & Newcomb** numbers
- Early half dimes by **Logan-McCloskey** numbers
- Early dimes by **John Reich** numbers
- Early quarters by **Browning** numbers
- Early half dollars by **Overton** numbers
- Early dollars by **Bowers-Borckardt** and **Bolender** numbers

To receive a variety of attribution with your grading submission to NGC, just add $7 per coin. For coins already encapsulated by NGC, the variety attribution can be added under our Designation Review service at $10 per coin.

Call 800-NGC-COIN or visit www.NGCcoin.com.

Join the community
www.collectors-society.com

Official Grading Service of
ANA · P·N·G

A Rare Commitment to Numismatics.
NGC
Numismatic Guaranty Corporation

P.O. Box 4776 | Sarasota, FL 34230 | **800-NGC-COIN** (642-2646) | www.NGCcoin.com

An Independent Member of the Certified Collectibles Group

Dedication

Each volume of the *Cherrypickers' Guide* is dedicated to an individual from the error-variety segment of the hobby, for outstanding contributions to numismatics, especially from an educational standpoint. Our honoree for this volume— David W. Lange—epitomizes dedication to the sharing of numismatic knowledge.

Dave Lange was born in San Francisco in 1958. "Coin crazy" since earliest childhood, he discovered the hobby through an older brother who, like many kids at the time, had Whitman folders for Lincoln cents and Buffalo nickels. As his

DAVID W. LANGE

brother lost interest in coins, these small collections were secured through a combination of begging and whining. Dave also obtained at that time a one-volume numismatic library consisting of R.S. Yeoman's *Handbook of United States Coins* (the "Blue Book"), 1964 edition.

After gathering as many coins as he could find from circulation, and with silver nearly gone from pocket change, Dave discovered the magical world of the coin shop. Simple filling of holes in albums gave way to a serious study of coins only after high school, when a meeting with numismatic literature dealer Cal Wilson revealed to Dave the wide variety of books available. He began collecting in every area of numismatics as each book led him in a different direction, finally returning to United States coinage. Advanced collecting in particular series led him to begin writing articles for both the general numismatic press and various specialized journals.

With his growing involvement in the hobby, Dave became active in local and regional coin clubs. He served as president of the California State Numismatic Association, the Pacific Coast Numismatic Society, and the New Jersey Numismatic Society. The move to New Jersey was prompted when he realized that his nearly 15 years in the engineering field was time that could have been spent in a numismatic career. In 1994, Dave joined Numismatic Guaranty Corporation of America as its director of research, later following the company in its move to Sarasota, Florida. Today his responsibilities with NGC include variety attribution, counterfeit detection, numismatic research, and writing, as well as maintenance of the NGC Census and NGC Registry.

Dave is a frequent instructor at the American Numismatic Association's annual Summer Seminar, and he has written a monthly column for *Numismatist*, the ANA's journal, since 1988. He is the author of several books recognized as important references in their series. Dave is also a member of the Numismatic Literary Guild and has received numerous awards for his writing in the field of numismatics.

End-to-End Services
Redefined.

Conserve...Grade...Protect...Register

Just one of the ways our rare commitment is redefining the hobby.

NGC has invested millions of dollars and thousands of hours of research and development time in the end-to-end services that make collecting easier and more enjoyable for you.

Whether you need expert conservation services through our independent affiliate NCS, or objective grading, NGC seamlessly provides you with the best in the world. Once graded and protected in the industry's best holder, you can display your coins in the NGC online set registry, the most inclusive registry in the hobby. There you'll network with others who share your passion for the hobby.

Find out how NGC's end-to-end services can make collecting easier and more enjoyable for you. Call 1-800-NGC-COIN or visit www.ngccoin.com.

A Rare Commitment to Numismatics.

Join the community
www.collectors-society.com

NGC
Numismatic Guaranty Corporation
www.ngccoin.com

Contents

Specializing in Major Mint Errors and "One of a Kind" Pieces

We Buy Major Error Type Coins, Modern Coins, and Foreign Coins. A Single Rare Piece or a Large Collection!

Visit www.fredweinberg.com to view more than 600 PCGS/NGC Major Error Coins, and more than 500 "Raw" Major Error Coins for sale, or see us at all major coin shows.

Fred Weinberg & Co.
Dealer in Major Mint Error Coins & Currency

800.338.6533
818.986.3733 • fax: 818.986-2153
ATC FACTS C03 • email: fred@fredweinberg.com
16311 Ventura Blvd., Suite 1298 • Encino, CA 91436

C.O.N.E.C.A. LIFE MEMBER   ICTA   PCGS Professional Coin Grading Service   P.N.G.   ANA MEMBER

Why Trust Your Precious VAMS To Any Service Other Than SEGS?

Increase the value & desirability of your unique VAM Portfolio!

1878-8TF VAM 14-4 M$1

MS-65 PL

TM

Sovereign
■■■ ENTITIES ■■■
Grading Services, Inc.

"The Numismatic Grading Specialists"

Williamsburg Professional Center
6402 Suite "B" East Brainerd Road
Chattanooga, TN 37421

SEGS has attributed, graded, and encapsulated more VAM Varieties and VAM Discovery Coins than any other service!

Call SEGS Today For Your FREE Submittal Package!

1-888-768-7261

Or Visit Us At:
www.Segscoins.com
e-mail: SEGSI@bellsouth.net

JIM'S COINS & STAMPS
702 N. Midvale Blvd. LL-2
Madison, WI 53705
(608) 233-2118

ERROR AUCTIONS
Six per year for 22 years!
USPS Year subscription $8.00, Sample $2.50
Or send email for free email copy: errorsale@sbcglobal.net
We buy errors outright or will auction them for you
with no buy-back fee!

Len Roosmalen  James Essence

Foreword

Q. DAVID BOWERS

For any numismatic library, some books are interesting to have, perhaps for glancing through, setting aside, and possibly reading at a later time. Other books are a bit more useful, with listings, prices, and historical information that are very helpful to collecting endeavors. Then there are books that are *essential* (make that *absolutely essential*)—of which this is one.

In the years since the *Cherrypickers' Guide to Rare Die Varieties* first came out, the book has grown from interesting, to important, to now essential. I cannot imagine collecting or understanding the topics covered here—half dimes through dollars, gold, and commemoratives—without a copy of this book at hand. I refer to my older editions regularly, and this most recent volume will certainly be used even more—with the many new listings, photographs, and other improvements.

While this and previous editions have proved profitable to the authors and publishers (the present edition is the first under the Whitman Publishing imprint), a spirit of altruism on the part of Bill Fivaz and J.T. Stanton has been equally important to the *Cherrypickers'* project. In the past, portions of the books' profits have gone to numismatic education, the furthering of research, and even scholarships. As a quick perusal of the contents will suggest, excellent sales of the book alone could not make up for the countless hours spent in perfecting each listing, one by one. As if this were not enough, the appendices offer a lot of useful information, including tips on etiquette, common sense, and collecting more effectively. In fact, it is hard to envision anything that is necessary that is absent from the pages to follow—though, surely, when the fifth edition eventually comes out, there will be plenty of new content. If the field of die varieties is anything, it is *dynamic*, and scarcely a month goes by without new discoveries coming to light, including for current Mint products.

For a long time the team of Bill Fivaz and J.T. Stanton has been the focal point of verifying new varieties and finessing information (such as concerning rarity and value) of overdates, repunched mintmarks, die doublings, and other departures from the standard. As interest in die varieties increases—as it has been doing steadily for years—their books have become increasingly important.

A visual treat, a feast of information, and a delightful read, all come together in the *Cherrypickers' Guide*. Congratulations once again to Bill and J.T. for a job well done.

Q. David Bowers
Wolfeboro, New Hampshire

Preface

In about June of 1989, J. Woodside of Scotsman's Coins in St. Louis suggested to Bill Fivaz that Bill should produce a book illustrating all the neat varieties he was always searching for. Bill called friend and printer J.T. Stanton (another avid variety enthusiast) to discuss the possibility. They agreed that such a reference was needed in the hobby. Bill and J.T. were both novices when it came to publishing books, and certainly not prepared for what they were about to undertake.

Initially they decided to include only about 100 of the most worthy varieties—those that any enthusiast would certainly want. Those initial 100 varieties quickly turned into more than 160. With that, a format for the book was decided upon, and the *Cherrypickers' Guide* became a reality.

Being in the printing business, J.T. handled the production. The U.S. Postal Service was very busy for a while as copy was going back and forth between Bill (in Dunwoody, Georgia) and J.T. (in Savannah). (Many readers don't realize there are about 275 miles between the coauthors.)

> *The **Cherrypickers' Guide** proves that there are times when someone can get lucky, and tackle the right subject at the right time.*

The final copy went to press in November 1989, with hopes of having the book finished and ready for distribution in time for the Florida United Numismatists (FUN) convention the first weekend of January 1990. J.T. stopped at the bindery in Jacksonville, Florida, on his way to Tampa for that show to pick up a quantity they felt would be sufficient (about 500 copies). They were not sure how well the book would be received. When they left Tampa on Sunday, all 500 copies had been sold, with orders for more to be shipped and mailed as soon as possible.

The first edition was a great learning experience for Bill and J.T. both. An initial printing of 3,000 copies was produced, which was more than they had anticipated selling. They actually felt lucky when all the copies were sold in less than 10 months.

A second edition was planned, which would increase the number of listings and add values for the varieties listed, along with some other improvements. Thanks to the numismatic press and many variety enthusiasts, the word of the new edition spread. Dealers and wholesalers wanted the book to offer to their customers. The production of 5,000 copies was sold in about six months.

Bill and J.T. were very pleased with the overall acceptance of the book, and the fact that grading services were using the Fivaz/Stanton (FS) attribution numbers on their slabs. (To the best of the authors' knowledge, ANACS was the first to recognize a coin with a Fivaz/Stanton designation.) It seems that Bill and J.T. had luckily stumbled onto a book with the right topic at the right time.

They offered the second edition in a spiral-bound format. J.T. feels this might well have been the first numismatic book to be offered with the spiral or coil binding. This format makes perfect sense: it is easy to lay the book open to a particular variety and examine a coin for comparison without having to prop or hold the book open. The third edition was published primarily in the spiral format.

When it was time for that third edition, one big hurdle needed to be overcome. J.T. simply didn't have the time to handle the production. Therefore, the coauthors set out to find a willing publisher. Several were contacted, and several were interested. Bowers and Merena was the authors' choice, and they set out to provide what would become their best effort yet. The third edition, which offered about five times as many varieties as the first, went to six printings and more than 28,000 copies before volume one of the fourth edition finally came out.

Since J.T. was in the business of printing, and by this time some publishing, the authors asked famous numismatist Q. David Bowers (then a principal of Bowers and Merena) if they could produce the fourth edition themselves. Being the gentleman everyone knows, Bowers immediately agreed—if that's what they wanted, that's what he wanted.

The fourth edition would become by far the largest effort to that date, so large in fact that it had to be divided into two volumes so the spiral binding could be used. Volume one included half cents through nickels. Volume two—the book you now hold—picks up with half dimes and bigger denominations. The division was a natural one. Volume one contained all minor coinage, and there are a lot of people who are only concerned with cents and nickels. Volume two includes other popular series including silver half dimes through dollars (including Bust and Liberty Seated series), gold coinage, and commemoratives.

The *Cherrypickers' Guide* proves that there are times when someone can get lucky, and tackle the right subject at the right time. Bill and J.T. have enjoyed the experience of creating the *Cherrypickers' Guide*, and hope its readers have learned a lot from the contributions of all the people who have made the book possible—those who have provided varieties and information, and who have made other contributions, including values, rarity data, and other vital details.

Waffled State Quarters
The New, Hot Collectible!!

Waffled Coins have sold for hundreds of dollars on Ebay.

Indiana State Quarter

State Quarters are among the most popular coins with collectors but only a select group of people will be able to get State Quarters that contained an error or imperfection and had to be waffle cancelled by the U.S. Mint.

All Waffled Coins are available NGC Certified or sonically sealed in an attractive Global Certification Services holder, which contains a photo of the coin and tells the story of "Waffle Coins", the Millenium's hottest collectable.

As seen in the 2006 Redbook, CoinAge, the Numismatist and Coin World

Other waffle coins available in 2006 include:

We have the only Waffled Quarters from "The Philadelphia Waffle Hoard"

Kennedy Half Dollar   Missouri   Maine   Illinois (available Fall 2006)

To order online or to see a video presentation about the minting and waffling process, log onto

www.certifiedEnterprises.com

or call (908) 788 2646

Your #1 Source for Waffle Coins

Credits and Acknowledgements

The *Cherrypickers' Guide* lists Bill Fivaz and J.T. Stanton as its authors, but the fact is the contributions of hundreds of collectors, dealers, and specialists over the years are the backbone of the book. Without those very important people offering new listings, detailed descriptions, rarity information, values (updated on a constant basis), and basic knowledge of a variety or series, this volume and the entire set of books would not have become the popular reference that it is today.

All the recognition possible cannot adequately express the gratitude appropriately due these individuals, companies, and groups. Yet there are several key people and organizations that must be mentioned for their tremendous contributions.

We have kept and maintained documentation of the people who have submitted various varieties for inclusion in the *Cherrypickers' Guide* over the years. The primary purpose of maintaining these records is to adequately acknowledge those who have submitted varieties. In a very few instances we may have missed one, but for the most part these records have been well maintained since 1991. In a few cases more than one person has contributed the same variety.

With this volume, special thanks must begin with **Dave Lange**. Dave examines thousands of varieties each year, and shares information and photographs of new discoveries. He is always willing to examine manuscripts before printing, helping to find mistakes and offer corrections. Dave has always been a strong supporter of, but more importantly a very good friend to, all numismatists. Thanks, Dave, for your help and support over the years.

There is a special collector who seems to have a new, previously undiscovered variety every time he is seen at a coin show. **Lee Day** has contributed new varieties for several years, and his participation in this volume is no different.

Chris Pilliod has contributed to every edition produced so far. Chris is very knowledgeable in virtually every series, but is best known for his enthusiasm for Flying Eagle and Indian Head cents and all Liberty Seated coinage. His contributions to the *Cherrypickers' Guide* and the hobby in general are too numerous to list. His help and friendship over the years are greatly appreciated.

Well-known and respected dealer **Larry Briggs** is one of the greatest contributors to this series of books. He always has new varieties to share, and gladly shares his coins for study and photos. Dealers such as Larry have really helped to make our work much easier.

Matt Allman has worked tirelessly to help with the compilation of values, recording results from online and traditional auctions. It is with his help that so many of the listed values are from actual sales.

(continued)

Last but certainly not least, **Jeff Oxman** has spent tireless hours and shared many rare coins from his collection for the special Morgan dollar section of this volume. Jeff has also graciously written and proofed much of the copy for the Morgan and Peace dollar sections, which list more than 100 silver dollar varieties. There just are not enough complimentary words to adequately describe his contributions.

There are numerous collectors, dealers, and specialists who have contributed greatly since the inception of the *Cherrypickers' Guide*. We wish to thank all those variety enthusiasts who are willing to share their coins, photographs, knowledge, and experience. Those who have contributed to this and previous editions are noted here. If we have missed anyone it is with our most sincere apologies.

Bill Affanoto
Leonard Albrecht
Roger Alexander
Brian Allen
Matt Allman
Gary Alt
ANACS
Walter Anderson
Guy Araby
Richard Austin
Richard Bateson
Frank Baumann
Ed Becker
Jack Beymer
David Biglow
Dick Bland
Al Blythe
Don Bonser
Charlie Boyd
Mike Bozovich
Dan Brady
Jym Braun
Ken Bressett
Larry Briggs
David Brody
Robert Bruce
Gene Bruder
Mike Bruggeman
Paul Bucerel
B. Buholtz
Ty Buxton
Cameo Coin Gallery
David J. Camire
Will Camp
Terry Campbell*

Donald Cantrell
Rick Carpenter
Ken Chylinski
Ted Clark
Clem Clement
Mark Clewell
Coin World
Lou Coles
CONECA
Bert Corkhill
José Cortez
Billy Crawford
David Crawford
Whaden Curtis
Ray Davis
Lee Day
Tom DeLorey
George Derwart
Rick DeSanctis
Daniel Dodge
J.T. Donahue
Dave Druzisky
Elliott Durann
Edgewood Coin Co.
Brian Edwards
Harry Ellis*
Mike Ellis
Larry Emard
Bill Erdokos
Richard Evans
Michael "Skip" Fazzari
Joe Feld
Ronn Fern
Michael Fey
Ed Fletcher

Kevin Flynn
Geoffrey Fults
Paul Funaiole
Bill Gase
Paul Geiserbach
Ray Gelewski
Jamie Giello
Jack Gorby*
Don Gordon*
Rudy Gos
Mike Gourley
Jane Gray
David Greenfelder
Brian Greer
Bob Grellman
Robert Griffiths
Richard Hana
Joe Haney
Rob Hanks Jr.
B.D. Harding
Tom Hart
Donald Hauser
James W. Hay
Dennis Heard
Doug Heisler
John Hemphill
Alan Herbert
Ronald Hickman
Lee Hiemke
Doug Hill
Ken Hill
Robert Howden
Ross Humphrey
Dave Hur
ICG

Martin Jordan
Matt Juppo
Mike Jurek
Carl Kanoff
Jonathan Kern
Jeff Kierstead
Derry King
Joe Kirchgessner
Keith Klopfenstein*
Gerald Kochel
Bud Kolanda
Martin Krashoc
Howard Kuykendall
Jim Lafferty
Dave Lange
Frank Leone
Fred Lindsey
Akio Lis
Don Lommler
Carl R. Loyd
Roy Maines
Arnold Margolis
J.P. Martin
Aimee McCabe
Steve McCabe
Mark McWherter
R.A. Medina
Tom Mendonca
Tony Mesaros
Michael Michel
Ed Miller
Joe Miller
Tom Miller
Ward Miller
Warren Mills
Michael Morris
Wali Motorwalla
Allan C. Murphy
Dan Murray
NCG
Gene Nichols
Neil Niederman
P. Nilson
John Nogosek
Charlie Nowack
Numismatic News
numismedia.com
Jim O'Donnell

Old Pueblo Coin
  Exchange
Lynn Ourso
Jeff Oxman
Dick Painter
Mike Paradis
Dennis Paulsen
George Pauwells
Richard Pawley
Daniel Pazsint
PCGS
PCI
Karen Peterson
Larry Philbrick*
Chris Pilliod
Denny Polly
Ron Pope
Ken Potter
Wayne Rattray
RCNH
Roger Reiner
Paul Reitmeir
Doug Riley
Mike Ringo
Joe Rizdy
Emory Robinson
Del Romines
Lee Roschen
Scott Rubin
Bob Ryan
Rick Rybicki
Charles Schaefer
Jerry Sajbel
Steve Schmidt
Terry Searcy
SEGS
Mark Serafine
Gary Shaffstall
Blaise Sidor
Sue and Rich Sisti
E.O. Smith
Jim Smith
Les Leroy Smith
Ruben Smith
Richard Snow
Art Snyder
Terry Souder
Howard Spindel

Jeff Stahl
John Starr
Larry Steve
Bob Stimax
Tom Stott
Kim Stoutjesdyke
Eric Striegel
Dave Stutzman
Norm Talbert*
Sol Taylor
David Thacker
Dave Thomas
Carson Torpey
Lee Tucker
Leroy Van Allen
Marilyn Van Allen
John L. Veach
Michael Volz
Gary Wagnon
Dan Walker
Mike Wallace
J.R. Walters
Jonathan Warren
Richard Watts
Val Webb
Dave Welsh
Michael Werda
John Wexler
Paul Wheeler
Bill White
Bob White
C.C. Whitaker
John Whitworth
Dave Wilson
James Wiles
Al Windholtz
Chuck Wishon
Andy Wong
Jay Woodward
C.L. Wyatt
Jerry Wysong
Vicken Yegparian
Dan Zaporra
Anthony Zito

* deceased

How to Use This Book

As do most technical reference books (especially those involving numismatics), the *Cherrypickers' Guide* frequently uses abbreviations, acronyms, and numbering systems to identify and attribute its listings as clearly as possible. Most experienced collectors will recognize and understand the format used herein. However, novices will find this section very helpful.

Symbols Used in This Book

The *Pocket Change* symbol indicates a variety which may reasonably be expected to be found in circulation today.

Pocket Change varieties typically are cents dated after 1959, Jefferson nickels (other than silver wartime issues), dimes and quarters minted after 1964, half dollars minted after 1970, and some circulation-strike modern dollars.

The *Red Book* symbol indicates a variety that is listed in the most recent edition of the *Guide Book of United States Coins* (popularly known as the "Red Book"), the best-selling annual price guide of U.S. coins.

The *Young Numismatists* symbol indicates a variety that young and/or emerging collectors might want to focus on. Many of these fall into the Pocket Change category as well.

In most cases, coins marked with the YN symbol are varieties of coins that are very inexpensive when found in their "normal" format, either in Mint State or high circulated grades. They can usually be sold for significant premiums through private sale or through auctions (such as those held periodically by CONECA). Finding these varieties can help finance the collection of a numismatist with modest funds.

Abbreviations Used in This Book

Abbreviation	Meaning	Abbreviation	Meaning
DDO	doubled-die obverse	PUP	Pick Up Point
DDR	doubled-die reverse	R	rarity
I	Interest Factor	RPD	repunched date
L	Liquidity Factor	RPM	repunched mintmark
LD	large date	SD	small date
MPD	misplaced date	SMS	Special Mint Set
NA	No Arrows	TDO	tripled-die obverse
ND	No Drapery	TDR	tripled-die reverse
N/L	not listed	URS	Universal Rarity Scale
OMM	over mintmark	WA	With Arrows
PF	Proof	WD	With Drapery

Kolit Positions (K-)

Locations of various coin characteristics are sometimes denoted by their Kolit positions (so named for Kolman and Litman, two numismatists who devised this identification system). This is a shorthand reference based on the numbers on the face of a clock, expressed as K-3 (3 o'clock), K-7 (7 o'clock), etc.

Pick Up Points (PUPs)

A variety's Pick Up Point is its area most prone to exhibit whatever characteristic(s) makes the variety unique. In most cases, this will be the date, the mintmark, or legends. Other PUPs include denticles, stars, designer's initials, and various design elements. For a quick list of typical PUPs, see the appendix.

Variety Value and Normal Value

Throughout the guide we offer values for varieties in several grades of preservation. (For more information on grading, refer to the *Official American Numismatic Association Grading Standards for United States Coins*.)

Sources for the values of varieties include:

- actual sales reported to us, with the most recent sales bearing the most weight.
- our assessments comparing one variety to another similar in rarity, collectibility, interest, and other factors.
- recommendation by those who specialize in particular series or denominations.

Also included in this issue (for the first time) are fair-market values for each variety's *normal*-version coin. These values are derived from the *Guide Book of United States Coins* (the "Red Book"), www.numismedia.com (a web site that offers values for U.S. coins), and other sources. They reflect actual retail sales and offers from some of the most respected dealers across the country. These "normal coin" values provide an easy comparison for the amount or percentage of premium each variety can command.

As with any price guide, the values listed should be used strictly as a reference. Although great pains are taken to ensure as much accuracy as possible, values can and do change, especially among varieties that trade frequently.

Factors Affecting Value Always keep in mind the two major factors affecting the value of any item: supply and demand. That advice has never been proven wrong. If 10 people want a particular variety and only six examples are available, the value will be far greater than a similar variety desired by 10 people, with 20 examples available.

With numismatic varieties especially, add to those two factors a very important third: *eye appeal!* As a rule (there may be a very few exceptions), the more visually dramatic a variety, the greater its value. For instance, compare two different repunched dates, with similar rarity and in similar grade, on an 1868 Shield nickel—one with a wide degree of separation and one with a very close separation. The variety with the wide separation will always command a greater price.

Values are subject to change whenever a variety becomes more readily available or more desirable. Variety values certainly change with the normal fluctuations of the numismatic market. Remember that, generally speaking, the higher the numismatic value of a particular coin, the lower the premium associated with its varieties. For example, a nice doubled die on a Liberty Head $20 gold coin will (generally) command little, if any, premium for the knowledgeable collector.

Values for Actively Traded Varieties Some of the varieties listed in the *Cherrypickers' Guide* are also noted in other hobby price guides that are updated on a regular basis. The values for these varieties, such as the 1955 Doubled Die Lincoln cent, fluctuate quite often as a result of market trends. In these instances, we highly recommend that you refer to other *current* price guides to obtain an up-to-date value for the variety. Values for these varieties are included in the *Cherrypickers' Guide* for reference only. Collectors and dealers can compare the prices noted with current prices and use the difference as a guide for possibly adjusting the values of other similar varieties.

The New Fivaz/Stanton (FS) Numbering System

The Fivaz/Stanton (FS) numbering system has dramatically changed with this new volume.

In the old system, adding new listings was problematic as additional decimal places were required in many instances. Furthermore, an attribution number such as FS-05-003.752, or even FS-10c-0.008 was be very complicated, and not within the normal thought processes of most collectors. The old system simply left no room for additions. This new system will allow for additions to the listings on an ongoing basis, and *without any limitation!*

Reading the Fivaz/Stanton Number With the new Fivaz/Stanton numbering system, the complete listing number includes

- the **denomination**, followed by
- the **date** and **mintmark** (if there is a mintmark), and finally
- the sequential **"identifier" number**.

The identifiers essentially denote the type of variety, and/or the location of its point of interest. This number is usually three digits, but can be four digits.

A four-digit identifier is used for dates that include two or more major types. For instance, a date variety on an 1867 With Rays Shield nickel might be FS-05-1867-301, yet a date variety on an 1867 No Rays Shield nickel might be FS-05-1867-1301. There are a few instances when there are three or more distinctive types, such as the 1864 Indian Head cent (copper-nickel, bronze No L, and bronze With L). In these cases the first "type" will be three digits, with the second and third "types" being four digits, such as 1301 and 2301.

With two major types, such as the 1867 With Rays and No Rays nickels, the WR varieties would have three digits, such as 301. The NR varieties would have four digits, such as 1301. The 1 at the beginning of the NR varieties differentiate the second "type" from the first.

There is one major exception in the identifier number system. The Morgan and Peace dollar series use the Van Allen–Mallis (VAM) numbers (when available) as the identifier. For instance, with an 1878 VAM 44, the FS number is FS-S1-1878-044. This is more convenient for VAM enthusiasts and for the grading services.

Most third-party services will gladly change an existing slab with the old FS number for a newer slab with the new FS numbering system. A fee for this service can be expected, but usually lower than a normal submission.

Identifiers for New Fivaz/Stanton Numbers

Identifier	Meaning
101–299	obverse doubled die and/or obverse die variety
301–399	obverse date variety
401–499	obverse variety, miscellaneous
501–699	mintmark variety
701–799	miscellaneous variety
801–899	reverse doubled die
901–999	reverse variety, miscellaneous

Note: As mentioned, Morgan and Peace dollar varieties will have Van Allen–Mallis (VAM) numbers as the primary number sequence of their identifiers.

Old Fivaz/Stanton Numbers Included in the Listings For this volume the old FS numbers are included as a cross-reference. The new FS number is primary, and the old FS number (when available) is secondary.

Abbreviations for Denominations

Abbreviation	Denomination
HC	half cent
LC	large cent
01	small cent
02	two-cent piece
3S	three-cent piece (silver)
3N	three-cent piece (nickel)
05	nickel five-cent piece
H10	half dime
10	dime
20	twenty-cent piece
25	quarter dollar

Abbreviation	Denomination
50	half dollar
S1	silver dollar
T1	trade dollar
C1	clad dollar/ Sacagawea
G1	gold dollar
G2.5	$2.50 gold piece
G5	$5 gold piece
G10	$10 gold piece
G20	$20 gold piece
C50	commemorative half dollar

Rarity Factors

The rarity factors used in the *Cherrypickers' Guide* are based upon the Universal Rarity Scale developed by Q. David Bowers. This is the only rarity scale available that is reasonably accurate for die varieties of the late-19th and 20th centuries. Following you will find a background of the older Sheldon rarity scale, and details of Bowers' Universal Rarity Scale.

The Sheldon Scale For many years, the only method of reasonably identifying rarity was with the use of the Sheldon scale, designed by numismatic author William H. Sheldon to identify the rarity of large cent varieties. Put to that use, the Sheldon scale worked very well, as most varieties ranged from scarce to very rare. The Sheldon scale was further adapted for use with many other coin series and denominations, as it was the only common scale in existence. However, it was not quite appropriate for most series, most varieties, or even most errors.

The Sheldon scale was simply a progression of eight levels into which the populations of all large cent varieties were to fall. Each level was prefaced with the letter R, for Rarity.

Abbreviation	Meaning	Abbreviation	Meaning
R-1	common	R-5	rare (31–75 pieces)
R-2	not so common	R-6	very rare (13–30 pieces)
R-3	scarce	R-7	extremely rare (4–12 pieces)
R-4	very scarce (est. 76–200 pieces known)	R-8	unique, or nearly so (1–3 pieces)

Numismatic writers adopted this scale to represent coins that were considered scarce or rare. However, as one can imagine, the scale is not appropriate for many coins, especially those of the late-19th and 20th centuries, with their high mintages. For instance, using this scale, the 1955 Doubled Die Lincoln cent would be considered common or not so common. Yet we know it is in fact scarce or rare.

Bowers's Universal Rarity Scale (URS) Clearly another scale was needed by the hobby for indicating rarity of all coins. Leave it to numismatic historian Q. David Bowers to recognize the need and develop a method that could be used for any series, and any rarity. (In fact, it can be used not only for coins, but for virtually anything whose rarity, scarcity, or availability is important.) Bowers developed the Universal Rarity Scale (URS), which, as its name implies, is universal for any coin or item. He outlined this scale in the June 1992 issue of *The Numismatist*. It has already been adopted by many writers and catalogers, and is used throughout the *Cherrypickers' Guide*.

The URS is a simple and reasonable mathematical progression:

Abbreviation	Meaning	Abbreviation	Meaning
URS-0	none known	URS-11	501 to 1,000 known
URS-1	1 known, unique	URS-12	1,001 to 2,000 known
URS-2	2 known	URS-13	2,001 to 4,000 known
URS-3	3 or 4 known	URS-14	4,001 to 8,000 known
URS-4	5 to 8 known	URS-15	8,001 to 16,000 known
URS-5	9 to 16 known	URS-16	16,001 to 32,000 known
URS-6	17 to 32 known	URS-17	32,001 to 65,000 known
URS-7	33 to 64 known	URS-18	65,001 to 125,000 known
URS-8	65 to 125 known	URS-19	125,001 to 250,000 known
URS-9	126 to 250 known	URS-20	250,001 to 500,000 known
URS-10	251 to 500 known		etc.

When using rarity numbers with coins, there are a couple important factors to remember:

1. **Rarity generally differs from one grade to another.** If a coin is listed as URS-13 (2,001 to 4,000 known) it might be relatively common. However, if there are only two pieces known in grades above AU, it would be a true rarity (URS-2) in MS-63. Such is the case with the 1888-O Morgan dollar, Hot Lips variety. These are fairly common in VG and Fine, but virtually unknown above AU. Such an AU coin is often referred to as a *condition rarity.*

2. **Rarity and value are not always as closely related as one might suspect.** If there are 10 known examples of a particular variety, but only seven or eight collectors are interested in it, the coin would certainly be rare, but because of a relatively low interest factor (low demand), it would not command much of a premium. Conversely, there could be 10,000 pieces known of a variety, but if 20,000 collectors are interested in obtaining one, the premium over the normal value of the coin would be much greater, due to the high interest factor (high demand). This brings us back to the age-old theory of supply and demand.

Interest Factor

Interest Factor is a term we use to indicate just how much demand a particular coin or variety has.

- A variety with a very high Interest Factor is in high demand, with several thousands of collectors desiring it.
- A medium Interest Factor may indicate that the variety is desired by hundreds or a few thousand people.
- A low Interest Factor might indicate that the coin is sought by just a handful of collectors.

In this guide, we rate each variety's Interest Factor as follows:

Abbreviation	Meaning
I-5	very high interest (most general collectors interested)
I-4	high interest (most variety collectors interested)
I-3	moderate interest (most series collectors interested)
I-2	minimal interest (some collectors interested)
I-1	very low interest (only very specialized collectors interested)

The Interest Factor, combined with the rarity, helps to determine the value of a variety or error. However, eye appeal is also a very important factor and must be considered in the final evaluation. A critical part of eye appeal for a variety or error is the relative strength or visibility of its defining characteristic—how easily can it be seen?

As a variety receives more publicity within the numismatic press, its Interest Factor might rise as demand increases. This can cause the value to increase without any change in the estimated quantity available.

Liquidity Factor

The Liquidity Factor indicates how quickly or how easily a coin or variety *should* sell at auction, given normal market conditions.

- A coin with a high Liquidity Factor would be expected to sell right away, generally commanding full or inflated values.

- A coin with a low Liquidity Factor would not normally sell very easily or quickly, and then usually at a discount from suggested values.

Hot or highly active market conditions can inflate the Liquidity Factor of any coin, with a cold market having the opposite effect.

Our Liquidity Factor scale is as follows:

Abbreviation	Meaning
L-5	will easily sell, and often above listed value
L-4	will usually sell quickly at listed value (for variety enthusiasts)
L-3	will often sell in a reasonable time period, often to specialists
L-2	might sell in time, maybe at a discounted price
L-1	might sell provided the right buyer is available, but at a discount

Other Numbers and Abbreviations

Identification numbers and abbreviations appear more frequently in the study of mint errors (and especially die varieties) than within the regular segment of the hobby. Some are easy methods of precisely identifying different varieties. Others are used to describe rarity, or even a certain class or type of variety. The important fact is with the use of these numbers, most specialists will know right away exactly which variety is being discussed. At the very least, a dealer or collector can look in a reference and find the corresponding number along with photos or detailed descriptions, which can easily and accurately identify a certain variety.

Most of these identification systems are simply numbers listed after the date and denomination. Some are more complex identification listings and include letters or symbols to further identify the variety or error.

RPM and OMM Listing Numbers These are the original RPM (repunched mintmark) and OMM (over mintmark) listing numbers compiled by CONECA (Combined Organizations of Numismatic Error Collectors of America). You will notice most RPMs and OMMs are identified simply, such as 1949-D/S 5c, OMM #1. These numbers indicate that the coin is a 1949-D nickel, with an over mintmark (D over S), and is over mintmark #1. This indicates that it was the first OMM listed for that particular date by John Wexler and Tom Miller when they originally began to catalog these varieties in the early 1980s. This cataloging system soon became the *RPM Book*, published in 1982.

Just because a variety is listed as #1 in no way should suggest it is the strongest, the most desirable, or the most valuable (although that is often the case). Other publications listing all known varieties for a series will normally include newer listings for that series. These newer listings are being cataloged by Dr. James Wiles for CONECA.

Doubled Die Listing Numbers As with the RPMs and OMMs, doubled dies are also assigned numbers that correspond to the listing numbers in CONECA's files. This numbering system was originally developed by Alan Herbert and John Wexler. These numbers can be confusing to the beginner, but they have a very logical and important sequence for serious collectors, so a brief explanation is included herewith.

There are eight basic classes of doubled dies. These classes generally have little to do with the strength of the doubling. Rather, they indicate how the particular doubling occurred. (Because of the complexity, the "how" of the doubling is not covered in this general overview.) The strength of the doubling is generally more important to most collectors.

For example, there is a Lincoln cent listed as 1971-S PF 1c 1-O-II. These numbers indicate that the coin is a 1971-S Proof cent, listed as die #1, with the doubling on the obverse, and it is a Class II doubled die. As with the RPMs, if the coin is listed as die #1, it does not necessarily mean that it is the strongest doubled die for that date, only the first one listed. In this instance, die #2 for the 1971-S Proof cent is actually stronger, more valuable, and certainly in greater demand.

The sequence for these doubled die listing numbers will always be the same. Following the date of the coin will be the indication of a Proof (if it is a Proof), then the denomination, the die number (indicated by Arabic numerals), an O or R signifying the doubled die is on the obverse or reverse, and finally the class of doubled die (indicated by Roman numerals). There are some doubled dies that were made as a result of a combination of more than one class of doubled die, such as 1971S PF 1c 2-O-II+V-CW. The CW at the end indicates the spread of the doubling (from the Class V) is in a clockwise direction. Class I and Class V doubled dies use this CW or CCW direction indicator, meaning either a clockwise or counterclockwise spread. There are also cases in which a coin will have a doubled die on the obverse and reverse, such as 1963 25c 7-O-II+1R-I. As mentioned above, these identification numbers should become easy to understand.

A more detailed description of each doubled die, by class, is published in *The Lincoln Cent Doubled Die*, by John Wexler, a book highly recommended for all variety enthusiasts. Although published in 1984, it is still a valuable source of information, and a must for variety collectors. These classes are also included in the *Cherrypickers' Guide* (third edition, and fourth edition, volume one).

Other Identification Numbers

Other numbers are used from time to time in this book to indicate a variety is cataloged in another reference book. The list below might not be comprehensive, as more books and reference works are being produced constantly.

Abbreviation	Meaning
Breen	Walter Breen's Complete Encyclopedia of U. S. and Colonial Coins
FS (Fivaz/Stanton)	The Cherrypickers' Guide
Greer	Brian Greer's Complete Guide to Liberty Seated Dimes
L	David Lawrence's books on Barber coinage (as mentioned in the text)
VAM (Van Allen/Mallis)	Comprehensive Catalog and Encyclopedia of Morgan and Peace Dollars
WB (Wiley/Bugert)	Complete Guide to Liberty Seated Half Dollars

Average Die Life
This chart indicates the average number of strikes that each obverse and reverse die for current coin designs are expected to produce. These figures are simply averages and expectations for circulation strikes. Dies can and do last longer, or may be retired from service earlier due to damage.

Damage can and does occur early into the life of a die. Depending upon the severity of the damage, the die may be repaired, or (often) will be retired early. Retirement can also occur if an abnormality is discovered on a die. This abnormality might be doubling or some other inaccuracy.

Type and Denomination	
Lincoln Cents	1,400,000
Jefferson Nickels	200,000[1]
Roosevelt Dimes	300,000[2]
Washington Quarters	752,000
Washington Statehood Quarters	275,000
Kennedy Half Dollars	160,000
Sacagawea Dollars	250,000

[1] At the time of publication these figures are for the "Monticello" design of the 2006 nickels.
[2] At the time of publication Denver is averaging about 400,000, while Philadelphia is averaging about 230,000.

According to a U.S. Mint official (as reported to the authors in May 2006), a coin's redesign will negatively affect the expected life of a die by some 30 to 50 percent. The average will improve slightly over time, as technicians analyze problems from the preceding year and "tweak" dies to address cracking issues. Once a new design is in operation for three to five years, Mint personnel will have improved die life to its maximum.

The new Presidential dollar coins are expected to have an average die life of 150,000 to 200,000. This die life can't be predicted definitely until the Mint has more experience with the design.

Capped Bust Half Dimes, 1829–1837

Bust coinage varieties may be slightly different from what many of us are accustomed to encountering in late-19th-century and later coinage. During the Bust era the die-making process was somewhat different from that of later years.

Often a template and punches were used to place many of the design elements, letters, and numbers into the working die, rather than the hub (as was used for later coinage). Therefore, it is not uncommon to see slight differences in positioning of these elements. In some cases individual letter or number punches were used, which can account for one or more letters or numbers appearing over another.

Clubs and Educational Information

One of the most active and educational specialty clubs in the United States is the John Reich Collectors Society. Bust half dimes, dimes, quarters, half dollars, and dollars are all within the focus of this excellent group.

At the time of this publication, membership is $20 annually. However, it is always suggested to write first, as dues and other requirements can change. Take a tip from us—membership in any numismatic specialty club is always highly educational and worth the modest cost of membership.

The JRCS has a fabulous web site, www.jrcs.org, with a membership application, club details, and educational information. Contact the society at

John Reich Collectors Society
Attn: Brad Karoleff
P.O. Box 135
Harrison OH 45040

1829, 9 OVER 3
FS-H10-1829-301 (1/2-10¢-000.1)

Variety: Overdate
PUP: 9 of date
URS-2 · I-5 · L-5

No other attribution

Description: This is an unusual overdate, with what we refer to as *surface doubling*. The first punch of the 3 is evident only on the top surface of the 9. This type of overdate is similar in appearance to the 1877/6 Liberty Seated half dollar.

	G-4	VG-8	F-12	VF-20	EF-40	AU-50	MS-60
VARIETY:	n/a	n/a	n/a	n/a	n/a	n/a	n/a
NORMAL:	$21	$24	$27	$52	$105	$165	$267

Comments: This is a new discovery with no sales records. Values are estimated at 150% to 350% of the normal coin, possibly even more for a higher-grade example. There is little doubt of the numeral 3 on the top surface of the 9. A logical assumption is that at least one 1823 die was made, never used, then punched with an 1829 date. This type of overdate can be difficult to comprehend for those not familiar with metal flow.

1834, 3 OVER INVERTED 3
FS-H10-1834-301 (1/2-10¢-000.3)

Variety: RPD
PUP: 3 of date
URS-6 · I-2 · L-3

Valentine 5, Breen 2997

Description: The 3 of the date was first punched into the die in an inverted position, then corrected without any attempt to remove the initial punching.

	VG-8	F-12	VF-20	EF-40	AU-50	MS-63	MS-65
VARIETY:	$50	$70	$100	$175	$275	$750	$2,800
NORMAL:	$24	$29	$31	$60	$120	$198	$300

Comments: Although this variety has been known for some time, collector interest only started to grow about 1997.

Liberty Seated Half Dimes, 1837–1873

To quote Al Blythe, a good friend and specialist in these coins, "The Liberty Seated half dime series is rich in varieties, overdates, repunched dates, and blundered dies. This provides a fertile ground for collectors who enjoy this facet of numismatics." Truer words could not be spoken.

Typically, specialists who collect any one of the Liberty Seated denominations will collect them all. The design is arguably one of the most interesting in United States numismatics. In addition, there were numerous changes during the many years the design was in use.

Liberty Seated half dimes contain numerous varieties, including some that are considered very rare by specialists. In addition, a large percentage of the varieties in the series are in great demand, and are almost always easy to sell.

Clubs and Educational Information

For those seriously interested in the series, we strongly recommend membership in the Liberty Seated Collectors Club, one of the best specialized clubs in numismatics. The *Gobrecht Journal*, the official publication of the club, is issued three times annually. This 52-page newsletter is loaded with excellent educational articles. The club also has a web site at www.numismalink.com/lscc.html. For membership information, contact

Liberty Seated Collectors Club
Mark Sheldon, Secretary/Treasurer
P.O. Box 261
Wellington OH 44090

1838
FS-H10-1838-901

Variety: Rusted Reverse Die
PUP: Reverse at K-3 and K-4
URS-4 · I-4 · L-4

No other attribution

Description: Rough, pebbly appearance on the reverse.

	G-4	VG-8	F-12	VF-20	EF-40	AU-50	MS-60
VARIETY:	n/a	n/a	n/a	n/a	n/a	n/a	n/a
NORMAL:	$9	$11	$14	$21	$47	$120	$200

Comments: Generally speaking, evidence of rust on working dies is very rare. Only a very few examples are known to exist for some obverse dies. But this is the reverse of an 1838 dime, rarely encountered. Very little information is available for this variety. Its value is subjective at this point. Collectors of Liberty Seated coinage consider this one of the more desirable varieties.

1840-O, NO DRAPERY
FS-H10-1840o-901 (000.5)

Variety: Transitional Reverse
PUP: Reverse letters, buds, and leaf clusters by DIME
URS-6 · I-5 · L-5

Valentine 6

Description: This rare transitional variety exhibits large letters and open or split buds on the reverse die, along with a small O mintmark. The key diagnostic of the variety is three leaf clusters on either side of the word DIME, while the common reverse has four leaf clusters.

	G-4	VG-8	F-12	VF-20	EF-40	AU-50	MS-60
VARIETY:	$90	$175	$250	$450	$800	$1,250	$1,600
NORMAL:	$12	$14	$22	$41	$77	$234	$590

Comments: The Open Buds reverse was intended for use from 1841 through 1853.

1842-O

FS-H10-1842o-301

Variety: Repunched Date
PUP: Date
URS-4 · I-4 · L-3

No other attribution

Description: Very slight doubling is evident on the 1, 8, and 2 of the date.

	G-4	VG-8	F-12	VF-20	EF-40
VARIETY:	$50	$95	$130	$250	$450
NORMAL:	$25	$41	$70	$178	$372

Comments: This variety will no doubt gain in popularity.

1843

FS-H10-1843-301 (000.06)

Variety: Repunched Date
PUP: Date
URS-8 · I-4 · L-4

Valentine 6a

Description: A very nice repunched date, most evident with secondary numerals 1, 8, and 4 south of the primary date.

	G-4	VG-8	F-12	VF-20	EF-40	AU-50	MS-60	MS-63
VARIETY:	$15	$25	$35	$50	$85	$140	$200	$375
NORMAL:	$10	$12	$15	$23	$52	$108	$156	$300

Comments: High-grade examples are always in demand. This is a well-known RPD, and very popular among Liberty Seated specialists.

1844 FS-H10-1844-301 (000.063)

Variety: Repunched Date
PUP: Date
URS-7 · I-4 · L-4

Valentine 3c

Description: This is a wonderful RPD, with secondary images evident north and south of the primary 1 and 8, and secondary images evident south on the first 4. Overlapping images are also evident on the last 4 of the date.

	G-4	VG-8	F-12	VF-20	EF-40	AU-50	MS-60	MS-63
VARIETY:	$20	$25	$35	$50	$95	$150	$250	$650
NORMAL:	$10	$12	$15	$23	$52	$108	$150	$500

Comments: This variety is always popular among Liberty Seated specialists.

1845 FS-H10-1845-301 (000.65)

Variety: Repunched Date
PUP: Date
URS-2 · I-5 · L-5

No other attribution

Description: This variety exhibits an 8 and a 4 clearly protruding from the rock above the date.

	G-4	VG-8	F-12	VF-20	EF-40	AU-50	MS-60	MS-63
VARIETY:	$75	$100	$150	$250	$750	$150	$250	$375
NORMAL:	$10	$12	$14	$22	$47	$101	$180	$372

Comments: Discovered in 1997 by Bill Fivaz, this should be considered very rare due to the length of time it remained unknown. Only two specimens are known to date!

1845 — FS-H10-1845-302 (000.66)

Variety: Repunched Date   Valentine 5
PUP: Date
URS-7 · I-5 · L-5

Description: All four digits of the date are repunched, with the secondary image slightly northwest of the primary date.

	VG-8	F-12	VF-20	EF-40	AU-50	MS-60	MS-63
VARIETY:	$40	$60	$100	$175	$300	$450	$750
NORMAL:	$12	$14	$22	$47	$101	$180	$372

Comments: This variety is a well-known repunched date; it is in high demand by Liberty Seated specialists.

1848 — FS-H10-1848-301 (001)

Variety: Large Date   Valentine 1a
PUP: Date
URS-11 · I-5 · L-5

Description: The digits of the date are much larger than normal. It is very obvious a 4-digit logotype punch intended for a dime was used. The digits protrude well into the rock. A secondary 8 is evident between the 4 and second 8.

	VG-8	F-12	VF-20	EF-40	AU-50	MS-60	MS-63
VARIETY:	$40	$70	$100	$150	$300	$450	$900
NORMAL:	$12	$14	$22	$47	$101	$180	$372

Comments: Beware of coins listed as the large date, which are not!

1848   FS-H10-1848-302 (001.3)

Variety: Overdate   **No other attribution**
PUP: Date
URS-6 · I-4 · L-4

Description: Many specialists believe this to be a tripled overdate, 8/7/6. Further study may prove this to be a normal RPD as the "spike" believed to be that of the 7 appears very much like a portion of an underlying 8, partially polished off.

	VG-8	F-12	VF-20	EF-40	AU-50	MS-60	MS-63
VARIETY:	$70	$100	$150	$225	$375	$450	$750
NORMAL:	$12	$14	$22	$47	$101	$180	$372

Comments: The lower portion of a repunched 4 is evident left of the primary 4.

1849, 9 OVER 8   FS-H10-1849-301 (001.5)

Variety: Overdate   **Valentine 1**
PUP: Date
URS-8 · I-5 · L-4

Description: The 4 of the date is at least triple punched, with one secondary 4 south and one east of the primary 4. There is also a secondary numeral east of the lower portion of the 9, which some specialists believe may be an 8. Some believe it to be an inverted 6 (improbable), and still others believe it to be a 9.

	VG-8	F-12	VF-20	EF-40	AU-50	MS-60	MS-63
VARIETY:	$20	$35	$75	$125	$225	$400	$1,000
NORMAL:	$18	$32	$62	$106	$192	$390	$900

Comments: Coauthor J.T. Stanton believes the image below the 9 is that of an 8.

1849, 9 OVER 8 — FS-H10-1849-302 (001.55)

Variety: Overdate
PUP: Date
URS-7 · I-5 · L-5

Valentine 2

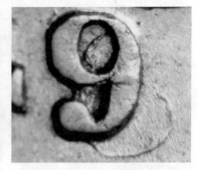

Description: Long described and listed as a 9/6 overdate, it is quite evident this is actually a 9/8. The underlying digit exhibits an inward curve midway up on the left side, indicative of an 8. A 6 would have a relatively straight left side.

	VG-8	F-12	VF-20	EF-40	AU-50	MS-60	MS-63
VARIETY:	$40	$60	$100	$175	$250	$600	$1,300
NORMAL:	$15	$29	$54	$82	$162	$250	$1,260

Comments: This is a very popular variety among Liberty Seated specialists.

1853, ARROWS — FS-H10-1853-301 (001.8)

Variety: Misplaced Date
PUP: Date
URS-5 · I-4 · L-4

No other attribution

Description: The lower portions of numerals 8, 5, and 3 are visible protruding from the lower portion of the rock above the primary date. Al Blythe says that remains of a 2 can be seen behind the upper portion of the primary 3.

	VG-8	F-12	VF-20	EF-40	AU-50	MS-60	MS-63
VARIETY:	$30	$60	$75	$125	$225	$300	$450
NORMAL:	$12	$13	$15	$46	$108	$170	$300

Comments: Certainly a nice MPD; this may prove to be an overdate.

9

1856   FS-H10-1856-301 (001.9)

Variety: Misplaced Date   No other attribution
PUP: Rock above date
URS-6 · I-4 · L-4

Description: A portion of an 8 is quite evident in the rock just above the primary 8.

	VG-8	F-12	VF-20	EF-40	AU-50	MS-60	MS-63
VARIETY:	$30	$50	$75	$100	$150	$200	$300
NORMAL:	$12	$13	$18	$47	$102	$150	$250

Comments: This is one of the many nice varieties discovered by Joe Miller. Two of the most significant discoveries in years are a 1964-D dime and 1964-D quarter, both with greatly misplaced mintmarks; these are also attributed to Miller.

1858   FS-H10-1858-301 (002)

Variety: Repunched Date   Breen 3090
PUP: Date
URS-8 · I-5 · L-5

Description: The date was first punched into the die very high, then corrected and punched in the normal location. The original high-date punch remains very evident within the upper portions of the primary date.

	VG-8	F-12	VF-20	EF-40	AU-50	MS-60	MS-63
VARIETY:	$60	$100	$150	$225	$325	$600	$900
NORMAL:	$12	$13	$18	$47	$90	$144	$270

Comments: This is considered one of the rarest and most desirable Liberty Seated half dime varieties.

1858 — FS-H10-1858-302 (003)

Variety: Date/Inverted Date
PUP: Date
URS-10 · I-5 · L-5

Breen 3091

Description: The first date punch was punched into the die in an inverted orientation, then corrected. The bases of the secondary digits are visible above the primary digits.

	VG-8	F-12	VF-20	EF-40	AU-50	MS-60	MS-63
VARIETY:	$60	$100	$150	$200	$300	$500	$750
NORMAL:	$12	$13	$18	$47	$90	$144	$270

Comments: Although one of the most well-known varieties of the series, and very spectacular, this can still be cherrypicked at times.

1861, 1 OVER 0 — FS-H10-1861-301 (003.6)

Variety: Overdate
PUP: Date
URS-9 · I-5 · L-5

Valentine 5

Description: An 1860 date was first punched into the die, after which an 1861 date was punched into the die over the 0.

	VG-8	F-12	VF-20	EF-40	AU-50	MS-60	MS-63
VARIETY:	$30	$50	$85	$230	$350	$575	$900
NORMAL:	$12	$13	$18	$32	$73	$138	$240

Comments: This is one of the top five varieties for the series, with more demand than supply. Some specialists feel this is not an overdate.

1865
FS-H10-1865-301 (003.8)

Variety: Repunched Date
PUP: Date
URS-6 · I-4 · L-3

Valentine 1

Description: The RPD is evident with a secondary 5 south of the primary 5, and secondary 1 and 6 north of those numbers.

	VG-8	F-12	VF-20	EF-40	AU-50	MS-60	MS-63
VARIETY:	$350	$425	$575	$700	$775	$1,000	$1,150
NORMAL:	$328	$391	$540	$650	$700	$950	$1,050

Comments: Due to the scarcity of the date, this variety may prove to be a large percentage of the existing population.

1871
FS-H10-1871-301 (003.9)

Variety: Misplaced Date
PUP: Rock
URS-5 · I-4 · L-3

No other attribution

Description: A spike, which is likely the base of a 1, is evident protruding from the base of the rock, above and right of the last 1.

	VG-8	F-12	VF-20	EF-40	AU-50	MS-60	MS-63
VARIETY:	$30	$50	$85	$230	$350	$575	$900
NORMAL:	$12	$13	$18	$32	$73	$138	$240

Comments: This is a fairly recent discovery.

1872 — FS-H10-1872-101 (004)

Variety: Doubled Die Obverse
PUP: AMERICA
URS-8 · I-5 · L-5

Valentine 6

Description: Doubling is evident on UNITED STATES OF AMERICA and on most elements of Miss Liberty. AMERICA is the strongest point.

	VG-8	F-12	VF-20	EF-40	AU-50	MS-60	MS-63
VARIETY:	$50	$75	$100	$200	$300	$550	$800
NORMAL:	$12	$13	$16	$32	$66	$132	$240

Comments: This is one of the more popular varieties of the series.

1872-S, MINTMARK BELOW BOW — FS-H10-1872S-301 (005)

Variety: Misplaced Date
PUP: Skirt
URS-5 · I-3 · L-2

No other attribution

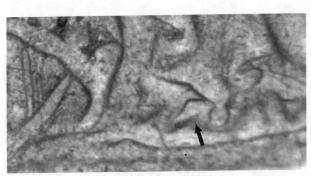

Description: The top of a numeral is evident in the skirt just below and right of the Y in LIBERTY. This has been reported as being a 7, but most certainly is a 1.

	VG-8	F-12	VF-20	EF-40	AU-50	MS-60	MS-63
VARIETY:	$20	$25	$50	$75	$125	$175	$300
NORMAL:	$12	$13	$20	$35	$66	$114	$220

Comments: This is a somewhat recent discovery whose Interest and Liquidity factors may increase.

The PCGS Variety Service

If varieties are the spice of life, then PCGS can make your collecting experience a little bit spicier. PCGS authenticates, grades, and attributes over 325 of the most popular VAM varieties of U.S. Morgan and Peace silver dollars. In addition to the Van Allen and Mallis reference guide, these varieties are listed in several other numismatic books: *The Top 100 Morgan Dollar Varieties: The VAM Keys; SSDC Official Guide to the Hot 50 Morgan Dollar Varieties; The Official Guide to the Top 50 Peace Dollars;* and *The 1878 Morgan Dollar 8 Tail Feathers Attribution Guide.* The service offers:

1) **World-Class Grading.** PCGS employs the best graders in the world. PCGS coins are recognized and accepted throughout the world for the accuracy and consistency of their grades.

2) **Guaranteed Authentication.** PCGS guarantees the authenticity of every coin we grade and we support our promise with a money-back guarantee.

3) **Guaranteed Attributions.** PCGS is so confident in the ability of our experts to get it right every time that we guarantee the attribution of any variety encapsulated under the PCGS Variety Service.

4) **Added Value.** Many VAM varieties carry significant value premiums. PCGS helps build and solidify value by identifying rare varieties and instilling confidence in both buyers and sellers.

5) **Prompt Service.** PCGS treats your coins with the respect they deserve, offering prompt, professional service on all orders.

For details on pricing and to submit your coins under the PCGS Variety Service, visit our website at **www.pcgs.com** or contact one of our helpful Customer Service representatives at **800-447-8848.**

A Division of Collectors Universe
Nasdaq: CLCT

©2006 Collectors Universe, Inc. 613501

The Standard for the Rare Coin Industry

Capped Bust Dimes, 1809—1837

Bust coinage varieties may be slightly different from what many of us are accustomed to encountering in late-19th-century and later coinage. During the Capped Bust era the die-making process was somewhat different from that of later years.

Often a template and punches were used to place many of the design elements, letters, and numbers into the working die, rather than the hub (as was

used for later coinage). Therefore, it is not uncommon to see slight differences in positioning of these elements. In some cases individual letter or number punches were used, which can account for one letter or number appearing over another.

Clubs and Educational Information

One of the most active and educational specialty clubs in the United States is the John Reich Collectors Society. Capped Bust half dimes, dimes, quarters, half dollars, and dollars are all within the focus of this excellent group.

At the time of this publication, membership is $20 annually. However, it is always suggested to write first, as dues and other requirements can change. Take a tip from us—membership in any numismatic specialty club is always highly educational and well worth the modest cost of membership.

The JRCS has a fabulous web site, www.jrcs.org, with a membership application, club details, and educational information. Contact the society at

John Reich Collectors Society
Attn: Brad Karoleff
P.O. Box 135
Harrison OH 45040

1829
FS-10-1829-301 (10¢-001)

Variety: Curl Base 2
PUP: 2 of date
URS-6 · I-5 · L-5

Breen 3188

RB

Description: The base of a typical 2 for this date is flat with a slight serif. This rare variety exhibits a wavy or "curled" base on the 2. Only one working die had this curled base 2, and was obviously used for a short press run.

	G-4	VG-8	F-12	VF-20	EF-40	AU-50	AU-55
VARIETY:	$2,500	$4,000	$6,000	$7,000	$8,000	$12,000	$25,000
NORMAL:	$21	$28	$43	$88	$215	$335	$420

Comments: Almost all specimens are low grade, i.e., Fine or below. A small number are known in VF, and fewer than four in EF. To date only one, an AU-50, has been reported higher than EF. Demand is very high for any grade and the coin sells virtually immediately when offered.

1829
FS-10-1829-901 (10¢-002)

Variety: Small Over Large 10 C
PUP: Denomination 10 C
URS-7 · I-5 · L-5

Breen 3187

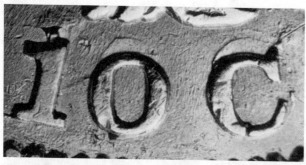

Description: The denomination, 10 C, on the reverse die was punched first with a large 10 C, then again with a smaller 10 C. The large 10 C is clearly evident north of the primary small 10 C.

	G-4	VG-8	F-12	VF-20	EF-40	AU-50	MS-60	MS-63
VARIETY:	$35	$50	$75	$150	$300	$425	$950	$1,600
NORMAL:	$21	$28	$43	$88	$215	$335	$800	$1,340

Comments: Although this variety has been known for some time, interest in it increased around 1997. It is highly salable.

1830, 30 OVER 29   FS-10-1830-301 (10¢-003)

Variety: Overdate
PUP: Date
URS-8 · I-3 · L-3

Breen 3194

RB

Description: Portions of the underlying 2 and 9 are evident behind the 3 and 0 in the date. The tail of the 2 is evident to the right of the lower curve of the 3. The very top of the 9 is evident above the 0. Surface doubling from the initial 1829 punch is also evident on the 8.

	VG-8	F-12	VF-20	EF-40	AU-50	MS-60	MS-63
VARIETY:	$75	$125	$175	$400	$650	$1,250	$3,500
NORMAL:	$70	$94	$156	$385	$610	$1,230	$3,470

Comments: There are three or four known dies of this overdate. All are similar and command similar prices. This variety was first publicized in *Scott's Comprehensive Catalogue and Encyclopedia of U.S. Coins*, 1971. Then considered exceedingly rare, today it is regarded as common.

THE CHERRYPICKERS' GUIDE **HELPFUL HINTS**

Read and re-read the appendix on die doubling.

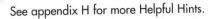

See appendix H for more Helpful Hints.

Nashville Coin Gallery

~ Always Buying & Selling ~

- Coin Collections, Accumulations and Estates
- Gold, Silver & Platinum Bullion
- All US Mint products (Proof Sets, Mint Sets, Modern Commems, Etc.)
- US Paper Money
- Sterling Silver Flatware Sets, & More

*** **Honesty** *** **Integrity** *** **Trust** ***

Please Call **Pete Dodge** Today At **(615) 832-9904** (Cell)

View Our Buy Prices Or Order Coins Online At:
www.CoinBidders.com

Authorized Dealer: PCGS (#548744)
NGC (#1945)
Life Member: American Numismatic Association (ANA LM #5839)
Tennessee State Numismatic Society (TSNS LM #290)
Member: Industry Council for Tangible Assets (ICTA)
CCE/FACTS Network (CB9)

Liberty Seated Dimes, 1837–1891

L iberty Seated dimes are a paradise for variety enthusiasts. Significant varieties are known and can be found for virtually every date and mint. From minor repunched mintmarks to major doubled dies, and even major design changes, the varieties are abundant.

Virtually all of the varieties within the series are in high demand by the large number of Liberty Seated specialists. In general, values for the varieties have been increasing at an even faster rate than for the normal coins. An eagle-eyed cherrypicker can easily earn a significant income by picking the varieties that go unnoticed by most non-specialist dealers.

Clubs and Educational Information

For those seriously interested in the series, we strongly recommend membership in the Liberty Seated Collectors Club (LSCC), one of the best specialty clubs in numismatics. The club issues its official publication, the *Gobrecht Journal*, three times each year. This 52-page newsletter is loaded with excellent educational articles.

The club has an outstanding web site at www.numismalink.com/lscc.html. As of this writing, the annual dues are $15—a bargain, considering the amount of information available. If you join the LSCC, you will be connecting with the most serious and knowledgeable collectors and dealers in the hobby. For more information, contact

Liberty Seated Collectors Club
Mark Sheldon, Secretary/Treasurer
P.O. Box 261
Wellington OH 44090

1838, SMALL STARS — FS-10-1838-801 (Small Stars)

Variety: Doubled Die Reverse   Greer—Identified
PUP: Bow on reverse
URS-20 · I-3 · L-3

Description: Doubling is evident on the D of DIME, the bow, and lower portions of the wreath. All of this date and type exhibit the DDR.

	G-4	VG-8	F-12	VF-20	EF-40	AU-50	MS-60
VARIETY:	$25	$35	$50	$125	$175	$325	$500
NORMAL:	$21	$32	$49	$104	$168	$325	$480

Comments: The same reverse die was used for a few of the 1838, Large Stars variety.

1838, LARGE STARS — FS-10-1838-802

Variety: Doubled Die Reverse   Greer 101
PUP: D of DIME
URS-7 · I-4 · L-4

Description: The same die was used for the 1838 Small Stars DDR. Doubling is evident on D of DIME, the bow, and lower portions of the wreath.

	G-4	VG-8	F-12	VF-20	EF-40	AU-50	MS-60
VARIETY:	$25	$35	$50	$125	$175	$325	$500
NORMAL:	$9	$11	$17	$26	$52	$170	$300

Comments: The value is for the doubled die, as it is for the Small Stars issue.

1839-O
FS-10-1839o-501 (003.28)

Variety: Repunched Mintmark
PUP: Mintmark
URS-7 · I-4 · L-4

Greer 102

Description: On the Large O variety, the secondary O mintmark is evident southeast of the primary O. This O mintmark variety has a very slight tilt to the right.

	G-4	VG-8	F-12	VF-20	EF-40	AU-50	MS-60
VARIETY:	$25	$35	$50	$75	$150	$325	$750
NORMAL:	$12	$14	$24	$47	$97	$265	$630

Comments: This very strong RPM is listed as Greer 102.

THE CHERRYPICKERS' GUIDE HELPFUL HINTS

Don't get hung up on just the varieties listed in this book. There are many nice, yet-to-be-discovered "cherries" out there waiting for you to pick!

See appendix H for more Helpful Hints.

1841-O

FS-10-1841o-901 (003.3)

Variety: Transitional Reverse (Small O Reverse)

Greer 102

PUP: Reverse, buds and leaf by U of UNITED

URS-3 · I-5 · L-5

Description: This die pair was struck with a reverse die that was to have been discontinued in 1840, but continued to see limited use into 1841. Note the closed buds and the second leaf from the left in the group of four to the left of the bow knot. The leaf on the Closed Bud reverse reaches only halfway across the bottom of the U of UNITED.

	G-4	VG-8	F-12	VF-20	EF-40	AU-50	MS-60
VARIETY:					$6,000		
NORMAL:	$9	$12	$20	$39	$94	$252	$930

Comments: This is a very rare and important variety in this series. It has the Smalll O mintmark. (Compare it to the next listing.)

1841-O

FS-10-1841o-902 (003.3)

Variety: Transitional Reverse (Large O Reverse)

Greer 102

PUP: Reverse, buds and leaf by U of UNITED

URS-6 · I-5 · L-5

Description: This die pair was struck with a reverse die that was to have been discontinued in 1840, but continued to see limited use into 1841. Note the closed buds and the second leaf from the left in the group of four to the left of the bow knot. The leaf on the Closed Bud reverse reaches only halfway across the bottom of the U of UNITED.

	G-4	VG-8	F-12	VF-20	EF-40	AU-50	MS-60
VARIETY:	$75	$125	$175	$225	$350	$600	$1,500
NORMAL:	$9	$12	$20	$39	$94	$252	$930

Comments: This is a very rare and important variety in this series. It has the large, or Normal O, mintmark. (Compare it to the preceding listing.)

1843　　　　　　　　　　　　　　　　FS-10-1843-301

Variety: Repunched Date　　　　　　　　　　**Greer 101**
PUP: Date
URS-7 · I-3 · L-3

Description: This is a nice repunched date, with a secondary 1 and 8 evident north, and a secondary 4 and 3 evident northeast of the primary numerals.

	G-4	VG-8	F-12	VF-20	EF-40	AU-50	MS-60
VARIETY:	$25	$35	$50	$75	$150	$250	$350
NORMAL:	$8	$10	$13	$16	$34	$115	$250

Comments: This is a vivid repunched date.

1853, ARROWS　　　　　　　　　　　　　FS-10-1853-130

Variety: Repunched Date　　　　　　　　　　**Greer 103**
PUP: Date
URS-6 · I-3 · L-3

Description: The secondary image is evident on all four digits, to the east.

	VG-8	F-12	VF-20	EF-40	AU-50	MS-55	MS-60
VARIETY:	$9	$11	$14	$35	$110	$125	$225
NORMAL:	$25	$50	$75	$100	$175	$225	$300

Comments: This is the most evident RPD for this date and the 1853–1855 type.

1856, SMALL DATE
FS-10-1856-1101

Variety: Doubled Die Obverse
Greer 101
PUP: Shield
URS-5 · I-4 · L-4

Description: Doubling is evident with a close spread on the right side and top of the shield, on the banner across the shield, and as a doubled pole.

	VG-8	F-12	VF-20	EF-40	AU-50	MS-60
VARIETY:	$25	$50	$75	$100	$200	$400
NORMAL:	$9	$12	$14	$34	$115	$210

Comments: This doubled die is difficult to notice on lower-grade pieces. There is also a Proof doubled die that is very similar, but commands little or no premium.

1856-O
FS-10-1856o-2301

Variety: Repunched Date
Greer 101
PUP: Date
URS-6 · I-3 · L-3

Description: This is one of the stronger repunched dates in the series, and can be located in lower grades.

	VG-8	F-12	VF-20	EF-40	AU-50	MS-60
VARIETY:	$25	$50	$75	$125	$300	$750
NORMAL:	$10	$12	$23	$68	$233	$685

Comments: This obverse is paired with a die exhibiting the Large O mintmark.

1872 — FS-10-1872-101 (003.4)

Variety: Doubled Die Obverse
PUP: Shield, lower robe
URS-4 · I-4 · L-4

Greer—N/L

Description: Doubling is evident on the shield, the banner across shield, the lower folds of the robe, and the lower edges of the rock.

	VG-8	F-12	VF-20	EF-40	AU-50	MS-60
VARIETY:	$25	$50	$75	$100	$125	$225
NORMAL:	$9	$11	$16	$31	$81	$130

Comments: This variety is not yet well known.

1872 — FS-10-1872-301

Variety: Repunched Date
PUP: Date
URS-9 · I-3 · L-2

Greer 101

Description: The weaker secondary date is visible south and west of the primary date. Most evident is the upper loop of the secondary 2 within the loop of the primary 2.

	VG-8	F-12	VF-20	EF-40	AU-50	MS-60
VARIETY:	$25	$50	$75	$100	$125	$225
NORMAL:	$9	$11	$16	$31	$81	$130

Comments: This variety is somewhat common.

1872

FS-10-1872-801

Variety: Doubled Die Reverse

Greer—N/L

PUP: Entire reverse

URS-3 · I-5 · L-5

Description: The first hubbing was almost totally obliterated by the second, which was rotated about 170° from the first. The key indicators are inside the opening of the D and the center arm of the E of ONE. The tip of the weaker lower-left leaf is evident above the primary E of ONE. Other elements are also clearly visible

	VG-8	F-12	VF-20	EF-40	AU-50	MS-60
VARIETY:	$50	$75	$150	$250	$350	$750
NORMAL:	$9	$11	$16	$31	$81	$130

Comments: This is one of the most dramatic doubled dies ever discovered. Lee Day reported this variety to J.T. Stanton in 1997, but Dave Thomas confirmed the type.

1873, CLOSE 3

FS-10-1873-301 (003.6)

Variety: Repunched Date
PUP: Date
URS-6 · I-3 · L-3

Greer 101

Description: This strong repunched date shows secondary digits west of the primary digits.

	VG-8	F-12	VF-20	EF-40	AU-50	MS-60
VARIETY:	$25	$50	$75	$175	$275	$500
NORMAL:	$15	$18	$32	$36	$78	$158

Comments: This variety is still very scarce.

THE CHERRYPICKERS' GUIDE **HELPFUL HINTS**

Remember, if you can't see the characteristics of a coin clearly, you'll likely miss the important one. Don't take a chance. Always use a good, triplet magnifier (7x or 10x). The added expense will be more than offset by just one nice find. There are additional magnifying suggestions in appendix B.

See appendix H for more Helpful Hints.

1873 (WITH ARROWS)
FS-10-1873-2101

Variety: Doubled Die Obverse
PUP: Shield
URS-4 · I-5 · L-5

Greer 101

Description: This is an extremely rare doubled die. Doubling is evident on the shield and on the banner across the shield.

	VG-8	F-12	VF-20	EF-40	AU-50	MS-60
VARIETY:	$250	$400	$700	$1,400	$1,800	$2,700
NORMAL:	$12	$20	$36	$120	$205	$383

Comments: Although well known for decades, very few specimens have been reported.

1875
FS-10-1875-301

Variety: Misplaced Date
PUP: Denticles below date
URS-6 · I-3 · L-3

Greer 104

Description: The top of a 1 is clearly evident protruding from the denticles below the date.

	VG-8	F-12	VF-20	EF-40	AU-50	MS-60
VARIETY:	$25	$35	$50	$75	$100	$200
NORMAL:	$10	$11	$13	$19	$63	$105

Comments: Chris Pilliod discovered this variety in January 1991.

1876-CC

FS-10-1876CC-101, 102, 103 (004)

Variety: Doubled Die Obverse
PUP: OF AMERICA
URS-6 · I-4 · L-4

Greer 101a

FS-101 Level CC

FS-102 Right C High

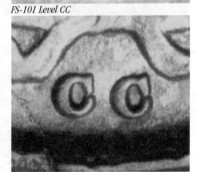

FS-103 Right C Low (Rarest)

Description: Doubling with a very strong spread is evident on OF AMERICA. Doubling is also visible on the lower folds of the gown and on the lower portion of the rock.

	VG-8	F-12	VF-20	EF-40	AU-50	MS-60
VARIETY:						
NORMAL:	$14	$22	$32	$55	$115	$230

Comments: Value depends upon the reverse die pairing. The doubled-die obverse shown here has been paired with three different reverse dies. FS-101 has a level CC mintmark; FS-102 has the second C high; FS-103 has the second C low.

1876-CC
FS-10-1876CC-301 (003.7)

Variety: Misplaced Date
PUP: Gown by shield
URS-4 · I-3 · L-3

Greer 104

Description: The bases of two 6's are evident in the gown by the shield, overlapping one another.

	VG-8	F-12	VF-20	EF-40	AU-50	MS-60
VARIETY:	$25	$35	$50	$75	$100	$250
NORMAL:	$10	$11	$14	$29	$55	$185

Comments: This variety shows another very massive misplaced date.

1876-CC
FS-10-1876CC-901 (005)

Variety: Type II Reverse
PUP: Reverse ribbon
URS-7 · I-4 · L-4

Greer—Listed

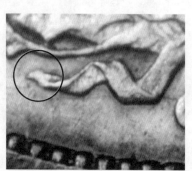 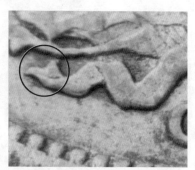

Description: This scarce Type II reverse exhibits a single point to the left ribbon end; the common Type I reverse exhibits a split of the left ribbon end.

	VG-8	F-12	VF-20	EF-40	AU-50	MS-60
VARIETY:	$100	$150	$200	$250	$350	$600
NORMAL:	$10	$11	$14	$29	$55	$185

Comments: This has become a highly collectible variety.

1887-S
FS-10-1887S-501

Variety: Repunched Mintmark
Greer—N/L
PUP: Mintmark
URS-3 · I-3 · L-3

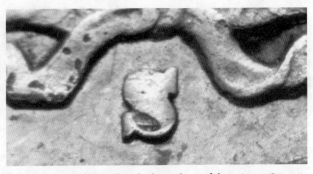

Description: The secondary S is evident within the lower loop of the primary S.

	VG-8	F-12	VF-20	EF-40	AU-50	MS-60
VARIETY:	$25	$35	$50	$75	$125	$225
NORMAL:	$10	$11	$14	$23	$61	$110

Comments: This does not appear to match the photos of CONECA RPM 2, which is also listed as Greer 102.

1888-S
FS-10-1888S-501

Variety: Repunched Mintmark
Greer 101
PUP: Mintmark
URS-7 · I-3 · L-3

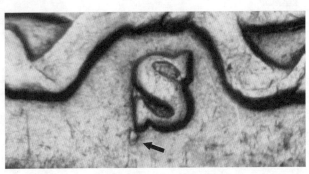

Description: The secondary S is evident just below the primary S, showing only the lower serif. The left curve of the secondary S is also visible in the lower opening of the primary S.

	VG-8	F-12	VF-20	EF-40	AU-50	MS-60
VARIETY:	$25	$35	$50	$75	$125	$325
NORMAL:	$11	$12	$14	$29	$80	$220

Comments: Greer lists this variety as very scarce.

1889
FS-10-1889-801 (005.3)

Variety: Doubled Die Reverse   Greer 101
PUP: Left wreath on reverse.
URS-11 · I-3 · L-3

Description: The doubling is evident on the wreath between K-7 and K-11.

	VG-8	F-12	VF-20	EF-40	AU-50	MS-60
VARIETY:	$25	$35	$50	$75	$100	$225
NORMAL:	$9	$11	$14	$18	$57	$100

Comments: The doubling is also evident on the O and D of ONE DIME.

1890
FS-10-1890-301 (005.5)

Variety: Misplaced Date   Greer 101
PUP: Gown by shield
URS-11 · I-3 · L-3

Description: The top of a digit—probably a 9—is evident in the gown just right of the banner across the shield.

	VG-8	F-12	VF-20	EF-40	AU-50	MS-60
VARIETY:	$25	$35	$50	$75	$125	$250
NORMAL:	$9	$11	$13	$18	$64	$100

Comments: This is another wildly misplaced date.

1890 FS-10-1890-302 (005.6)

Variety: Misplaced Date
PUP: Gown by shield
URS-6 · I-3 · L-3

Greer 102

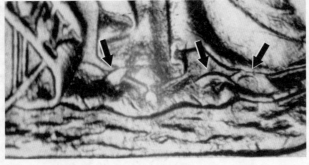

Description: The tops of several digits are evident in the gown.

	VG-8	F-12	VF-20	EF-40	AU-50	MS-60
VARIETY:	$25	$35	$50	$75	$125	$250
NORMAL:	$9	$11	$13	$18	$64	$100

Comments: This is also a wildly misplaced date.

1890-S FS-10-1890S-501 (006)

Variety: Repunched Mintmark
PUP: Mintmark
URS-7 · I-3 · L-3

Greer 101

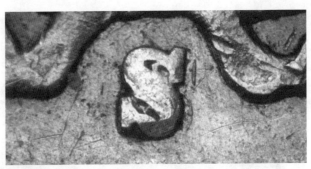

Description: The primary S mintmark, larger and centered over the initial smaller S, is evident within and to the right of the upper loop of the primary S.

	VG-8	F-12	VF-20	EF-40	AU-50	MS-60
VARIETY:	$25	$50	$75	$100	$225	$400
NORMAL:	$14	$23	$36	$57	$140	$300

Comments: This is a very tough variety to locate in any grade. (Note: the wrong photo was shown in the third edition of the *CPG*.)

1890-S
FS-10-1890S-501 (006)

Variety: Repunched Mintmark
PUP: Mintmark
URS-7 · I-3 · L-3

Greer 101

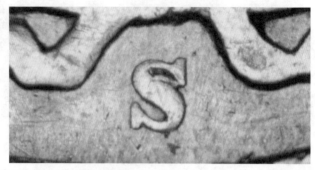

Description: The primary S mintmark, larger and centered over the initial smaller S, is evident within the upper loop of the primary S.

	VG-8	F-12	VF-20	EF-40	AU-50	MS-60
VARIETY:	$25	$50	$75	$100	$225	$400
NORMAL:	$14	$23	$36	$57	$140	$300

Comments: This is a very tough variety to locate in any grade. (Note: the wrong photo was shown in the third edition of the *CPG*.)

1891
FS-10-1891-301

Variety: Misplaced Date
PUP: Denticles below date
URS-6 · I-3 · L-3

Greer 101

Description: The top of a digit—most likely an 8—is evident in the denticles below the 8 and 9 in the date.

	VG-8	F-12	VF-20	EF-40	AU-50	MS-60
VARIETY:	$25	$35	$50	$75	$100	$200
NORMAL:	$9	$11	$13	$18	$63	$104

Comments: The misplaced date is very evident even in lower grades.

1891-O
FS-10-1891o-501 (005.6)

Variety: Repunched Mintmark
PUP: Mintmark
URS-8 · I-3 · L-3

Greer 101

Description: The primary mintmark was punched over a previously punched horizontal O.

	VG-8	F-12	VF-20	EF-40	AU-50	MS-60
VARIETY:	$25	$35	$50	$75	$100	$200
NORMAL:	$10	$12	$16	$23	$68	$125

Comments: Though very rare, this has always been a very popular variety.

1891-S
FS-10-1891S-501 (007)

Variety: Repunched Mintmark
PUP: Mintmark
URS-9 · I-3 · L-3

Greer 101

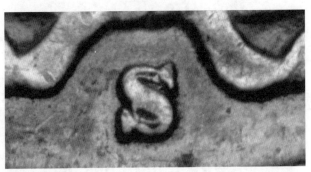

Description: As on the 1890 coin, the larger primary S mintmark (known as the medium S) was punched squarely over the smaller initial S, and is evident within both loops of the primary S.

	VG-8	F-12	VF-20	EF-40	AU-50	MS-60
VARIETY:	$25	$35	$50	$75	$100	$250
NORMAL:	$9	$11	$15	$32	$66	$150

Comments: This is another extremely popular variety.

Take A Good Look At Your Coins!
Find Varieties & Errors Quickly.

Worlds Brightest Halogen Top And Fluorescent Bottom Light Built-In.

Show Buyers Exactly What You're Selling On Ebay Or Your Website!
Document your Find.

Microscope Adapters For
Most Digital Cameras
And The Famous
Coin-Dome For Coin
Micro/Macro Photography.

Over 7500 Sold At Major Coin Shows During Past 12 Years.

Stereo Microscopes $139.00 - $699.00
Photo Domes $79.00 - $199.00
Microscope Camera Adapters $60.00

5 YEAR WARRANTY!

www.CoinOptics.com
Applied Scientific Devices Corp.
9655 SW Ventura Ct.
Tigard, OR 97223-9168

Call Toll Free 877-235-4946

Barber or Liberty Head Dimes, 1892–1916

Only a limited number of varieties in the Barber series were reported when the third edition of the *Cherrypickers' Guide* went to press. Furthermore, some varieties were known but were not included in that edition. Since that time a significant number of new varieties have been reported, and there are undoubtedly many varieties yet to be discovered. Therefore, we encourage close inspection of all Barber coins.

Clubs and Educational Information

To obtain more knowledge of Barber coins in general and Barber varieties in particular, we suggest membership in the Barber Coin Collectors' Society. Annual dues are $15. For more information, contact

BCCS
Eileen Ribar
2053 Edith Place
Merrick NY 11566
Email: emcrib@optonline.net

The society's quarterly publication, the *Journal*, contains educational information on all denominations of the Barber design. The web site address is www.barbercoins.org. Visitors to the site can find educational articles; membership information; and general information concerning the Barber design, the three Barber silver series, and Liberty Head nickels.

1892 — FS-10-1892-301 (10¢-008.3)

Variety: Repunched Date
PUP: Date
URS-3 · I-3 · L-3

Lawrence—N/L

Description: The secondary digits 8, 9, and 2 are visible left of the primary numbers. Although this variety is extremely similar to Lawrence 102 (Breen 3472), the difference is discernible by comparing the alignment of the 8 and 9 with the denticles below the date.

	F-12	VF-20	EF-40	AU-50	AU-55	MS-60	MS-63
VARIETY:	$30	$40	$65	$100	$125	$150	$225
NORMAL:	$13	$19	$22	$55	$60	$85	$132

Comments: This specimen is different from the better-known RPD as indicated above, and should be considered rarer because few examples have been reported.

1892 — FS-10-1892-302 (10¢-008.4)

Variety: Repunched Date
PUP: Date
URS-4 · I-3 · L-3

Lawrence 102

Description: This RPD is evident with secondary numbers left of the primary numbers on the 8, 9, and 2. Additional doubling is visible south of the 2.

	F-12	VF-20	EF-40	AU-50	AU-55	MS-60	MS-63
VARIETY:	$30	$40	$65	$100	$125	$150	$225
NORMAL:	$13	$19	$22	$55	$60	$85	$132

Comments: As with many repunched dates of the series, value is subjective.

1892-O   FS-10-1892o-301 (10¢-008.5)

Variety: Repunched Date   Lawrence 101
PUP: Date
URS-4 · I-3 · L-2

Description: This is another somewhat typical RPD, with secondary digits visible west of the primary digits. The secondary 2 is weaker than the other numbers.

	F-12	VF-20	EF-40	AU-50	AU-55	MS-60	MS-63
VARIETY:	$40	$50	$75	$110	$150	$200	$350
NORMAL:	$13	$19	$22	$55	$60	$85	$132

Comments: This is a fairly well known variety.

1893-S   FS-10-1893S-501 (10¢-009)

Variety: Repunched Mintmark   Lawrence 101
PUP: Mintmark
URS-6 · I-3 · L-3

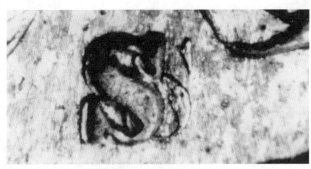

Description: A well-known RPM among variety and Barber specialists, the secondary S is evident east of the primary S.

	F-12	VF-20	EF-40	AU-50	AU-55	MS-60	MS-63
VARIETY:	$55	$75	$125	$175	$200	$300	$700
NORMAL:	$29	$37	$80	$112	$133	$225	$550

Comments: There are two other interesting repunched mintmarks known for this date. We would like to examine them for photos! Strike doubling is evident to the left of the primary S.

1895-S
FS-10-1895S-301 (10¢-009.2)

Variety: Repunched Date
PUP: Date
URS-5 · I-3 · L-2

Lawrence 101

Description: The secondary 9 and 5 are evident north of the primary numbers.

	F-12	VF-20	EF-40	AU-50	AU-55	MS-60
VARIETY:	$125	$175	$225	$275	$325	$550
NORMAL:	$109	$148	$183	$233	$275	$446

Comments: To the best of our knowledge, this RPD is rather scarce.

1896
FS-10-1896-301 (10¢-009.3)

Variety: Repunched Date
PUP: Date
URS-5 · I-3 · L-2

Lawrence—N/L

Description: A secondary 8, 9, and 5 are evident south of the primary digits. The secondary 8 is primarily visible within the lower loop of the primary 8.

	VG-8	F-12	VF-20	EF-40	AU-50	AU-55	MS-60
VARIETY:	$35	$60	$75	$100	$125	$150	$200
NORMAL:	$19	$44	$60	$78	$89	$94	$150

Comments: This is a very attractive RPD!

1897 | FS-10-1897-301

Variety: Repunched Date
PUP: Date
URS-6 · I-3 · L-2

Lawrence 101

Description: The secondary digits of the date are evident west of the primary digits.

	VG-8	F-12	VF-20	EF-40	AU-50	AU-55	MS-60
VARIETY:	$25	$40	$60	$75	$100	$125	$175
NORMAL:	$3	$7	$11	$23	$57	$65	$96

Comments: This is one of the most dramatic RPDs of the series.

1897 | FS-10-1897-302 (10¢-009.51)

Variety: Repunched Date
PUP: Date
URS-6 · I-2 · L-2

Lawrence—N/L

Description: Like the FS-301, this variety shows the secondary digits west of the primary, but they are slightly different and somewhat less evident.

	VG-8	F-12	VF-20	EF-40	AU-50	AU-55	MS-60
VARIETY:	$25	$40	$60	$75	$100	$125	$175
NORMAL:	$3	$7	$11	$23	$57	$65	$96

Comments: Demand for this variety is moderate.

1899-O · FS-10-1899o-301 (10¢-009.83)

Variety: Repunched Date
PUP: Date
URS-6 · I-3 · L-2

Lawrence—N/L

Description: The loop of a secondary 9 is visible within the loop of the last 9.

	F-12	VF-20	EF-40	AU-50	AU-55	MS-60
VARIETY:	$80	$125	$175	$225	$325	$500
NORMAL:	$57	$77	$110	$179	$242	$375

Comments: This variety is most evident on higher-grade specimens.

1899-O · FS-10-1899o-501 (10¢-009.8)

Variety: Repunched Mintmark
PUP: Mintmark
URS-7 · I-3 · L-2

Lawrence 103

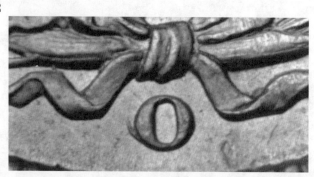

Description: The secondary mintmark is evident west of the primary. The upper portion of the left side of the secondary O apparently was polished away.

	F-12	VF-20	EF-40	AU-50	AU-55	MS-60
VARIETY:	$90	$150	$190	$250	$325	$500
NORMAL:	$57	$77	$110	$179	$242	$375

Comments: This is a very well known variety!

1901-O

FS-10-1901o-501 (10¢-010)

Variety: Repunched Mintmark

Lawrence—N/L

PUP: Mintmark

URS-2 · I-3 · L-3

Description: This variety is commonly referred to as an O Over Horizontal O. The mintmark was punched into the die horizontally and later corrected.

	F-12	VF-20	EF-40	AU-50	AU-55	MS-60
VARIETY:	$110	$135	$225	$350	$450	$700
NORMAL:	$85	$109	$183	$317	$367	$610

Comments: This is a relatively newly discovered variety for the date.

1903

FS-10-1903-301 (10¢-010.025)

Variety: Repunched Date

Lawrence—N/L

PUP: Date

URS-2 · I-3 · L-2

Description: Secondary digits are visible west of the primary digits, with the 1 and 0 being the most prominent.

	VG-8	F-12	VF-20	EF-40	AU-50	AU-55	MS-60
VARIETY:	$25	$40	$60	$75	$100	$125	$175
NORMAL:	$2	$4	$7	$19	$50	$55	$108

Comments: The image at the lower left of the 0 is likely a small die chip. A higher grade specimen is necessary for further study.

1903-O
FS-10-1903o-301

Variety: Repunched Date
Lawrence—N/L
PUP: Date
URS-5 · I-3 · L-2

Description: A secondary 3 is evident west of the primary 3.

	VG-8	F-12	VF-20	EF-40	AU-50	AU-55	MS-60
VARIETY:	$25	$40	$60	$75	$100	$125	$275
NORMAL:	$6	$10	$14	$27	$78	$110	$233

Comments: Although some collectors believe this to be a 3 over 2, the detail of this early die state clearly shows a 3 over 3.

1906
FS-10-1906-301 (10¢-010.085)

Variety: Repunched Date
Lawrence 103
PUP: Date
URS-8 · I-3 · L-2

Description: The last two digits of the date are repunched, with the secondary digits evident west of the primary digits. The secondary 0 in this photo does not show well.

	VG-8	F-12	VF-20	EF-40	AU-50	AU-55	MS-60
VARIETY:	$15	$20	$30	$40	$75	$90	$125
NORMAL:	$2	$3	$6	$17	$50	$55	$85

Comments: Because of low liquidity, expect only higher-grade specimens to sell easily.

1906-D

FS-10-1906D-301 (10¢-010.088)

Variety: RPD and RPM
PUP: Date, Mintmark
URS-4 · I-3 · L-3

Lawrence—N/L

Description: Several secondary numbers are evident in various directions. A secondary 1 is visible west of the primary, a secondary 9 slightly north, a barely evident secondary 0 far south, and a secondary 6 west within the loop of the primary 6. The secondary D mintmark is evident east of the primary D.

	VG-8	F-12	VF-20	EF-40	AU-50	AU-55	MS-60
VARIETY:	$20	$30	$40	$60	$100	$125	$200
NORMAL:	$4	$7	$12	$26	$63	$78	$150

Comments: This may become a very popular variety.

1906-D

FS-10-1906D-302 (10¢-010.089)

Variety: RPD and RPM
PUP: Date, Mintmark
URS-4 · I-3 · L-3

Lawrence—N/L

Description: This variety is similar to the previous listing, but differs in several aspects. The secondary date digits are visible very slightly south on all digits. The lower right side of the secondary D mintmark is evident east and slightly north of the primary D.

	VG-8	F-12	VF-20	EF-40	AU-50	AU-55	MS-60
VARIETY:	$20	$30	$40	$60	$100	$125	$200
NORMAL:	$4	$7	$12	$26	$63	$78	$150

Comments: As with the previous listing, this may prove to be a very popular variety.

1906-D
FS-10-1906D-303 (10¢-010.089)

Variety: RPD and MPD
PUP: Date, Mintmark
URS-1 · I-4 · L-3

Lawrence—N/L

Description: This very interesting variety features a repunched date showing a secondary 9 within the loop of the primary 9, a secondary 0 far south but barely evident within the lower portion of the primary 0, and a secondary 6 within the loop of the primary 6. The most remarkable features of this variety, though, are the numerous date digits protruding from the denticles below the primary date. We've counted as many as nine digits in the denticles.

	VG-8	F-12	VF-20	EF-40	AU-50	AU-55	MS-60
VARIETY:	$20	$30	$40	$60	$100	$125	$200
NORMAL:	$4	$7	$12	$26	$63	$78	$150

Comments: To date we know of only the one specimen, so please let us know if you find others!

1906-O
FS-10-1906o-301

Variety: RPD and MPD
PUP: Date
URS-3 · I-3 · L-2

Lawrence—N/L

 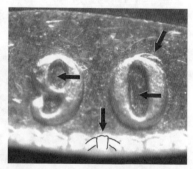

Description: All four digits are repunched, with the secondary 1 and 9 east, the secondary 0 northeast, and the secondary 6 evident within the loop of the primary 6. Another digit, possibly an 0, is visible within the denticles between the 9 and the 0.

	VG-8	F-12	VF-20	EF-40	AU-50	AU-55	MS-60
VARIETY:	$25	$50	$75	$100	$175	$225	$275
NORMAL:	$10	$38	$52	$73	$121	$142	$179

Comments: Values shown above are estimates.

1906-S

FS-10-1906S-301

Variety: RPD and RPM
PUP: Date, Mintmark
URS-4 · I-3 · L-3

Lawrence—N/L

Description: A secondary digit is evident within the lower loop of the 9 and within the upper loop of the 6. The earlier die states show a secondary S north of the primary S, indicating that there may have been more than one repunched S.

	VG-8	F-12	VF-20	EF-40	AU-50	AU-55	MS-60
VARIETY:	$20	$30	$40	$75	$125	$150	$275
NORMAL:	$5	$9	$14	$36	$80	$125	$192

Comments: This is certainly a variety worth searching for.

1907

FS-10-1907-301

Variety: Repunched Date
PUP: Date
URS-4 · I-3 · L-3

Lawrence 103

Description: This very interesting repunched date shows secondary images north of the primary 1 and 9.

	VG-8	F-12	VF-20	EF-40	AU-50	AU-55	MS-60
VARIETY:	$20	$30	$40	$60	$75	$125	$175
NORMAL:	$2	$3	$6	$18	$50	$55	$80

Comments: This is one of the more attractive RPDs in the series.

1907-D

FS-10-1907D-301

Variety: Repunched Date
PUP: Date
URS-5 · I-2 · L-2

Lawrence 101

Description: Secondary images are visible within the lower loop of the 9 and below the tail of the 7.

	VG-8	F-12	VF-20	EF-40	AU-50	AU-55	MS-60
VARIETY:	$20	$30	$40	$60	$125	$175	$300
NORMAL:	$4	$8	$13	$32	$90	$108	$232

Comments: This variety can be located with some searching.

1907-O

FS-10-1907o-501

Variety: Repunched Mintmark
PUP: Mintmark
URS-6 · I-3 · L-3

Lawrence—N/L

Description: The weaker O mintmark is evident south of the primary mintmark.

	VG-8	F-12	VF-20	EF-40	AU-50	AU-55	MS-60
VARIETY:	$25	$45	$65	$90	$125	$175	$225
NORMAL:	$6	$25	$37	$45	$70	$110	$167

Comments: This is a very collectible variety!

1908
FS-10-1908-301

Variety: Repunched Date
PUP: Date
URS-6 · I-3 · L-3

Lawrence 101

Description: This is a fairly well known repunched date, with secondary images evident south on the 9, 0 and 8.

	VG-8	F-12	VF-20	EF-40	AU-50	AU-55	MS-60
VARIETY:	$20	$30	$40	$60	$75	$125	$175
NORMAL:	$2	$3	$6	$17	$50	$70	$84

Comments: This is another nice RPD for the series.

1908
FS-10-1908-302

Variety: Repunched Date
PUP: Date
URS-7 · I-3 · L-3

Lawrence—N/L

Description: A secondary 0 is clearly evident inside the lower left portion of the 0. There is also a secondary image of some type within the upper loop of the 8.

	VG-8	F-12	VF-20	EF-40	AU-50	AU-55	MS-60
VARIETY:	$20	$30	$40	$60	$75	$125	$175
NORMAL:	$2	$3	$6	$18	$50	$55	$80

Comments: This is one of the more attractive RPDs in the series.

1908 — FS-10-1908-303

Variety: Repunched Date
PUP: Date
URS-5 · I-2 · L-2

Lawrence—N/L

Description: This is a nice repunched date, with multiple secondary images evident on all four digits southeast of the primary digits.

	VG-8	F-12	VF-20	EF-40	AU-50	AU-55	MS-60
VARIETY:	$20	$30	$40	$60	$125	$175	$300
NORMAL:	$4	$8	$13	$32	$90	$108	$232

Comments: There may be as many as four complete dates punched into this die.

1908-D — FS-10-1908D-301 (10¢-010.220)

Variety: Repunched Mintmark
PUP: Mintmark
URS-4 · I-3 · L-3

Lawrence—N/L

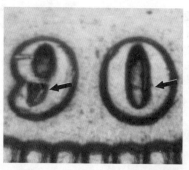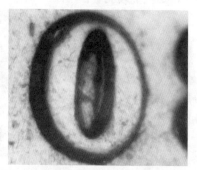

Description: This is another variety considered by some to be an overdate. A secondary image, which may be a low 0, is evident within the lower loop of the 0. Secondary images are also evident within the lower loop of the 9 and within the 8.

	VG-8	F-12	VF-20	EF-40	AU-50	AU-55	MS-60
VARIETY:	$25	$45	$65	$90	$125	$175	$225
NORMAL:	$2	$6	$10	$24	$50	$63	$104

Comments: This may become a highly sought-after variety!

1908-D   FS-10-1908D-302 (10¢-010.210)

Variety: Repunched Date

Lawrence—N/L

PUP: Date

URS-3 · I-3 · L-3

Description: Secondary digits are evident within the 0 and the 8, south of the primary digits.

	VG-8	F-12	VF-20	EF-40	AU-50	AU-55	MS-60
VARIETY:	$20	$30	$40	$60	$75	$125	$175
NORMAL:	$2	$6	$10	$24	$50	$63	$104

Comments: Please let us know if you locate other specimens!

1908-D   FS-10-1908D-303 (10¢-010.200)

Variety: Overdate

Lawrence 104

PUP: Date

URS-7 · I-3 · L-3

Description: This is another very attractive overdate with multiple punchings. Secondary digits are evident within the 9, the 0, and the 8.

	VG-8	F-12	VF-20	EF-40	AU-50	AU-55	MS-60
VARIETY:	$20	$30	$40	$60	$100	$175	$360
NORMAL:	$2	$6	$10	$24	$50	$63	$104

Comments: This is another very collectible overdate.

1908-D   FS-10-1908D-304 (10¢-010.225)

Variety: Repunched Date   Lawrence 105
PUP: Date
URS-7 · I-3 · L-3

Description: The top of an 0 is evident within the loop of the 0.

	VG-8	F-12	VF-20	EF-40	AU-50	AU-55	MS-60
VARIETY:	$20	$30	$40	$60	$75	$125	$175
NORMAL:	$2	$6	$10	$24	$50	$63	$104

Comments: A very dramatic variety.

1908-D   FS-10-1908D-305 (10¢-010.230)

Variety: Repunched Date   Lawrence 101
PUP: Date
URS-6 · I-3 · L-3

Description: This RPD shows evidence of multiple date punches, particularly within the opening of the 0 and within both loops of the 8. Very little repunching is evident on the 1.

	VG-8	F-12	VF-20	EF-40	AU-50	AU-55	MS-60
VARIETY:	$20	$30	$40	$60	$75	$125	$175
NORMAL:	$2	$6	$10	$24	$50	$63	$104

Comments: This RPD may be difficult to detect in low grades.

1908-D   FS-10-1908D-306 (10¢-010.235)

Variety: Repunched Date   Lawrence—N/L
PUP: Date
URS-6 · I-3 · L-3

Description: The initial date was punched too low and then corrected. Secondary images are evident within the 0 and within both loops of the 8.

	VG-8	F-12	VF-20	EF-40	AU-50	AU-55	MS-60
VARIETY:	$20	$30	$40	$60	$125	$175	$300
NORMAL:	$2	$6	$10	$24	$50	$63	$104

Comments: This variety may also be difficult to determine in lower grades.

1908-D   FS-10-1908D-307 (10¢-010.240)

Variety: Repunched Date   Lawrence—N/L
PUP: Date
URS-3 · I-3 · L-3

Description: On this particular specimen, the only visible evidence of a repunched date is the protruding 1 below the primary 1. This is the only known 1908-D with a strong repunched 1.

	VG-8	F-12	VF-20	EF-40	AU-50	AU-55	MS-60
VARIETY:	$20	$30	$40	$60	$125	$175	$300
NORMAL:	$2	$6	$10	$24	$50	$63	$104

Comments: We really need to see a higher-grade specimen.

53

1908-O
FS-10-1908o-301 (10¢-010.250)

Variety: Repunched Date
PUP: Date area, above-right of the 8
URS-2 · I-4 · L-5

Lawrence—N/L

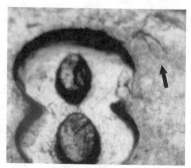

Description: This is a very dramatic repunched date, with remnants of an underlying 8 evident above and far right of the primary 8. There is evidence that other numbers were repunched as well.

	VG-8	F-12	VF-20	EF-40	AU-50	AU-55	MS-60
VARIETY:	$40	$60	$75	$125	$200	$275	$400
NORMAL:	$10	$34	$45	$72	$125	$175	$275

Comments: We need to see a higher-grade specimen of this variety, too!

1908-O
FS-10-1908o-302 (10¢-010.260)

Variety: Repunched Date
PUP: Date
URS-6 · I-3 · L-3

Lawrence—N/L

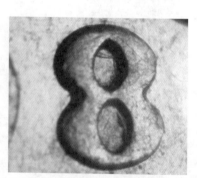

Description: Secondary images are evident within the loops of the 8. Remnants of other underlying numbers can be seen within the 9 and the 0.

	VG-8	F-12	VF-20	EF-40	AU-50	AU-55	MS-60
VARIETY:	$30	$50	$75	$100	$175	$225	$350
NORMAL:	$10	$34	$45	$72	$125	$175	$275

Comments: These variations may be difficult to detect in low grades.

1912-S

FS-10-1912S-101 (10¢-010.250)

Lawrence—N/L

Variety: Doubled Die Obverse
PUP: UNITED
URS-3 · I-4 · L-4

Description: The doubling is evident on all lettering of UNITED STATES OF AMERICA, most notably on UNITED.

	VG-8	F-12	VF-40	EF-40	AU-50	AU-55	MS-60
VARIETY:	$25	$35	$45	$75	$150	$225	$350
NORMAL:	$3	$5	$10	$27	$74	$86	$142

Comments: This is certain to become a popular variety.

THE CHERRYPICKERS' GUIDE **HELPFUL HINTS**

Strike doubling can often be confused with the more valuable die doubling, such as a doubled die or repunched mintmark. To help ensure you know the difference, take time to read, read, and re-read appendix A.

See appendix H for more Helpful Hints.

Eagle Eye
Rare Coins

Knowledge, Fairness, Integrity

RICHARD SNOW

Building a quality Flying Eagle and Indian Cents collection, regardless whether its XF, MS-63RB, MS-65RD or Proof, takes time and knowledge and most important - access to the right coins. Rick Snow travels the country looking for the top quality coins you desire for your collection. You will be pleasantly surprised at the quality of coins you will receive when forming your collection through Eagle Eye.

If you are interested in selling your Flying Eagle and Indian Cents, you can expect to be treated with the utmost integrity. Whether it is an outright purchase, consignment, or through an auction, Rick Snow can advise you as to the best way to sell your collection.

Regardless if it's a MS65RD or XF, we are always in need of your cherished coins in order to form the collections of tomorrow.

Please contact Rick Snow today to discover the joys of collecting Flying Eagle and Indian Cents!

Eagle Eye Rare Coins, Inc.   Richard Snow
P.O. Box 65645   Tucson, AZ 85728
Toll Free 866-323-2646   (520) 498-4615
rick@indiancent.com

www.indiancent.com

Mercury Dimes, 1916–1945

Mercury dimes are one of the most widely collected series of the 20th century. Both the artistic design and the fact that the coins were still in circulation during the collecting boom of the 1950s have served to intensify collector interest. Unlike Jefferson nickels, Roosevelt dimes, or Lincoln cents, this series has relatively few varieties. Several of them, however, are quite dramatic and in very high demand. Serious collectors are obviously interested in the scarce and rare dates, but also among those specimens are some well-struck coins that exhibit "full split bands" on the reverse. Even some of the most notable varieties are of great interest!

The most remarkable and well-known varieties are certainly the overdates of 1942 and 1942-D, though other significant varieties do exist. The 1945-D, D Over Horizontal D, and the 1945-S, S Over Horizontal S, are highly prized finds. Other varieties include repunched mintmarks, doubled dies, and a very likely S Over D variety from 1945.

Clubs and Educational Information

As of this publication date there are no clubs devoted strictly to the study of the Mercury dime. However, for those interested primarily in the varieties within the series, we suggest membership in CONECA, the national error and variety club. Each issue of their bi-monthly publication, the *Errorscope*, contains articles on errors and varieties of all type, and even from other countries. You can visit this organization's web site at www.conecaonline.org.

1928-S

FS-10-1928S-501 (10¢-010.26)

Variety: Large S Mintmark
PUP: Mintmark
URS-5 · I-4 · L-4

No other attribution

| *Scarce Large S* | *Common Small S* |

Description: The mintmark on this variety is relatively large, with two distinct serifs.

	VF-20	EF-40	AU-50	MS-60	MS-63
VARIETY:	$10	$50	$100	$250	$400
NORMAL:	$5	$13	$32	$100	$208

Comments: This variety has proven quite rare in Mint State. The normal or "small" mintmark is the typical size for the era. About 80% of the coins of this date are the Small S variety.

1929-S

FS-10-1929S-101 (10¢-010.3)

Variety: Doubled Die Obverse
PUP: Date, IN GOD WE TRUST
URS-4 · I-3 · L-2

CONECA 1-O-II

Description: This doubled die is evident with moderate doubling on the date and IN GOD WE TRUST.

	VF-20	EF-40	AU-50	MS-60	MS-63
VARIETY:	$30	$45	$60	$100	$150
NORMAL:	$3	$6	$17	$28	$38

Comments: This variety has not attracted a lot of interest.

1931-D
FS-10-1931D-101

Variety: Doubled Die Obverse and Doubled Die Reverse
PUP: Date
URS-3 · I-2 · L-2

CONECA—N/L

Description: Light doubling is evident on the date, and very light doubling on the leaves by OF on the reverse.

	VF-20	EF-40	AU-50	MS-60	MS-63
VARIETY:	$60	$75	$85	$125	$175
NORMAL:	$13	$25	$44	$62	$88

Comments: The doubling is not very dramatic, and the variety has not been previously listed anywhere.

1931-S
FS-10-1931S-101

Variety: Doubled Die Obverse
PUP: Date
URS-4 · I-2 · L-3

CONECA 1-O-II

Description: This is a moderate doubled die, with the doubling evident on the date and IN GOD WE TRUST.

	VF-20	EF-40	AU-50	MS-60	MS-63
VARIETY:	$20	$30	$50	$125	$175
NORMAL:	$5	$10	$32	$71	$91

Comments: This is one of the few doubled dies known in the series.

1935-S

FS-10-1935S-501 (10¢-010.5)

Variety: Repunched Mintmark
PUP: Mintmark
URS-9 · I-3 · L-3

CONECA RPM 2

Description: The secondary S is evident south of the primary S.

	VF-20	EF-40	AU-50	MS-60	MS-63
VARIETY:	$20	$30	$40	$65	$95
NORMAL:	$2	$5	$8	$21	$24

Comments: On the specimen examined, strike doubling was also evident on the north side of the primary mintmark.

1936

FS-10-1936-101 (10¢-010.5)

Variety: Doubled Die Obverse
PUP: Date, IN GOD WE TRUST
URS-9 · I-3 · L-3

CONECA 1-O-II

Description: Moderate doubling is evident on IN GOD WE TRUST and the date. Lesser doubling is also visible on LIBERTY.

	VF-20	EF-40	AU-50	AU-55	MS-60	MS-63	MS-65
VARIETY:	$20	$30	$40	$50	$65	$95	$125
NORMAL:	$2	$3	$4	$5	$6	$11	$28

Comments: This is one of the stronger doubled dies known for this series.

1936-S

FS-10-1936S-110

Variety: Possible Overdate
CONECA—N/L
PUP: Date
URS-1 · I-5 · L-5

Description: The secondary image of a 2 is evident beneath the 3 of the date. Most evident is the flat portion of the base of the underlying 2. Remains of what is likely a secondary 9 is evident to the left of the primary 9. Many die polish marks are also evident throughout the surface of the obverse. No doubling is evident on other elements.

	EF-40	AU-50	AU-55	MS-60	MS-63	MS-65
VARIETY:	$60	$75	$100	$150	$350	$500
NORMAL:	$3	$8	$10	$13	$17	$28

Comments: Discovered by Bill Fivaz, this variety will likely stir a lot of interest. The length of time between the striking of the last 1929-dated coins and this 1936 coin would seem to eliminate the possibility of a 2 underlying the 3. However, examination has matched the shapes on the image under the 3 to that of the 2 on 1929-dated dimes. Stranger things have happened. Keep in mind that 1936 was during the Great Depression, when Mint personnel wanted to save money whenever possible.

THE CHERRYPICKERS' GUIDE **HELPFUL HINTS**

Don't get discouraged if you haven't found any significant varieties for a while—they're out there, and eventually you'll uncover some. Remember, knowledge is power, but it's only relevant when you use it!

1937
FS-10-1937-101

Variety: Doubled Die Obverse
PUP: IN GOD WE TRUST
URS-8 · I-2 · L-2

CONECA 1-O-II

Description: A very close spread is evident on IN GOD WE TRUST, the date, and designer's initials.

	EF-40	AU-50	AU-55	MS-60	MS-63	MS-65
VARIETY:	$10	$15	$20	$25	$45	$65
NORMAL:	$3	$4	$5	$6	$10	$24

Comments: Although exhibiting somewhat minor doubling, the variety is collectible.

1937-S
FS-10-1937S-101

Variety: Doubled Die Obverse
PUP: Date, IN GOD WE TRUST
URS-4 · I-3 · L-3

CONECA 1-O-II

Description: Doubling is evident on the date, IN GOD WE TRUST, and the designer's initials.

	EF-40	AU-50	AU-55	MS-60	MS-63	MS-65
VARIETY:	$8	$10	$15	$30	$45	$75
NORMAL:	$5	$6	$10	$16	$23	$35

Comments: This variety attracts premiums of about 60% to 100% of the normal coin's value.

1939
FS-10-1939-101

Variety: Doubled Die Obverse
CONECA 1-O-II

PUP: Date
URS-6 · I-2 · L-2

Description: Light doubling is evident on the date, and IN GOD WE TRUST.

	EF-40	AU-50	AU-55	MS-60	MS-63	MS-65
VARIETY:	$8	$10	$12	$15	$25	$40
NORMAL:	$3	$4	$6	$8	$12	$25

Comments: This variety can be located with a little searching.

1939-D
FS-10-1939D-501

Variety: Repunched Mintmark
CONECA RPM 1

PUP: Mintmark
URS-4 · I-3 · L-3

Description: The secondary D is evident south of the primary D.

	EF-40	AU-50	AU-55	MS-60	MS-63	MS-65
VARIETY:	$10	$15	$20	$30	$50	$75
NORMAL:	$3	$5	$8	$10	$14	$24

Comments: RPMs in this series are highly collectible.

1940-S

FS-10-1940S-501

Variety: Repunched Mintmark
PUP: Mintmark
URS-5 · I-3 · L-3

CONECA RPM 1

Description: This S/S/S/S quadruple-punched mintmark is evident with secondary images west, and several split serifs.

	EF-40	AU-50	AU-55	MS-60	MS-63	MS-65
VARIETY:	$10	$15	$20	$30	$50	$75
NORMAL:	$1	$2	$4	$8	$11	$26

Comments: This is a very nice RPM—the nicest for the date, and one of the nicest seen so far in the series.

1941

FS-10-1941-101

Variety: Doubled Die Obverse
PUP: TRUST
URS-4 · I-3 · L-3

CONECA 2-O-IV+VIII

Description: Strong doubling is evident on the RUS of TRUST. Other doubling is evident on the nose, the truncation of the bust, and the base of the 1 on the date. Strong die polish is also evident through the S and T.

	EF-40	AU-50	AU-55	MS-60	MS-63	MS-65
VARIETY:	$20	$35	$50	$65	$90	$150
NORMAL:	$1	$2	$3	$4	$9	$20

Comments: This variety commands strong premiums over the normal coin's value.

1941-D

FS-10-1941D-101

Variety: Doubled Die Obverse, Doubled Die Reverse
PUP: Date, IN GOD WE TRUST
URS-6 · I-2 · L-2

CONECA 1-O-V+1-R-II

Description: The doubling is most evident on IN GOD WE TRUST, the date, and OF AMERICA.

	EF-40	AU-50	AU-55	MS-60	MS-63	MS-65
VARIETY:	$20	$25	$30	$35	$75	$100
NORMAL:	$1	$3	$4	$5	$10	$25

Comments: Having a doubled die on both obverse and reverse is somewhat unusual and increases interest in this variety.

1941-S

FS-10-1941S-501

Variety: Repunched Mintmark
PUP: Mintmark
URS-5 · I-3 · L-3

CONECA RPM 1

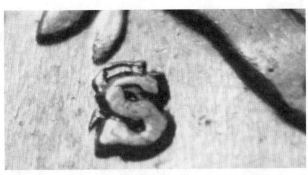

Description: The secondary S is evident north of the primary S.

	EF-40	AU-50	AU-55	MS-60	MS-63	MS-65
VARIETY:	$8	$10	$15	$20	$25	$50
NORMAL:	$1	$2	$4	$6	$10	$28

Comments: RPMs in this series are highly collectible.

1941-S

FS-10-1941S-502

Variety: Repunched Mintmark
PUP: Mintmark
URS-3 · I-3 · L-3

CONECA—Unknown

Description: A slightly tilted secondary S is evident east.

	EF-40	AU-50	AU-55	MS-60	MS-63	MS-65
VARIETY:	$8	$10	$15	$20	$25	$50
NORMAL:	$1	$2	$4	$6	$10	$28

Comments: This is another very nice RPM for the series.

1941-S

FS-10-1941S-511

Variety: Large S Mintmark
PUP: Mintmark
URS-7 · I-5 · L-5

CONECA—N/L

Scarce Large S

Common Small S

Description: The upper serif points downward and the lower serif is rounded, like the bell of a trumpet.

	EF-40	AU-50	AU-55	MS-60	MS-63	MS-65
VARIETY:	$35	$75	$100	$125	$175	$300
NORMAL:	$1	$2	$4	$6	$10	$28

Comments: This is the "trumpet tail" S, which is rare for this date. The Large S variety has long been overlooked by collectors, but has gained popularity in recent years. There are several dies known for the Large S dime, including one that is repunched.

1941-S

FS-10-1941S-801

Variety: Doubled Die Reverse
PUP: E PLURIBUS UNUM
URS-4 · I-2 · L-1

CONECA 1-R-II

Description: Very light doubling is evident on E PLURIBUS UNUM, on the right side of DIME, and on AMERICA.

	EF-40	AU-50	AU-55	MS-60	MS-63	MS-65
VARIETY:	$5	$7	$10	$15	$20	$45
NORMAL:	$1	$2	$4	$6	$10	$28

Comments: Lacking strong doubling, this variety will probably be tough to sell for much profit.

THE CHERRYPICKERS' GUIDE HELPFUL HINTS

The varieties listed in this book are only the tip of the iceberg. Even more are yet to be discovered. Always examine closely any coin you obtain. You may soon discover that one great variety wanted by every collector in the hobby! And let us know when you do.

See appendix H for more Helpful Hints.

THE *Variety* COLLECTOR'S FRIEND

BUY - SELL - TRADE
RARE VARIETIES

A Trusted Name in Numismatics and Varieties Since 1983.

DAVE'S
DCW COLLECTION
P.O. Box 500850 • San Diego, CA 92150-0850

(800) 346-6718

We are a contributor to the *Cherrypickers' Guide.*

1942/1   FS-10-1942-101 (010.7)

Variety: Doubled Die Obverse   CONECA 1-O-III
PUP: Date
URS-12 · I-5 · L-5

Description: The doubling is evident as the 42 over 41 overdate, and slightly evident on IN GOD WE TRUST.

	EF-40	AU-50	AU-55	MS-60	MS-63	MS-65
VARIETY:	$750	$1,050	$1,200	$1,600	$3,500	$9,400
NORMAL:	$1	$2	$3	$5	$10	$21

Comments: The values for this variety will fluctuate. Be sure to check current price guides.

1942-D, 2 OVER 1   FS-10-1942D-101 (010.8)

Variety: Doubled Die Obverse, Repunched Mintmark   CONECA 1-O-III, RPM 4
PUP: Date
URS-11 · I-5 · L-5

Description: Doubling is evident as the 42 over 41 overdate, slightly evident on IN GOD WE TRUST, and as a D over D slanted west.

	EF-40	AU-50	AU-55	MS-60	MS-63	MS-65
VARIETY:	$750	$1,000	$1,100	$2,000	$3,200	$5,750
NORMAL:	$1	$2	$3	$5	$10	$21

Comments: The values for this variety will fluctuate. Be sure to check current price guides.

1942-D
FS-10-1942D-501

Variety: Repunched Mintmark
PUP: Mintmark
URS-6 · I-3 · L-3

CONECA RPM 5

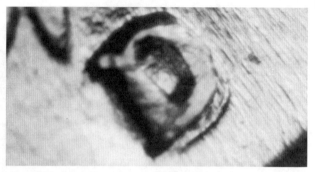

Description: The repunched mintmark is southeast of the primary D, making this another very evident D over D RPM.

	EF-40	AU-50	AU-55	MS-60	MS-63	MS-65
VARIETY:	$8	$10	$15	$20	$25	$50
NORMAL:	$1	$2	$3	$5	$10	$21

Comments: This variety commands strong premiums, especially in lower grades.

1943-S
FS-10-1943S-501

Variety: Repunched Mintmark
PUP: Mintmark
URS-5 · I-3 · L-3

CONECA RPM 1

Description: This is an S/S/S/S, with secondary mintmarks visible north, northeast, and southwest of the primary S.

	EF-40	AU-50	AU-55	MS-60	MS-63	MS-65
VARIETY:	$8	$10	$15	$20	$25	$50
NORMAL:	$1	$3	$4	$6	$13	$26

Comments: This may be the nicest RPM for this date.

1943-S

FS-10-1943S-511

Variety: Trumpet Tail Mintmark

CONECA—N/L

PUP: Mintmark

URS-3 · I-4 · L-4

Description: The top serif of the S points downward, with the lower serif rounded, much like the bell of a trumpet.

	EF-40	AU-50	AU-55	MS-60	MS-63	MS-65
VARIETY:	$75	$95	$125	$150	$225	$400
NORMAL:	$1	$3	$4	$6	$13	$26

Comments: This variety is considerably rarer than the 1941-S Large S, and is extremely rare in Mint State. Specimens with full bands demand a significant premium.

1944-D

FS-10-1944D-501

Variety: Repunched Mintmark

CONECA RPM 3

PUP: Mintmark

URS-5 · I-3 · L-3

Description: The secondary D is evident southeast of the primary D.

	EF-40	AU-50	AU-55	MS-60	MS-63	MS-65
VARIETY:	$8	$10	$15	$20	$25	$50
NORMAL:	$1	$2	$3	$4	$9	$20

Comments: This is a very nice D over D variety.

1945-D

FS-10-1945D-501

Variety: Repunched Mintmark
CONECA RPM 1
PUP: Mintmark
URS-5 · I-3 · L-3

Description: The secondary D is evident northeast of the primary D.

	EF-40	AU-50	AU-55	MS-60	MS-63	MS-65
VARIETY:	$8	$10	$15	$20	$25	$50
NORMAL:	$1	$2	$3	$4	$11	$21

Comments: This variety commands strong premiums, especially in the lower grades.

1945-D

FS-10-1945D-506 (010.95)

Variety: D Over Horizontal D
CONECA RPM 6
PUP: Mintmark
URS-4 · I-5 · L-5

Description: The first D mintmark was punched into the die horizontally and then corrected.

	EF-40	AU-50	AU-55	MS-60	MS-63	MS-65
VARIETY:	$225	$350	$400	$450	$600	$850
NORMAL:	$1	$2	$3	$4	$11	$21

Comments: This discovery was made in the late 1990s.

1945-S

FS-10-1945S-503 (011)

Variety: S Over Horizontal S
PUP: Mintmark
URS-5 · I-5 · L-5

CONECA RPM 3

Description: The first S mintmark was punched into the die horizontally and then corrected.

	EF-40	AU-50	AU-55	MS-60	MS-63	MS-65
VARIETY:	$225	$350	$400	$450	$600	$850
NORMAL:	$1	$2	$3	$5	$12	$24

Comments: This variety was discovered after the previous 1945-D, D Over Horizontal D and is considered very rare.

1945-S

FS-10-1945S-511

Variety: Possible S Over D Mintmark
PUP: Mintmark
URS-2 · I-4 · L-4

CONECA—N/L

Description: The primary S mintmark is evident; however, what may be an underlying D is evident within the upper and lower loops of the S.

	EF-40	AU-50	AU-55	MS-60	MS-63	MS-65
VARIETY:	$15	$25	$45	$75	$100	$150
NORMAL:	$1	$2	$3	$5	$12	$24

Comments: The discovery and examination of a higher-grade example may determine whether this variety shows die cracks or, in fact, an underlying D.

1945-S

FS-10-1945S-512

Variety: Micro S Mintmark
PUP: Mintmark
URS-10 · I-4 · L-4

CONECA RPM 1

Scarce Micro S   Common Knob Tail S

Description: The S is significantly smaller than the normal S punches.

	EF-40	AU-50	AU-55	MS-60	MS-63	MS-65
VARIETY:	$5	$10	$20	$25	$35	$95
NORMAL:	$1	$2	$3	$5	$12	$24

Comments: This variety has the only mintmark punch of this type and size known to have been used during the 1940s, and is beginning to generate increased interest among collectors.

THE CHERRYPICKERS' GUIDE HELPFUL HINTS

Always check coins produced between 1941 and 1945. Most of the dramatic varieties from the 20th century were produced during WWII, when the U.S. government was trying to conserve metals, energy, and time. There are still significant discoveries to be made.

See appendix H for more Helpful Hints.

Roosevelt Dimes, 1946 to Date

A s of our publication date, there are no clubs devoted strictly to the study of the Roosevelt dime. However, with the rapidly growing interest in this series, a Roosevelt dime club is sure to be formed soon. This series is widely collected, both as a series and for varieties. And if you're interested in varieties, this is certainly an area that can hold a pot of gold.

Varieties include visually attractive doubled dies, repunched mintmarks, over mintmarks, and even missing mintmarks. In fact, the CONECA Die Variety Master

Listing shows 99 doubled dies and 48 repunched mintmarks for the year 1946 alone! Some of the most attractive and desirable doubled dies include a 1950-D reverse, 1960 Proof obverse, and 1968-S Proof obverse. The over mintmarks include a 1947-S, S Over D; and 1950-D, D Over S. Also included are a really attractive and scarce 1953-D Over Horizontal D; a 1959-D, D Over inverted D; and a 1962-D, D Over Horizontal D. The majority of the most valuable varieties in the series are illustrated in this section.

Repunched mintmarks are abundant, and RPM collectors are growing constantly. Together, with the numerous RPMs appearing, and the growth of collectors, RPMs in this and other series are becoming more popular—and valuable!

Clubs and Educational Information

For those interested primarily in the varieties within the series, we would suggest membership in CONECA, the national error and variety club. Each issue of their bi-monthly publication, the *Errorscope*, contains articles on errors and varieties of all type, and even from other countries. An application is available online at www.conecaonline.org/join, or by contacting Paul Funaiole at

CONECA
Paul Funaiole, Membership
35 Leavitt Lane
Glenburn ME 04401-1013

1946   FS-10-1946-101

Variety: DDO and DDR   **CONECA 4-O-V+3-R-II**
PUP: Date, LIBERTY, ONE DIME
URS-3 · I-3 · L-3

Description: Strong doubling is evident on all obverse lettering, on the date and on the designer's initials. Doubling on the reverse is evident on OF AMERICA, ONE DIME, UNUM, and the dot to the right of UNUM.

	EF-40	AU-50	MS-60	MS-63	MS-65	MS-66
VARIETY:	$10	$20	$50	$75	$125	$200
NORMAL:			$1	$3	$15	$25

Comments: This is one of the more popular varieties of the 1946 dime.

1946   FS-10-1946-102

Variety: Doubled Die Obverse   **CONECA 4-O-V**
PUP: Date, IN GOD WE TRUST, LIBERTY, designer's initials
URS-2 · I-4 · L-4

Description: This is the same obverse die as the previous listing, but without the matching doubled-die reverse.

	EF-40	AU-50	MS-60	MS-63	MS-65	MS-66
VARIETY:	$10	$25	$50	$100	$150	$250
NORMAL:			$1	$3	$15	$25

Comments: No additional specimens have been reported to date.

1946   FS-10-1946-103

Variety: Doubled Die Obverse   **CONECA—Unknown**
PUP: Date, IN GOD WE TRUST
URS-3 · I-3 · L-3

Description: Strong doubling is evident on LIBERTY, the motto, the date, and the designer's initials.

	EF-40	AU-50	MS-60	MS-63	MS-65	MS-66
VARIETY:	$10	$25	$50	$100	$150	$250
NORMAL:			$1	$3	$15	$25

Comments: Several other doubled dies for this date are somewhat similar to this one.

1946   FS-10-1946-104

Variety: Doubled Die Obverse   **CONECA—Unknown**
PUP: Date, IN GOD WE TRUST, LIBERTY, designer's initials
URS-4 · I-3 · L-3

Description: Strong doubling is evident on IN GOD WE TRUST, the date, the designer's initials. A medium counterclockwise spread is evident on LIBERTY.

	EF-40	AU-50	MS-60	MS-63	MS-65	MS-66
VARIETY:	$10	$30	$60	$125	$200	$350
NORMAL:			$1	$3	$15	$25

Comments: This variety was previously attributed unofficially as CONECA 28-O-V, but the CONECA Master Listing only shows 26 obverse dies.

1946 — FS-10-1946-801

Variety: Doubled Die Reverse
PUP: UNITED
URS-1 · I-3 · L-3

CONECA 6-R-II+V

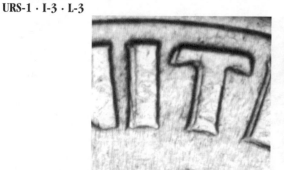

Description: Strong doubling is evident on UNITED, the olive branches, and the leaves.

	EF-40	AU-50	MS-60	MS-63	MS-65	MS-66
VARIETY:	$10	$20	$50	$75	$125	$200
NORMAL:			$1	$3	$15	$25

Comments: A strong die crack is evident through the T of STATES and the oak leaf.

1946 — FS-10-1946-802

Variety: Doubled Die Reverse
PUP: Olive stem
URS-2 · I-3 · L-3

CONECA 7-R-IV+VIII

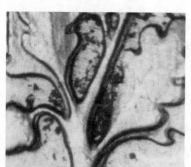

Description: Very strong doubling is evident on the olive stem, branches, and leaves; with very close doubling visible on UNUM.

	EF-40	AU-50	MS-60	MS-63	MS-65	MS-66
VARIETY:	$15	$30	$60	$125	$200	$350
NORMAL:			$1	$3	$15	$25

Comments: This variety is unusual in that the very strong doubling is evident only in this area.

1946-D   FS-10-1946D-501

Variety: Repunched Mintmark   CONECA—Unknown
PUP: Mintmark
URS-3 · I-3 · L-3

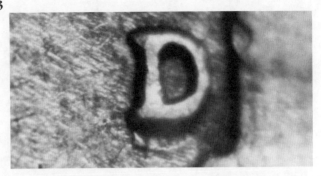

Description: A strong RPM is evident south.

	EF-40	AU-50	MS-60	MS-63	MS-65	MS-66
VARIETY:	$5	$10	$20	$25	$35	$50
NORMAL::			$1	$3	$16	$26

Comments: This RPM may now be listed by CONECA.

1946-D   FS-10-1946D-502

Variety: Repunched Mintmark   CONECA—Unknown
PUP: Mintmark
URS-3 · I-3 · L-3

Description: A secondary D is evident north of the primary D mintmark.

	EF-40	AU-50	MS-60	MS-63	MS-65	MS-66
VARIETY:	$5	$10	$20	$25	$35	$50
NORMAL:			$1	$3	$16	$26

Comments: This RPM was not listed in the RPM book by Tom Miller and John Wexler.

1946-D

Variety: Repunched Mintmark
PUP: Mintmark
URS-3 · I-3 · L-3

CONECA—Unknown

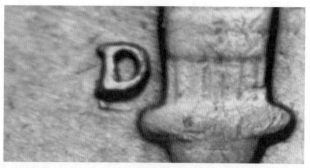

Description: This variety has a very strong RPM with the secondary D south of the primary D.

	EF-40	AU-50	MS-60	MS-63	MS-65	MS-66
VARIETY:	$5	$10	$20	$25	$35	$50
NORMAL:			$1	$3	$16	$26

Comments: This RPM may now be listed by CONECA.

1946-S

Variety: RPM, DDR
PUP: Mintmark
URS-5 · I-4 · L-3

CONECA RPM 1 + 1-R-II+V

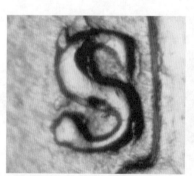 

Description: The doubled die is most evident on AMERICA, the right branch, the leaves, UNUM, and DIME. The RPM is quadrupled, with the remnants of three secondary S mintmarks north of the primary.

	EF-40	AU-50	MS-60	MS-63	MS-65	MS-66
VARIETY:	$10	$20	$35	$60	$100	$150
NORMAL:			$1	$4	$15	$24

Comments: Most of the value for this variety is for the significant RPM.

1946-S
FS-10-1946S-502 (011.6)

Variety: RPM, DDR
PUP: Mintmark, UNITED STATES
URS-6 · I-3 · L-3

CONECA RPM 2 + DDR 2-R-IV

Description: The secondary mintmark is evident southeast of the primary S. Doubling is most noticeable on UNITED STATES and E PLURIBUS.

	EF-40	AU-50	MS-60	MS-63	MS-65	MS-66
VARIETY:	$10	$20	$35	$60	$100	$150
NORMAL:			$1	$3	$16	$26

Comments: As with the previous listing, most of the value is for the RPM.

1946-S
FS-10-1946S-503

Variety: Repunched Mintmark
PUP: Mintmark
URS-3 · I-3 · L-3

CONECA—Unknown

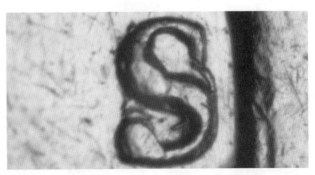

Description: This is a very strong RPM—actually, a triple punched mintmark—with the secondary images evident north and north of the primary S.

	EF-40	AU-50	MS-60	MS-63	MS-65	MS-66
VARIETY:	$5	$10	$20	$25	$35	$50
NORMAL:			$1	$3	$16	$26

Comments: This may be listed in CONECA as RPM 13.

1946-S

FS-10-1946S-504

Variety: Sans Serif Mintmark
PUP: Mintmark
URS-2 · I-5 · L-5

CONECA—N/L

Description: The mintmark on this one die is the sans serif type, i.e., without serifs.

	MS-60	MS-63	MS-65	MS-66
VARIETY:	n/a	n/a	n/a	n/a
NORMAL:	$1	$3	$16	$26

Comments: Until the discovery of this piece, the sans serif S mintmark was only known on 1947 dated dimes. This and one other are the only known examples to date. Any other finds should be considered extremely rare.

1947

FS-10-1947-101

Variety: Doubled Die Obverse
PUP: Mintmark
URS-3 · I-3 · L-3

CONECA 2-O-II+VI

Description: Very strong doubling is evident on the date, the motto, the designer's initials, and LIBERTY.

	EF-40	AU-50	MS-60	MS-63	MS-65	MS-66
VARIETY:	$5	$10	$20	$25	$35	$50
NORMAL:			$1	$5	$17	$27

Comments: This is a very strong DDO, especially when compared to others of the series. This variety was illustrated in *Cherrypickers' News*, number 13.

1947-S

Variety: S Over D Mintmark
CONECA OMM 1
PUP: Mintmark
URS-6 · I-4 · L-4

Description: The S mintmark was punched over a D mintmark. Remnants of the initial D mintmark are evident only across the opening of the lower loop, and slightly right of the lower loop.

	EF-40	AU-50	MS-60	MS-63	MS-65	MS-66
VARIETY:	$25	$50	$100	$200	$300	$500
NORMAL:		$2	$7	$17	$27	

Comments: This variety and the next are very similar; however, number 501 is the sans serif S mintmark, and number 502 is the "trumpet tail" S mintmark.

1947-S

Variety: S Over D Mintmark
CONECA OMM 2
PUP: Mintmark
URS-6 · I-4 · L-4

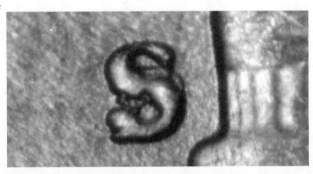

Description: The S mintmark was punched over a D mintmark. Remnants of the initial D mintmark are evident within the upper loop of the S, and across the opening of the lower loop.

	EF-40	AU-50	MS-60	MS-63	MS-65	MS-66
VARIETY:	$25	$50	$100	$200	$300	$500
NORMAL:		$2	$7	$17	$27	

Comments: This variety and the previous are very similar; however, number 501 is the sans serif S mintmark, and number 502 is the "trumpet tail" S mintmark.

1947-S
FS-10-1947S-503

Variety: Repunched Mintmark
PUP: Mintmark
URS-7 · I-3 · L-3

CONECA RPM 2

Description: The secondary S is evident protruding north of the primary S.

	EF-40	AU-50	MS-60	MS-63	MS-65	MS-66
VARIETY:	$3	$5	$10	$15	$35	$50
NORMAL:			$2	$7	$17	$27

Comments: There are several nice RPMs for 1946 and 1947, in both D- and S-mintmark coins.

1947-S
FS-10-1947S-504

Variety: Repunched Mintmark
PUP: Mintmark
URS-8 · I-3 · L-3

CONECA RPM 4

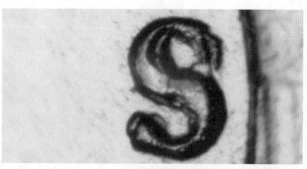

Description: The secondary S is somewhat centered under the primary S, with a rotation clockwise, showing right of the primary upper loop and left of the primary second loop.

	EF-40	AU-50	MS-60	MS-63	MS-65	MS-66
VARIETY:	$3	$5	$10	$15	$35	$50
NORMAL:			$2	$7	$17	$27

Comments: CONECA has six RPMs listed for the 1947-S dime. There are probably others. Try to locate them all!

1947-S

FS-10-1947S-801 (013.5)

Variety: Doubled Die Reverse
CONECA 1-R-II+V
PUP: E PLURIBUS UNUM
URS-5 · I-3 · L-3

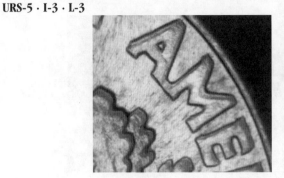

Description: The very strong doubling is evident on all reverse lettering, E PLURIBUS UNUM, on almost all leaves and branches, and especially on the flame.

	EF-40	AU-50	MS-60	MS-63	MS-65	MS-66
VARIETY:	$10	$20	$35	$50	$100	$150
NORMAL:			$2	$7	$17	$27

Comments: On the few specimens we have examined, there is a spike protruding from the top of the R in PLURIBUS. EDS specimens should command a higher premium.

1948

FS-10-1948-801

Variety: Doubled Die Reverse
CONECA 1-R-I
PUP: UNITED STATES OF AMERICA, flame
URS-4 · I-3 · L-3

Description: Strong doubling is evident on all outer letters, on the flame tips, and slightly on the branches and leaves.

	EF-40	AU-50	MS-60	MS-63	MS-65	MS-66
VARIETY:	$10	$20	$35	$50	$100	$150
NORMAL:			$3	$6	$18	$30

Comments: This variety is not well known, but is a very nice doubled die reverse.

1950, PROOF
FS-10-1950-801

Variety: Doubled Die Reverse
CONECA PF-1-R-II
PUP: AMERICA
URS-5 · I-2 · L-2

Description: Moderate doubling is evident on UNUM, DIME, and OF AMERICA.

	PF-63	PF-65	PF-66
VARIETY:	$25	$50	$90
NORMAL:	$21	$38	$75

Comments: Although on a Proof specimen, this may be difficult to sell.

1950-D/S
FS-10-1950D-501

Variety: D Over S Mintmark
CONECA—N/L
PUP: Mintmark
URS-1 • I-5 • L-5

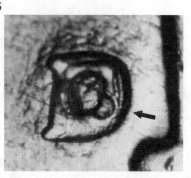 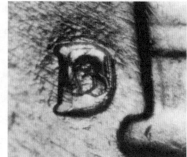

Description: The diagonal stroke of the initially punched S mintmark is visible within the opening of the primary D mintmark. The lower curve of the S is evident on the lower right curve of the D.

	EF-40	AU-50	MS-60	MS-63	MS-65	MS-66
VARIETY:	$125	$175	$250	$400	$650	$850
NORMAL:		$2	$8	$18	$28	

Comments: It is remarkable that this variety escaped notice for so long. One would think the late discovery would be a clear indication of rarity. As there are no clear sales records, the values shown are estimates based upon other OMMs.

1950-D

FS-10-1950D-801 (014)

Variety: Doubled Die Reverse

CONECA 1-R-III

PUP: E PLURIBUS UNUM

URS-8 · I-4 · L-4

Description: Strong doubling is evident on E PLURIBUS UNUM, the lower portions of the oak and olive branches, and the lower left portion of the torch.

	EF-40	AU-50	MS-60	MS-63	MS-65	MS-66
VARIETY:	$50	$100	$125	$175	$250	$500
NORMAL:			$2	$8	$18	$28

Comments: This variety has been known for a long time, but is still very much in demand.

1950-S

FS-10-1950S-501

Variety: S Over D Mintmark

CONECA RPM 5

PUP: Mintmark

URS-7 · I-4 · L-4

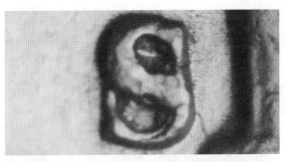

Description: The S mintmark is punched squarely over a previously punched D.

	EF-40	AU-50	MS-60	MS-63	MS-65	MS-66
VARIETY:	$25	$50	$125	$250	$400	$750
NORMAL:			$20	$24	$36	$45

Comments: There has been a lot of discussion about this variety over the past couple of years. CONECA now lists this as an S over inverted S, indicating that the line enclosing the lower loop is that of the long upper serif on an inverted S. However, we still believe this to be an OMM (actually S/S/D) because the long upper serif of an S would not enclose the lower opening. In addition, the curve of the face of a D is clearly evident in the upper opening.

1953-D
FS-10-1953D-501

Variety: D Over Horizontal D
PUP: Mintmark
URS-4 · I-4 · L-4

CONECA RPM 3

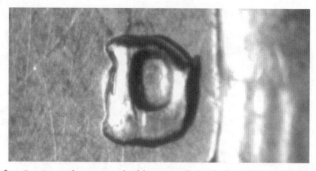

Description: The first D mintmark was punched horizontally, with the primary mintmark punched in the correct (vertical) orientation. The variety can easily be identified by the upper serif of the underlying D, which appears as a spike protruding from the upper part of the curve.

	EF-40	AU-50	MS-60	MS-63	MS-65	MS-66
VARIETY:	$15	$25	$50	$75	$100	$150
NORMAL:			$1	$4	$15	$28

Comments: This variety is a relatively new discovery.

1954, PROOF
FS-10-1954-101

Variety: Doubled Die Obverse
PUP: Date
URS-6 · I-3 · L-3

CONECA 1-O-VI

Description: The doubling is evident as extreme extra thickness on all obverse lettering, especially on the 9 and 4 of the date.

	PF-63	PF-65	PF-66
VARIETY:	$20	$35	$50
NORMAL:	$14	$26	$34

Comments: This variety can be easily detected by the die chip at the base of the 4.

1954
FS-10-1954-801

Variety: Doubled Die Reverse
PUP: Right side of torch base and oak stem
URS-1 · I-4 · L-5

CONECA Unlisted

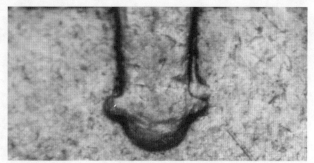

Description: The doubling is evident at the bottom of the torch and on the oak stem, rotated slightly in a counterclockwise direction.

	EF-40	AU-50	MS-60	MS-63	MS-65	MS-66
VARIETY:	$25	$50	$75	$100	$150	$200
NORMAL:			$1	$3	$15	$30

Comments: This is a very exciting new discovery. Because it is new, the values are subjective. Further study and improved photographs will require a higher-grade specimen.

1954-S
FS-10-1954S-501

Variety: Repunched Mintmark
PUP: Mintmark
URS-5 · I-3 · L-3

CONECA RPM 1

Description: Secondary S mintmarks are evident northwest of the primary S, and very slightly south of the primary S.

	EF-40	AU-50	MS-60	MS-63	MS-65	MS-66
VARIETY:	$8	$10	$15	$25	$35	$50
NORMAL:			$1	$3	$16	$29

Comments: RPMs in this series are comparatively marketable.

1956, PROOF
FS-10-1956-101

Variety: Doubled Die Obverse
PUP: IN GOD WE TRUST, date
URS-7 · I-3 · L-3

CONECA 2-O-VI

Description: Extreme extra thickness, typical of the Class VI doubled dies, is evident on IN GOD WE TRUST, LIBERTY, the date, and designer's initials.

	PF-63	PF-65	PF-66
VARIETY:	$20	$35	$50
NORMAL:	$8	$17	$20

Comments: For more on Class VI doubled dies, refer to the *Cherrypickers' Guide* web site at www.cherrypickersguide.com.

1959-D
FS-10-1959D-502

Variety: Repunched Mintmark
PUP: Mintmark
URS-4 · I-3 · L-3

CONECA RPM 4

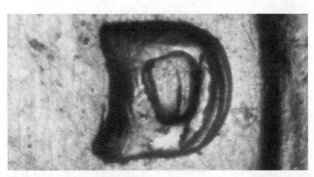

Description: This RPM exhibits a secondary curve west evident within the primary loop, and portions of the secondary vertical to the left of the primary.

	EF-40	AU-50	MS-60	MS-63	MS-65	MS-66
VARIETY:	$8	$10	$15	$20	$30	$40
NORMAL:			$1	$3	$15	$22

Comments: This is one of many recently listed Roosevelt dime RPMs. The primary D exhibits strike doubling on the right.

1959-D

FS-10-1959D-503

Variety: Repunched Mintmark
PUP: Mintmark
URS-4 · I-3 · L-3

CONECA RPM 3

Description: Portions of a secondary D mintmark are evident west of the primary D, most noticeably the lower serif of the weaker D left of the primary D.

	EF-40	AU-50	MS-60	MS-63	MS-65	MS-66
VARIETY:	$8	$10	$15	$20	$30	$40
NORMAL:			$1	$3	$15	$22

Comments: This is one of many recently listed Roosevelt dime RPMs.

1959-D

FS-10-1959D-511

Variety: Repunched Mintmark
PUP: Mintmark
URS-4 · I-4 · L-5

CONECA Unknown

Description: The D mintmark was punched into the die inverted, then punched with the D correct.

	EF-40	AU-50	MS-60	MS-63	MS-65	MS-66
VARIETY:	$25	$40	$50	$75	$100	$175
NORMAL:			$1	$3	$15	$22

Comments: This is an extremely tough variety to locate.

1960, PROOF   FS-10-1960-102a

Variety: Doubled Die Obverse, Early Die State   **Early Die State CONECA 5-O-V**
PUP: Date, IN GOD WE TRUST
URS-5 · I-4 · L-4

Description: Extremely strong doubling is evident on all obverse lettering and on the date.

	PF-63	PF-65	PF-66	PF-67
VARIETY:	$200	$350	$500	$750
NORMAL:	$3	$7	$9	$21

Comments: Because it has been well known for many years, this variety may be difficult to cherry-pick! The early die state is many times rarer than the late die state. The specimen shown is early- to mid-die state.

1960, PROOF   FS-10-1960-102b

Variety: Doubled Die Obverse Late Die State   **CONECA 5-O-V**
PUP: Date, IN GOD WE TRUST
URS-9 · I-3 · L-2

Description: Extremely strong doubling is evident on all obverse lettering and on the date. The late die state specimens exhibit a very weak date.

	PF-63	PF-65	PF-66	PF-67
VARIETY:	$200	$350	$500	$750
NORMAL:	$3	$7	$9	$21

Comments: Values for late die state (LDS) specimens are much lower than the values for early die state (EDS) specimens.

1960, PROOF FS-10-1960-801

Variety: Doubled Die Reverse CONECA 1-R-V
PUP: UNITED
URS-4 · I-3 · L-2

Description: Moderate doubling is evident on all reverse lettering, with the strongest spread on UNITED, ONE, and E PLU.

	PF-63	PF-65	PF-66
VARIETY:	$35	$75	$125
NORMAL:	$3	$7	$9

Comments: Relatively few specimens of this variety have been reported to date.

1960-D FS-10-1960D-501

Variety: Repunched Mintmark CONECA RPM 3
PUP: Mintmark
URS-5 · I-3 · L-3

Description: This RPM is evidenced by two secondary vertical lines within the opening of the main D, and a spike right of the primary D.

	EF-40	AU-50	MS-60	MS-63	MS-65	MS-66
VARIETY:	$8	$10	$15	$20	$30	$40
NORMAL:			$1	$3	$15	$22

Comments: This is one of many recently listed Roosevelt dime RPMs.

1961-D

FS-10-1961D-801

Variety: Doubled Die Reverse
CONECA 1-R-1
PUP: UNITED
URS-5 · I-3 · L-2

Description: Moderate doubling is evident on UNITED, and ONE DIME, with a lighter spread on STATES OF AMERICA and E PLURIBUS UNUM.

	EF-40	AU-50	MS-60	MS-63	MS-65	MS-66
VARIETY:	$5	$10	$15	$20	$30	$50
NORMAL:			$1	$3	$15	$20

Comments: Relatively few specimens have been reported to date.

1962-D

FS-10-1962D-501

Variety: Repunched Mintmark
CONECA RPM 5
PUP: Mintmark
URS-4 · I-5 · L-5

 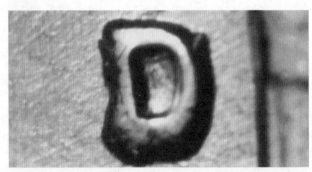

Description: The D was punched into the die horizontally first, then corrected.

	EF-40	AU-50	MS-60	MS-63	MS-65	MS-66
VARIETY:	$20	$25	$35	$50	$75	$125
NORMAL:			$1	$3	$15	$20

Comments: This is a new discovery; few specimens have been reported.

1963
FS-10-1963-101

Variety: Doubled Die Obverse   CONECA 1-O-II+V
PUP: Date
URS-5 · I-3 · L-2

Description: The doubling is evident on the date, LIBERTY, and IN GOD WE TRUST.

	EF-40	AU-50	MS-60	MS-63	MS-65	MS-66
VARIETY:	$5	$10	$15	$20	$30	$50
NORMAL:			$1	$3	$15	$20

Comments: This variety can be found in Mint sets. Referred to as the "forked-tail" variety.

1963, PROOF
FS-10-1963-801 (017)

Variety: Doubled Die Reverse   CONECA 7-R-V
PUP: UNITED
URS-7 · I-3 · L-3

Description: The doubling is evident with a strong spread on UNITED, and to a lesser degree, on STATES OF AMERICA, E PLURIBUS UNUM, the leaves, and ONE DIME.

	PF-63	PF-65	PF-66
VARIETY:	$35	$50	$75
NORMAL:	$3	$7	$9

Comments: This variety was incorrectly listed in *CPG* (third edition) as CONECA 5-R-II+V.

1963, PROOF FS-10-1963-802 (017.5)

Variety: Doubled Die Reverse CONECA 9-R-1
PUP: UNITED
URS-9 · I-3 · L-3

Description: Very strong doubling is evident on all lettering, but strongest on UNITED and ONE DIME.

	PF-63	PF-65	PF-66
VARIETY:	$175	$250	$350
NORMAL:	$3	$7	$9

Comments: This is likely the most impressive reverse doubled die for the date in Proof.

1963, PROOF FS-10-1963-803 (018)

Variety: Doubled Die Reverse CONECA 12-R-V
PUP: UNITED
URS-6 · I-3 · L-3

Description: The doubling is evident on UNITED STATES, and E PLU, with weaker doubling visible on OF AMERICA, ONE DIME, and other elements.

	PF-63	PF-65	PF-66
VARIETY:	$35	$50	$75
NORMAL:	$3	$7	$9

Comments: There are 21 different doubled dies listed by CONECA for the 1963 Roosevelt reverse. Eighteen of those are on Proof coinage.

1963, PROOF

FS-10-1963-804

Variety: Doubled Die Reverse
PUP: UNITED
URS-6 · I-3 · L-3

CONECA 4-R-I

Description: The doubling is very strong on UNITED, with split serifs on most other reverse letters.

	PF-63	PF-65	PF-66
VARIETY:	$50	$75	$125
NORMAL:	$3	$7	$9

Comments: This variety is somewhat similar to FS-10-1963-801 (017).

1963

FS-10-1963-805

Variety: Doubled Die Reverse
PUP: UNITED
URS-6 · I-3 · L-2

CONECA 14-R-V

Description: Doubling is evident on UNITED, E PLURIBUS, the olive branch, and the stem. Lesser doubling is also visible on ONE DIME.

	EF-40	AU-50	MS-60	MS-63	MS-65	MS-66
VARIETY:	$5	$10	$20	$30	$50	$75
NORMAL:			$1	$3	$15	$20

Comments: Reminder—this is not a Proof coin!

1963-D
FS-10-1963D-801

Variety: Doubled Die Reverse
CONECA 1-R-IV
PUP: AMERICA
URS-5 · I-3 · L-3

 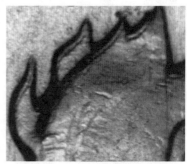

Description: Doubling is evident on all reverse lettering, with the most evident doubling on AMERICA and the top of the flame.

	EF-40	AU-50	MS-60	MS-63	MS-65	MS-66
VARIETY:	$10	$20	$50	$100	$175	$250
NORMAL:			$1	$3	$15	$20

Comments: Most Mint State specimens will be MS-63 or lower.

1964, PROOF
FS-10-1964-101 (018.4)

Variety: Doubled Die Obverse
CONECA 5-O-V
PUP: IN GOD WE TRUST, LIBERTY
URS-3 · I-4 · L-4

Description: Strong doubling is evident on IN GOD WE TRUST, LIBERTY, and on the designer's initials.

	PF-63	PF-65	PF-66
VARIETY:	$350	$550	$750
NORMAL:	$3	$6	$8

Comments: There are at least four weaker obverse doubled dies for 1964 Proof dimes.

1964 — FS-10-1964-801

Variety: Doubled Die Reverse
PUP: DIME, AMERICA
URS-4 · I-3 · L-3

CONECA 6-R-I

Description: The doubling is evident on all reverse lettering, oak stems and leaves, and the flame, with a clockwise (CW) spread. Doubling is strongest on DIME and AMERICA.

	EF-40	AU-50	MS-60	MS-63	MS-65	MS-66
VARIETY:	$50	$75	$100	$175	$250	$375
NORMAL:			$1	$3	$13	$24

Comments: This variety and the next are similar, but the doubling is in different directions.

1964 — FS-10-1964-802 (018.3)

Variety: Doubled Die Reverse
PUP: DIME, AMERICA
URS-4 · I-3 · L-3

CONECA 8-R-I

Description: The doubling is evident on all reverse lettering, oak stems, and the flame, with a counterclockwise (CCW) spread. Doubling is strongest on AMERICA.

	EF-40	AU-50	MS-60	MS-63	MS-65	MS-66
VARIETY:	$20	$30	$40	$50	$75	$100
NORMAL:			$1	$3	$13	$24

Comments: Compare the direction of the doubling with that of the previous listing.

1964-D

FS-10-1964D-501

Variety: Repunched Mintmark
PUP: Mintmark
URS-5 · I-3 · L-3

CONECA RPM 3

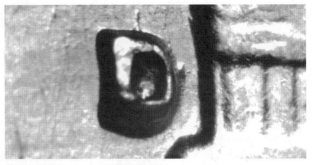

Description: The secondary mintmark is visible with a wide spread toward the northeast. The left upright and lower right curve of the weaker D are evident.

	EF-40	AU-50	MS-60	MS-63	MS-65	MS-66
VARIETY:	$5	$7	$10	$15	$25	$35
NORMAL:			$1	$3	$13	$24

Comments: Specimens above MS65 are rare.

1964-D

FS-10-1964D-502 (018.7)

Variety: Misplaced Mintmark
PUP: Mintmark—torch area
URS-3 · I-4 · L-5

CONECA RPM 6

Description: A trace of a secondary mintmark is evident protruding from the left side of the torch.

	EF-40	AU-50	MS-60	MS-63	MS-65	MS-66
VARIETY:	$25	$50	$75	$125	$250	$400
NORMAL:			$1	$3	$13	$24

Comments: This variety was discovered in 1996 by Joe Miller, and is one of the most dramatic RPMs ever found!

1964-D
FS-10-1964D-503

Variety: Repunched Mintmark
PUP: Mintmark
URS-4 · I-3 · L-3

CONECA RPM 4

Description: The secondary mintmark is visible south of the primary, but is somewhat weak. The lower serif on the secondary D is most prominent.

	EF-40	AU-50	MS-60	MS-63	MS-65	MS-66
VARIETY:	$5	$7	$10	$15	$25	$35
NORMAL:			$1	$3	$13	$24

Comments: This is a relatively new discovery.

1964-D
FS-10-1964D-504

Variety: Repunched Mintmark
PUP: Mintmark
URS-4 · I-3 · L-3

CONECA—Unknown

Description: The secondary D is visible south of the primary, but is very weak. Only the left upright and a small portion of the right lower curve of the secondary D are evident.

	EF-40	AU-50	MS-60	MS-63	MS-65	MS-66
VARIETY:	$5	$7	$10	$15	$25	$35
NORMAL:			$1	$3	$13	$24

Comments: This is a relatively new discovery.

1964-D

FS-10-1964D-505

Variety: Repunched Mintmark
PUP: Mintmark
URS-4 · I-3 · L-3

CONECA—Unknown

Description: This RPM is very similar to FS-503, yet the underlying mintmark on FS-505 is positioned just slightly further left than on 503.

	EF-40	AU-50	MS-60	MS-63	MS-65	MS-66
VARIETY:	$5	$7	$10	$15	$25	$35
NORMAL:			$1	$3	$13	$24

Comments: This variety is also a relatively new discovery.

1964-D

FS-10-1964D-506

Variety: Repunched Mintmark
PUP: Mintmark
URS-4 · I-3 · L-3

CONECA RPM 9

Description: The secondary D is evident south of the primary D. The most evident portion of the underlying D is the lower serif.

	EF-40	AU-50	MS-60	MS-63	MS-65	MS-66
VARIETY:	$5	$7	$10	$15	$25	$35
NORMAL:			$1	$3	$13	$24

Comments: This is another relatively new discovery.

1964-D
FS-10-1964D-801

Variety: Doubled Die Reverse
CONECA 1-R-I
PUP: UNITED STATES OF AMERICA
URS-5 · I-3 · L-3

Description: Doubling is evident on all reverse lettering, the top of the flame, and the tips of the leaves on higher-grade specimens.

	EF-40	AU-50	MS-60	MS-63	MS-65	MS-66
VARIETY:	$30	$50	$75	$100	$150	$250
NORMAL:			$1	$3	$13	$24

Comments: Specimens above MS-65 are rare.

1964-D
FS-10-1964D-802

Variety: Doubled Die Reverse
CONECA 3-R-V
PUP: ONE, E PLU
URS-6 · I-3 · L-3

Description: The doubling is most evident on ONE DIME, UNITED, E PLU, and the oak stems. Lesser doubling is visible on RIBUS UNUM and AMERICA.

	EF-40	AU-50	MS-60	MS-63	MS-65	MS-66
VARIETY:	$30	$50	$75	$100	$150	$250
NORMAL:			$1	$3	$13	$24

Comments: This variety may be undervalued.

1964-D

FS-10-1964D-803

Variety: Doubled Die Reverse

CONECA—N/L

PUP: AMERICA

URS-1 · I-3 · L-3

Description: Moderate doubling is evident on OF AMERICA, DIME, US UNUM, and the oak leaves on the right.

	EF-40	AU-50	MS-60	MS-63	MS-65	MS-66
VARIETY:	$30	$50	$75	$100	$150	$250
NORMAL:			$1	$3	$13	$24

Comments: This is the only specimen that has been reported to date.

1967

FS-10-1967-101 (019)

Variety: Doubled Die Obverse

CONECA 1-O-II

PUP: IN GOD WE TRUST

URS-3 · I-4 · L-5

Description: Doubling is evident on IN GOD WE TRUST, the date, and designer's initials.

	EF-40	AU-50	MS-60	MS-63	MS-65	MS-66
VARIETY:	$75	$100	$150	$250	$400	$550
NORMAL:			$1	$2	$7	$18

Comments: Although it has been known for years, this remains a very rare doubled die.

1968 — FS-10-1968-101

Variety: Doubled Die Obverse
CONECA 1-O-V
PUP: LIBERTY
URS-5 · I-3 · L-2

Description: The doubling is evident on LIBERTY, IN GOD WE TRUST, the date, and the designer's initials.

	EF-40	AU-50	MS-60	MS-63	MS-65	MS-66
VARIETY:	$20	$30	$40	$50	$75	$125
NORMAL:				$1	$5	$11

Comments: Discovered by James Wiles, this variety can be found in some Mint sets.

1968-S, PROOF — FS-10-1968S-101 (020)

Variety: Doubled Die Obverse
CONECA 2-O-V
PUP: LIBERTY
URS-3 · I-4 · L-4

Description: The doubling is evident on LIBERTY and IN GOD WE TRUST, and slightly on the date.

	PF-63	PF-65	PF-66
VARIETY:	$250	$350	$500
NORMAL:	$2	$3	$4

Comments: Although it has been known for years, this remains a very rare variety.

1968-S, PROOF
FS-10-1968S-102 (020.2)

Variety: Doubled Die Obverse
CONECA 8-O-I
PUP: IN GOD WE TRUST, date
URS-3 · I-4 · L-4

Description: There is moderate doubling on IN GOD WE TRUST, the designer's initials, and the date, with a light spread on LIBERTY.

	PF-63	PF-65	PF-66
VARIETY:	$250	$350	$500
NORMAL:	$2	$3	$4

Comments: This is also a very rare variety.

1968, PROOF, NO S
FS-10-1968S-501

Variety: Missing Mintmark
CONECA—N/L
PUP: IN GOD WE TRUST
URS-5 · I-5 · L-5

Description: The S mintmark was inadvertently omitted from the die.

	PF-63	PF-65	PF-66	PF-67
VARIETY:	$6,000	$6,500	$7,500	$8,500
NORMAL:	$3	$6	$8	$20

Comments: The defective die was probably discovered before the end of the die's life.

1968-S, PROOF

FS-10-1968S-502

Variety: Repunched Mintmark
PUP: Mintmark
URS-4 · I-3 · L-3

CONECA RPM 1

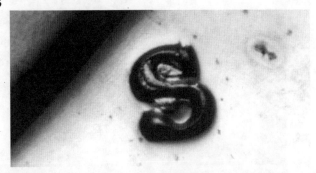

Description: The secondary mintmark is very close to and west of the primary S.

	PF-63	PF-65	PF-66
VARIETY:	$10	$15	$25
NORMAL:	$3	$6	$8

Comments: The obverse is also a very minor doubled die, but does not increase the coin's value.

1968-S, PROOF

FS-10-1968S-801 (020.3)

Variety: Doubled Die Reverse
PUP: UNITED, DIME
URS-4 · I-3 · L-3

CONECA 1-R-I

Description: The doubling is evident on UNITED STATES, ONE DIME, and E PLURIBUS UNUM. Weaker doubling is evident on AMERICA and on the olive stems.

	PF-63	PF-65	PF-66
VARIETY:	$125	$250	$350
NORMAL:	$3	$6	$8

Comments: This variety is considered very rare.

1968-S, PROOF

FS-10-1968S-802

Variety: Doubled Die Reverse
PUP: UNITED
URS-2 · I-3 · L-2

CONECA 4-R-I

Description: Moderate doubling is clear on UNITED STATES OF AMERICA, but lesser doubling is visible on ONE DIME.

	PF-63	PF-65	PF-66
VARIETY:	$25	$50	$75
NORMAL:	$3	$6	$8

Comments: This variety may be difficult to find.

1969-D

FS-10-1969D-501 (020.4)

Variety: Repunched Mintmark
PUP: Mintmark
URS-5 · I-3 · L-3

CONECA RPM 1

Description: This RPM has a very wide spread to the northeast.

	EF-40	AU-50	MS-60	MS-63	MS-65	MS-66
VARIETY:	$10	$15	$20	$25	$50	$75
NORMAL:				$1	$5	$10

Comments: Look in those Mint sets for this variety!

1970 — FS-10-1970-801 (020.6)

Variety: Doubled Die Reverse
PUP: UNITED STATES OF AMERICA
URS-3 · I-4 · L-5

CONECA 1-R-V

Description: Doubling is evident on all reverse lettering, especially on UNITED STATES OF AMERICA, with slightly weaker doubling on ONE DIME.

	EF-40	AU-50	MS-60	MS-63	MS-65	MS-66
VARIETY	$25	$75	$150	$225	$300	$400
NORMAL:				$1	$5	$10

Comments: This variety is extremely rare. The values shown may be low.

1970-D — FS-10-1970D-801 (020.6)

Variety: Doubled Die Reverse
PUP: DIME, AMERICA
URS-8 · I-3 · L-2

CONECA 1-R-V

PC

Description: Doubling is evident on UNITED STATES OF AMERICA, the flame, the tops of the oak leaves, and very slightly on UNUM.

	EF-40	AU-50	MS-60	MS-63	MS-65	MS-66
VARIETY:	$5	$10	$15	$20	$25	$35
NORMAL:				$1	$5	$10

Comments: This is one of three different reverse doubled dies known that have been found in Mint sets.

1970-D

FS-10-1970D-802

Variety: Doubled Die Reverse
PUP: UNITED STATES OF AMERICA
URS-7 · I-3 · L-2

PC

Description: Moderate doubling is evident on all reverse lettering, the flame, and the tops of the oak leaves.

	EF-40	AU-50	MS-60	MS-63	MS-65	MS-66
VARIETY:	$10	$15	$20	$25	$50	$75
NORMAL:				$1	$5	$10

Comments: This is arguably the nicest of all the 1970-D reverse doubled dies. This variety can also be found in Mint sets.

1975-S

FS-10-1975S-501

Variety: Repunched Mintmark
PUP: Mintmark
URS-6 · I-3 · L-3

YN

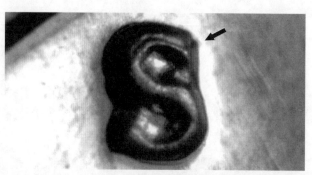

Description: The secondary mintmark north is very close, visible at the top of the S.

	PF-63	PF-65	PF-66
VARIETY:	$10	$15	$25
NORMAL:	$2	$5	$7

Comments: There are at least two different RPMs for this date and mint.

1982, NO P   FS-10-1982-501 (021)

Variety: Missing Mintmark   CONECA—N/L
PUP: Mintmark
URS-10 · I-4 · L-4

Description: The mintmark (P) was omitted from this working die. There are two versions of this variety: one with a strong strike and one with a weak strike. The strong strike is far more valuable and in demand than the weak strike.

	AU-50	MS-60	MS-63	MS-65	MS-66
VARIETY:	$75	$95	$125	$200	$600
NORMAL:		$2	$4	$8	$18

Comments: Compare the strong strike here with the weak strike in the next listing.

1982, NO P   FS-10-1982-502

Variety: Missing Mintmark   CONECA—N/L
PUP: Mintmark
URS-11 · I-2 · L-2

Description: The mintmark (P) was omitted from this working die. This is the weak strike, which is less interesting and commands far less value than the previous listing.

	AU-50	MS-60	MS-63	MS-65	MS-66
VARIETY:	$10	$30	$40	$75	$95
NORMAL:		$2	$4	$8	$18

Comments: This weak strike is listed here so that collectors will be able to make comparisons and offer values for the weak-strike version.

1983-D

FS-10-1983D-501

Variety: Repunched Mintmark
PUP: Mintmark
URS-5 · I-3 · L-3

CONECA RPM 1

Description: A secondary D is visible protruding from the primary D. Only a small portion of the left upright bar of the underlying D is visible.

	EF-40	AU-50	MS-60	MS-63	MS-65	MS-66
VARIETY:	$10	$15	$20	$25	$50	$75
NORMAL:				$3	$5	$8

Comments: This is one of the lastest-dated RPMs for the series!

Questionable Varieties

We have included the next three listings for several reasons. These varieties do catch the eye of many collectors, both novice and seasoned. Some variety enthusiasts believe them to be misplaced mintmark varieties; however, while all three varieties show an image that appears to be a misplaced mintmark, in our opinion there is simply not enough evidence to classify them conclusively. We do not intend to state categorically that they are not misplaced mintmarks; we simply can't state for sure they are. We have not assigned on FS number to them.

All the specimens we have seen come from very late die states, as evidenced by the "orange-peel" effect clearly visible on the coins' surfaces. We have not seen any of these in an earlier die state.

The inclusion of these varieties will provide a reference for understanding or describing the variety. Additionally, the novice collector will recognize that there are still questions about their validity.

1985-P

No FS#

Variety: Possible Misplaced Mintmark
CONECA—N/L
PUP: Area on neck and field
URS-N/A · I-2 · L-2

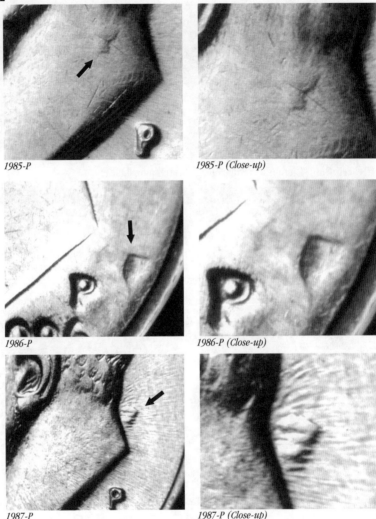

| 1985-P | 1985-P (Close-up) |

| 1986-P | 1986-P (Close-up) |

| 1987-P | 1987-P (Close-up) |

Description: For the 1985-P, a faint image, which some enthusiasts believe is a misplaced P mintmark, is visible on the neck just below the hairline. For the 1986-P, a faint image, which some enthusiasts believe is a misplaced P mintmark is visible in the field just right of the primary mintmark. For the 1987-P, a faint image, which some enthusiasts feel is a misplaced P mintmark, is visible in the field by the neck on an even level with the lower ear.

	MS-63	MS-65	MS-66
VARIETY:	n/a	n/a	n/a
NORMAL:	$3	$5	$8

Comments: Please read the commentary on the preceding page.

2004-D
FS-10-2004D-701

Variety: Curved Image
PUP: Ear
URS-2 · I-4 · L-4

CONECA—N/L

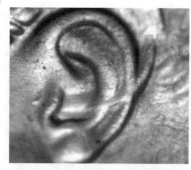

Description: There is a circular image overlapping the ear.

	MS-63	MS-65	MS-66
VARIETY:	n/a	n/a	n/a
NORMAL:	$3	$5	$8

Comments: An employee of the Denver Mint probably added the circular image to the die deliberately. The size and shape of this added image are very similar to those known on the reverse of the two different Wisconsin D-Mint quarters, also featured in this volume.

PCI, Inc.

Certified Coin Grading Service

P.O. Box 486, Rossville, GA 30741
(800) 277-2646
www.pcicoins.com

CERTIFIED CAPSULE®
PCI
COIN GRADING SERVICE

Twenty-Cent Pieces, 1875–1878

This abbreviated denomination was produced for circulation only in 1875 and 1876, but Proof coinage was also struck in 1877 and 1878. Mintages were low for the circulation coinage, meaning very few production dies were used. As a result, the varieties that do exist are relatively common. In fact, the major variety, a misplaced date for 1875-S, is far more common than the date without the misplaced date.

Clubs and Educational Information

For those seriously interested in the series, we strongly recommend membership in the Liberty Seated Collectors Club (LSCC), which we believe to be one of the very best specialty clubs in numismatics. The club issues its official publication, the *Gobrecht Journal*, three times each year. This 52-page newsletter is loaded with excellent educational articles. The club has an outstanding web site at www .numismalink.com/lscc.html. As of this writing, the annual dues are $15—a bargain, considering the amount of information available. If you join the LSCC, you will be connecting with some of the most serious and knowledgeable collectors and dealers in the hobby. For more information, contact

Liberty Seated Collectors Club
Mark Sheldon, Secretary/Treasurer
P.O. Box 261
Wellington OH 44090

1875-S

FS-20-1875S-301

Variety: Misplaced Date
PUP: Denticles below date
URS-14 · I-3 · L-2

No other attribution

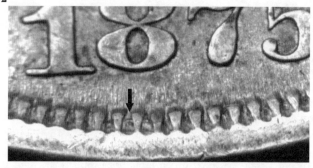

Description: The top of a digit, likely an 8, is visible in the denticles below the primary 8.

	VG-8	F-12	VF-20	EF-40	AU-50	MS-60	MS-63
VARIETY:	$50	$81	$92	$125	$283	$442	$925
NORMAL:	$50	$81	$92	$125	$283	$442	$925

Comments: Don't expect a premium on this variety or the next. This date without an MPD is actually scarcer than one with the digits in the denticles.

1875-S

FS-20-1875S-302

Variety: Misplaced Date
PUP: Denticles below date, mintmark
URS-tk · I-tk · L-tk

CONECA RPM 1

Description: The top of a digit, likely a 5, is visible in the denticles below the primary 7. The S mint-mark is repunched, with the secondary S evident and tilted.

	VG-8	F-12	VF-20	EF-40	AU-50	MS-60	MS-63
VARIETY:	$50	$81	$92	$125	$283	$442	$925
NORMAL:	$50	$81	$92	$125	$283	$442	$925

Comments: Don't expect a premium on this variety or the previous. This date without an MPD is actually scarcer than one with the digits in the denticles.

Capped Bust Quarters, 1815–1838

Capped Bust coinage varieties may be slightly different from what many of us are accustomed to encountering in late-19th-century and later coinage. During the Bust era the die-making process was somewhat different from that of later years.

Often a matrix and punches were used to place many of the design elements, letters, and numbers into the working die, rather than the hub (as was used for later coinage). Therefore, it is not uncommon to see slight differences in positioning of these elements. In some cases individual letter or number punches were used, which can account for one letter or number appearing over another.

Clubs and Educational Information

Membership in a specialty club is always informative and well worth the relatively modest cost. The John Reich Collectors Society, which focuses on Capped Bust half dimes, dimes, quarters, halves, and dollars, is one of the most active and educational clubs in the United States. A membership application is available online at www.jrcs.org, or by writing to

John Reich Collectors Society
Attn: Brad Karoleff
P.O. Box 135
Harrison OH 45040

1831

FS-25-1831-301

Variety: Repunched Date
Breen 3919
PUP: Numeral 1's in date
URS-7 · I-3 · L-3

Description: A large-date logo punch was used over a small-date logo punch. The 1's and the 8 are clearly repunched.

	VF-20	EF-40	AU-50	MS-60	MS-63
VARIETY:	$150	$325	$650	$900	$2,600
NORMAL:	$104	$267	$555	$820	$2,425

Comments: This variety brings a small premium over the normal coin.

1833

FS-25-1833-901

Variety: Repunched Letters Reverse
Breen 3924
PUP: OF AMERICA on reverse
URS-8 · I-3 · L-3

Description: The letters OF and AM on the reverse have been repositioned.

	VF-20	EF-40	AU-50	MS-60	MS-63
VARIETY:	$150	$350	$675	$1,250	$2,800
NORMAL:	$125	$308	$610	$1,175	$2,675

Comments: This variety can be found with a little looking!

1834

FS-25-1834-901

Variety: Repunched Letters Reverse
PUP: OF AMERICA on reverse
URS-4 · I-4 · L-3

Breen—N/L

Description: Very similar to the previous listing, the OF is re-engraved with the letters connected at the top, and the first A in AMERICA is also re-engraved. Other identifying characteristics: no period after C in denotation; 5 and C are farther apart.

	VF-20	EF-40	AU-50	MS-60	MS-63
VARIETY:	n/a	n/a	n/a	n/a	n/a
NORMAL:	$125	$308	$610	$1,175	$2,675

Comments: This is a rare variety, especially if very sharp. Too little information is available to value this variety.

Specializing in Major Mint Errors and "One of a Kind" Pieces

We Buy Major Error Type Coins, Modern Coins, and Foreign Coins. A Single Rare Piece or a Large Collection!

Visit www.fredweinberg.com to view more than 600 PCGS/NGC Major Error Coins, and more than 500 "Raw" Major Error Coins for sale, or see us at all major coin shows.

Fred Weinberg & Co.
Dealer in Major Mint Error Coins & Currency
800.338.6533

fax: 818.986-2153 • email: fred@fredweinberg.com • 16311 Ventura Blvd., Suite 1298 • Encino, CA 91436

LBRC

Seated Liberty & Variety Specialist

Larry Briggs Rare Coins

BUYING • SELLING • TRADING

Liberty Seated, Early Date and Rare Coins a Speciality

Want Lists Solicited

GIVE US A CALL TODAY FOR THOSE HARD-TO-FIND
DOUBLED DIES, RPMS & MPDS

CHOOSE FROM THOUSANDS OF UNIQUE
CHOICE ERROR AND VARIETY COINS

**OFFCENTERS • BROADSTRIKES
DOUBLESTRIKES • TRIPLESTRIKES**

LBRC
Larry Briggs Rare Coins
205 W. High Street - Suite 201
Lima, Ohio 45801

TELEPHONE: 419-228-3831
EMAIL: LBRC@BRIGHT.NET • FAX: 419-228-0137

Experience In Coins Since 1954

Liberty Seated Quarters, 1838–1891

L iberty Seated quarters are a paradise for variety enthusiasts. Significant varieties are known and can be found for virtually every date and mint. From minor repunched mintmarks to major doubled dies, and even major design changes, the varieties are abundant

Virtually all of the varieties within the series are in high demand by the large number of Liberty Seated specialists. In general, values for the varieties have been increasing at an even faster rate than for the normal coins. An eagle-eyed cherrypicker can easily earn a significant income by picking the varieties that go unnoticed by most dealers.

Clubs and Educational Information

For those seriously interested in the series, we strongly recommend membership in the Liberty Seated Collectors Club (LSCC), which we believe to be one of the very best specialty clubs in numismatics. The club issues its official publication, The *Gobrecht Journal,* three times each year. This 52-page newsletter is loaded with excellent educational articles.

The club has an outstanding web site at www.numismalink.com/lscc.html. As of this writing, the annual dues are $15—a bargain, considering the amount of information available. If you join the LSCC, you will be connecting with some of the most serious and knowledgeable collectors and dealers in the hobby. For more information, contact

Liberty Seated Collectors Club
Mark Sheldon, Secretary/Treasurer
P.O. Box 261
Wellington OH 44090

1840-O, WITH DRAPERY

FS-25-1840o-501

Variety: Large O Mintmark

Briggs Rev A

PUP: Mintmark

URS-7 · I-3 · L-3

Description: The O mintmark punch used on this reverse die is about 25% larger than the others of this date and type.

	F-12	VF-20	EF-40	AU-50	MS-60	MS-63
VARIETY:	$500	$750	$1,500	$2,000	$3,000	
NORMAL:	$57	$117	$233	$400	$850	$2,725

Comments: There are two known reverse dies, with one showing doubled denticles.

1841-O, WITH DRAPERY

FS-25-1841o-101 (001)

Variety: Doubled Die Obverse

Briggs Obv 2

PUP: Shield

URS-7 · I-3 · L-3

Description: Doubling is evident on the shield, ribbon, rock, and lower gown.

	F-12	VF-20	EF-40	AU-50	MS-60	MS-63
VARIETY:	$100	$200	$350	$650	$1,000	$3,000
NORMAL:	$57	$117	$233	$400	$850	$2,725

Comments: The first three stars on the left are also doubled.

1843-O   FS-25-1843o-301

Variety: Repunched Date   Briggs Obv 2
PUP: Date
URS-8 · I-3 · L-3

Description: The secondary digits are evident north of the primary 1 and 8.

	F-12	VF-20	EF-40	AU-50	MS-60	MS-63
VARIETY:	$100	$200	$350	$800	$2,100	$5,100
NORMAL:	$45	$92	$258	$700	$1,925	$4,850

Comments: The crossbar of the 4 is doubled on higher-grade specimens.

1843-O   FS-25-1843o-501 (001.5)

Variety: Large O Mintmark   Briggs Rev F
PUP: Mintmark
URS-8 · I-3 · L-3

Description: The O mintmark was probably intended for a half dollar die.

	F-12	VF-20	EF-40	AU-50	MS-60	MS-63
VARIETY:	$175	$250	$500	$1,250	$2,000	
NORMAL:	$45	$92	$258	$700	$1,925	$4,850

Comments: Notice the die rust evident on the reverse by the mintmark.

1845

FS-25-1845-301

Variety: Repunched Date
PUP: Date
URS-6 · I-3 · L-3

Briggs Obv 3

Description: The primary 5 was punched over a smaller secondary 5, evident north.

	F-12	VF-20	EF-40	AU-50	MS-60	MS-63
VARIETY:	$75	$125	$200	$300	$500	$900
NORMAL:	$27	$36	$68	$133	$450	$675

Comments: A secondary 8 and 4 can be seen north on higher-grade specimens. These digits also appear smaller, supporting our theory that the initial date punch was likely intended for a half dime or dime.

1847

FS-25-1847-301 (002.3)

Variety: Misplaced Date
PUP: Rock area above 8 of date
URS-8 · I-3 · L-3

Briggs Obv 3

Description: The lower portion of an 8 is evident protruding from the rock above the primary 8.

	F-12	VF-20	EF-40	AU-50	MS-60	MS-63
VARIETY:	$50	$75	$100	$200	$450	$900
NORMAL:	$27	$35	$70	$167	$350	$775

Comments: Remember to look in the rock and gown on all Liberty Seated coins for misplaced digits.

1847

FS-25-1847-801 (002)

Variety: Doubled Die Reverse, RPD
PUP: UNITED STATES
URS-9 · I-3 · L-3

Briggs Obv 2, Rev A

Description: This variety is most valuable for the doubled-die reverse, which is evident on UNITED STATES OF AMERICA and QUAR. DOL., the olive leaves, the eagle's left talon and eye, and the horizontal shield lines. The RPD is evident with a secondary 7 left of the primary 7.

	F-12	VF-20	EF-40	AU-50	MS-60	MS-63
VARIETY:	$50	$70	$95	$325	$575	$900
NORMAL:	$27	$35	$70	$167	$350	$775

Comments: Although somewhat strong, the RPD is not as important as the DDR.

1850

FS-25-1850-301

Variety: Misplaced Digit
PUP: Denticles below date
URS-11 · I-3 · L-3

Briggs Obv 1

Description: The lower base of a 1 is evident protruding from the denticles.

	F-12	VF-20	EF-40	AU-50	MS-60	MS-63
VARIETY:	$75	$100	$200	$400	$950	
NORMAL:	$55	$77	$150	$333	$835	$2,150

Comments: This variety is considered somewhat common.

1853, NO ARROWS — FS-25-1853-301

Variety: Repunched Date — Briggs Obv 1
PUP: Date
URS-7 · I-3 · L-3

Description: This RPD is evident with the secondary 5 and 3 south of the primary digits.

	F-12	VF-20	EF-40	AU-50	MS-60
VARIETY:	$725	$865	$1,125	$1,650	$2,500
NORMAL:	$725	$865	$1,125	$1,650	$2,500

Comments: At one time, this variety was erroneously attributed as a 53/2. This is the only die known for 1853 that lacks the arrows and rays.

1853, ARROWS AND RAYS — FS-25-1853-1301 (003)

Variety: Overdate — Briggs Obv 1
PUP: Date and right arrow shaft
URS-6 · I-4 · L-4

Description: The 3 of the date is punched over a 4. Also evident are the repunched 8 and 5, with the weaker images slightly north and west. The right arrow shaft is also doubled north of the primary.

	F-12	VF-20	EF-40	AU-50	MS-60	MS-63
VARIETY:	$150	$200	$450	$525	$2,125	$4,150
NORMAL:	$29	$43	$121	$250	$710	$1,625

Comments: On well worn or late-die-state specimens, the doubling of the arrow shaft may be the only evidence of the overdate. This is the only quarter dollar date known to be punched over the *following* year!

1853-O, ARROWS AND RAYS
FS-25-1853o-501

Variety: O Over Horizontal O
Briggs—N/L
PUP: Mintmark
URS-4 · I-4 · L-4

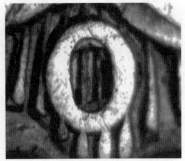

Description: A somewhat new discovery, the first O mintmark punch entered the die horizontally, with a subsequent punch in the correct orientation. The horizontal O is evident within the opening of the primary O and can also be seen right of the primary O.

	F-12	VF-20	EF-40	AU-50	MS-60	MS-63
VARIETY:	$75	$150	$400	$1,000	$3,500	
NORMAL:	$31	$55	$225	$730	$2,625	$8,340

Comments: This variety commands a fair premium.

1854-O, ARROWS
FS-25-1854o-501 (004)

Variety: Huge O Variety
Briggs Rev A
PUP: Mintmark
URS-7 · I-4 · L-4

Description: This particular O mintmark is very large, extremely thick on left side, and most irregular. This suggests that the O may have been carved into the die by hand.

	VG-8	F-12	VF-20	EF-40	AU-50	AU-55	MS-60	MS-63
VARIETY:	$1,100	$1,875	$3,250	$5,500	$8,250	$9,650		
NORMAL:		$28	$45	$100	$200	$550	$750	$1,025

Comments: There are other characteristics unique to this reverse die. Only one example has been reported in Mint State.

1856
FS-25-1856-301

Variety: Misplaced Date
Briggs—N/L
PUP: Robe right of Y of LIBERTY
URS-3 · I-3 · L-3

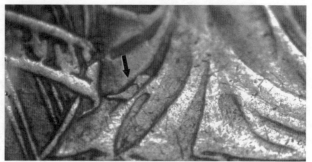

Description: The top left and bottom of a 1 is evident in the gown immediately right of the Y of LIBERTY. The top curve of a 6 is visible protruding from the rock below the foot.

	F-12	VF-20	EF-40	AU-50	MS-60	MS-63
VARIETY:	n/a	n/a	n/a	n/a	n/a	n/a
NORMAL:	$21	$27	$45	$130	$285	$435

Comments: Although the true rarity of this new variety is not yet known, it must be assumed to be extremely rare. It is too new to have established market values.

1856-S
FS-25-1856S-501 (005)

Variety: Repunched Mintmark
Briggs Rev E
PUP: Mintmark
URS-4 · I-3 · L-3

Description: A larger S mintmark is punched over a much smaller S mintmark. The smaller S mintmark was probably intended for a half dime.

	F-12	VF-20	EF-40	AU-50
VARIETY:	$150	$300	$750	$1,500
NORMAL:	$92	$180	$475	$1,275

Comments: This is one of the more desirable mintmark varieties in the series.

1857
FS-25-1857-901 (006)

Variety: Clashed Reverse Die
Briggs Rev F
PUP: Reverse by eagle's neck
URS-6 · I-4 · L-4

Description: The reverse of this 1857 Large Date quarter clashed with the reverse die of an 1857 Flying Eagle cent. Images of the FE cent reverse die are easily seen on either side of the eagle's neck, within the shield, and below the eagle's left (viewer's right) wing.

	F-12	VF-20	EF-40	AU-50	MS-60	MS-63
VARIETY:	$150	$300	$500	$750		
NORMAL:	$24	$27	$45	$125	$270	$510

Comments: Refer also to the 1857 Flying Eagle cent with muled clashed dies, in *CPG*, fourth ed., volume one.

1857-O
FS-25-1857o-301 (006.2)

Variety: Misplaced Digit
Briggs—N/L
PUP: Denticles below date
URS-3 · I-3 · L-3

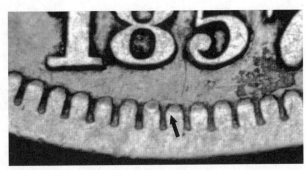

Description: The upper portion of an 8 is evident protruding from the denticles below the right side of the primary 8.

	F-12	VF-20	EF-40	AU-50	MS-60
VARIETY:	$50	$75	$100	$400	$750
NORMAL:	$25	$45	$68	$310	$635

Comments: This coin from Larry Briggs was discovered after the publication of his book on Seated Liberty quarters.

1872

FS-25-1872-301

Variety: Repunched Date
PUP: Date
URS-3 · I-3 · L-3

Briggs—N/L

Description: The digits are repunched, with the secondary images south of the primary. On the coin examined, the secondary 7 is not noticeable, but the 1, 8, and 2 are all dramatic.

	F-12	VF-20	EF-40	AU-50	MS-60
VARIETY:	$100	$150	$250	$400	$700
NORMAL:	$54	$77	$135	$225	$500

Comments: This is another variety discovered after the publication of *Comprehensive Encyclopedia of United States Liberty Seated Quarters* by Larry Briggs.

1875

FS-25-1875-301 (006.75)

Variety: Misplaced Date
PUP: Denticles below date
URS-3 · I-3 · L-3

Briggs—N/L

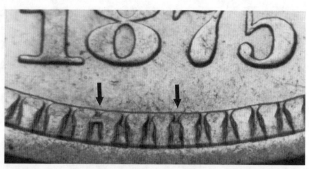

Description: The upper portion of an 8 and a 7 can be seen within the denticles below the primary date.

	F-12	VF-20	EF-40	AU-50	MS-60	MS-63
VARIETY:	$50	$75	$100	$200	$300	$500
NORMAL:	$23	$27	$45	$110	$221	$392

Comments: This is another variety discovered after the publication of the Briggs encyclopedia.

1876   FS-25-1876-301

Variety: Misplaced Date   Briggs—N/L
PUP: Denticles below date
URS-3 · I-2 · L-2

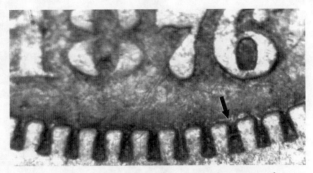

Description: The upper 6 can be seen within the denticles below the primary 6.

	F-12	VF-20	EF-40	AU-50	MS-60	MS-63
VARIETY:	$50	$75	$100	$200	$300	$500
NORMAL:	$23	$27	$45	$110	$221	$392

Comments: This variety was also discovered after the publication of the Briggs encyclopedia.

1876   FS-25-1876-302 (006.8)

Variety: Repunched Date   Briggs—N/L
PUP: Date
URS-3 · I-4 · L-4

Description: The "flag" of a secondary 1 is evident south and west of the primary 1, and a third 1 is south and west of the primary 8.

	F-12	VF-20	EF-40	AU-50	MS-60	MS-63
VARIETY:	$75	$150	$225	$300	$450	$600
NORMAL:	$23	$27	$45	$110	$221	$392

Comments: This variety, too, was discovered after the publication of the Briggs encyclopedia.

1876   FS-25-1876-303 (006.85)

Variety: Misplaced Date   Briggs—N/L
PUP: Rock above date
URS-3 · I-3 · L-3

Description: The base of a number (likely a 6) is evident protruding from the rock above the date, between the 8 and the 7.

	F-12	VF-20	EF-40	AU-50	MS-60	MS-63
VARIETY:	$50	$75	$100	$200	$300	$500
NORMAL:	$23	$27	$45	$110	$221	$392

Comments: Always check the rock and skirt on Liberty Seated coins.

1876   FS-25-1876-304

Variety: Repunched Date   Briggs Obv 6
PUP: Date
URS-5 · I-3 · L-3

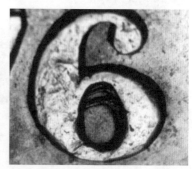

Description: Repunching is evident as a triple punched 6, seen within the loop of the 6, and very slightly north on the base of the 1.

	F-12	VF-20	EF-40	AU-50	MS-60	MS-63
VARIETY:	$75	$150	$225	$300	$450	$600
NORMAL:	$23	$27	$45	$110	$221	$392

Comments: Always check all elements on all Liberty Seated coins.

1876   FS-25-1876-305

Variety: Misplaced Date   **Briggs Obv 2**
PUP: Denticles below date
URS-5 · I-3 · L-3

Description: The tops of a 1 and an 8 are evident in the denticles below the date.

	F-12	VF-20	EF-40	AU-50	MS-60	MS-63
VARIETY:	$50	$75	$100	$200	$300	$500
NORMAL:	$23	$27	$45	$110	$221	$392

Comments: Always check the denticles on Liberty Seated coins.

1876-S   FS-25-1876S-301

Variety: Misplaced Date   **Briggs—N/L**
PUP: Denticles below date
URS-5 · I-3 · L-3

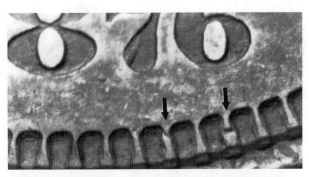

Description: The tops of a 7 and a 6 can be seen in the denticles below the date.

	F-12	VF-20	EF-40	AU-50	MS-60	MS-63
VARIETY:	$50	$75	$100	$200	$300	$500
NORMAL:	$22	$27	$55	$120	$225	$371

Comments: The reverse type is unknown, but is probably Type 2.

1876-S
FS-25-1876S-302

Variety: Misplaced Date   Briggs—N/L
PUP: Denticles below date
URS-5 · I-3 · L-3

Description: The tops of two 8's are evident below the primary 8.

	F-12	VF-20	EF-40	AU-50	MS-60	MS-63
VARIETY:	$50	$75	$100	$200	$300	$500
NORMAL:	$22	$27	$55	$120	$225	$371

Comments: The reverse type is unknown, but is probably Type 2.

1876-CC
FS-25-1876CC-301

Variety: Repunched Date   Briggs—N/L
PUP: Date
URS-3 · I-3 · L-3

Description: Secondary digits for the 1, 8, and 7 are evident south of the primary digits. The secondary digits are very close to the primary.

	F-12	VF-20	EF-40	AU-50	MS-60	MS-63
VARIETY:	$75	$100	$150	$200	$425	$750
NORMAL:	$23	$33	$82	$140	$371	$650

Comments: The reverse type is unknown, but is probably Type 2.

1877-CC   FS-25-1877CC-301

Variety: Repunched Date   Briggs Obv 2
PUP: Date
URS-5 · I-3 · L-3

 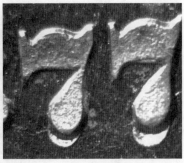

Description: The two 7's of the date are strongly repunched south.

	F-12	VF-20	EF-40	AU-50	MS-60	MS-63
VARIETY:	$75	$100	$150	$200	$425	$750
NORMAL:	$26	$30	$85	$145	$300	$590

Comments: A second, very similar RPD is also known for this date.

1877-S   FS-25-1877S-501

Variety: Repunched Mintmark   Briggs Rev D
PUP: Mintmark
URS-6 · I-4 · L-4

Description: The initial S mintmark was punched into the die horizontally, then corrected with an
upright S mintmark.

	F-12	VF-20	EF-40	AU-50	MS-60	MS-63
VARIETY:	$100	$200	$300	$400	$650	$1,500
NORMAL:	$23	$27	$50	$120	$220	$350

Comments: This is one of the most collectible mintmark varieties in the series, of longstanding
fame—cherrypicked back to the 1950s.

1891

Variety: Misplaced Date
PUP: Denticles below the date
URS-7 · I-3 · L-3

Briggs Obv 7

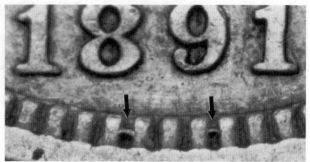

Description: The tops of an 8 and 9 are very evident protruding from the denticles below the primary date.

	F-12	VF-20	EF-40	AU-50	MS-60	MS-63
VARIETY:	$50	$100	$150	$300	$400	$550
NORMAL:	$22	$27	$45	$115	$204	$392

Comments: This is one of the more evident MPDs in this series.

THE CHERRYPICKERS' GUIDE **HELPFUL HINTS**

The varieties listed in this book are only the tip of the iceberg. Even more are yet to be discovered. Always examine closely any coin you obtain. You may soon discover that one great variety wanted by every collector in the hobby! And let us know when you do.

See appendix H for more Helpful Hints.

Barber or Liberty Head Quarter Dollars, 1892–1916

The three series of the Barber design have long been neglected when one considers the typical varieties, such as doubled dies, repunched mintmarks, overdates, and the like. For many collectors, the Barber quarter series has been somewhat of an afterthought when searching for nice varieties. But all that is changing now that many new varieties are discovered and reported, and some of the known varieties are becoming more popular. We encourage close inspection of all Barber coins.

Only a limited number of varieties in the Barber quarter series were known when the third edition of the *Cherrypickers' Guide* went to press. In this volume of the *Cherrypickers' Guide* we have included 12 varieties that are rapidly gaining in popularity. Compared to the previous four listings, one can easily see the increased interest. More varieties will certainly be included in the fifth edition. New listings are also included for the Barber dimes and Barber half dollars. Be sure to check those sections for other new listings.

Clubs and Educational Information

To obtain more knowledge on Barber coins in general, and Barber varieties in particular, we suggest membership in the Barber Coin Collectors Society. Annual dues are $15. You may make contact through

Eileen Ribar
2053 Edith Place
Merrick NY 11566
Email: emcrib@optonline.net

Their quarterly publication, the *Journal,* contains educational information on all denominations of the Barber design. The society also has a web site at www.barbercoins.org. Visitors to the site can find educational articles; membership information; and general information concerning the Barber design, the three Barber series, and Liberty Head nickels.

1892
FS-25-1892-101 (007.7)

Variety: Doubled Die Obverse
PUP: Motto
URS-8 · I-2 · L-2

Lawrence 104

Description: Doubling is very evident on IN GOD WE TRUST.

	VG-8	F-12	VF-20	EF-40	AU-50	MS-60	MS-63
VARIETY:	$25	$50	$75	$100	$200	$250	$350
NORMAL:	$7	$18	$28	$60	$98	$139	$204

Comments: This variety commands healthy premiums.

1892
FS-25-1892-301

Variety: Repunched Date, TDO
PUP: Date, Motto
URS-4 · I-2 · L-2

Lawrence—N/L

Description: The repunched date is most evident below the primary 8. The TDO is a very close spread, mostly visible on TRUST.

	VG-8	F-12	VF-20	EF-40	AU-50	MS-60	MS-63
VARIETY:	$15	$25	$50	$75	$100	$200	$250
NORMAL:	$7	$18	$28	$60	$98	$139	$204

Comments: The tripled obverse die is relatively minor; therefore, most of the value is for the repunched date.

1892

FS-25-1892-801

Variety: Tripled Die Reverse
Lawrence 105
PUP: Reverse lettering
URS-7 · I-4 · L-3

 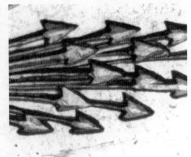

Description: Tripling is evident on all outer lettering, with doubling visible on several stars, the ribbon ends, and the arrows.

	VG-8	F-12	VF-20	EF-40	AU-50	MS-60	MS-63
VARIETY:	$25	$50	$75	$100	$200	$250	$350
NORMAL:	$7	$18	$28	$60	$98	$139	$204

Comments: Two different die states are known. Later states appear with chips evident on the upper loops of the first and last S of STATES. Die chips are common.

1892-O

FS-25-1892o-101 (007.8)

Variety: Doubled Die Obverse
Lawrence 103
PUP: Motto
URS-8 · I-3 · L-3

Description: Doubling is very evident on IN GOD WE TRUST and the ribbon ends.

	VG-8	F-12	VF-20	EF-40	AU-50	MS-60	MS-63
VARIETY:	$25	$50	$100	$150	$250	$350	$500
NORMAL:	$11	$29	$37	$63	$110	$200	$360

Comments: The reverse is a minor DDR, hardly worth the mention.

1892-O
FS-25-1892o-501

Variety: Repunched Date
Lawrence 102
PUP: Date
URS-9 · I-3 · L-3

Description: Secondary digits are visible south on all numbers, but most noticeable on the 2 of the date.

	VG-8	F-12	VF-20	EF-40	AU-50	MS-60	MS-63
VARIETY:	$25	$50	$100	$150	$250	$350	$500
NORMAL:	$11	$29	$37	$63	$110	$200	$360

Comments: This variety will bring a substantial premium.

1892-S
FS-25-1892S-501

Variety: Repunched Mintmark
Lawrence 101
PUP: Mintmark
URS-7 · I-3 · L-3

Description: The secondary S is evident northwest of the primary S.

	VG-8	F-12	VF-20	EF-40	AU-50	MS-60	MS-63
VARIETY:	$75	$100	$125	$225	$325	$500	$950
NORMAL:	$36	$63	$76	$121	$242	$367	$775

Comments: This is a very evident and popular RPM.

1902-O

Variety: Misplaced Date
PUP: Denticles below date
URS-4 · I-2 · L-2

Lawrence—N/L

Description: The top of a digit (likely a 0) can be seen in the denticles below the primary 0 of the date.

	VG-8	F-12	VF-20	EF-40	AU-50	MS-60	MS-63
VARIETY:	$25	$50	$75	$125	$200	$375	$1,000
NORMAL:	$13	$29	$60	$88	$160	$335	$940

Comments: This is one of the few listed MPDs for the Barber quarter series.

1907-D

Variety: Repunched Date, DDO
PUP: Date
URS-4 · I-3 · L-3

Lawrence 102

Description: Secondary digits are evident south on all four digits, most noticeable on the 9, 0, and 7. Minor doubling is evident on the first two stars on left and ribbon ends.

	VG-8	F-12	VF-20	EF-40	AU-50	MS-60	MS-63
VARIETY:	$25	$50	$75	$100	$200	$350	$700
NORMAL:	$7	$23	$39	$68	$155	$280	$600

Comments: You can double or triple your money if you cherrypick this variety.

1907-S

Variety: Repunched Mintmark
PUP: Mintmark
URS-7 · I-3 · L-3

Lawrence 102

Description: This RPM is evident on the notched serifs on the S. The secondary S is rotated slightly.

	VG-8	F-12	VF-20	EF-40	AU-50	MS-60	MS-63
VARIETY:	$25	$50	$75	$125	$275	$425	$950
NORMAL:	$9	$36	$50	$90	$210	$335	$835

Comments: There are at least two other RPMs known for this date.

1908-D

Variety: Misplaced Date
PUP: Denticles below the date
URS-4 · I-2 · L-2

Lawrence—N/L

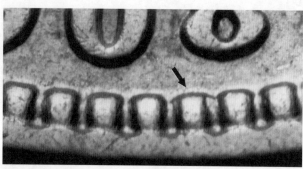

Description: The top of a digit (likely a 0) is visible in the denticles below the space between the 0 and 8.

	VG-8	F-12	VF-20	EF-40	AU-50	MS-60	MS-63
VARIETY:	$20	$35	$50	$75	$125	$225	$375
NORMAL:	$5	$17	$25	$55	$90	$185	$320

Comments: Very few MPDs are listed in this series.

1914-D

FS-25-1914D-101 (007.99)

Variety: Doubled Die Obverse
PUP: Motto
URS-5 · I-3 · L-3

Lawrence 102

Description: Doubling is evident on all obverse lettering, ribbon ends, and stars.

	VG-8	F-12	VF-20	EF-40	AU-50	MS-60	MS-63
VARIETY:	$25	$50	$75	$100	$200	$250	$400
NORMAL:	$5	$16	$26	$55	$90	$146	$236

Comments: This is a very nice doubled die, and still findable!

1916-D

FS-25-1916D-501 (008)

Variety: Repunched Mintmark
PUP: Mintmark
URS-8 · I-4 · L-4

Lawrence 102

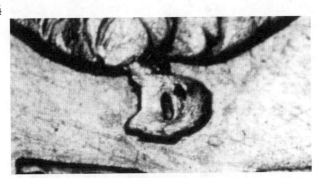

Description: The secondary D mintmark is evident within the opening of the primary mintmark. We believe this is a large D over a small D.

	VG-8	F-12	VF-20	EF-40	AU-50	MS-60	MS-63
VARIETY:	$15	$25	$50	$75	$125	$175	$225
NORMAL:	$5	$14	$25	$57	$90	$135	$204

Comments: There are at least three other RPMs known for the date.

143

Now in the Red Book!

1998 - 1999 - 2000
Lincoln Cent "Wide AM Reverse"

In John Wexler's front-page Coin World story of Jan. 22, 2001, he reported on the discovery of a 2000 dated circulation-strike Lincoln cent minted with a Proof style reverse. Shortly after his announcement the same variety was found on a 1998 cent. Even later the variety was discovered on a 1999 dated cent (as seen in my *Coin World* column)! As noted by Wexler, since 1993, the reverse for the Lincoln cent has bore noticeable differences between the dies used for circulation strikes vs. those prepared for Proof coinage. In a VIP tour of the Philadelphia Mint, (which Wexler and I attended together in 1998); a Mint spokesman said that the dies for Proof cents were different from circulation-strike dies, with special enhancements implemented for cosmetic reasons. It was obvious that the Proof style dies were never intended to be used for business-strike coinage. So far, finds of the Type-2 variety for both dates have proven very few and far between; the 1998 appearing several times scarcer than the 2000 and the 1999 downright rare!

Type 1 Diagnostics: This is the regular common design used for circulation coins; the letters AM of AMERICA are close together and virtually touching, the designer's initials, FG, at the right base of the Lincoln Memorial building, are spaced well away from the building.

Type 2 Diagnostics: This is the scarce/rare variety struck with Proof style reverse; the letters AM of AMERICA are spaced significantly further apart; the designer's initials, FG, are close to the building. Scarce to very scarce on 1998 and 2000 dated cents; rare on 1999 cents.

1998 Type-2 Wide AM Rev: MS63RD $35, MS64RD $45, MS65RD $55, ICG-65RD $65*

1999 Type-2 Wide AM Rev: MS63RD $425, MS64RD $495, MS65RD $650, PCGS Cert - Call

2000 Type-2 Wide AM Rev: MS64RD $35, MS65RD $45, ICG65RD $49.95, ICG66RD $55.

*ANACS/PCGS Grades – Call

24-Page Catalog of: Error/Variety Coins $2.00 pp.
22-Page Catalog of: Medals/Bars/Rounds $2.00 pp.
54-Page Catalog of: Rare Coin Reproductions $3.00 pp.

14 days return privilege.
Please add $3.65 postage.
PayPal (MC, VISA, DISC)

Ken Potter
P.O. Box 760232-CP, Lathrup Village, MI 48076

Phone: (313)255-8907 Cell: (313)268-3280 Email: ken@koinpro.com

ANA-LM, NLG, CONECA-LM, NCADD-FM, MSNS-LM

Numismatist Since 1959 • www.koinpro.com • Serving Collectors Since 1973

Standing Liberty Quarters, 1916–1930

For some unknown reason, there are very few varieties in the Standing Liberty quarter series. In this volume, we have included only the varieties of which we are certain. Obviously, the most dramatic variety in the series is the 1918-S, 8 Over 7, which is a very rare variety, especially in high grade.

As we have mentioned elsewhere in the text, major varieties for the 20th century seem to occur during wartime years, and the monster overdate of 1918 is a good example. One obvious reason, which is very well known, is the U.S.

government will do anything and everything possible to conserve metal for use with ammunition and equipment. This could possibly explain the use of overdated dies for production during these times.

Clubs and Educational Information

More information about varieties in the series can be obtained from the CONECA web site. CONECA is the national error/variety club devoted to the study of numismatic errors and varieties. James Wiles is the primary attributor of 20th-century die varieties for the organization. Dr. Wiles maintains a complete list of all varieties listed in the CONECA register. This list is available to Internet users.

If you're interested in learning as much as possible about errors and varieties, we highly suggest membership in CONECA. A membership application can be found on the Internet at www.conecaonline.org/join. You can also contact the membership chairman by writing to

Paul Funaiole
CONECA Membership
35 Leavitt Lane
Glenburn, ME 04401-1013

1918-S, 8 OVER 7

FS-25-1918S-101 (008.5)

Variety: Overdate/Doubled Die Obverse

Breen 4235

PUP: Date

URS-11 · I-5 · L-5

Description: This clear overdate, 1918/7, was caused by using two different dated hubs when the die was made. Because of the boldness of the 7, this variety can be confirmed easily in low grades.

	VG-8	F-12	VF-20	EF-40	AU-50	MS-60	MS-63	MS-65
VARIETY:	$1,550	$2,825	$3,350	$5,450	$9,150	$13,250	$25,000	$77,500
NORMAL:	$18	$22	$35	$40	$50	$100	$185	$300

Comments: This variety is extremely rare in high grades. We recommend authentication because alterations do exist. Genuine specimens have a small die chip above the pedestal, just to the left of the lowest star on the right.

1928-S

FS-25-1928S-501

Variety: Inverted Mintmark

Breen—N/L

PUP: Mintmark

URS-3 · I-3 · L-3

Description: An inverted S mintmark was clearly punched into the die.

	VG-8	F-12	VF-20	EF-40	AU-50	MS-60	MS-63
VARIETY:	$10	$15	$20	$50	$125	$175	$225
NORMAL:	$4	$5	$12	$27	$98	$139	$156

Comments: Inverted S-mintmark varieties are rapidly gaining in popularity.

1928-S

FS-25-1928S-502

Variety: Repunched Mintmark
PUP: Mintmark
URS-3 · I-3 · L-3

Breen 4259

Description: The primary S is punched over a slightly east and tilted S.

	VG-8	F-12	VF-20	EF-40	AU-50	MS-60	MS-63
VARIETY:	$35	$50	$75	$100	$200	$300	$450
NORMAL:	$4	$5	$12	$27	$98	$139	$156

Comments: Only six RPMs are listed by CONECA in this series.

1929-S

FS-25-1929S-401

Variety: Clashed Obverse Die
PUP: Right of Liberty's right leg
URS-3 · I-3 · L-3

Breen—N/L

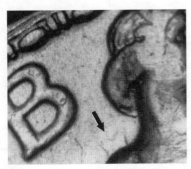 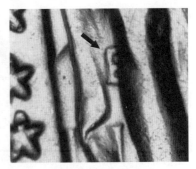

Description: This obverse die shows typical elements of a strong clashed die. An inverted B of PLURIBUS is evident protruding from the viewer's left of Liberty's right leg. The letter I of AMERICA is also evident below this B. Stars are visible left of Liberty's head.

	VG-8	F-12	VF-20	EF-40	AU-50	MS-60	MS-63
VARIETY:	$10	$15	$20	$50	$125	$175	$225
NORMAL:	$4	$5	$12	$27	$98	$139	$156

Comments: This is becoming a popular variety!

1930-S

FS-25-1930S-501

Variety: Likely Repunched Mintmark

Breen—N/L

PUP: Mintmark

URS-3 · I-3 · L-3

Description: The S mintmark appears to be punched over another S mintmark, but other possible explanations exist. This is definitely not the common shearing seen on many mintmarks. In all likelihood, this is a small S over a larger S.

	VG-8	F-12	VF-20	EF-40	AU-50	MS-60	MS-63
VARIETY:	$15	$25	$35	$75	$150	$200	$275
NORMAL:	$4	$5	$12	$27	$98	$139	$156

Comments: We would like to examine a higher-grade specimen!

THE CHERRYPICKERS' GUIDE HELPFUL HINTS

Don't forget to inspect the denticles of a coin, especially those near and beneath the date, for variety characteristics. Dozens of significant varieties exhibit portions of numbers within or protruding from the denticle. Most of these are prized additions to a collection.

See appendix H for more Helpful Hints.

Washington Quarters, 1932 to Date

Collectors of Washington quarter varieties are as avid as any group of variety specialists, and very serious in their quest for the most popular and rare specimens. They will actively compete for a hard-to-find variety.

When the first edition of the *Cherrypickers' Guide* was published in 1989, this series was one of the "sleepers" for variety specialists. At that time, many of the better varieties were known only to a few collectors, so the pickings were relatively easy. However, since about 1990, the series has become increasingly more popular, making the searches much more challenging.

Interesting and rare varieties in the Washington quarter series include some spectacular doubled dies, significant repunched mintmarks, over mintmarks, and master die alterations. One of the few known totally separated, repunched mintmarks, the 1940-D and D, is still considered one of the most elusive varieties. A couple of other very significant misplaced mintmarks have also been found in this series.

Very few reference books specializing in this series contain significant details of varieties. The most complete work is that of James Wiles, former president of the Combined Organizations of Numismatic Error Collectors of America (CONECA).

The varieties listed in this volume of the *Cherrypickers' Guide* are generally considered the best of the best. However, some of the lesser varieties are also included so that our Young Numismatists (YNs) and other novice enthusiasts can find some of the many nice varieties known in the series.

Major Design Alterations for Washington Quarters

Washington quarter specialist José Cortez, one of only a handful of people who have studied this series extensively, graciously provided this research. Not only has he shared this important information, he has also contributed several varieties for inclusion in this volume. His experience and guidance have been invaluable in the development of this section, including in its valuations.

In 1932 the U.S. Mint began production of the George Washington quarter dollar. Initially intended to commemorate the 200th anniversary of the president's birth, its popularity was the basis for the Mint's decision to retain the design for regular coin production from that date forward.

Between 1932 and 1964 there were three obverse design alterations, and three reverse design alterations—all relatively minor, but all significant in the minds of collectors.

The Obverse Design Alterations
Oddly, all three obverse design alterations occurred in 1934. Initial production began with the obverse design as adopted in 1932, now referred to as the Light Motto. The letters of the motto are very weak and mushy, and become progressively lighter from the rim to the portrait. The letters of the word WE are often so light that it is difficult to discern them clearly from the field in macro photos.

In an effort to enhance the motto, the Mint designed a new master hub with what is now referred to as the Heavy Motto variety. This alteration had a much bolder motto than the first effort. It is easily identified by viewing the center stroke of the W in WE of the motto, which rises above the two outer strokes. This motto was used from 1936 forward on Proof and circulation-strike coinage. Philadelphia and Denver also used this variety in 1934.

In the same year (1934), another master hub was used, also with a bolder motto, but with the center stroke of the W in WE below the two outer strokes. This design, referred to as the Medium Motto, was used at Philadelphia and Denver in 1934 and 1935, and at San Francisco in 1935. Therefore, 1935 is the only year that the Medium Motto variety was used at all three mints. It was also the last year this variety was used, as the Heavy Motto variety was adopted permanently in 1936.

The Reverse Design Alterations
The reverse design changes began in 1936 with production of the first Proof coins of the series. The design alteration, or rather *enhancement*, produced a bolder view of the eagle's tail feathers, the leaves, and the arrows. The alteration also resulted in wider separation between the E and S of STATES. This design is referred to as the Type B reverse for the series. This design was intended for use on Proof issues from 1936 to 1964, and 1968 to 1972.

The Type B reverse also exists on regular circulation-strike issues for Philadelphia from 1956 to 1964. All are considered scarce to very scarce. Mint sets of 1959 and 1960 are known with Type B reverse quarters.

Another reverse alteration began to be used with the introduction of the new copper-nickel clad series in 1965. This variety became known as the Type C reverse. Close examination shows that it is a bolder version of the Type A reverse.

It differs from the Type A in that the leaves are bolder and more distinct. The leaf above the first L in DOLLAR is very distinct and almost touches the L. The leaf that disappeared in front of the bundle of arrow tips on the Type A reverse is now very bold and comes to a noticeable point at the tip of the top arrow. The tail feathers are bolder, showing lines in the center of the feathers that are more distinct.

Although adopted for use on clad issues beginning with coins dated 1965, one Type C reverse die was mistakenly punched with a D mintmark and sent to the Denver Mint. This was actually used to produce silver quarters dated 1964. These 1964-D quarters with the Type C reverse are considered very scarce. The Type C reverse was also used for some Proof issues of 1968-S, and was eventually adopted for all Proof issues from 1973 through 1998.

There has been speculation over the years that there may be Denver-minted Washington quarters with the Type B reverse from 1956 to 1964 and 1968 to 1972, however, none have yet been confirmed.

The only year in which all three reverse types are known to have been used is 1964. This became possible when the lone Type C die bearing the D mintmark was sent to Denver for production of 1964 circulation-strike coins.

THE CHERRYPICKERS' GUIDE HELPFUL HINTS

Please read the information in the front of this book. It sets the tone for the material that follows and makes it easier to interpret the information for each listing.

See appendix H for more Helpful Hints.

Reverse Hub Comparisons

Comparing the different reverse hubs of the Washington quarter is relatively easy once one has the opportunity to compare the differences. Below we illustrate photos of the three key areas of the three hubs, side by side.

Type A Reverse _____

- The overall reverse is somewhat weak.
- The leaf at the arrow tips is weak, somewhat blunt, and does not rise above the tips.
- The leaf below the left end of the arrow shafts is weak, and does not touch the shafts.
- The tail feathers are weak and ill-defined.
- The E and S of STATES almost touch.

Type A   Arrow Points   *Type A   Tail Feathers*   *Type A   ES of STATES*

Type B Reverse _____

- The design is strengthened, all elements are sharp.
- The leaf at the arrow tips is strengthened, pointed, and rises slightly above the arrow tips.
- The leaf below the left end of the arrow shafts is strengthened, and barely touches the shafts.
- The tail feathers are sharp.
- The E and S of STATES are well separated.

Type B   Arrow Points   *Type B   Tail Feathers*   *Type B   ES of STATES*

Type C Reverse _____

- The reverse is similar to the Type A, but sharp.
- The leaf at the arrow tips is strengthened, pointed, but does not rise above the tips.
- The leaf below the left end of the arrow shafts is strengthened, pointed, and touches the shafts.
- The tail feathers are sharp with center veins added.
- The E and S of STATES almost touch.

 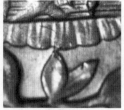 

Type C   Arrow Points   *Type C   Tail Feathers*   *Type C   ES of STATES*

1932

FS-25-1932-101

Variety: Doubled Die Obverse
PUP: Earlobe
URS-4 · I-3 · L-3

CONECA 1-O-IV

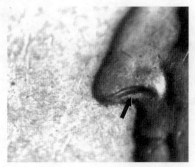 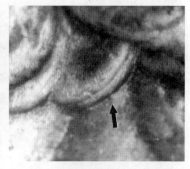

Description: The doubling is evident as a doubled earlobe, with additional doubling visible on the nostril and back of queue.

	VF-20	EF-40	AU-50	MS-60	MS-63	MS-65
VARIETY:	$150	$200	$250	$350	$500	$750
NORMAL:	$3	$4	$8	$20	$30	$75

Comments: The reverse of this variety is also a minor doubled die, listed as CONECA 1-R-VI.

THE CHERRYPICKERS' GUIDE HELPFUL HINTS

Check all the coins in your 1960 and 1968 Proof sets. These are known to have nice doubled dies for each denomination, some on the obverse and some on the reverse. For a complete list of known Mint set and Proof set varieties, refer to appendix C.

See appendix H for more Helpful Hints.

1934 — FS-25-1934-101

Variety: Doubled Die Obverse — CONECA 1-O-I
PUP: IN GOD WE TRUST
URS-10 · I-4 · L-4

Description: Very strong doubling is evident on the motto, LIBERTY, and date. This is a Medium Motto variety. (See FS-25-1934-402.)

	VF-20	EF-40	AU-50	MS-60	MS-63	MS-65
VARIETY:	$250	$325	$750	$1,500	$2,500	n/a
NORMAL:	$3	$4	$8	$20	$30	$75

Comments: This obverse, one of the strongest and most popular of all Washington quarter varieties, is also found matched with a minor Class VI reverse doubled die.

1934 — FS-25-1934-401

Variety: Light Motto — Breen 4270
PUP: IN GOD WE TRUST
URS-13 · I-3 · L-4

Description: Notice the considerable weakness in the letters of the motto. In addition, the center point of the W is pointed.

	VF-20	EF-40	AU-50	AU-55	MS-60	MS-63	MS-65
VARIETY:	$15	$20	$30	$50	$75	$100	$400
NORMAL:	$3	$4	$8	$10	$19	$30	$75

Comments: Of the three primary 1934 obverse hubs, this is the one that will command a premium.

1934   FS-25-1934-402

Variety: Medium Motto   **Breen 4271**
PUP: IN GOD WE TRUST
URS-22 · I-2 · L-1

Description: The motto is more pronounced than the Light Motto. The center point of the W is somewhat squared off, not pointed like on the Light Motto.

	VF-20	EF-40	AU-50	AU55	MS-60	MS-63	MS-65
VARIETY:	$3	$4	$8	$10	$19	$30	$75
NORMAL:	$3	$4	$8	$10	$19	$30	$75

Comments: This is the most common of the three primary 1934 obverse designs.

1934   FS-25-1934-403

Variety: Heavy Motto   **Breen 4272**
PUP: IN GOD WE TRUST
URS-21 · I-2 · L-1

Description: The motto has very thick letters. The center point of the W is pointed and rises slightly above the other letters.

	VF-20	EF-40	AU-50	AU-55	MS-60	MS-63	MS-65
VARIETY:	n/a	n/a	n/a	n/a	n/a	n/a	n/a
NORMAL:	$3	$4	$8	$10	$19	$30	$75

Comments: This variety is also classified as Breen 4272.

1934-D
FS-25-1934D-501

Variety: Mintmark of 1932
Breen—N/L
PUP: Mintmark
URS-3 · I-3 · L-4

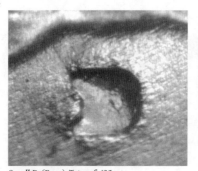 

Small D (Rare) Type of '32   *Normal D (Common) Type of '34*

Description: The D mintmark is smaller than the common D of 1934.

	VF-20	EF-40	AU-50	AU-55	MS-60	MS-63	MS-65
VARIETY:	$50	$75	$100	$150	$250	$400	$1,650
NORMAL:	$7	$13	$65	$74	$183	$250	$1,225

Comments: This is the D mintmark of 1932, and is likely the result of a single die left over from that year. This is a very rare variety by any standard.

1935
FS-25-1935-101

Variety: Doubled Die Obverse
CONECA 1-O-II+V
PUP: IN GOD WE TRUST
URS-4 · I-2 · L-2

Description: Doubling is evident on the motto and on the L of LIBERTY.

	VF-20	EF-40	AU-50	AU-55	MS-60	MS-63	MS-65
VARIETY:	$10	$15	$25	$45	$60	$75	$125
NORMAL:	$3	$4	$7	$9	$17	$24	$92

Comments: We would very much like to examine a higher-grade specimen.

1936   FS-25-1936-101 (011)

Variety: Doubled Die Obverse   CONECA 1-O-I
PUP: IN GOD WE TRUST
URS-7 · I-4 · L-5

Description: Very strong doubling is evident on the motto, LIBERTY, and the date.

	EF-40	AU-50	AU-55	MS-60	MS-63	MS-65
VARIETY:	$300	$375	$450	$500	$750	$3,000
NORMAL:	$4	$7	$9	$16	$31	$82

Comments: This very rare variety is always in high demand.

1937   FS-25-1937-101 (012)

Variety: Doubled Die Obverse   CONECA 1-O-V
PUP: IN GOD WE TRUST
URS-8 · I-5 · L-5

Description: Very strong doubling on the motto, LIBERTY, the date, and the end of the ribbons.

	VF-20	EF-40	AU-50	AU-55	MS-60	MS-63	MS-65
VARIETY:	$350	$700	$1,250	$1,400	$1,500	$2,100	$3,200
NORMAL:	$3	$4	$14	$16	$20	$29	$78

Comments: This variety is considered one of the most important in the series.

1939-D
FS-25-1939D-501 (012.3)

Variety: D/S Mintmark
PUP: Mintmark
URS-2 · I-3 · L-4

CONECA—N/L

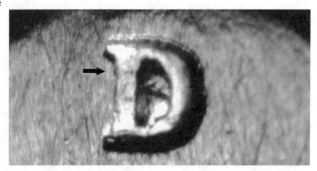

Description: This particular reverse die illustrates a D mintmark punched over an S mintmark. The center curve of the S is clearly evident within the opening of the D, and the left-most upper curve of the S is evident immediately left of the upright of the D.

	EF-40	AU-50	AU-55	MS-60	MS-63	MS-65
VARIETY:	$100	$125	$200	$250	$350	$650
NORMAL:	$8	$15	$18	$33	$40	$90

Comments: There is a coin listed as FS-12.3 by Flynn and Wexler in their book *Over Mintmarks and Hot Repunched Mintmarks*. That coin is shown as being a refuted over mintmark, but is *not* the same die as listed here.

1939-S
FS-25-1939S-101

Variety: Doubled Die Obverse
PUP: IN GOD WE TRUST
URS-7 · I-2 · L-2

CONECA 1-O-V

Description: Doubling is evident on the motto, LIBERTY, and date.

	VF-20	EF-40	AU-50	AU-55	MS-60	MS-63	MS-65
VARIETY:	$20	$30	$50	$60	$75	$125	$300
NORMAL:	$6	$13	$41	$45	$73	$96	$260

Comments: This variety may not be very difficult to find.

1940-D   FS-25-1940D-101

Variety: Doubled Die Obverse   CONECA 1-O-II
PUP: IN GOD WE TRUST
URS-6 · I-3 · L-4

Description: Strong doubling is evident on the motto, and lesser doubling is visible on LIBERTY and the date.

	VF-20	EF-40	AU-50	AU-55	MS-60	MS-63	MS-65
VARIETY:	$50	$75	$100	$125	$150	$225	$350
NORMAL:	$9	$19	$46	$50	$84	$121	$252

Comments: This is a very attractive doubled die!

1940-D   FS-25-1940D-501 (012.4)

Variety: Repunched Mintmark   CONECA RPM 002
PUP: Mintmark
URS-3 · I-5 · L-5

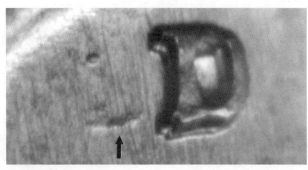

Description: This highly unusual repunched mintmark shows a secondary D totally separated and west of the primary D.

	EF-40	AU-50	AU-55	MS-60	MS-63	MS-65
VARIETY:	$200	$250	$275	$300	$450	$750
NORMAL:	$19	$46	$50	$84	$121	$252

Comments: This is one of about 10 known repunched mintmarks that are totally separated. Discovered by Lee Iliemke, this is a very rare variety and is in very high demand.

1941 — FS 25-1941-101 (012.7)

Variety: Doubled Die Obverse — CONECA 3-O-V
PUP: IN GOD WE TRUST
URS-7 · I-2 · L-2

Description: The doubling is most evident on GOD WE and the UST of TRUST. The doubling is very obvious.

	EF-40	AU-50	MS-60	MS-63	MS-65
VARIETY:	$25	$50	$75	$100	$125
NORMAL:	$2	$3	$5	$13	$48

Comments: This listing was formerly cross-referenced in CPG #3 as CONECA 1-O-III, when in fact it should have been 3-O-V.

1941 — FS-25-1941-102 (012.9)

Variety: Doubled Die Obverse — CONECA 6-O-I
PUP: IN GOD WE TRUST
URS-7 · I-3 · L-3

Description: Doubling is very evident on the motto, slightly on LIBERTY, and slightly west on the date.

	EF-40	AU-50	MS-60	MS-63	MS-65
VARIETY:	$50	$60	$75	$100	$125
NORMAL:	$2	$3	$5	$13	$48

Comments: There are several other 1941 obverse doubled dies. The two illustrated here are those in highest demand.

1941   FS-25-1941-801 (013)

Variety: Doubled Die Reverse   CONECA 1-R-V
PUP: Eagle's Beak
URS-5· I-3 · L-4

Description: Doubling is evident on the eagle's beak, doubled south. Other doubling is also visible on portions of QUARTER DOLLAR.

	EF-40	AU-50	MS-60	MS-63	MS-65
VARIETY:	$50	$60	$75	$100	$125
NORMAL:	$2	$3	$5	$13	$48

Comments: CONECA lists at least 15 other reverse doubled dies for 1941-(P) that are somewhat similar to this variety. All command a nice premium. It is suggested to have any similar variety accurately attributed.

1941-D   FS-25-1941D-801

Variety: Doubled Die Reverse   CONECA 1-R-V
PUP: Reverse lettering
URS-7· I-3 · L-4

Description: The doubling is most evident on STATES OF AMERICA, with a light spread on the D of UNITED and the AR of DOLLAR.

	EF-40	AU-50	MS-60	MS-63	MS-65
VARIETY:	$50	$60	$100	$150	$200
NORMAL:	$4	$8	$30	$50	$65

Comments: This reverse doubled die is considered rare and in demand by Washington variety enthusiasts.

1941-S   FS-25-1941S-501 (013.5)

Variety: Large S Mintmark   **CONECA MMS-002**
PUP: Mintmark
URS-7 · I-5 · L-5

Large S (Scarce)   *Small S (Normal)*

Description: The S mintmark on a very few 1941-S coins exhibits the large S, or trumpet-tail style mintmark. Compare to the normal or small S mintmark. Some of the large S varieties have a filled upper loop.

	EF-40	AU-50	MS-60	MS-63	MS-65
VARIETY:	$50	$75	$150	$250	$400
NORMAL:	$3	$7	$20	$27	$72

Comments: There are four or five reverse dies with this large S mintmark. One Large S die has the same style S as on the Large S nickels, with a triangular lower serif (see photo below).

1941-S   FS-25-1941S-503

Variety: Large S Mintmark   **CONECA RPM-002**
PUP: Mintmark
URS-5 · I-5 · L-5

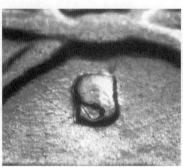 

Large Triangular Serif S   *Normal, Small S*

Description: This Large S mintmark, with triangular shaped lower serif, is the same Large S as found on scarce 1941-S Large S nickels.

	EF-40	AU-50	MS-60	MS-63	MS-65
VARIETY:	$50	$75	$175	$300	$500
NORMAL:	$3	$7	$20	$27	$72

Comments: Only one reverse die is known as of this writing.

1942 — FS-25-1942-101

Variety: Doubled Die Obverse

CONECA 3-O-V

PUP: IN GOD WE TRUST

URS-5 · I-3 · L-4

Description: Doubling is evident on the lower portions of the motto. Secondary images are especially evident on GOD and TRUST.

	EF-40	AU-50	MS-60	MS-63	MS-65
VARIETY:	$25	$50	$75	$100	$150
NORMAL:	$2	$3	$4	$7	$30

Comments: Other obverse doubled dies are known for this date, but all are less evident.

1942 — FS-25-1942-801 (014)

Variety: Doubled Die Reverse

CONECA 2-R-V

PUP: Reverse lettering

URS-6 · I-4 · L-5

Description: Doubling is extremely strong on UNITED STATES OF AMERICA, with lesser doubling, although evident, on QUARTER DOLLAR.

	EF-40	AU-50	MS-60	MS-63	MS-65
VARIETY:	$125	$200	$300	$500	$1,000
NORMAL:	$2	$3	$4	$7	$30

Comments: Be careful not to confuse this variety with the next one.

1942 FS-25-1942-802 (014.3)

Variety: Doubled Die Reverse CONECA 5-R-I
PUP: Reverse lettering
URS-7 · I-4 · L-5

Description: This is one of the strongest reverse doubled dies known for the Washington series. The doubling is evident on all reverse lettering, with a clockwise spread.

	EF-40	AU-50	MS-60	MS-63	MS-65
VARIETY:	$125	$200	$300	$500	$1,000
NORMAL:	$2	$3	$4	$7	$30

Comments: This variety is extremely rare in high grade!

1942 FS-25-1942-803

Variety: Doubled Die Reverse CONECA 6-R-IV
PUP: Eagle's beak
URS-6 · I-3 · L-4

Description: The doubling on this variety can be seen on the eagle's right side (viewer's left), and is most evident as a strongly doubled beak.

	EF-40	AU-50	MS-60	MS-63	MS-65
VARIETY:	$75	$100	$150	$225	$350
NORMAL:	$2	$3	$4	$7	$30

Comments: This is a very attractive and elusive variety.

1942-D

FS-25-1942D-101 (015)

Variety: Doubled Die Obverse

CONECA 1-O-I

PUP: IN GOD WE TRUST, LIBERTY

URS-9 · I-5 · L-5

Description: Doubling is evident, with a very strong spread, on LIBERTY, the date, and the motto. This is one of the most popular Washington quarter varieties.

	EF-40	AU-50	MS-60	MS-63	MS-65
VARIETY:	$350	$750	$1,250	$1,750	$2,500
NORMAL:	$3	$7	$12	$16	$46

Comments: If you can locate a high-grade example, you will have no trouble selling it.

1942-D

FS-25-1942D-801 (016)

Variety: Doubled Die Reverse

CONECA 1-R-IV

PUP: Eagle's beak, branch

URS-6 · I-5 · L-5

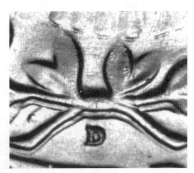

Description: The doubling on this variety is most prominent on the eagle's beak, the arrows, and the branch above the mintmark.

	EF-40	AU-50	MS-60	MS-63	MS-65
VARIETY:	$200	$350	$500	$750	$1,500
NORMAL:	$3	$7	$12	$16	$46

Comments: This is another of the most popular Washington varieties.

1943
FS-25-1943-101 (16.5)

Variety: Doubled Die Obverse
CONECA 5-O-II
PUP: IN GOD WE TRUST
URS-7 · I-2 · L-2

Description: The doubling is very strong northwest on the motto, and to a lesser degree on LIBERTY.

	EF-40	AU-50	MS-60	MS-63	MS-65
VARIETY:	$75	$125	$200	$300	$500
NORMAL:	$2	$3	$4	$11	$36

Comments: This variety was discovered by Glenn Jeong.

1943
FS-25-1943-102

Variety: Doubled Die Obverse
CONECA 6-O-I
PUP: LIBERTY
URS-3 · I-3 · L-3

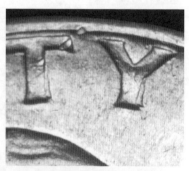

Description: Doubling is very strong on LIBERTY, with lesser doubling on the date and the motto.

	EF-40	AU-50	MS-60	MS-63	MS-65
VARIETY:	$75	$125	$200	$300	$500
NORMAL:	$2	$3	$4	$11	$36

Comments: This variety is very popular among Washington specialists.

1943   FS-25-1943-103 (016.7)

Variety: Doubled Die Obverse   CONECA 11-O-I
PUP: IN GOD WE TRUST
URS-2 · I-5 · L-5

Description: This very strong doubled die was only discovered about 1993 or 1994 by Eric Striegel. The doubling is very strong on the motto, LIBERTY, and the date, and appears very similar to the popular and well-known 1943-S.

	EF-40	AU-50	MS-60	MS-63	MS-65
VARIETY:	$300	$500	$750	$1,250	$1,750
NORMAL:	$2	$3	$4	$11	$36

Comments: Any grade would likely sell in a heartbeat!

1943-D   FS-25-1943D-101

Variety: Doubled Die Obverse   CONECA 4-O-IV
PUP: Ear
URS-3 · I-3 · L-3

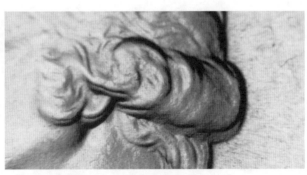

Description: The doubling is evident on the chin, ear, hair curls, and queue.

	EF-40	AU-50	MS-60	MS-63	MS-65
VARIETY:	$35	$50	$75	$150	$250
NORMAL:	$3	$9	$18	$24	$42

Comments: This is a most interesting variety.

1943-S

FS-25-1943S-101 (17)

Variety: Doubled Die Obverse
PUP: IN GOD WE TRUST, LIBERTY
URS-9 · I-5 · L-5

CONECA 1-O-I

Description: Very strong doubling is evident on the motto, LIBERTY, designer's initials, and the date.

	EF-40	AU-50	MS-60	MS-63	MS-65
VARIETY:	$200	$350	$500	$750	$1,500
NORMAL:	$5	$11	$17	$22	$46

Comments: This dramatic doubled die has long been known to collectors. Values for this variety are generally firm, but do change with market conditions and demand fluctuations.

1943-S

FS-25-1943S-501

Variety: Trumpet Tail S
PUP: Mintmark
URS-5 · I-4 · L-5

CONECA—N/L

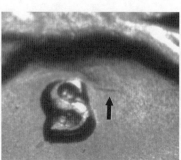

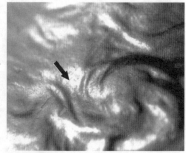

Trumpet Tail　　　　　　　　*Diagnostic*

Description: The upper serif is pointed downward, not up and down as on the Large S varieties common to this date.

	EF-40	AU-50	MS-60	MS-63	MS-65
VARIETY:	$75	$150	$250	$500	$650
NORMAL:	$5	$11	$17	$22	$46

Comments: This variety is infinitely rarer than the 1941-S trumpet tail. As of 04/02, fewer than 10 AU specimens and only three Mint State specimens are known. All are from the same die pair, exhibiting a die gouge in the hair, a doubled 4, and a die scratch just right of the mintmark.

1943-S

FS-25-1943S-502

Variety: Medium S Mintmark　　　　　　　　　　　　　CONECA—N/L
PUP: Mintmark
URS-4 · I-4 · L-4

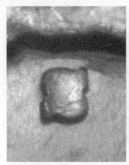 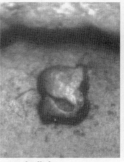 

Filled　　　　　　　　*Partial Filled*　　　　　　　*Large S (Common)*

Description: This variety exhibits a slightly smaller medium S mintmark. Shown for comparison is the Large S (common).

	EF-40	AU-50	MS-60	MS-63	MS-65
VARIETY:	n/a	n/a	n/a	n/a	n/a
NORMAL:	$5	$11	$17	$22	$46

Comments: This variety was unknown for this date until recently. Its track record is too short to assign fair market values.

1943-S

FS-25-1943S-503

Variety: Repunched Mintmark　　　　　　　　　　　　CONECA RPM 2
PUP: Mintmark
URS-4 · I-3 · L-4

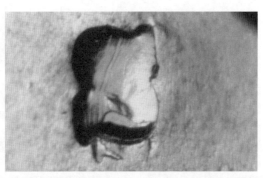

Description: A secondary S mintmark is evident south of the primary S on the large S variety.

	EF-40	AU-50	MS-60	MS-63	MS-65
VARIETY:	$30	$35	$75	$125	$175
NORMAL:	$5	$11	$17	$22	$46

Comments: The filled primary S mintmark is common for this date.

1943-S
FS-25-1943S-504

Variety: Repunched Mintmark
CONECA—N/L
PUP: Mintmark
URS-2 · I-3 · L-4

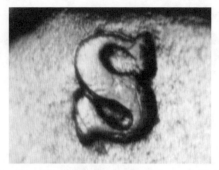

Description: A secondary S mintmark is visible south of the primary S. The lower left knob of that secondary S is barely visible south of the primary.

	EF-40	AU-50	MS-60	MS-63	MS-65
VARIETY:	$30	$35	$75	$125	$175
NORMAL:	$5	$11	$17	$22	$46

Comments: Actual rarity is still unknown.

1944
FS-25-1944-101

Variety: Doubled Die Obverse
CONECA 6-O-I
PUP: IN GOD WE TRUST
URS-7 · I-2 · L-3

Description: Doubling is evident south on the motto IN GOD WE TRUST, with a medium spread, and somewhat evident on LIBERTY.

	EF-40	AU-50	MS-60	MS-63	MS-65
VARIETY:	$20	$25	$35	$50	$75
NORMAL:	$2	$3	$4	$8	$34

Comments: All 1944 quarters are from a doubled master die (nose, earlobe). There are several similar doubled dies for this date. Keep searching!

1944-D

FS-25-1944D-101

Variety: Doubled Die Obverse
PUP: LIBERTY
URS-8 · I-3 · L-3

CONECA 2-O-I

Description: Doubling is most evident on ERTY of LIBERTY, slightly on the date and the designer's initials.

	EF-40	AU-50	MS-60	MS-63	MS-65
VARIETY:	$10	$20	$40	$75	$125
NORMAL:	$2	$6	$11	$15	$31

Comments: This is another of the many doubled dies known for this series.

1944-S

FS-25-1944S-101 (017.5)

Variety: Tripled Die Obverse
PUP: IN GOD WE TRUST
URS-19 · I-2 · L-2

CONECA 1-O-I

Description: Doubling is evident south on the motto, and slightly on LIBERTY, the date and the designer's initials.

	EF-40	AU-50	MS-60	MS-63	MS-65
VARIETY:	$20	$25	$35	$50	$75
NORMAL:	$2	$3	$7	$12	$33

Comments: This variety, although very evident, is considered very common.

1945 FS-25-1945-101 (018)

Variety: Doubled Die Obverse
PUP: IN GOD WE TRUST
URS-7 · I-2 · L-2

CONECA 1-O-I

Description: Doubling is most evident slightly northwest on the motto, on LIBERTY, and on the date.

	EF-40	AU-50	MS-60	MS-63	MS-65
VARIETY:	$50	$60	$100	$150	$225
NORMAL:	$2	$3	$4	$8	$32

Comments: This variety is tough to locate in high grade.

1945-S FS-25-1945S-101

Variety: Tripled Die Obverse
PUP: IN GOD WE TRUST
URS-6 · I-2 · L-3

CONECA 2-O-I

Description: Doubling is most evident on IN GOD WE TRUST, slightly on the date and LIBERTY. Tripling is evident on the designer's initials.

	EF-40	AU-50	MS-60	MS-63	MS-65
VARIETY:	$20	$25	$35	$50	$75
NORMAL:	$2	$3	$4	$7	$33

Comments: This variety has proven to be very elusive!

1945-S

FS-25-1945S-102

Variety: Doubled Die Obverse
PUP: IN GOD WE TRUST
URS-5 · I-3 · L-4

CONECA 4-O-VI

Description: Extreme extra thickness is evident on the motto, with doubling also evident on LIBERTY.

	EF-40	AU-50	MS-60	MS-63	MS-65
VARIETY:	$35	$50	$75	$125	$275
NORMAL:	$2	$3	$4	$7	$33

Comments: This is another very tough variety to locate.

1946

FS-25-1946-101

Variety: Doubled Die Obverse
PUP: IN GOD WE TRUST
URS-4 · I-3 · L-3

CONECA 2-O-I

Description: Doubling is evident on the motto and the date, and slightly on LIBERTY and the ribbon.

	EF-40	AU-50	MS-60	MS-63	MS-65
VARIETY:	$25	$50	$75	$100	$150
NORMAL:	$1	$2	$3	$5	$37

Comments: This variety seems to be relatively scarce at this time.

1946
FS-25-1946-801 (018.2)

Variety: Doubled Die Reverse
CONECA 2-R-V

PUP: IN GOD WE TRUST
URS-4 · I-2 · L-2

Description: The doubling is most evident on E PLURIBUS UNUM, STATES OF, and slightly on AMER-ICA. There is a very minor DDO paired with this reverse die, listed as CONECA 8-O-V.

	EF-40	AU-50	MS-60	MS-63	MS-65
VARIETY:	$20	$25	$35	$50	$75
NORMAL:	$1	$2	$3	$5	$37

Comments: This is yet another variety that may be very difficult to locate in high grade.

1946-D
FS-25-1946D-501

Variety: Repunched Mintmark
CONECA—N/L

PUP: Mintmark
URS-2 · I-3 · L-3

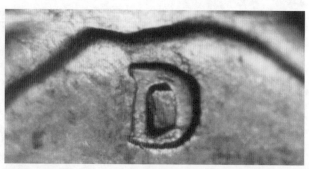

Description: The secondary D is weak but evident north of the primary D, and touching the branch above.

	EF-40	AU-50	MS-60	MS-63	MS-65
VARIETY:	$10	$15	$25	$50	$140
NORMAL:	$1	$3	$5	$8	$35

Comments: This RPM is not currently listed by CONECA.

1946-S

FS-25-1946S-501

Variety: Repunched Mintmark
CONECA RPM 2
PUP: Mintmark
URS-7 · I-3 · L-3

Description: A secondary S is evident north of the primary, with only the left most portion of the secondary S visible.

	EF-40	AU-50	MS-60	MS-63	MS-65
VARIETY:	$10	$15	$25	$35	$50
NORMAL:	$2	$3	$4	$7	$37

Comments: This RPM is in fairly high demand.

1947

FS-25-1947-101

Variety: Doubled Die Obverse
CONECA 1-O-I
PUP: LIBERTY
URS-3 · I-3 · L-3

Description: Doubling is evident *mainly* on LIBERTY, with an extremely weak spread on the date, the designer's initials, and the motto IN GOD WE TRUST.

	EF-40	AU-50	MS-60	MS-63	MS-65
VARIETY:	$25	$50	$75	$100	$150
NORMAL:	$2	$3	$4	$7	$35

Comments: To date this is a very rare variety!

1947-S

FS-25-1947S-501

Variety: Repunched Mintmark
PUP: Mintmark
URS-5 · I-3 · L-3

CONECA RPM 1

Description: The weaker S is evident west of the primary S. The most prominent portion of the underlying S is the upper left loop, protruding left of the primary.

	EF-40	AU-50	MS-60	MS-63	MS-65
VARIETY:	$15	$20	$25	$35	$50
NORMAL:		$3	$4	$7	$32

Comments: This is a highly collectible RPM.

1947-S

FS-25-1947S-502

Variety: Repunched Mintmark
PUP: Mintmark
URS-2 · I-4 · L-4

CONECA—N/L

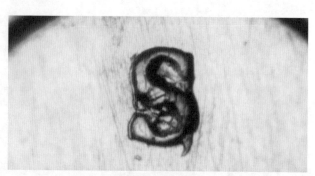

Description: The secondary S is evident south of the primary S. There is also a third S mintmark protruding from the upper left loop of the primary S mintmark.

	EF-40	AU-50	MS-60	MS-63	MS-65
VARIETY:	$15	$20	$25	$50	$75
NORMAL:		$3	$4	$7	$32

Comments: Although somewhat similar to CONECA RPM 2, the third mintmark protruding from the left upper loop is significantly different.

1948-S

FS-25-1948S-501 (018.4)

Variety: Repunched Mintmark
CONECA RPM 2
PUP: Mintmark
URS-2 · I-4 · L-4

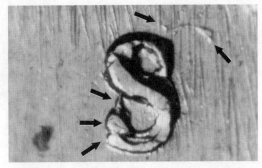

Description: The top of two different S mintmarks are visible north of the primary, and a total of at least three are evident within the lower loop of the primary. It seems there are four different mintmark punches on this die.

	EF-40	AU-50	MS-60	MS-63	MS-65
VARIETY:	$15	$25	$50	$100	$200
NORMAL:		$3	$4	$7	$40

Comments: This is one of the most dramatic repunched mintmarks in the entire series, and was only recently discovered! It will certainly become a highly sought-after variety.

1949-D

FS-25-1949D-501

Variety: Repunched Mintmark
CONECA—N/L
PUP: Mintmark
URS-2 · I-4 · L-4

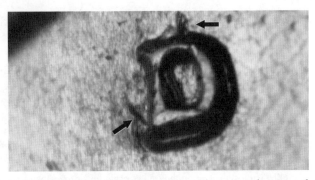

Description: This very interesting RPM shows what appears to be a secondary D northeast of the primary, and another west of the primary. The image west may be the remains of either an inverted D or a horizontal D. Further study may prove the image west as one way or the other.

	EF-40	AU-50	MS-60	MS-63	MS-65
VARIETY:	$10	$25	$35	$50	$100
NORMAL:		$5	$10	$14	$45

Comments: This variety will certainly be in demand by specialists.

1949-D

FS-25-1949D-601 (018.8)

Variety: Over Mintmark

CONECA—N/L

PUP: Mintmark

URS-2 · I-4 · L-4

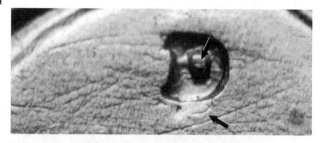

Description: The remnants of a secondary mintmark are evident south of the primary D. Some specialists believe this to be a D/D and not a D/S. However, it is still the opinion of the authors that the underlying mintmark is an S, as evidenced by the curvature of the lower bar on the underlying image. Additionally, the overall width of the underlying image appears too narrow to be that of a D.

	EF-40	AU-50	MS-60	MS-63	MS-65
VARIETY:	$35	$50	$75	$150	$250
NORMAL:		$5	$10	$14	$45

Comments: The coin illustrated above is obviously a later die state. Questions about the underlying mintmark may be answered definitively if an earlier die state is discovered.

1950

FS-25-1950-801 (019)

Variety: Doubled Die Reverse

CONECA 1-R-IV

PUP: Eagle's beak

URS-10 · I-3 · L-2

Description: Doubling is most evident on the eagle's beak, lower left wing edges, and the leaves and stems on the left side.

	EF-40	AU-50	MS-60	MS-63	MS-65
VARIETY:	$15	$20	$25	$35	$50
NORMAL:		$2	$3	$6	$29

Comments: An early die state specimen will command about twice the stated values.

1950-D

FS-25-1950D-801 (020)

Variety: Doubled Die Reverse
PUP: Eagle's talons
URS-9 · I-2 · L-2

CONECA 1-R-IV

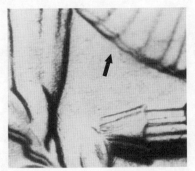 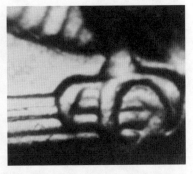

Description: Doubling is evident on the eagle's talons, arrow points, and the feathers on the legs.

	EF-40	AU-50	MS-60	MS-63	MS-65
VARIETY:	$25	$50	$75	$100	$150
NORMAL:		$2	$3	$8	$31

Comments: Discovered by Del Romines, this variety can be found with some searching.

1950-D

FS-25-1950D-802

Variety: Doubled Die Reverse
PUP: Reverse lettering
URS-5 · I-2 · L-2

CONECA 2-R-VI

Description: As with all Class VI doubled dies, this variety exhibits the typical extra thickness on all reverse lettering. This extra thickness is especially strong on UNITED and QUARTER DOLLAR, where some separation in the letters may be evident.

	EF-40	AU-50	MS-60	MS-63	MS-65
VARIETY:	$15	$25	$35	$50	$75
NORMAL:		$2	$3	$8	$31

Comments: This is a very dramatic class VI doubled die.

1950-D

Variety: Repunched Mintmark
PUP: Mintmark
URS-6 · I-3 · L-3

CONECA RPM 2

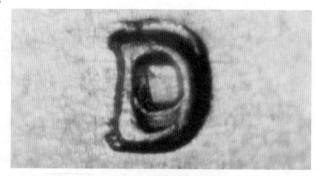

Description: The secondary mintmark is evident north of the primary D.

	EF-40	AU-50	MS-60	MS-63	MS-65
VARIETY:	$15	$20	$25	$35	$50
NORMAL:		$2	$3	$8	$31

Comments: This variety is one of the more attractive RPMs for the date.

1950-D

Variety: Over Mintmark
PUP: Mintmark
URS-9 · I-5 · L-5

CONECA OMM 1

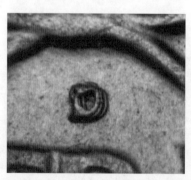 

Description: The upper left curve of the underlying S is evident west and north of the D.

	EF-40	AU-50	MS-60	MS-63	MS-65
VARIETY:	$150	$200	$300	$500	$700
NORMAL:		$2	$3	$8	$31

Comments: Most specimens exhibit strike doubling on the D, and have brilliant surfaces.

1950-S   FS-25-1950S-801

Variety: Doubled Die Reverse   CONECA—N/L
PUP: Arrows on reverse
URS-4 · I-2 · L-2

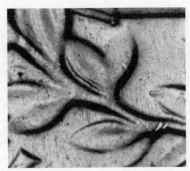 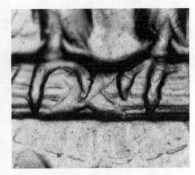

Description: Doubling is visible on the lower arrows and on some of the lower leaves.

	EF-40	AU-50	MS-60	MS-63	MS-65
VARIETY:	$15	$20	$25	$35	$50
NORMAL:		$2	$4	$8	$38

Comments: Although a relatively minor doubled die, this one is featured as an example of some of the varieties that are still to be found!

1950-S   FS-25-1950S-501

Variety: Repunched Mintmark   CONECA RPM 1
PUP: Mintmark
URS-7 · I-3 · L-3

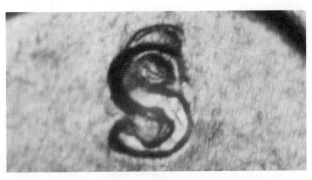

Description: The weaker S mintmark is evident wide north of the primary S.

	EF-40	AU-50	MS-60	MS-63	MS-65
VARIETY:	$15	$20	$25	$35	$50
NORMAL:		$2	$4	$8	$38

Comments: This is considered a very wide repunching on a mintmark.

1950-S

Variety: Over Mintmark
CONECA OMM 1
PUP: Mintmark
URS-9 · I-5 · L-5

Description: The underlying D mintmark is clearly visible beneath the primary S.

	EF-40	AU-50	MS-60	MS-63	MS-65
VARIETY:	$200	$250	$350	$550	$850
NORMAL:		$2	$4	$8	$38

Comments: Certainly one of the most popular Washington varieties. Most UNC specimens have a frosty luster, compared to the brilliant surfaces on most UNC 1950-D/S quarters.

1951-D

Variety: Doubled Die Obverse
CONECA 2-O-V
PUP: LIBERTY
URS-5 · I-3 · L-3

Description: The doubling is most evident on LIBERTY, and on IN GOD WE TRUST.

	EF-40	AU-50	MS-60	MS-63	MS-65
VARIETY:	$35	$45	$60	$75	$95
NORMAL:		$2	$3	$6	$32

Comments: This is a most underrated doubled die.

1952, PROOF FS-25-1952-901

Variety: Engraving Error (?)
PUP: Eagle's breast
URS-9 · I-3 · L-3

CONECA—N/L

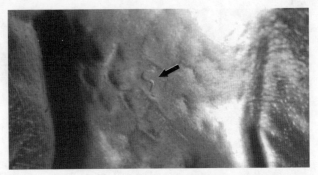

Description: There is an unusual S-shaped mark on the breast of the Eagle. The cause of this mark is unknown.

	PF-63	PF-65	PF-66
VARIETY:	$100	$250	$500
NORMAL:	$24	$41	$52

Comments: The nickname for this well-known variety is, suitably, "Superbird!"

1952-D FS-25-1952D-101

Variety: Doubled Die Obverse
PUP: LIBERTY
URS-4 · I-2 · L-2

No other attribution

Description: Moderate doubling is evident on the date, the motto, and LIBERTY.

	EF-40	AU-50	MS-60	MS-63	MS-65
VARIETY:	$50	$75	$100	$150	$225
NORMAL:		$2	$3	$6	$31

Comments: This variety can still be located with a little searching.

1952-D

FS-25-1952D-501

Variety: Huge Mintmark
PUP: Mintmark
URS-1 · I-3 · L-4

CONECA—N/L

Huge D   Medium D   Small D

Description: The huge D mintmark is considered very rare, with only three specimens known to the authors as of publication. A medium and small D are shown for comparison. The size of this D mintmark is unknown on any other U.S. coin.

	EF-40	AU-50	MS-60	MS-63	MS-65
VARIETY:	$75	$100	$200	$300	$500
NORMAL:		$2	$3	$6	$31

Comments: Again, to date only three examples have been reported.

1952-S

FS-25-1952S-501

Variety: Repunched Mintmark
PUP: Mintmark
URS-7 · I-3 · L-3

CONECA RPM 1

Description: A triple punched mintmark, with a secondary S is evident north of the primary, and another overlaps the primary.

	EF-40	AU-50	MS-60	MS-63	MS-65
VARIETY:	$15	$20	$25	$35	$50
NORMAL:		$2	$7	$10	$32

Comments: RPMs in this series are becoming highly collectible.

1952-S

FS-25-1952S-502

Variety: Repunched Mintmark
PUP: Mintmark
URS-4 · I-3 · L-3

CONECA RPM 2

Description: The secondary mintmark is evident north of the primary.

	EF-40	AU-50	MS-60	MS-63	MS-65
VARIETY:	$15	$20	$25	$35	$50
NORMAL:		$2	$7	$10	$32

Comments: New RPMs in this series are being reported every year!

1953, PROOF

FS-25-1953-101 (022.1)

Variety: Doubled Die Obverse
PUP: IN GOD WE TRUST
URS-9 · I-3 · L-3

CONECA 1-O-V

Description: Doubling is evident on all obverse lettering, very strong on the motto and date.

	PF-63	PF-65	PF-66
VARIETY:	$150	$250	$350
NORMAL:	$16	$30	$40

Comments: This is a fairly well known variety, but it can still be cherrypicked!

1953-D   FS-25-1953D-101 (022.2)

Variety: Doubled Die Reverse   CONECA 1-R-I
PUP: UNITED STATES OF AMERICA
URS-6 · I-3 · L-3

Description: Doubling is evident on all reverse lettering, strongest on UNITED STATES OF AMERICA, and weaker on QUARTER DOLLAR.

	EF-40	AU-50	MS-60	MS-63	MS-65
VARIETY:	$50	$75	$100	$150	$225
NORMAL:		$2	$3	$9	$38

Comments: This variety is one of the strongest reverse doubled dies in the series.

1953-D   FS-25-1953D-501

Variety: Repunched Mintmark (Inverted)   CONECA RPM 1
PUP: Mintmark
URS-3 · I-5 · L-5

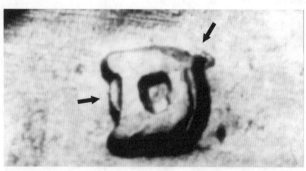

Description: The primary D mintmark is punched over what is believed to be an inverted mintmark. Further study may determine the underlying D to be horizontal, but the current photos lean more toward the inverted orientation.

	EF-40	AU-50	MS-60	MS-63	MS-65
VARIETY:	$35	$50	$75	$150	$250
NORMAL:		$2	$3	$9	$38

Comments: This is an extremely popular variety.

1953-D

FS-25-1953D-601 (022.3)

Variety: D over S Mintmark
PUP: Mintmark
URS-3 · I-5 · L-4

CONECA OMM 1

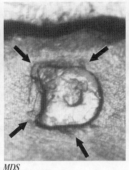

EDS   *MDS*   *LDS*

Description: Multiple mintmark punches produced this fascinating variety, creating a D/D/D/S/S over mintmark. Some specialists consider only one underlying S, but these photos clearly show at least two S mintmark punches.

	EF-40	AU-50	MS-60	MS-63	MS-65
VARIETY:	$35	$50	$75	$150	$250
NORMAL:		$2	$3	$9	$38

Comments: This variety is not very well known, but can be found with some searching. The late die stage (illustrated above) is often overlooked, and not as saleable.

1956

FS-25-1956-701

Variety: Reverse Die Gouge
PUP: Reverse under talons
URS-2 · I-3 · L-3

CONECA—N/L

Description: A very unusual die gouge is evident on the arrows below the eagle's right talons. Another die scratch is evident under the eagle's left talons.

	EF-40	AU-50	MS-60	MS-63	MS-65
VARIETY:	$25	$35	$50	$75	$100
NORMAL:		$2	$3	$5	$29

Comments: The causes of these gouges are unknown, but they are extremely interesting.

1956 — FS-25-1956-901

Variety: Type B Reverse
CONECA—N/L
PUP: Eagle's tail feathers, STATES
URS-4 · I-3 · L-4

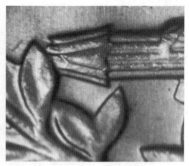

Description: The reverse die was inadvertently produced using a Type B hub, intended for use with Proof dies from 1936 to 1964, and from 1968 to 1972. The Type B reverse exhibits enhanced eagle feathers, and greater separation between the E and S of STATES.

	AU-50	MS-60	MS-63	MS-65
VARIETY:	$50	$75	$100	$150
NORMAL:	$2	$3	$5	$29

Comments: More detailed photos are shown in the front of this section.

1956-D — FS-25-1956D-501 (022.4)

Variety: Repunched Mintmark (Inverted)
CONECA RPM 1
PUP: Mintmark
URS-7 · I-4 · L-4

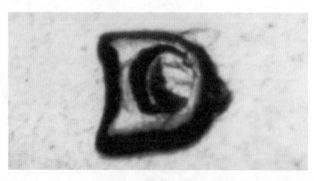

Description: The initial mintmark was punched into the die inverted, and then the second (primary) mintmark was punched correctly, creating this variety.

	AU-50	MS-60	MS-63	MS-65
VARIETY:	$50	$75	$150	$250
NORMAL:	$2	$3	$5	$33

Comments: This is also a very interesting and popular variety.

1957   FS-25-1957-901

Variety: Type B Reverse   CONECA—N/L
PUP: Eagle's tail feathers, STATES
URS-4 · I-3 · L-4

Description: The reverse die was inadvertently produced using a Type B hub, intended for use with Proof dies from 1936 to 1964, and from 1968 to 1972. The Type B reverse exhibits enhanced eagle feathers, stronger leaves, and greater separation between the E and S of STATES.

	AU-50	MS-60	MS-63	MS-65
VARIETY:	$50	$75	$100	$150
NORMAL:	$2	$3	$5	$23

Comments: See the detailed comparison photos on page 152.

1958   FS-25-1958-901

Variety: Type B Reverse   CONECA—N/L
PUP: Eagle's tail feathers, STATES
URS-4 · I-3 · L-4

Description: The reverse die was inadvertently produced using a Type B hub, intended for use with Proof dies from 1936 to 1964, and from 1968 to 1972. The Type B reverse exhibits enhanced eagle feathers, stronger leaves, and greater separation between the E and S of STATES.

	AU-50	MS-60	MS-63	MS-65
VARIETY:	$50	$75	$100	$150
NORMAL:	$2	$3	$5	$23

Comments: See the detailed comparison photos on page 152.

1959, PROOF

FS-25-1959-101

Variety: Doubled Die Obverse
PUP: IN GOD WE TRUST
URS-5 · I-3 · L-3

CONECA 3-O-II

Description: Doubling is dramatic on all obverse lettering, especially on IN GOD WE TRUST.

	PF-63	PF-65	PF-66
VARIETY:	$100	$150	$250
NORMAL:	$6	$11	$14

Comments: There are at least five different obverse doubled dies for the 1959 Proofs, but this is by far the nicest.

1959

FS-25-1959-901

Variety: Type B Reverse
PUP: Eagle's tail feathers, STATES
URS-4 · I-3 · L-4

CONECA—N/L

Description: The reverse die was inadvertently produced using a Type B hub, intended for use with Proof dies from 1936 to 1964, and from 1968 to 1972. The Type B reverse exhibits enhanced eagle feathers, stronger leaves, and greater separation between the E and S of STATES.

	AU-50	MS-60	MS-63	MS-65
VARIETY:	$20	$30	$50	$75
NORMAL:	$2	$3	$5	$22

Comments: See the detailed comparison photos on page 152.

1959-D

FS-25-1959D-501

Variety: Repunched Mintmark
PUP: Mintmark
URS-4 · I-3 · L-3

CONECA RPM 1

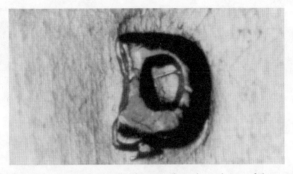

Description: The secondary D mintmarks are evident north and southeast of the primary D.

	AU-50	MS-60	MS-63	MS-65
VARIETY:	$8	$10	$15	$25
NORMAL:	$2	$3	$5	$22

Comments: This RPM is relatively new, and can likely be found with a little searching.

1960, PROOF

FS-25-1960-801

Variety: Doubled Die Reverse
PUP: QUARTER DOLLAR
URS-5 · I-3 · L-3

CONECA 2-R-II

Description: The doubling on this variety is evident on all reverse lettering, and many of the other design elements. A strong spread is evident on the eagle's wings, the leaf stems, and especially QUARTER DOLLAR.

	PF-63	PF-65	PF-66
VARIETY:	$50	$100	$200
NORMAL:	$6	$10	$14

Comments: This is one of the strongest Proof reverse doubled dies in the series.

1960

FS-25-1960-901

Variety: Type B Reverse

CONECA—N/L

PUP: Eagle's tail feathers, STATES

URS-4 · I-3 · L-4

Description: The reverse die was inadvertently produced using a Type B hub, intended for use with Proof dies from 1936 to 1964, and from 1968 to 1972. The Type B reverse exhibits enhanced eagle feathers, stronger leaves, and greater separation between the E and S of STATES.

	AU-50	MS-60	MS-63	MS-65
VARIETY:	$20	$30	$50	$75
NORMAL:	$2	$3	$5	$22

Comments: See the detailed comparison photos on page 152.

1961, PROOF

FS-25-1961-101

Variety: Doubled Die Obverse

CONECA 1-O-II

PUP: IN GOD WE TRUST

URS-5 · I-2 · L-2

Description: Moderate doubling is evident on the date, designer's initials, and the motto.

	PF-60	PF-63	PF-65
VARIETY:	$75	$100	$150
NORMAL:	$3	$5	$22

Comments: There are several other obverse doubled dies for the 1961 Proof.

1961

Variety: Type B Reverse
CONECA—N/L
PUP: Eagle's tail feathers, STATES
URS-4 · I-3 · L-4

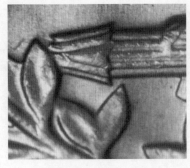 

Description: The reverse die was inadvertently produced using a Type B hub, intended for use with Proof dies from 1936 to 1964, and from 1968 to 1972. The Type B reverse exhibits enhanced eagle feathers, stronger leaves, and greater separation between the E and S of STATES.

	MS-60	MS-63	MS-65
VARIETY:	$75	$100	$150
NORMAL:	$3	$5	$22

Comments: See the detailed comparison photos on page 152.

1961-D

Variety: Repunched Mintmark
CONECA—N/L
PUP: Mintmark
URS-4 · I-3 · L-3

 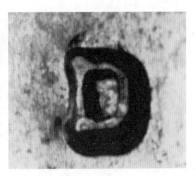

Description: The secondary D is evident north of the primary D.

	MS-60	MS-63	MS-65
VARIETY:	$10	$15	$45
NORMAL:	$3	$5	$22

Comments: This is a fairly strong RPM for the series.

1961-D

FS-25-1961D-502

Variety: Repunched Mintmark
PUP: Mintmark
URS-3 · I-3 · L-3

CONECA RPM 1

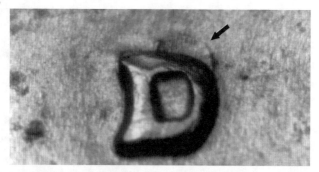

Description: The secondary D is evident north of the primary D.

	MS-60	MS-63	MS-65
VARIETY:	$10	$15	$45
NORMAL:	$3	$5	$22

Comments: This listing is clearly different from the previous one.

1962, PROOF

FS-25-1962-101

Variety: Doubled Die Obverse
PUP: IN GOD WE TRUST
URS-4 · I-4 · L-4

CONECA 4-O-VI

 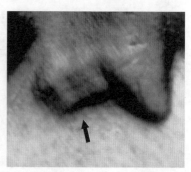

Description: The extra thickness on all lettering is typical of the Class VI doubled die. However, close examination will clearly show four separate hubbings, especially on the R of TRUST and the end of the ribbon.

	PF-63	PF-65	PF-66
VARIETY:	$75	$95	$150
NORMAL:	$6	$10	$14

Comments: This is an extremely strong Class VI variety.

1962
FS-25-1962-901

Variety: Type B Reverse
CONECA—N/L
PUP: Eagle's tail feathers, STATES
URS-4 · I-3 · L-4

YN

Description: The reverse die was inadvertently produced using a Type B hub, intended for use with Proof dies from 1936 to 1964, and from 1968 to 1972. The Type B reverse exhibits enhanced eagle feathers, stronger leaves, and greater separation between the E and S of STATES.

	MS-60	MS-63	MS-65
VARIETY:	$75	$100	$150
NORMAL:	$3	$5	$22

Comments: See the detailed comparison photos on page 152.

1962-D
FS-25-1962D-501

Variety: Repunched Mintmark
CONECA—N/L
PUP: Mintmark
URS-3 · I-3 · L-3

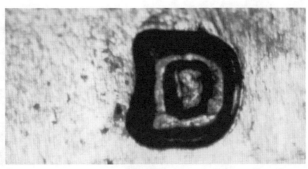

Description: Remnants of a secondary D mintmark are evident northeast of the primary D. The vertical of the secondary D is protruding from the upper right portion of the primary D.

	MS-60	MS-63	MS-65
VARIETY:	$10	$15	$45
NORMAL:	$3	$5	$22

Comments: An earlier die state of the RPM would be a great find!

1963   FS-25-1963-101 (023)

Variety: Doubled Die Obverse   CONECA 1-O-II
PUP: IN GOD WE TRUST
URS-10 · I-3 · L-2

Description: Doubling is evident on all obverse lettering and the date.

	MS-60	MS-63	MS-65
VARIETY:	$25	$35	$45
NORMAL:	$3	$5	$22

Comments: This variety can be found in Mint sets, if any remain. This has been a known packaged variety for several years.

1963   FS-25-1963-102

Variety: Doubled Die Obverse   CONECA 1-O-II+1-R-I
PUP: IN GOD WE TRUST, AMERICA
URS-6 · I-3 · L-3

Description: The obverse doubling is the same as FS-101. The reverse is doubled on all lettering around the rim.

	MS-60	MS-63	MS-65
VARIETY:	$75	$100	$150
NORMAL:	$3	$5	$22

Comments: This variety can also be found in Mint sets.

1963

FS-25-1963-103

Variety: Doubled Die Obverse
PUP: Date
URS-4 · I-3 · L-3

CONECA 3-O-V

Description: The doubling is only evident on the six and three of the date. The secondary six is clear to the right of the loop of the primary six.

	MS-60	MS-63	MS-65
VARIETY:	$25	$30	$50
NORMAL:	$3	$5	$22

Comments: This is one of the more interesting doubled dies for this date.

1963

FS-25-1963-801

Variety: Doubled Die Reverse
PUP: AMERICA
URS-4 · I-2 · L-2

CONECA 4-R-VIII

 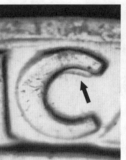 

Description: Doubling is evident only left of the left upright on M of AMERICA, inside the upper loop on C of AMERICA, and left of the first T of STATES.

	MS-60	MS-63	MS-65
VARIETY:	$50	$75	$100
NORMAL:	$3	$5	$22

Comments: This is a very unusual variety.

1963, PROOF
FS-25-1963-802

Variety: Doubled Die Reverse
PUP: AMERICA
URS-3 · I-2 · L-2

CONECA 6-R-II

Description: Doubling is evident on all reverse lettering, but strongest on AMERICA and DOLLAR.

	PF-63	PF-65	PF-66
VARIETY:	$75	$100	$150
NORMAL:	$6	$10	$14

Comments: The true rarity of this variety is still unknown.

1963
FS-25-1963-901

Variety: Type B Reverse
PUP: Eagle's tail feathers, STATES
URS-4 · I-3 · L-4

CONECA—N/L

Description: The reverse die was inadvertently produced using a Type B hub, intended for use with Proof dies from 1936 to 1964, and from 1968 to 1972. The Type B reverse exhibits enhanced eagle feathers, stronger leaves, and greater separation between the E and S of STATES.

	MS-60	MS-63	MS-65
VARIETY:	$75	$100	$150
NORMAL:	$3	$5	$22

Comments: See the detailed comparison photos on page 152.

1963-D

Variety: Doubled Die Obverse
PUP: LIBERTY
URS-4 · I-3 · L-3

FS-25-1963D-101

CONECA 4-O-II+V

Description: Doubling is evident on all obverse lettering, strongest on LIBERTY, lesser on IN GOD WE TRUST and date.

	MS-60	MS-63	MS-65
VARIETY:	$25	$30	$50
NORMAL:	$3	$5	$22

Comments: This should prove to be a relatively popular variety.

1964

Variety: Doubled Die Obverse
PUP: IN GOD WE TRUST
URS-3 · I-2 · L-2

FS-25-1964-101

CONECA—Unknown

Description: Doubling is evident on IN GOD WE TRUST, and very slightly on the date and the designer's initials.

	MS-63	MS65	MS-66
VARIETY:	$15	$25	$40
NORMAL:	$5	$14	$43

Comments: At this time, we haven't been able to match this variety to a CONECA listing.

1964
FS-25-1964-801

Variety: Doubled Die Reverse CONECA 1-R-I
PUP: QUARTER DOLLAR
URS-4 · I-4 · L-4

Description: Doubling is evident on all reverse lettering with a very strong spread, strongest on QUARTER DOLLAR.

	AU-55	MS-60	MS-63	MS-65	MS-66
VARIETY:	$50	$75	$100	$150	$300
NORMAL:		$2	$5	$14	$43

Comments: This variety is in extremely high demand by specialists.

1964
FS-25-1964-802 (024.5)

Variety: Doubled Die Reverse CONECA 2-R-II
PUP: QUARTER DOLLAR
URS-3 · I-3 · L-3

Description: Doubling is evident with a nice spread on QUARTER DOLLAR.

	AU-55	MS-60	MS-63	MS-65	MS-66
VARIETY:	$50	$75	$100	$125	$200
NORMAL:			$5	$14	$43

Comments: This is one of at least 11 reverse doubled dies for this date.

1964 FS-25-1964-803

Variety: Doubled Die Reverse CONECA 3-R-I
PUP: AMERICA
URS-3 · I-3 · L-3

Description: Doubling is moderate on UNITED STATES OF AMERICA, being strongest on STATES and AMERICA.

	AU-55	MS-60	MS-63	MS-65	MS-66
VARIETY:	$35	$50	$60	$75	$100
NORMAL:		$5	$14	$43

Comments: This variety is very scarce in high grade.

1964 FS-25-1964-804

Variety: Doubled Die Reverse CONECA 4-R-V
PUP: QUARTER DOLLAR
URS-3 · I-4 · L-5

Description: The doubling is very strong on QUARTER DOLLAR, weaker on UNITED, and very light on STATES.

	AU-55	MS-60	MS-63	MS-65	MS-66
VARIETY:	$100	$150	$200	$250	$350
NORMAL:		$5	$15	$42

Comments: This is a rare variety, and always in demand.

1964
FS-25-1964-901

Variety: Type B Reverse
CONECA—N/L
PUP: Eagle's tail feathers, STATES
URS-4 · I-3 · L-4

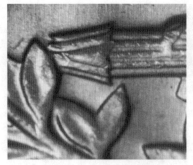

Description: The reverse die was inadvertently produced using a Type B hub, intended for use with Proof dies from 1936 to 1964, and from 1968 to 1972. The Type B reverse exhibits enhanced eagle feathers, and greater separation between the E and S of STATES.

	AU-55	MS-60	MS-63	MS-65	MS-66
VARIETY:	$50	$60	$75	$100	$150
NORMAL:			$5	$15	$42

Comments: See the detailed comparison photos on page 152.

1964-D
FS-25-1964D-101

Variety: Doubled Die Obverse
CONECA 1-O-II
PUP: IN GOD WE TRUST
URS-5 · I-2 · L-2

Description: The doubling is most evident on the motto.

	AU-55	MS-60	MS-63	MS-65	MS-66
VARIETY:	$15	$20	$25	$30	$40
NORMAL:			$5	$15	$42

Comments: This is very similar to the 1963-(P) FS-101.

1964-D FS-25-1964D-501

Variety: Repunched Mintmark CONECA RPM 3
PUP: Mintmark
URS-3 · I-3· L-3

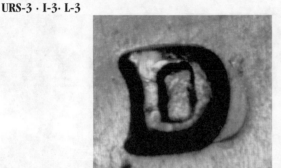 

Description: The secondary D mintmark is evident east of the primary D.

	AU-55	MS-60	MS-63	MS-65	MS-66
VARIETY:	$8	$10	$15	$25	$35
NORMAL:		$2	$5	$15	$24

Comments: This is one of the nicer RPMs for the date.

1964-D FS-25-1964D-502

Variety: Misplaced Mintmark CONECA—N/L
PUP: Branch above mintmark
URS-2 · I-4 · L-4

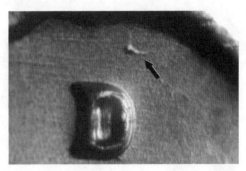

Description: On this very dramatic RPM, a secondary D mintmark is evident protruding from the branch above the mintmark area.

	AU-55	MS-60	MS-63	MS-65	MS-66
VARIETY:	$125	$150	$200	$300	$450
NORMAL:		$2	$5	$15	$42

Comments: This is one of the very few totally separated repunched mintmark varieties.

1964-D

FS-25-1964D-801 (025)

Variety: Doubled Die Reverse
PUP: AMERICA
URS-4 · I-3 · L-4

CONECA 1-R-V

Description: Doubling is very strong on OF AMERICA and DOLLAR, with a medium spread on STATES, QUARTER, and E PLURIBUS UNUM.

	AU-55	MS-60	MS-63	MS-65	MS-66
VARIETY:	$125	$150	$200	$300	$450
NORMAL:		$2	$5	$15	$42

Comments: This is a very dramatic doubled die reverse.

THE CHERRYPICKERS' GUIDE HELPFUL HINTS

Check the coins already in your collection. In many cases, collectors will find a variety they had no idea they had. In some cases, these unfound varieties can be quite valuable. This first happened to J.T. Stanton back in 1982, and it can happen to you!

See appendix H for more Helpful Hints.

1964-D

Variety: Type C Reverse

CONECA—N/L

PUP: Eagle's tail feathers, leaf at arrow tips

URS-4 · I-3 · L-4

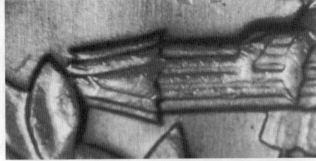
Type C

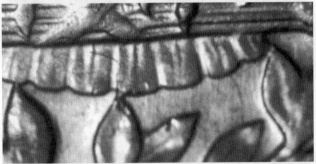
Type C

Type B

Description: A very few 1964-D coins are known to have the Type C reverse intended for use starting in 1965. These Type C reverse coins show the leaves above the AR of DOLLAR sharp and almost touching the letters, where the Type A is weak and the Type B is bold, but the one leaf does touch the A of DOLLAR. The tail feathers on the Type C reverse have a very distinct centerline. Additionally, the leaves below the tail feathers are sharp and barely touch those tail feathers. The leaf in front of the arrow tips comes to a distinct point in front of the arrow tips. On the Type B reverse, this leaf rises above the top arrow tip, and on the Type A it is very weak.

	AU-55	MS-60	MS-63	MS-65	MS-66
VARIETY:	$125	$150	$200	$300	$450
NORMAL:		$2	$5	$15	$42

Comments: The D-Mint coins from 1956 through 1964 are suspected with a Type B reverse. Keep a lookout for these!

1965

Variety: Doubled Die Obverse
PUP: IN GOD WE TRUST, LIBERTY
URS-3 · I-4 · L-5

CONECA 1-O-IV

Description: The doubling is very strong on all obverse lettering, the eye, and the date.

	AU-50	AU-55	MS-60	MS-63	MS-65	MS-66
VARIETY:	$350	$450	$550	$750	$1,000	$1,500
NORMAL:			$1	$1	$9	$21

Comments: This variety is extremely rare, and sells very quickly at auction.

1965

Variety: Doubled Die Obverse
PUP: LIBERTY
URS-3 · I-3 · L-3

CONECA 2-O-V

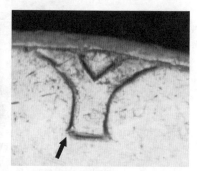

Description: Doubling is very strong on LIBERTY.

	AU-50	AU-55	MS-60	MS-63	MS-65	MS-66
VARIETY:	$50	$60	$75	$125	$200	$300
NORMAL:			$1	$1	$9	$21

Comments: This variety is typical of a Class V doubled die with doubling evident on one area only.

1965

FS-25-1965-801

Variety: Doubled Die Reverse
CONECA 1-R-II+VI
PUP: QUARTER DOLLAR
URS-3 · I-4· L-3

Description: The doubling is evident on all reverse lettering, some with the Class II spread, and some with the extra thickness normally associated with Class VI.

	AU-50	AU-55	MS-60	MS-63	MS-65	MS-66
VARIETY:	$25	$35	$50	$75	$125	$175
NORMAL:			$1	$1	$9	$21

Comments: This is a relatively new discovery.

1966

FS-25-1966-801 (026.3)

Variety: Doubled Die Reverse
CONECA 1-R-I
PUP: UNITED STATES OF AMERICA, QUARTER DOLLAR
URS-2 · I-5 · L-5

Description: Very strong doubling is evident on all reverse lettering, including E PLURIBUS UNUM. NOTE: This is not the SMS issue!

	AU-55	MS-60	MS-63	MS-65	MS-66
VARIETY:	$300	$600	$800	$1,250	$2,000
NORMAL:	$0.75	$1	$1	$6	$21

Comments: Discovered by Roger Gray, this has proven to be a very rare variety!

1967, SPECIAL MINT SET   FS-25-1967-101 (026.5)

Variety: Doubled Die Obverse   CONECA 2-O-I
PUP: IN GOD WE TRUST
URS-5 · I-4 · L-4

Description: Strong doubling is evident on the motto and LIBERTY, with moderate doubling evident on the date.

	MS-60	MS-63	MS-65	MS-66
VARIETY:	$550	$750	$1,000	$1,500
NORMAL:	$1	$1	$5	$24

Comments: This variety is known with strike doubling. Those specimens will command far less than values stated.

1967, SPECIAL MINT SET   FS-25-1967-801

Variety: Doubled Die Reverse   CONECA 2-R-II+VI
PUP: QUARTER DOLLAR
URS-3 · I-4 · L-4

Description: Moderate doubling is evident on the stems and QUARTER DOLLAR.

	MS-60	MS-63	MS-65	MS-66
VARIETY:	$25	$50	$75	$100
NORMAL:	$1	$1	$5	$24

Comments: More specimens of this variety are sure to be uncovered.

1968-D
FS-25-1968D-801

Variety: Doubled Die Reverse
CONECA 1-R-I
PUP: UNITED STATES OF AMERICA, QUARTER DOLLAR
URS-4 · I-4 · L-4

Description: Very strong doubling evident on all reverse lettering, leaves, branches, and wing tips.

	AU-55	MS-60	MS-63	MS-65	MS-66
VARIETY:	$300	$450	$600	$750	$1,000
NORMAL:	$0.75	$1	$1	$5	$11

Comments: Keep an eye open for this very strong doubled die.

1968-S, PROOF
FS-25-1968S-101 (027)

Variety: Doubled Die Obverse
CONECA 1-O-I
PUP: Date, LIBERTY
URS-3 · I-4 · L-4

Description: The doubling is evident on the motto, LIBERTY, and the date.

	PF-63	PF-65	PF-66
VARIETY:	$250	$500	$750
NORMAL:		$4	$5

Comments: This is an extremely rare variety!

1968-S, PROOF

FS-25-1968S-501

Variety: Repunched Mintmark
PUP: Mintmark
URS-3 · I-3 · L-3

CONECA RPM 3, 4

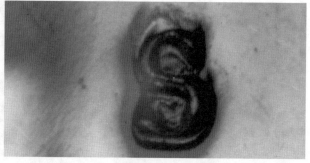

Description: The secondary mintmark is evident north of the primary S.

	PF-63	PF-65	PF-66
VARIETY:	$25	$50	$75
NORMAL:		$4	$5

Comments: This could possibly be CONECA RPM 4. Both 3 and 4 are listed as S/S north.

1968-S, PROOF

FS-25-1968S-801 (027)

Variety: Doubled Die Reverse
PUP: QUARTER DOLLAR
URS-6 · I-3 · L-3

CONECA 1-R-I

Description: The doubling is on all lettering around the rim and the left tips.

	PF-63	PF-65	PF-66
VARIETY:	$250	$500	$750
NORMAL:		$4	$5

Comments: Although well known for years, very few examples have surfaced!

1969-D

FS-25-1969D-501

Variety: Repunched Mintmark

CONECA RPM 1

PUP: Mintmark

URS-5 · I-3 · L-3

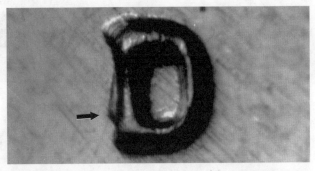

Description: The secondary mintmark is slanted slightly west of the primary D.

	MS-63	MS-65	MS-66
VARIETY:	$20	$25	$50
NORMAL:	$1	$5	$20

Comments: This variety can be found in Mint sets.

1969-D

FS-25-1969D-502

Variety: Repunched Mintmark

CONECA RPM 3

PUP: Mintmark

URS-4 · I-3 · L-3

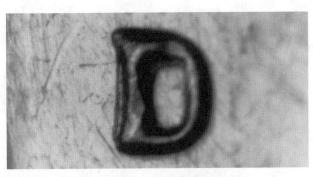

Description: The secondary mintmark is slightly west of the primary D.

	MS-63	MS-65	MS-66
VARIETY:	$20	$25	$50
NORMAL:	$1	$5	$20

Comments: Reported to have been found in Mint sets.

1969-S, PROOF
FS-25-1969S-101 (027.08)

Variety: Doubled Die Obverse
PUP: Date, LIBERTY
URS-4 · I-5 · L-5

CONECA 1-O-IV

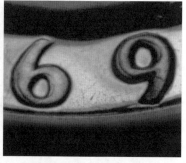

Description: The doubling is extremely strong on all obverse lettering and on the date.

	PF-63	PF-65	PF-66
VARIETY:	$600	$750	$1,000
NORMAL:		$4	$5

Comments: This very rare variety was pictured on the cover of *Cherrypickers' Guide* third edition, but omitted from the text of the book. Some eagle-eyed collectors wanted to know more.

1969-S, PROOF
FS-25-1969S-501 (27.1)

Variety: Repunched Mintmark
PUP: Mintmark
URS-4 · I-3 · L-3

CONECA RPM 2

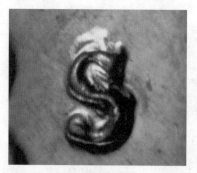

Description: This RPM exhibits an S/S/S, with both secondary punches slightly north of the primary S.

	PF-63	PF-65	PF-66
VARIETY:	$25	$50	$75
NORMAL:		$4	$5

Comments: Very few specimens have been reported.

1970-D · FS-25-1970D-101 (27.3)

Variety: Doubled Die Obverse
PUP: IN GOD WE TRUST
URS-3 · I-4· L-4

CONECA 1-O-V

Description: A very strong and rare doubled die, with doubling evident on the date, IN GOD WE TRUST, and the ERTY of LIBERTY.

	AU-55	MS-60	MS-63	MS-65	MS-66
VARIETY:	$400	$500	$600	$750	$1,000
NORMAL:		$1	$1	$6	$30

Comments: Again, this variety is considered extremely rare.

1970-D · FS-25-1970D-102

Variety: Doubled Die Obverse
PUP: LIBERTY
URS-2 · I-4 · L-4

CONECA 2-O-I

Description: The doubling on this extremely rare variety is evident on the date, the motto, and LIB-ERTY. Both hubbings were of equal depth, causing the differences in the two to be faint. However, the wide separation, evidenced by the split serifs, is very dramatic.

	AU-55	MS-60	MS-63	MS-65	MS-66
VARIETY:	$200	$300	$400	$500	$750
NORMAL:		$1	$1	$6	$30

Comments: This is extremely rare, with only two reported to date.

1970-D
FS-25-1970D-801

Variety: Doubled Die Reverse
PUP: QUARTER DOLLAR
URS-6 · I-3· L-3

CONECA 1-R-III+V

Description: Moderate doubling is evident on lower letters, branches, leaves, and slightly on UNITED.

	AU-55	MS-60	MS-63	MS-65	MS-66
VARIETY:	$50	$75	$150	$200	$300
NORMAL:		$1	$1	$6	$30

Comments: This variety has *reportedly* been found in Mint sets.

1970-D
FS-25-1970D-802

Variety: Doubled Die Reverse
PUP: AMERICA, DOLLAR
URS-5 · I-3· L-3

CONECA 2-R-III+I

Description: Strong doubling is evident around the rim, within the feathers, and on the lower wreath.

	AU-55	MS-60	MS-63	MS-65	MS-66
VARIETY:	$100	$150	$200	$250	$350
NORMAL:		$1	$1	$6	$30

Comments: We hope to be able to photograph a high-grade raw specimen. This variety can be found in Mint sets.

1971-D

FS-25-1971D-801 (027.8)

Variety: Doubled Die Reverse
PUP: UNITED STATES OF AMERICA
URS-3 · I-4 · L-4

CONECA 1-R-V

Description: Strong doubling is evident on UNITED STATES OF AMERICA.

	AU-55	MS-60	MS-63	MS-65	MS-66
VARIETY:	$200	$300	$400	$500	$750
NORMAL:		$1	$1	$3	$20

Comments: We would love to see a higher-grade specimen!

1976-D

FS-25-1976D-101 (028)

Variety: Doubled Die Obverse
PUP: LIBERTY
URS-6 · I-4 · L-4

CONECA 1-O-V

Description: Very strong doubling is evident on LIBERTY, and very slight doubling on the motto and date.

	AU-55	MS-60	MS-63	MS-65	MS-66
VARIETY:	$600	$750	$1,000	$1,250	$1,500
NORMAL:		$0.75	$1	$6	$25

Comments: Generally, only early die state specimens will show doubling on the motto.

1976-D

FS-25-1976D-102

Variety: Doubled Die Obverse
PUP: LIBERTY
URS-4 · I-3 · L-3

CONECA 2-O-V

Description: Moderate doubling is evident only on LIBERTY.

	AU-55	MS-60	MS-63	MS-65	MS-66
VARIETY:	$10	$20	$35	$50	$100
NORMAL:		$0.75	$1	$5	$7

Comments: This variety may prove very rare.

1979-S, PROOF

FS-25-1979S-501

Variety: Type II Mintmark
PUP: Mintmark
URS-10 · I-5 · L-5

No other attribution

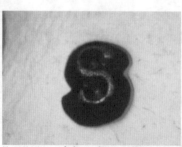

Type II Mintmark (Scarce)   Type I Mintmark (common)

Description: For the 1979-S Proof coins, the style mintmark was changed during the production, creating two distinctly different types. The Type II is the rare variety, and is easily distinguished from the common Type I. The Type I has a very indistinct blob, whereas the Type II shows a well-defined S.

	PF-63	PF-65	PF-66
VARIETY:	$3	$12	$16
NORMAL:		$6	$11

Comments: Complete government-sealed Proof sets in which all six coins are Type II command a substantial premium over the six individual coins. Of the six coins, the quarter dollar is one of the more common pieces.

1981-S, PROOF · FS-25-1981S-501

Variety: Type II Mintmark　　　　　　　　　　**No other attribution**
PUP: Mintmark
URS-10 · I-5 · L-5

Type II Mintmark (Scarce)　　　　　　*Type I Mintmark (common)*

Description: For the 1981-S Proof coins, the style mintmark was changed during the production, creating two distinct different types. The Type II is the rare variety, and is not easily distinguished from the common Type I. For most collectors, the easiest difference to discern on the Type II is the flatness on the top curve of the S, which is rounded on the Type I. Additionally, the surface of the Type II mintmark is frosted, and the openings in the loops slightly larger.

	PF-63	PF-65	PF-66
VARIETY:	$4	$11	$12
NORMAL:		$6	$8

Comments: Complete government-sealed Proof sets with all six coins being Type II command a substantial premium over the six individual coins. Of the six coins, the quarter dollar is one of the more common pieces.

1982-S, PROOF · FS-25-1982S-101

Variety: Doubled Die Obverse　　　　　　　　　　**CONECA—N/L**
PUP: Date
URS-2 · I-3 · L-3

Description: Doubling is visible on the motto, date, and LIBERTY.

	PF-63	PF-65	PF-66
VARIETY:	$25	$50	$75
NORMAL:		$3	$4

Comments: These later Proofs with a doubled die are somewhat difficult to pick up because of the relatively equal depth of the hubbings and the frosting on the letters and numbers.

1989-D FS-25-1989D-501

Variety: Repunched Mintmark CONECA RPM 1
PUP: Mintmark
URS-2 · I-3 · L-3

Description: The secondary D is evident west of the primary D.

	MS-60	MS-63	MS-65	MS-66
VARIETY:	$15	$20	$25	$50
NORMAL:	$0.60	$0.75	$3	$30

Comments: We'd love to see a higher-grade specimen!

1990-S, PROOF FS-25-1990S-101

Variety: Doubled Die Obverse CONECA 1-O-V
PUP: Date, mintmark
URS-4 · I-4 · L-4

Description: Very strong doubling is evident on the date, mintmark, and slightly on IN GOD
WE TRUST.

	PF-63	PF-65	PF-66
VARIETY:	$300	$450	$750
NORMAL:		$4	$5

Comments: Only a few examples have been reported. Check those 1990-S Proof sets!

1995-S, PROOF

FS-25-1995S-101

Variety: Doubled Die Obverse
PUP: Date, ribbon end
URS-2 · I-3 · L-3

CONECA—N/L

Description: Very close doubling is visible on the date, mintmark, ribbon, and hair.

	PF-63	PF-65	PF-66
VARIETY:	$125	$200	$300
NORMAL:		$8	$9

Comments: This may be difficult to pick up, as doubling is often hard to see on coins with heavy frosting.

1996-P

FS-25-1996P-701

Variety: Unknown die damage
PUP: Area in front of and behind head
URS-1 · I-2 · L-2

CONECA—N/L

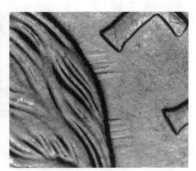

Description: Leave it to Tom Stott to find something so different that there is no real explanation, other than that it's very interesting.

	MS-60	MS-63	MS-65
VARIETY:	n/a	n/a	n/a
NORMAL:	$0.50	$0.60	$8

Comments: This may be the remnant of a lapped die. The variety is too new on the market to gauge fair values.

2004-D   FS-25-2004D-5901

Variety: Design Manipulation   **No other attribution**
PUP: Reverse—corn
URS-12 · I-5 · L-5

Upward Line Reverse   *Normal Reverse*

Description: An image was added to the working die, creating an upward line to the left cornhusk.

	AU-55	MS-60	MS-63	MS-65	MS-66
VARIETY:	$150	$250	$450	$750	$950
NORMAL:	$0.40	$0.50	$0.60	$1.25	$5

Comments: It is our belief that the additional lines on this and the next variety of the Wisconsin quarters were deliberately added to the reverse dies. Apparently, a tool with a rounded edge was impressed into the working dies to create images that were not a part of the intended design. Many collectors, dealers, etc., refer to these as an Extra Leaf variety. However, the lines are not the image of a leaf. (Compare with the next variety.)

2004-D   FS-25-2004D-5902

Variety: Design Manipulation   **No other attribution**
PUP: Reverse—corn
URS-13 · I-5 · L-5

Downward Lines Reverse   *Normal Reverse*

Description: Images were added to the working die, creating two downward lines to the left cornhusk.

	AU-55	MS-60	MS-63	MS-65	MS-66
VARIETY:	$100	$150	$250	$650	$850
NORMAL:	$0.40	$0.50	$0.60	$1.25	$5

Comments: See the comments for the previous listing.

More on the 2004-D Wisconsin Quarter varieties

The very interesting varieties of the 2004-D Wisconsin quarters were first reported by Rob Weiss of Old Pueblo Coin in Tucson, Arizona. Since the publication of these varieties, there has been a lot of discussion and disagreement over the cause of the extra lines on the reverse. These discussions will surely continue for many years. There is no clear consensus on either the purpose or the cause of the lines.

Some error/variety specialists think these two different coins occurred accidentally, caused by actual damage to the dies or die breaks. Other specialists believe the differences were created officially as an intentional design alteration.

It is our belief, however, that someone in the Denver Mint may have been celebrating something (perhaps a retirement, a little early) by intentionally adding an extra image to some dies. Our reasoning is that:

1. The additional images are concentric, very similar in appearance, and in an interesting location. The mathematical odds of this occurring entirely by accident are astronomical.

2. The concentric lines were most likely caused by an instrument, perhaps a small nut driver or similar implement. It would be very easy to make an impression into a working die with such a tool.

3. The lines are all the same length, a factor that depends on the angle and pressure with which the implement was placed against the die and, therefore, not likely to happen by accident.

4. While some specialists have suggested that only a die-room worker could have altered the die, we disagree, believing that anyone with access to the dies could have accomplished this deed.

5. A mark of very similar size and shape near the ear on a 2004-D dime provides virtually conclusive evidence that the lines were made intentionally.

We believe strongly that the lines on the reverse of the Wisconsin quarters do not represent a means of adding a leaf to the cornhusk. A location that would allow the added images to be identified was most likely chosen at random.

As attention to the varieties increased, many error/variety specialists tried to denounce the use of a nickname, as the error/variety hobby community generally deplores the use of them. However, nicknames are readily used these days by most numismatists. The Three-Legged Buffalo nickel of 1937 is probably the best example. This very popular variety was created by an over-polished die.

Many error/variety specialists also object to promoting the coins as a legitimate variety; yet for any promotion to be successful, dealers and collectors must both accept them as varieties.

Our feelings are very simple: if you like the coins as varieties, consider adding them to your collection. It's very clear, though, that these varieties are here to stay. And (in case you were wondering)—we love 'em!

Value, rarity, and estimated populations

As with any new variety, it takes at least a year for its true value to be established in the marketplace. One of the most critical components needed to establish value is rarity, and then only as influenced by demand.

Rob Weiss at Old Pueblo Coin in Tucson has been tracking the population reports of ANACS, NGC, PCGS, and the other grading services. His estimates, based on these populations and other factors (most notably known "raw" coins) indicate that about 4,000 occurrences of the upward lines ("Extra Leaf High") and about 6,000 of the downward lines ("Extra Leaf Low") have been reported in all grades. These reports are supported by the mix of the coins in the original rolls. Almost all original rolls came from the Tucson, Arizona, areas and San Antonio, Texas, and each was found to contain approximately three coins with upward lines, seven with downward lines, and 30 normal coins. Very few new specimens were reported during the last six months of 2005 and into 2006.

If these population reports turn out to be relatively accurate over time, it could be that Weiss's results indicate that the imperfect dies were discovered very early and subsequently removed from service. The higher estimate of 6,000 coins from the one die is actually a very low production quantity. The values offered by Weiss are as follows:

	AU-58	MS-60	MS-63	MS-64	MS-65	MS-66
EXTRA LEAF HIGH	$150	$250	$300	$320	$400	$600
EXTRA LEAF LOW	$100	$150	$200	$225	$250	$300

Values may further vary depending upon the eye appeal of the coin.

Regardless of where the value and populations settle, we are certain these varieties will be around for a long time to come. Just remember, don't ever let anyone tell you what you should or should not collect. The hobby should be fun for *you*!

Liberty Seated Half Dollars, 1839–1891

Liberty Seated half dollars contain numerous interesting and valuable die varieties. Significant varieties are known and can be found for virtually every date and mint. From minor repunched mintmarks to major doubled dies, and even major design changes, the varieties are abundant.

Virtually all varieties within the series are in high demand by the large number of Liberty Seated specialists. In general, values for the varieties have been increasing at an even faster rate than for the normal coins. An eagle-eyed cherrypicker can easily earn a significant income by picking the varieties that go unnoticed by most dealers.

The varieties listed in this edition of the *Cherrypickers' Guide* are but a percentage of those known in the series. More will be included in future editions. Many other varieties known in the series are documented in the *Complete Guide to Liberty Seated Half Dollars*, by Randy Wiley and Bill Bugert.

Clubs and Educational Information

For those seriously interested in the series, we strongly recommend membership in the Liberty Seated Collectors Club (LSCC), which we believe to be one of the very best specialty clubs in numismatics. The club issues its official publication, the *Gobrecht Journal*, three times each year. This 52-page newsletter is loaded with excellent educational articles. The club has an outstanding web site at www.numismalink.com/lscc.html. As of this writing, the annual dues are $15—a bargain, considering the amount of information available. If you join the LSCC, you will be connecting with some of the most serious and knowledgeable collectors and dealers in the hobby. For more information, contact

Liberty Seated Collectors Club
Mark Sheldon, Secretary/Treasurer
P.O. Box 261
Wellington OH 44090

Note: References to Wiley and Bugert (WB) in this volume apply to listings in their *Complete Guide to Liberty Seated Half Dollars*.

1840 (REVERSE OF 1839)

FS-50-1840-301

Variety: Repunched Date
PUP: Date
URS-9 · I-3 · L-3

WB 102

Description: This RPD shows with a secondary 4 and 0 evident south of the primary digits. The 0 is actually slightly southeast.

	VG-8	F-12	VF-20	EF-40	AU-50	MS-60
VARIETY:	$120	$150	$200	$300	$500	$750
NORMAL:	$32	$48	$68	$100	$225	$490

Comments: This is a reverse of the 1839 variety.

1840 (REVERSE OF 1839)

FS-50-1840-302

Variety: Repunched Date
PUP: Date
URS-8 · I-3 · L-3

WB 104

Description: This RPD shows a secondary 18 slightly west, a secondary 4 slightly north, and a secondary 0 evident north.

	VG-8	F-12	VF-20	EF-40	AU-50	MS-60
VARIETY:	$120	$150	$200	$300	$500	$750
NORMAL:	$32	$48	$68	$100	$225	$490

Comments: This is a reverse of the 1839 variety.

1842 — FS-50-1842-301

Variety: Repunched Date **WB 105**
PUP: Date
URS-11 · I-3 · L-3

Description: Another RPD, with secondary digits visible south on the 8, the 4, and the 2.

	VG-8	F-12	VF-20	EF-40	AU-50	MS-60
VARIETY:	$120	$150	$200	$300	$500	$750
NORMAL:	$31	$47	$56	$82	$170	$460

Comments: There are at least three other RPDs known for the date.

1842 — FS-50-1842-801 (000.5)

Variety: Doubled Die Reverse **WB 103**
PUP: UNITED STATES OF AMERICA
URS-7 · I-3 · L-3

Description: A very nice doubled die is evident on all reverse lettering, leaves, and arrow tips.

	VG-8	F-12	VF-20	EF-40	AU-50	MS-60
VARIETY:	$120	$150	$200	$300	$500	$750
NORMAL:	$31	$47	$56	$82	$170	$460

Comments: This is one of the more popular varieties of the series.

1843-O
FS-50-1843o-301

Variety: Repunched Date
WB 103
PUP: Date
URS-11 · I-3 · L-3

Description: The secondary 1 and 8 are visible south of the primary digits, while the secondary 4 and 3 are visible north of the primary digits.

	VG-8	F-12	VF-20	EF-40	AU-50
VARIETY:	$75	$100	$125	$200	$350
NORMAL:	$26	$43	$60	$82	$180

Comments: This is a reverse of the 1839 variety.

1844-O
FS-50-1844o-301 (001)

Variety: Misplaced Date
WB 103
PUP: Date
URS-7 · I-4 · L-4

Description: This is one of the more dramatic misplaced dates in this series. All four digits are evident protruding from the rock above the date.

	VG-8	F-12	VF-20	EF-40	AU-50	MS-60
VARIETY:	$700	$1,100	$1,500	$2,200	$4,500	$10,000
NORMAL:	$24	$43	$50	$78	$180	$650

Comments: This variety is considered rare and highly collectible.

1845-O
FS-50-1845o-301 (001.5)

Variety: Repunched Date
PUP: Date
URS-7 · I-4 · L-4

WB 104

Description: The strong repunched date is evident with a secondary 5 far east of the primary 5. Other secondary numbers are not visible.

	VG-8	F-12	VF-20	EF-40	AU-50	MS-60
VARIETY:	$700	$1,000	$1,500	$2,500	$4,500	$10,000
NORMAL:	$24	$38	$53	$120	$240	$500

Comments: This variety is sometimes errantly called a tripled date.

1845-O
FS-50-1845o-302 (002)

Variety: Repunched Date
PUP: Date
URS-6 · I-4 · L-4

WB 106

Description: This RPD is clearly tripled on all four digits. Below the primary 8 are three distinct lower loops. Below the primary 4, one can see the bases of two different 4s punched into the die.

	VG-8	F-12	VF-20	EF-40	AU-50	MS-60
VARIETY:	$300	$500	$800	$1,200	$1,800	$2,400
NORMAL:	$24	$38	$53	$120	$240	$500

Comments: This variety can be detected in low grades.

1845-O

FS-50-1845o-303

Variety: Repunched Date
PUP: Date
URS-9 · I-3 · L-3

WB 108

Description: Another RPD with all four digits clearly repunched, with the secondary digits west of the primary digits.

	VG-8	F-12	VF-20	EF-40	AU-50	MS-60
VARIETY:	$300	$500	$800	$1,200	$1,800	$2,400
NORMAL:	$24	$38	$53	$120	$240	$500

Comments: This variety can be detected in low grades.

1845-O

FS-50-1845o-501 (002.5)

Variety: O Over Horizontal O Mintmark
PUP: Mintmark
URS-10 · I-3 · L-3

WB 103

Description: The primary mintmark was punched into the die over a previously punched horizontal mintmark. The underlying horizontal O is evident within the opening at the top, and slightly right at the top of the primary O.

	VG-8	F-12	VF-20	EF-40	AU-50	MS-60
VARIETY:	$150	$300	$500	$750	$1,000	$1,500
NORMAL:	$24	$38	$53	$120	$240	$500

Comments: This variety can be detected in low grades.

1846   FS-50-1846-301 (003)

Variety: Repunched Date   **WB 104**
PUP: Date
URS-10 · I-5 · L-5

Description: With this RPD, the primary 6 was punched over a 6 previously punched into the die horizontally.

	VG-8	F-12	VF-20	EF-40	AU-50	MS-60
VARIETY:	$215	$270	$365	$565	$1,020	
NORMAL:	$25	$42	$47	$85	$185	$475

Comments: This variety can be detected in low grades.

1847   FS-50-1847-101

Variety: Doubled Die Obverse   **WB N/L**
PUP: Shield, LIBERTY
URS-1 · I-3 · L-3

Description: Doubling is evident on the shield and LIBERTY.

	VG-8	F-12	VF-20	EF-40	AU-50	MS-60
VARIETY:			$500			
NORMAL:	$23	$41	$54	$72	$140	$475

Comments: The next item, (1847/6) is listed in WB as a doubled die in early die states. It is unknown at this time whether this listing is a later state (without evidence of the over-date). David Camire is very knowledgeable with varieties and would most likely have noted that when these photos were sent. However, the authors have not seen this coin and can't discount the doubled die being from the overdate die. Liberty Seated coin specialist Larry Briggs stated this was most likely a late die state of the overdate die, yet still worth a modest premium.

1847, 7 OVER 6 — FS-50-1847-301 (004)

Variety: Overdate
PUP: Date
URS-6 · I-5 · L-5

WB 102

Description: Remains of an underlying 6 can be seen below and between the primary 4 and 7.

	VG-8	F-12	VF-20	EF-40	AU-50	MS-60
VARIETY:	$2,500	$3,500	$4,500	$6,500	$10,000	
NORMAL:	$23	$41	$54	$72	$140	$475

Comments: The overdate might not be evident on later die states. This is a very popular variety!

1849 — FS-50-1849-301 (004.5)

Variety: Repunched Date
PUP: Date
URS-6 · I-4 · L-4

WB 102

Description: The lower portions of all four secondary digits are evident west of the primary digits. Most notable will be the lower 1 and 4 just left of the primary numbers.

	VG-8	F-12	VF-20	EF-40	AU-50	MS-60
VARIETY:	$2,000	$3,000	$4,000	$6,000	$8,500	
NORMAL:	$33	$46	$70	$135	$330	$685

Comments: This variety is considered by many to be one of the true rarities of the entire series.

1853, ARROWS AND RAYS — FS-50-1853-401

Variety: Clashed Obverse Die WB—N/L
PUP: Date area
URS-2 · I-4 · L-4

Description: This obverse die was clashed with a reverse die, exhibiting the rays protruding from the rock on the obverse.

	VG-8	F-12	VF-20	EF-40	AU-50	MS-60
VARIETY:	n/a	n/a	n/a	n/a	n/a	n/a
NORMAL:	$26	$40	$73	$190	$400	$975

Comments: To date we've only heard of two examples of this variety, but we're certain others have been located. Remember this is a one-year type coin.

1853, ARROWS AND RAYS — FS-50-1853-801 (004.7)

Variety: Doubled Die Reverse WB—N/L
PUP: UNITED STATES OF AMERICA
URS-6 · I-3 · L-3

Description: The reverse doubling has a clockwise spread on UNITED STATES OF AMERICA, but very little doubling elsewhere.

	VG-8	F-12	VF-20	EF-40	AU-50	MS-60
VARIETY:	$120	$150	$200	$300	$500	$975
NORMAL:	$26	$40	$73	$190	$400	$750

Comments: To date, only a few specimens have been reported.

1853, ARROWS AND RAYS · FS-50-1853-801 (004.7)

Variety: Doubled Die Reverse WB—N/L
PUP: UNITED, HALF
URS-6 · I-3 · L-3

Description: Doubling is evident on UNITED STATES OF AMERICA, and very slightly on HALF DOL.

	VG-8	F-12	VF-20	EF-40	AU-50	MS-60
VARIETY:	$120	$150	$200	$300	$500	$975
NORMAL:	$26	$40	$73	$190	$400	$750

Comments: To date, only a few specimens have been reported.

1853, ARROWS AND RAYS · FS-50-1853-802

Variety: Doubled Die Reverse WB—N/L
PUP: HALF DOL
URS-3 · I-3 · L-3

Description: The doubling is evident on HALF DOL, AMERICA, and some rays.

	VG-8	F-12	VF-20	EF-40	AU-50	MS-60
VARIETY:	$120	$150	$200	$300	$500	$975
NORMAL:	$26	$40	$73	$190	$400	$750

Comments: Doubling can also be seen on some of the denticles.

1853, ARROWS AND RAYS

FS-50-1853-803

Variety: Doubled Die Reverse

WB—N/L

PUP: STATES

URS-3 · I-3 · L-3

Description: The doubling is evident on UNITED STATES OF AMERICA, with a slight spread toward the center.

	VG-8	F-12	VF-20	EF-40	AU-50	MS-60
VARIETY:	$120	$150	$200	$300	$500	$975
NORMAL:	$26	$40	$73	$190	$400	$750

Comments: The doubling on this variety is slightly weaker than on the previous one.

1855, 5 OVER 4, W/ARROWS

FS-50-1855-301 (005)

Variety: Overdate

WB 102

PUP: Date

URS-7 · I-4 · L-5

Description: The 1855 date was punched over an 854.

	VG-8	F-12	VF-20	EF-40	AU-50	MS-60
VARIETY:	$75	$125	$200	$350	$600	$1,625
NORMAL:	$27	$38	$55	$100	$260	$675

Comments: This is certainly one of the top three varieties of the series.

1855-O

FS-50-1855o-501 (006)

Variety: Repunched Mintmark
PUP: Mintmark
URS-6 · I-4 · L-3

WB 102

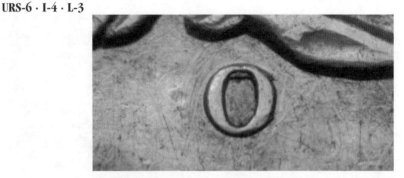

Description: The initial mintmark was punched into the die in a horizontal orientation, with a subsequent punch correctly vertical.

	VG-8	F-12	VF-20	EF-40	AU-50	MS-60
VARIETY:	$100	$150	$200	$300	$600	$1,000
NORMAL:	$26	$42	$47	$91	$242	$479

Comments: This is listed as CONECA RPM 1.

1856-O

FS-50-1856o-501 (006.5)

Variety: Repunched Date
PUP: Date
URS-9 · I-3 · L-3

WB 102

Description: The initial date was punched into the die angled slightly upward, with the subsequent punch being more level, creating the repunched date. The secondary 1 is evident south, with a secondary 5 and 6 evident north.

	VG-8	F-12	VF-20	EF-40	AU-50	MS-60
VARIETY:	$75	$100	$150	$200	$350	$750
NORMAL:	$25	$39	$47	$68	$170	$450

Comments: This variety can be spotted in lower grades!

1858 — FS-50-1858-101

Variety: Doubled Die Obverse

WB 102

PUP: Left rock and skirt

URS-6 · I-3 · L-3

Description: Doubling is most evident on the shield, left rock, and skirt; and is also visible on the foot, the hand and the right side of the rock.

	VG-8	F-12	VF-20	EF-40	AU-50	MS-60
VARIETY:	$100	$200	$300	$450	$600	$900
NORMAL:	$22	$38	$44	$68	$140	$375

Comments: This is still a very rare variety.

1858 — FS-50-1858-301

Variety: Repunched Date

WB 105

PUP: Date

URS-6 · I-3 · L-3

Description: Evidence of secondary numbers is evident both left and right of the primary 5. Wiley and Bugert indicate the image right of the 5 is an inverted 1, and that may well be accurate.

	VG-8	F-12	VF-20	EF-40	AU-50	MS-60
VARIETY:	$100	$200	$300	$450	$600	$900
NORMAL:	$22	$38	$44	$68	$140	$375

Comments: This is a very scarce variety.

1858 — FS-50-1858-302

Variety: Misplaced Date
PUP: Date
URS-3 · I-3 · L-3

WB—N/L

Description: A portion of an 8 is visible protruding from the skirt above the first 8.

	VG-8	F-12	VF-20	EF-40	AU-50	MS-60
VARIETY:	$100	$200	$300	$450	$600	$900
NORMAL:	$22	$38	$44	$68	$140	$375

Comments: This variety is not listed in WB.

1858-O — FS-50-1858o-301

Variety: Misplaced Date
PUP: Date
URS-8 · I-3 · L-3

WB 108

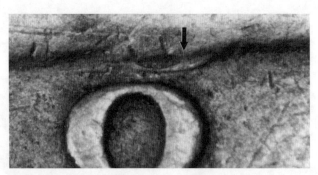

Description: The lower portion on an 8 is evident protruding from the rock above the final primary 8.

	VG-8	F-12	VF-20	EF-40	AU-50	MS-60
VARIETY:	$75	$125	$200	$300	$500	$750
NORMAL:	$32	$48	$68	$100	$155	$340

Comments: This and other MPDs are abundant in all Liberty Seated coinage series.

1859-O

FS-50-1859o-301

Variety: Repunched Date
PUP: Date
URS-7 · I-3 · L-3

WB 104

Description: A secondary 1 is evident slightly south of the primary, and a secondary 9 is visible very slightly north, showing only as a doubled serif.

	VG-8	F-12	VF-20	EF-40	AU-50	MS-60
VARIETY:	$50	$75	$100	$150	$300	$500
NORMAL:	$23	$36	$45	$68	$175	$345

Comments: This and other RPDs are abundant in all Liberty Seated coinage series.

1861-O

FS-50-1861o-401 (007)

Variety: Confederate Obverse
PUP: Die crack in front of head
URS-6 · I-4 · L-4

WB 102

Description: The die crack from the denticles to the right of the sixth star down to Liberty's nose (actually to her shoulder below her jaw) is the diagnostic for this rare variety.

	VG-8	F-12	VF-20	EF-40	AU-50	MS-60
VARIETY:	$150	$200	$300	$500	$1,000	$2,000
NORMAL:	$25	$38	$60	$90	$190	$333

Comments: In 1861, the New Orleans Mint produced a very few half dollars using this obverse die in the striking of Confederate half dollars. This same obverse die, when paired with the normal reverse, is quite desirable, and the higher the grade, the rarer the coin.

1865 — FS-50-1865-301

Variety: Repunched Date WB 102
PUP: Date
URS-7 · I-3 · L-3

Description: A secondary 1 is evident north of the primary 1, and a secondary 5 is evident south of the primary 5.

	VG-8	F-12	VF-20	EF-40	AU-50	MS-60
VARIETY:	$75	$150	$200	$300	$400	$650
NORMAL:	$36	$54	$72	$130	$242	$492

Comments: The 8 and 6 are also repunched, although very closely.

1866 — FS-50-1866-301

Variety: Misplaced Date WB—N/L
PUP: Date
URS-3 · I-3 · L-3

Description: The base of three digits (likely a 6) can be seen protruding from the rock. Two images are together above the first 6, and the third is barely visible above the 8.

	VG-8	F-12	VF-20	EF-40	AU-50	MS-60
VARIETY:	$75	$125	$200	$300	$500	$750
NORMAL:	$27	$39	$61	$88	$160	$375

Comments: This variety is not listed in WB.

1866 — FS-50-1866-302

Variety: Misplaced Date   WB 102
PUP: Date
URS-7 · I-3 · L-3

Description: The top of a 6 is evident protruding from the denticles below the last 6.

	VG-8	F-12	VF-20	EF-40	AU-50	MS-60
VARIETY:	$75	$125	$200	$300	$500	$750
NORMAL:	$27	$39	$61	$88	$160	$375

Comments: This variety can be detected in low grades.

1867 — FS-50-1867-801

Variety: Doubled Die Reverse   WB 102
PUP: Eagle's beak
URS-6 · I-4 · L-4

Description: The ribbon, IN GOD WE TRUST, and the eagle's beak and eye are all visibly doubled.

	VG-8	F-12	VF-20	EF-40	AU-50	MS-60
VARIETY:	$150	$200	$300	$500	$750	$1,000
NORMAL:	$39	$58	$100	$140	$225	$420

Comments: This variety is different from that associated with the 1867-S doubled die reverse.

1873 ARROWS
FS-50-1873-1101 (007.1)

Variety: Doubled Die Obverse "Quad Stripes"
PUP: Shield
URS-8 · I-4 · L-4

WB 109

Description: The doubling is evident on Liberty's gown, foot, and shield, the scroll, and the lower stars, but is most notable by the sets of four vertical stripes in the shield.

	VG-8	F-12	VF-20	EF-40	AU-50	MS-60
VARIETY:	$100	$200	$300	$450	$600	$900
NORMAL:	$25	$38	$70	$174	$308	$675

Comments: This is likely the strongest doubled obverse die in the series.

1873 ARROWS
FS-50-1873-1301 (007.2)

Variety: Misplaced Date
PUP: Denticles under right arrow
URS-3 · I-3 · L-3

WB—N/L

Description: The top of a digit (likely a 3) is evident protruding from the denticles under the tip of the right arrow.

	VG-8	F-12	VF-20	EF-40	AU-50	MS-60
VARIETY:	$50	$75	$100	$250	$450	$900
NORMAL:	$25	$38	$70	$174	$308	$675

Comments: This variety is not listed in WB.

1876

Variety: Large/Small Date
PUP: Date
URS-3 · I-4 · L-4

WB 106

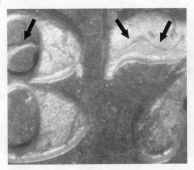

Description: This repunched date, confirmed by overlays, is a normal (large) date over a smaller date, likely a logo punch intended for a 20-cent or 25-cent denomination. The initial smaller numbers are evident between and on top of the primary numbers.

	VG-8	F-12	VF-20	EF-40	AU-50	MS-60
VARIETY:	$100	$150	$200	$350	$600	$1,000
NORMAL:	$22	$36	$42	$62	$150	$321

Comments: This variety is considered very rare.

THE CHERRYPICKERS' GUIDE **HELPFUL HINTS**

Study and learn the Pick-Up-Points (PUPs) for each series so that you can focus your initial attention on these areas to find varieties. Don't forget the denticle area and the design above the date (especially on 19th-century coinage such as the Liberty Seated series) for misplaced numbers, etc. They hide, so use a good loupe and good light.

See appendix H for more Helpful Hints.

1876

FS-50-1876-302

Variety: Repunched Date

WB 105

PUP: Date

URS-8 · I-3 · L-3

Description: The remains of two underlying numbers are evident at the lower left of the 7 and 6 of the primary date.

	VG-8	F-12	VF-20	EF-40	AU-50	MS-60
VARIETY:	$50	$75	$100	$150	$250	$500
NORMAL:	$22	$36	$42	$62	$150	$321

Comments: This is another very rare variety.

1876

FS-50-1876-303 (007.3)

Variety: Misplaced Date

WB—N/L

PUP: Date

URS-5 · I-3 · L-3

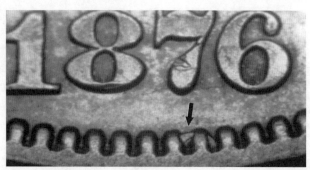

Description: The upper portion of a number (likely a 6) is evident protruding from the denticles below the 7.

	VG-8	F-12	VF-20	EF-40	AU-50	MS-60
VARIETY:	$50	$75	$100	$150	$250	$500
NORMAL:	$22	$36	$42	$62	$150	$321

Comments: This variety can be detected even in low grades.

1876

FS-50-1876-304

Variety: Misplaced Date
PUP: Date
URS-5 · I-3 · L-3

WB—N/L

Description: The upper portion of two numbers can be detected protruding from the denticles below the primary 1 and 8.

	VG-8	F-12	VF-20	EF-40	AU-50	MS-60
VARIETY:	$50	$75	$100	$150	$250	$500
NORMAL:	$22	$36	$42	$62	$150	$321

Comments: This variety can be detected even in low grades.

1876, PROOF

FS-50-1876-401

Variety: C in neck
PUP: Neck of Liberty
URS-2 · I-4 · L-4

WB—N/L

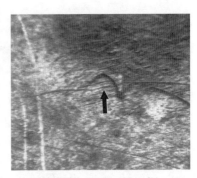

Description: On this Proof die, the remnants of a C are evident in Liberty's neck. The style of the C is identical to that of a CC mintmark.

	PF-60	PF-63	PF-65
VARIETY:	$500	$750	n/a
NORMAL:	$379	$575	$2,950

Comments: Because this variety is a Proof, the chance is very high that several of them will be identified.

1877, 7 OVER 6

FS-50-1877-301

Variety: Overdate
PUP: Date
URS-4 · I-4 · L-4

WB—N/L

Description: The top portion of a 6 is evident on the upper surface of the last 7. This type of overdate is well known in the Morgan dollar series.

	VG-8	F-12	VF-20	EF-40	AU-50	MS-60
VARIETY:	$350	$500	$750	$1,000	$1,500	$2,500
NORMAL:	$22	$36	$41	$62	$125	$361

Comments: This variety is sure to become very popular among Liberty Seated specialists.

THE CHERRYPICKERS' GUIDE **HELPFUL HINTS**

Don't forget to inspect the denticles of a coin, especially those near and beneath the date, for variety characteristics. Dozens of significant varieties exhibit portions of numbers within or protruding from the denticles. Most of these are prized additions to a collection.

See appendix H for more Helpful Hints.

Barber or Liberty Head Half Dollars, 1892–1915

The three series of the Barber design have long been neglected when one considers the typical varieties, such as doubled dies, repunched mintmarks, overdates, and the like. For many collectors, the Barber quarter series has been somewhat of an afterthought when searching for nice varieties. But all that is changing now that many new varieties are discovered and reported, and some of the known varieties are becoming more popular. We encourage close inspection of all Barber coins.

Only a limited number of varieties in the Barber series were known when the third edition of the *Cherrypickers' Guide* went to press. Furthermore, some varieties were known but were not included in that edition. Since that time a significant number of new varieties have been reported, and there are undoubtedly many varieties yet to be discovered. Therefore, we encourage close inspection of all Barber coins.

Clubs and Educational Information

To obtain more knowledge of Barber coins in general and Barber varieties in particular, we suggest membership in the Barber Coin Collector's Society. Annual dues are $15. For more information, contact

BCCS
Eileen Ribar
2053 Edith Place
Merrick NY 11566
Email: emcrib@optonline.net

The society's quarterly publication, the *Journal,* contains educational information on all denominations of the Barber design. The Web address is www.barbercoins.org. Visitors to the site will find educational articles, membership information, and general information concerning the Barber design, the three Barber series, and Liberty Head nickels.

1892   FS-50-1892-301 (007.7)

Variety: Repunched Date   Lawrence 101
PUP: Date
URS-3 · I-3 · L-3

Description: All four digits of the date are dramatically repunched south.

	VG-8	F-12	VF-20	EF-40	AU-50	MS-60	MS-63
VARIETY:	$75	$100	$200	$300	$400	$600	$900
NORMAL:	$30	$55	$93	$154	$229	$354	$640

Comments: This impressive RPD has yet to yield many specimens.

1892   FS-50-1892-801 (007.8)

Variety: Tripled Die Reverse   Lawrence 102
PUP: Reverse lettering
URS-6 · I-3 · L-3

Description: Tripling is evident on all outer lettering, with doubling visible on several stars, the ribbon ends, and the arrows.

	VG-8	F-12	VF-20	EF-40	AU-50	MS-60	MS-63
VARIETY:	$75	$100	$200	$400	$600	$750	$1,000
NORMAL:	$30	$55	$93	$154	$229	$354	$640

Comments: This has become a very popular variety among Barber specialists.

1892-O
FS-50-1892o-501 (007.9)

Variety: Small O Mintmark
PUP: Mintmark
URS-8 · I-3 · L-3

Lawrence 101

Description: Most often referred to as a micro O, this variety was created when an O mintmark punch for quarters was used in place of the regular, larger mintmark intended for use on half dollar dies.

	F-12	VF-20	EF-40	AU-50	MS-60	MS-63
VARIETY:	$1,000	$1,500	$2,500	$4,000	$6,000	$8,000
NORMAL:	$367	$400	$425	$450	$720	$1,175

Comments: Many examples show strong strike doubling on reverse.

1909-S
FS-50-1909S-501

Variety: Inverted S Mintmark
PUP: Mintmark
URS-3 · I-3 · L-3

Lawrence—N/L

Description: The S mintmark was punched into the die in an inverted orientation. The base of a correct S is slightly wider than the top.

	VG-8	F-12	VF-20	EF-40	AU-50	MS-60	MS-63
VARIETY:	$50	$75	$150	$250	$400	$600	$1,100
NORMAL:	$12	$29	$76	$158	$292	$458	$960

Comments: Inverted S mintmarks are being discovered more frequently as of late, in many series.

1911-S

FS-50-1911S-501

Variety: Repunched Mintmark
PUP: Mintmark
URS-7 · I-3 · L-3

Lawrence—N/L

Description: The lower serif of the underlying mintmark is evident protruding from the primary serif.

	VG-8	F-12	VF-20	EF-40	AU-50	MS-60	MS-63
VARIETY:	$50	$75	$150	$250	$400	$700	$1,400
NORMAL:	$13	$33	$76	$142	$271	$525	$1,175

Comments: This is a good example of one of the newly discovered varieties, especially among RPMs.

24-Page Catalog of:
Error/Variety Coins
$2.00 pp.
22-Page Catalog of:
Medals/Bars/Rounds
$2.00 pp.
54-Page Catalog of:
Rare Coin Reproductions
$3.00 pp.

When Thinking About Buying or Selling Error-Variety Coins, Think Ken Potter!

Ken Potter

P.O. Box 760232-CP, Lathrup Village, MI 48076
Phone: (313)255-8907 • Cell: (313)268-3280
Email: ken@koinpro.com
ANA-LM, NLG, CONECA-LM, NCADD-FM, MSNS-LM

Numismatist Since 1959 • **www.koinpro.com** • Serving Collectors Since 1973

Liberty Walking Half Dollars, 1916–1947

The Liberty Walking half dollars contain many significant and very rare varieties. These include doubled dies, RPMs, and of course missing and hand-carved designer's initials.

Likely the rarest of all the varieties in the series is a very strong obverse doubled die known on a 1936-(P) specimen. The specimen we've illustrated in this volume comes to us from Dave Hur. Unknown to us above the grade of Fine, this variety has proven to be very rare and elusive, with fewer than five examples known to exist.

Other significant varieties include visually significant and rare repunched mintmarks, hand-engraved initials on a 1944-D, missing initials on a 1945-(P), and an inverted S mintmark on a 1944-S specimen.

Clubs and Educational Information

As of this publication date there are no clubs devoted strictly to the study of Liberty Walking half dollars. Yet this design is one of the most popular for series collectors, and does hold a number of really nice varieties. For those interested primarily in the varieties within the series, we suggest membership in CONECA, the national error and variety club. Each issue of their bimonthly publication, *Errorscope*, contains articles on errors and varieties of all types, including those on coins from other countries. An application is available online at www.conecaonline.org/join, or by contacting Paul Funaiole at

CONECA
Paul Funaiole, Membership
35 Leavitt Lane
Glenburn ME 04401-1013

1916-D

FS-50-1916D-501

Variety: Repunched Mintmark   Fox V-101
PUP: Mintmark
URS-8 · I-3 · L-3

Description: The secondary D is evident southwest of the primary D.

	VG-8	F-12	VF-20	EF-40	AU-50	MS-60	MS-63
VARIETY:	$75	$100	$200	$275	$400	$500	$750
NORMAL:	$38	$58	$93	$158	$192	$283	$436

Comments: This dramatic RPM has yet to yield many specimens.

1936

FS-50-1936-101 (008.4)

Variety: Doubled Die Obverse   Fox—N/L
PUP: Date
URS-2 · I-4 · L-4

YN

Description: Extremely strong doubling is evident on the date. Lesser doubling is evident on IN GOD WE TRUST, the skirt, and some other elements.

	VG-8	F-12	VF-20	EF-40	AU-50
VARIETY:	$300	$400	$500	$600	$750
NORMAL:	$4	$5	$6	$7	$19

Comments: Unknown above Fine, this variety will be very elusive.

1936
FS-50-1936-102

Variety: Doubled Die Obverse
PUP: Date, IN GOD WE TRUST
URS-11 · I-2 · L-2

Fox V-101

Description: Doubling is evident on the date, IN GOD WE TRUST, the lower folds of the skirt, the shoes, and the ground.

	VG-8	F-12	VF-20	EF-40	AU-50	MS-60	MS-63
VARIETY:	$10	$15	$20	$25	$30	$60	$100
NORMAL:	$4	$5	$6	$7	$19	$33	$66

Comments: This variety is still easy to locate. Some of the doubled dies of 1936 are from a doubled master die.

1936-D
FS-50-1936D-101

Variety: Doubled Die Obverse
PUP: Date, IN GOD WE TRUST
URS-11 · I-2 · L-2

Fox V-101

Description: Doubling is evident on the date, IN GOD WE TRUST, the lower folds of the skirt, the shoes, and the ground.

	VG-8	F-12	VF-20	EF-40	AU-50	MS-60	MS-63
VARIETY:	$10	$15	$20	$25	$50	$85	$150
NORMAL:	$4	$5	$6	$16	$36	$62	$100

Comments: This and the previous variety are from a doubled master die.

1936-S   FS-50-1936S-101

Variety: Doubled Die Obverse   Fox V-101
PUP: Date, IN GOD WE TRUST
URS-11 · I-2 · L-2

Description: Doubling is evident on the date, IN GOD WE TRUST, the lower folds of the skirt, the shoes, and the ground.

	VG-8	F-12	VF-20	EF-40	AU-50	MS-60	MS-63
VARIETY:	$10	$15	$20	$30	$75	$150	$200
NORMAL:	$4	$5	$6	$18	$53	$108	$167

Comments: This variety is also from a doubled master die.

1939-D   FS-50-1939D-101 (008.45)

Variety: Doubled Die Obverse   Fox V-103
PUP: Date, IN GOD WE TRUST
URS-11 · I-2 · L-2

Description: Doubling is evident on the date, IN GOD WE TRUST, the lower folds of the skirt, the shoes, and the ground.

	VG-8	F-12	VF-20	EF-40	AU-50	MS-60	MS-63
VARIETY:	$10	$15	$20	$25	$35	$75	$100
NORMAL:	$4	$5	$6	$7	$20	$33	$75

Comments: This variety is extremely similar to the previous three listings.

1939-D
FS-50-1939D-501

Variety: Repunched Mintmark
Fox V-101

PUP: Mintmark
URS-5 · I-3 · L-3

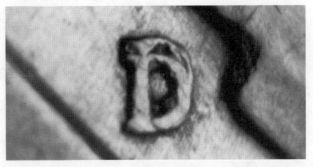

Description: The secondary mintmark is evident north of the primary mintmark.

	VG-8	F-12	VF-20	EF-40	AU-50	MS-60	MS-63
VARIETY:	$15	$20	$25	$35	$50	$75	$100
NORMAL:	$4	$5	$6	$7	$20	$33	$75

Comments: CONECA lists this very prominent RPM as RPM 1.

1941-D
FS-50-1941D-501

Variety: Repunched Mintmark
Fox V-101

PUP: Mintmark
URS-7 · I-3 · L-3

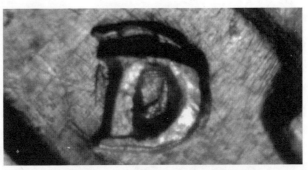

Description: The secondary mintmark is evident northwest of the primary mintmark.

	VG-8	F-12	VF-20	EF-40	AU-50	MS-60	MS-63
VARIETY:	$15	$20	$25	$35	$50	$75	$100
NORMAL:	$3	$4	$5	$6	$15	$30	$55

Comments: CONECA lists this very prominent repunched mintmark as RPM 1.

1941-S

FS-50-1941S-501

Variety: Repunched Mintmark
PUP: Mintmark
URS-6 · I-3 · L-3

Fox V-102

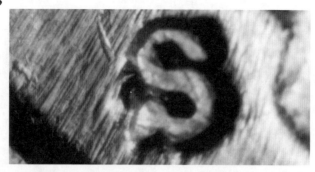

Description: The secondary mintmark is evident northwest of the primary mintmark.

	VG-8	F-12	VF-20	EF-40	AU-50	MS-60	MS-63
VARIETY:	$10	$15	$20	$25	$35	$75	$100
NORMAL:	$3	$4	$5	$6	$13	$30	$55

Comments: Fox incorrectly lists this variety as an S over horizontal S.

1942

FS-50-1942-101 (008.5)

Variety: Doubled Die Obverse
PUP: Liberty's breast
URS-12 · I-2 · L-2

Fox V-103

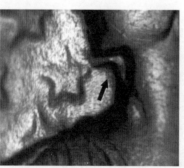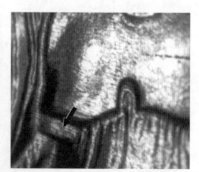

Description: The doubling is evident on Liberty's breast and neck, and on the bottom of the gown.

	VG-8	F-12	VF-20	EF-40	AU-50	MS-60	MS-63
VARIETY:	$10	$15	$20	$25	$35	$75	$100
NORMAL:	$3	$4	$5	$6	$9	$28	$39

Comments: This doubled die was caused by a doubled master die.

1942 — FS-50-1942-801 (009)

Variety: Doubled Die Reverse
Fox V-101
PUP: HALF DOLLAR
URS-8 · I-4 · L-4

Description: Doubling is evident on HALF DOLLAR, UNITED STATES OF AMERICA, the olive branch and the lower eagle.

	VG-8	F-12	VF-20	EF-40	AU-50	MS-60	MS-63
VARIETY:	$15	$25	$35	$50	$75	$100	$250
NORMAL:	$3	$4	$5	$6	$9	$28	$39

Comments: This is one of two very popular DDRs in this series.

1942-D — FS-50-1942D-101

Variety: Doubled Die Obverse
Fox V-106
PUP: Liberty's breast
URS-8 · I-2 · L-2

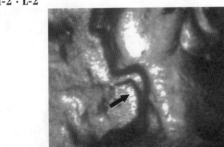 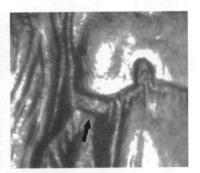

Description: The doubling is evident on Liberty's breast and neck, and on the bottom of the gown.

	VG-8	F-12	VF-20	EF-40	AU-50	MS-60	MS-63
VARIETY:	$10	$15	$20	$25	$35	$75	$100
NORMAL:	$3	$4	$5	$6	$14	$30	$78

Comments: This doubled die was caused by a doubled master die.

1942-D

No FS#

Variety: No Variety
PUP: Mintmark
URS-15 · I-1 · L-1

Fox V-101

Description: Once considered a "D over S" mintmark variety, further study has confirmed that the area thought to be an underlying S is the result of either metal fatigue or die damage.

	VG-8	F-12	VF-20	EF-40	AU-50	MS-60	MS-63
VARIETY:	$3	$4	$5	$6	$14	$30	$78
NORMAL:	$3	$4	$5	$6	$14	$30	$78

Comments: Several reported dies of a possible D/S have been examined, but as of this writing none have been confirmed.

1942-S

FS-50-1942S-101

Variety: Doubled Die Obverse
PUP: Liberty's breast
URS-4 · I-2 · L-2

Fox V-106

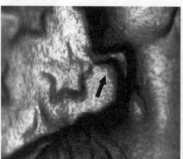 

Description: The doubling is evident on Liberty's breast and neck, and on the bottom of the gown.

	VG-8	F-12	VF-20	EF-40	AU-50	MS-60	MS-63
VARIETY:	$10	$15	$20	$25	$35	$75	$100
NORMAL:	$3	$4	$5	$6	$14	$30	$78

Comments: This doubling was caused by a doubled master die.

1943 — FS-50-1943-101

Variety: Master Die DDO
PUP: IN GOD WE TRUST, date
URS-20 · I-1 · L-1

Fox V-101, 102, 103, 106

Description: The doubling is evident on IN GOD WE TRUST and on the date.

	VG-8	F-12	VF-20	EF-40	AU-50	MS-60	MS-63
VARIETY:	$3	$4	$5	$6	$9	$28	$39
NORMAL:	$3	$4	$5	$6	$9	$28	$39

Comments: This and many other 1943 doubled dies (from all three mints) are the result of a doubled master die. Almost all 1943-dated halves will exhibit some form of this doubling. On some specimens the last number is clearly doubled. Although some people believe it to be 1943 over 1942, this has not been confirmed. We believe that the upper curve of the underlying digit more closely matches that of a 3.

1943-D — FS-50-1943D-101

Variety: Master Die DDO
PUP: IN GOD WE TRUST, date
URS-20 · I-1 · L-1

Fox V-101, 102, 104, 107

Description: The doubling is evident on IN GOD WE TRUST and on the date.

	VG-8	F-12	VF-20	EF-40	AU-50	MS-60	MS-63
VARIETY:	$3	$4	$5	$6	$18	$32	$75
NORMAL:	$3	$4	$5	$6	$18	$32	$75

Comments: This and many other 1943 doubled dies (from all three mints) are the result of a doubled master die. Almost all 1943-dated halves will exhibit some form of this doubling. On some specimens the last number is clearly doubled. Although some people believe it to be 1943 over 1942, this has not been confirmed. We believe that the upper curve of the underlying digit more closely matches that of a 3.

1943-S

FS-50-1943S-101

Variety: Master Die DDO
PUP: IN GOD WE TRUST, date
URS-20 · I-1 · L-1

Fox V-101, 102, 103, 105, 107, 108, 115

Description: The doubling is evident on IN GOD WE TRUST and on the date.

	VG-8	F-12	VF-20	EF-40	AU50	MS-60	MS-63
VARIETY:	$3	$4	$5	$6	$17	$30	$74
NORMAL:	$3	$4	$5	$6	$17	$30	$74

Comments: This and many other 1943 doubled dies (from all three mints) are the result of a doubled master die. Almost all 1943 dated halves will exhibit some form of this doubling. On some specimens the last number is clearly doubled. Although some people believe it to be 1943 over 1942, this has not been confirmed. We believe that the upper curve of the underlying digit more closely matches that of a 3.

1943-D

No FS#

Variety: No Variety
PUP: Mintmark
URS-5 · I-1 · L-1

Fox—N/L

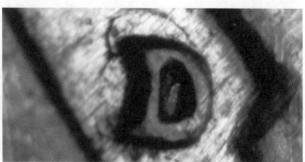

Description: As with the 1942-D (FS-50-1942D-501), this reverse die has been misinterpreted as a D over S, however, the area around the mintmark was most likely caused by die fatigue.

	VG-8	F-12	VF-20	EF-40	AU-50	MS-60	MS-63
VARIETY:	$3	$4	$5	$6	$18	$32	$75
NORMAL:	$3	$4	$5	$6	$18	$32	$75

Comments: This listing is included to help prevent inaccurate D over S attributions.

1944-D   FS-50-1944D-901

Variety: Hand Engraved Initials   Fox—N/L
PUP: Designer's initials
URS-4 · I-4 · L-4

Hand Engraved   Normal Hub/Die Transfer

Description: The designer's initials on the reverse were omitted from the original die and were subsequently hand engraved.

	VG-8	F-12	VF-20	EF-40	AU-50	MS-60	MS-63
VARIETY:	$30	$50	$75	$150	$300	$500	$750
NORMAL:	$3	$4	$5	$6	$9	$28	$39

Comments: The cause of the missing initials is unclear. The initials are not punched into each die, as many think, but are a part of the master hub and die series, and would normally have been transferred onto the working dies. Other dates and mints within the series are known and will be added to our listings as we can examine them.

1944-S   FS-50-1944S-501

Variety: Repunched Mintmark   Fox—N/L
PUP: Mintmark
URS-6 · I-3 · L-3

Description: The secondary mintmark is evident north of the primary mintmark.

	VG-8	F-12	VF-20	EF-40	AU-50	MS-60	MS-63
VARIETY:	$15	$20	$25	$35	$50	$75	$125
NORMAL:	$3	$4	$5	$6	$14	$31	$63

Comments: CONECA lists this very prominent repunched mintmark as RPM 4.

1944-S

FS-50-1944S-502

Variety: Repunched Mintmark
PUP: Mintmark
URS-6 · I-3 · L-3

Fox V-101

 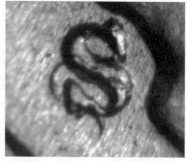

Description: The secondary mintmark is evident southwest, north, and east of the primary mintmark.

	VG-8	F-12	VF-20	EF-40	AU-50	MS-60	MS-63
VARIETY:	$15	$20	$25	$35	$50	$75	$125
NORMAL:	$3	$4	$5	$6	$14	$31	$63

Comments: CONECA lists this very prominent repunched mintmark as RPM 2.

1944-S

FS-50-1944S-511

Variety: Inverted Mintmark
PUP: Mintmark
URS-5 · I-3 · L-3

Fox—N/L

Description: The S mintmark was punched into the die in an inverted orientation.

	VG-8	F-12	VF-20	EF-40	AU-50	MS-60	MS-63
VARIETY:	$15	$20	$25	$35	$50	$75	$125
NORMAL:	$3	$4	$5	$6	$14	$31	$63

Comments: This variety will certainly be very popular.

1945 FS-50-1945-901

Variety: Missing Designer's Initials Fox V-102
PUP: Designer's initials
URS-5 · I-4 · L-4

Description: The designer's initials on this die are missing.

	VG-8	F-12	VF-20	EF-40	AU-50	MS-60	MS-63
VARIETY:	$30	$50	$75	$100	$200	$300	$500
NORMAL:	$3	$4	$5	$6	$9	$28	$38

Comments: This is a very underrated variety.

1946 FS-50-1946-101

Variety: Doubled Die Obverse Fox—N/L
PUP: Fold of flag
URS-3 · I-3 · L-3

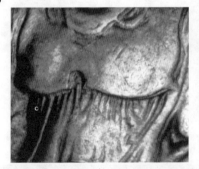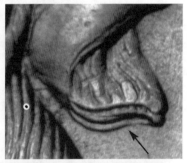

Description: The doubling is evident on Liberty's breast and left arm, and on the fold of the flag.

	VG-8	F-12	VF-20	EF-40	AU-50	MS-60	MS-63
VARIETY:	$10	$15	$20	$25	$50	$75	$100
NORMAL:	$3	$4	$5	$6	$11	$28	$41

Comments: CONECA lists this variety as 1-O-IV+VIII.

1946

FS-50-1946-801 (011.1)

Variety: Doubled Die Reverse

Fox V-101

PUP: EPU, feathers

URS-7 · I-4 · L-4

Description: Very strong doubling is evident on E PLURIBUS UNUM, the eagle's wing feathers, the eagle's left wing, and the branch.

	VG-8	F-12	VF-20	EF-40	AU-50	MS-60	MS-63
VARIETY:	$15	$25	$35	$50	$100	$175	$300
NORMAL:	$3	$4	$5	$6	$11	$28	$41

Comments: This is the second of the two most popular doubled dies of the series.

Franklin Half Dollars, 1948–1963

Compared with other series, the Franklin half dollars contain few significant varieties, yet one of the rarest Proof doubled reverse dies comes from this series. The 1961 Proof doubled-die reverse (FS-801) is extremely rare and in very high demand, with values continually on the rise. Without a doubt, this is one of the most significant varieties of the last half of the 20th century.

Other varieties in the series are known, and are highly collectible. However, some of these are on low-mintage dates, such as a quadrupled obverse die on a

1950 Proof. Obviously, being a low-mintage Proof, this variety will likely be found on a large percentage of the population.

Clubs and Educational Information

As of this publication date there are no clubs devoted strictly to the study of Franklin half dollars. However, for those interested primarily in the varieties within the series, we suggest membership in CONECA, the national error and variety club. Each issue of their bimonthly publication, *Errorscope*, contains articles on errors and varieties of all type, and even from other countries. An application is available online at www.conecaonline.org/join, or by contacting Paul Funaiole at

CONECA
Paul Funaiole, Membership
35 Leavitt Lane
Glenburn ME 04401-1013

1948
FS-50-1948-801

Variety: Doubled Die Reverse
PUP: E PLURIBUS UNUM
URS-8 · I-3 · L-3

CONECA 1-R-IV+VIII

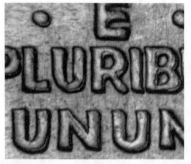 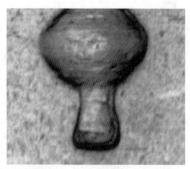

Description: Doubling is evident on E PLURIBUS UNUM, UNITED, HALF DOLLAR, the dots, and the clapper.

	EF-40	AU-50	MS-60	MS-63	MS-65	MS-66
VARIETY:	$15	$25	$45	$60	$75	$150
NORMAL:	$5	$6	$7	$12	$24	$64

Comments: There are several similar, yet lesser, DDRs for this date.

1948-D
FS-50-1948D-801

Variety: Doubled Die Reverse
PUP: E PLURIBUS UNUM
URS-8 · I-3 · L-3

CONECA 1-R-IV+VIII

Description: Doubling is evident on E PLURIBUS UNUM, UNITED, HALF DOLLAR, the dots, and the clapper.

	EF-40	AU-50	MS-60	MS-63	MS-65	MS-66
VARIETY:	$15	$25	$45	$60	$75	$150
NORMAL:	$5	$6	$7	$12	$21	$124

Comments: There are several similar, yet lesser, DDRs for this date.

1949-S

FS-50-1949S-501 (011.3)

Variety: Repunched Mintmark
PUP: Mintmark
URS-5 · I-3 · L-3

CONECA RPM 2

 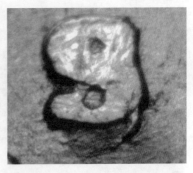

Description: The secondary mintmark is evident south of the primary.

	EF-40	AU-50	MS-60	MS-63	MS-65	MS-66
VARIETY:	$15	$25	$50	$75	$100	$200
NORMAL:	$5	$10	$15	$36	$45	$100

Comments: CONECA has two other RPMs listed for the date.

1950, PROOF

FS-50-1950-101

Variety: Quadrupled Die Obverse
PUP: Date, Liberty
URS-4 · I-3 · L-3

CONECA 1-O-II

Description: Quadrupling is evident on the date and LIBERTY.

	PF-63	PF-65
VARIETY:	$250	$500
NORMAL:	$232	$440

Comments: Close examination of the R in LIBERTY clearly indicates this is actually a quadrupled obverse die.

1951-S
FS-50-1951S-801

Variety: Doubled Die Reverse
CONECA 2-R-VIII
PUP: E PLURIBUS UNUM
URS-6 · I-3 · L-3

Description: Doubling is evident on E PLURIBUS UNUM, as well as on the eagle's left wing and tail feathers.

	EF-40	AU-50	MS-60	MS-63	MS-65	MS-66
VARIETY:	$15	$20	$30	$50	$75	$125
NORMAL:	$4	$10	$12	$20	$30	$75

Comments: There is another similar DDR for this date.

1953-S
FS-50-1953S-501

Variety: Repunched Mintmark
CONECA—Unknown
PUP: Mintmark
URS-5 · I-3 · L-3

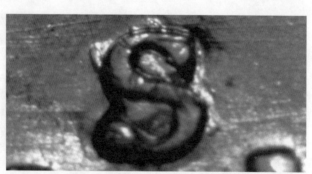

Description: The secondary S is evident northwest of the primary S. Strike doubling can be detected at the top of the primary S on the specimen examined.

	EF-40	AU-50	MS-60	MS-63	MS-65	MS-66
VARIETY:	$15	$20	$30	$50	$75	$125
NORMAL:	$5	$9	$11	$18	$25	$60

Comments: CONECA has one 1953-S RPM listed as S/S west; however, this RPM appears in more of a northwest direction, and doesn't match the CONECA description.

1954, PROOF
FS-50-1954-101

Variety: Doubled Die Obverse
PUP: UST of TRUST
URS-4 · I-3 · L-3

CONECA—N/L

Description: Doubling is evident on the 54 of the date and UST of TRUST.

	PF-63	PF-65	PF-66
VARIETY:	$75	$125	$175
NORMAL:	$40	$80	$94

Comments: This variety is somewhat minor, but rarely found.

1955
FS-50-1955-401

Variety: Clashed Obverse Die
PUP: Mouth of Franklin
URS-13 · I-3 · L-3

CONECA—N/L

Description: This variety is affectionately known as the "Bugs Bunny." There is evidence of clash marks that appear as two buck teeth on Franklin (similar to the buck teeth commonly seen on cartoon characters).

	AU-50	AU-55	MS-60	MS-63	MS-65	MS-66
VARIETY:	$20	$25	$35	$50	$75	$175
NORMAL:	$9	$13	$19	$25	$46	$148

Comments: Although very common, this variety is still in demand! Other "Bugs Bunny" varieties include 1951-P, 1952-P, 1953-P, 1954-P, 1954-D, and 1956.

1956, PROOF   FS-50-1956-101

Variety: Doubled Die Obverse   CONECA 3-O-II+VI
PUP: Date, TRUST
URS-5 · I-3 · L-3

Description: Doubling is evident on the date and WE TRUST, with extra thickness on the letters of IN GOD WE TRUST.

	PF-65	PF-66
VARIETY:	$75	$100
NORMAL:	$40	$65

Comments: The Proof varieties in this series will likely prove to be moderately rare.

1956, PROOF   FS-50-1956-801

Variety: Doubled Die Reverse   CONECA 1-R-II+VI
PUP: E PLURIBUS UNUM
URS-5 · I-3 · L-3

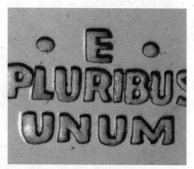

Description: The doubling appears as extreme extra thickness on all perimeter letters, with moderate separation on E PLURIBUS UNUM and the bell clapper.

	PF-65	PF-66
VARIETY:	$75	$100
NORMAL:	$40	$65

Comments: The Proof varieties in this series will likely prove to be moderately rare.

1957, PROOF   FS-50-1957-801

Variety: Tripled Die Reverse
PUP: E PLURIBUS UNUM, HALF DOLLAR
URS-5 · I-3 · L-3

CONECA 4-R-II+VI

Description: A close tripled image can be seen on E PLURIBUS UNUM, portions of UNITED STATES OF AMERICA, and on HALF DOLLAR.

	PF-65	PF-66
VARIETY:	$75	$125
NORMAL:	$23	$29

Comments: This is one of the more collectible reverse varieties of the decade.

1957-D   FS-50-1957D-501

Variety: Repunched Mintmark
PUP: Mintmark
URS-6 · I-3 · L-3

CONECA RPM 1

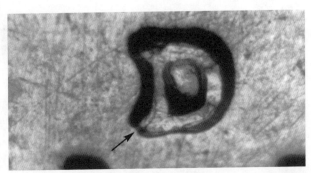

Description: This RPM is rotated slightly, with the secondary D evident at lower left of the primary D.

	AU-55	MS-60	MS-63	MS-65	MS-66
VARIETY:	$15	$35	$50	$75	$100
NORMAL:	$4	$5	$12	$39	$72

Comments: As of this writing, this is the only known RPM for the date.

1959

FS-50-1959-801

Variety: Doubled Die Reverse
PUP: E PLURIBUS UNUM, eagle
URS-5 · I-3 · L-3

CONECA 1-R-IV+VIII

Description: There is evidence of doubling on E PLURIBUS UNUM, UNITED, and portions of the bell. Doubling also appears strong on the eagle.

	AU-55	MS-60	MS-63	MS-65	MS-66
VARIETY:	$25	$50	$75	$100	$500
NORMAL:	$4	$5	$11	$65	$400

Comments: This may become a very popular variety!

1960, PROOF

FS-50-1960-101 (012)

Variety: Doubled Die Obverse
PUP: Date, TRUST
URS-8 · I-3 · L-3

CONECA 3-O-V

Description: Doubling is evident on LIBERTY, TRUST, and the date.

	PF-65	PF-66
VARIETY:	$75	$125
NORMAL:	$16	$22

Comments: This can be found with some searching!

1961, PROOF — FS-50-1961-801 (013)

Variety: Doubled Die Reverse
CONECA 3-R-V
PUP: E PLURIBUS UNUM
URS-7 · I-5 · L-5

Description: Very strong doubling is visible on UNITED STATES OF AMERICA and HALF DOLLAR.

	PF-65	PF-66
VARIETY:	$2,500	$3,500
NORMAL:	$15	$20

Comments: This is by far the strongest doubled die in the series, and is easily sold!

1961, PROOF — FS-50-1961-802

Variety: Doubled Die Reverse
CONECA—N/L
PUP: E PLURIBUS UNUM
URS-3 · I-3 · L-3

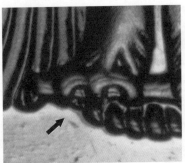

Description: The doubling is evident on all perimeter lettering (with a clockwise spread), and shows very nicely on the eagle's tail and E PLURIBUS UNUM.

	PF-65	PF-66
VARIETY:	$50	$75
NORMAL:	$15	$20

Comments: While looking for the previous double die reverse, you may find one of these!

1961, PROOF   FS-50-1961-803

Variety: Doubled Die Reverse   CONECA 4-R-II
PUP: E PLURIBUS UNUM
URS-6 · I-3 · L-3

Description: Doubling is very evident on E PLURIBUS UNUM, and also visible on perimeter lettering and eagle.

	PF-65	PF-66
VARIETY:	$30	$50
NORMAL:	$15	$20

Comments: While looking for the biggie, you may find one of these!

1962, PROOF   FS-50-1962-101

Variety: Doubled Die Obverse   CONECA 2-O-II
PUP: Date, TRUST
URS-5 · I-3 · L-3

Description: The doubling is evident on the 62 of the date and on WE TRUST.

	PF-65	PF-66
VARIETY:	$30	$50
NORMAL:	$14	$19

Comments: This variety is worthwhile to look for!

Kennedy Half Dollars, 1964 to Date

This series boasts the portrait of one of our most popular presidents. The popularity of the design is likely the result of two important factors—a president assassinated during the lifetime of many budding collectors, and the subsequent removal of silver from most circulating U.S. coinage immediately after the release of the design. Fortunately for collectors, the Kennedy design contains many interesting die varieties.

Coins dated 1964-D display evidence of several different obverse die doublings or triplings; some of these are relatively easy to locate. Proof obverse doubled dies are also dramatic for 1968 and 1969. Certain specimens of a 1968-S Proof half dollar are known with an inverted S mintmark; repunched mintmarks are also known for several dates, most significantly 1964-D.

An excellent reference on these varieties is from James Wiles who has authored a wonderful, highly detailed book on the entire series, *The Kennedy Half Dollar Book*, which has hundreds of superb photos illustrating almost every known variety within the series. Additionally, a list of the doubled dies and repunched mintmarks can be found on the CONECA website (www.conecaonline.org).

Clubs and Educational Information

As of this publication date there are no clubs devoted strictly to the study of Kennedy half dollars. However, for those interested primarily in the varieties within the series, we suggest membership in CONECA, the national error and variety club. Each issue of their bi-monthly publication, the *Errorscope*, contains articles on errors and varieties of all type, and even from other countries. An application is available online at www.conecaonline.org/join, or by contacting Paul Funaiole at

CONECA
Paul Funaiole, Membership
35 Leavitt Lane
Glenburn ME 04401-1013

1964, PROOF
FS-50-1964-101 (013.2)

Variety: Doubled Die Obverse
CONECA 2-O-V
PUP: WE TRUST
URS-7 · I-3 · L-2

Description: Doubling is evident on WE TRUST, RTY (of LIBERTY), and the upper hair, with lesser doubling on IN GOD and the date.

	PF-63	PF-65	PF-66	PF-67
VARIETY:	$10	$25	$50	$75
NORMAL:	$5	$9	$12	$17

Comments: This is a Normal Hair variety. See FS-50-1964-401.

1964
FS-50-1964-102

Variety: Doubled Die Obverse
CONECA 7-O-II
PUP: WE TRUST
URS-6 · I-3 · L-3

Description: Doubling is very strong on WE TRUST, LIBERTY, and the date.

	MS-63	MS-65	MS-66	MS-67
VARIETY:	$25	$35	$100	$150
NORMAL:	$5	$9	$12	$17

Comments: Extremely high grades (MS-66+) are almost impossible to find.

1964, PROOF — FS-50-1964-103

CONECA—Unknown

Variety: Doubled Die Obverse
PUP: IN GOD, LIBERTY
URS-3 · I-3 · L-3

Description: Doubling is moderate on IN GOD WE TRUST, LIBERTY, the date, and the upper hair.

	PF-63	PF-65	PF-66	PF-67
VARIETY:	$20	$25	$35	$50
NORMAL:	$5	$9	$12	$17

Comments: This is an Accented Hair variety. See FS-50-1964-401.

1964, PROOF — FS-50-1964-401

CONECA ODV-001

Variety: Accented Hair Variety
PUP: Hair, I of LIBERTY
URS-19 · I-4 · L-3

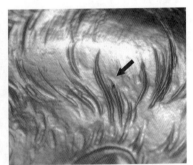

Description: The Accented Hair variety is identifiable by the enhanced hairline in the central area of the hair, just below the part. However, the easiest way to identify the variety is the weak or broken lower left serif of the I (in LIBERTY).

	PF-65	PF-66	PF-67
VARIETY:	$20	$35	$50
NORMAL:	$9	$12	$17

Comments: Although somewhat common in variety terms, this variety is desirable!

1964
FS-50-1964-801

Variety: Doubled Die Reverse
CONECA 1-R-II
PUP: UNITED STATES OF AMERICA
URS-4 · I-3 · L-3

Description: Doubling is evident on UNITED STATES OF AMERICA, the rays and stars above E PLURIBIS UNUM, and (slightly) the banner and E PLURIBUS UNUM.

	MS-63	MS-65	MS-66	MS-67
VARIETY:	$25	$35	$100	$150
NORMAL:	$5	$9	$12	$17

Comments: This is the best of several doubled reverse dies for 1964-P.

1964-D
FS-50-1964D-101 (013.4)

Variety: Doubled Die Obverse
CONECA 1-O-V
PUP: IN GOD WE TRUST
URS-9 · I-3 · L-3

Description: Doubling is evident on the date, IN GOD WE TRUST, LI and TY (of LIBERTY), and the designer's initials.

	MS-63	MS-65	MS-66	MS-67
VARIETY:	$35	$75	$150	$400
NORMAL:	$4	$22	$38	

Comments: This is a very popular variety. It is extremely rare above MS-65. Note: FS-50-1964D-102 is reserved for future use.

1964-D

FS-50-1964D-103 (013.5)

Variety: Tripled Die Obverse
CONECA 3-O-V
PUP: IN GOD WE TRUST
URS-7 · I-4 · L-3

Description: The tripled image is evident on WE TRUST, with strong doubling visible on IN GOD, the L and TY (of LIBERTY), and the date.

	MS-63	MS-65	MS-66	MS-67
VARIETY:	$35	$75	$150	$400
NORMAL:	$4	$22	$38	

Comments: This is well known in grades below MS-65.

1964-D

FS-50-1964D-104

Variety: Doubled Die Obverse
CONECA 4-O-II
PUP: IN GOD
URS-6 · I-2 · L-2

Description: Doubling is evident on IN GOD WE TRUST, but strongest on IN GOD. Doubling is also evident on letters of LIBERTY and portions of the date.

	MS-63	MS-65	MS-66	MS-67
VARIETY:	$25	$50	$100	$350
NORMAL:	$4	$22	$38	

Comments: All 1964-D halves are very scarce in MS-65 and above.

1964-D FS-50-1964D-105 (013.6)

Variety: Quadrupled Die Obverse CONECA 5-O-II
PUP: IN GOD WE TRUST
URS-8 · I-4 · L-3

Description: A quadrupled image is evident on IN GOD WE TRUST, the hair, and TY (of LIBERTY).

	MS-63	MS-65	MS-66	MS-67
VARIETY:	$35	$75	$150	$400
NORMAL:	$4	$22	$38	

Comments: This is somewhat similar to FS-50-1964D-103. However, the multiple images on the upper right of U in TRUST are slanted down *to the right*, whereas the multiple images on the same area on FS-103 slant straight down.

1964-D FS-50-1964D-106

Variety: Doubled Die Obverse CONECA 4-O-II
PUP: WE TRUST
URS-4 · I-2 · L-2

Description: Doubling is evident on WE TRUST and TY (in LIBERTY).

	MS-63	MS-65	MS-66	MS-67
VARIETY:	$25	$50	$100	$350
NORMAL:	$4	$22	$38	

Comments: All 1964-D halves are very scarce in MS-65 and above. Note: FS-50-1964D-107 is reserved for future use.

1964-D
FS-50-1964D-108

Variety: Doubled Die Obverse
CONECA 8-O-II
PUP: IN GOD WE TRUST
URS-4 · I-2 · L-2

 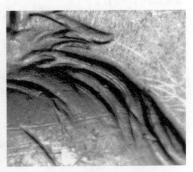

Description: Doubling is evident on IN GOD WE TRUST, the date, and portions of the hair.

	MS-63	MS-65	MS-66	MS-67
VARIETY:	$25	$50	$100	$350
NORMAL:	$4	$22	$38	

Comments: All 1964-D halves are very scarce in MS-65 and above.

1964-D
FS-50-1964D-501

Variety: Repunched Mintmark
CONECA RPM 1
PUP: Mintmark
URS-6 · I-4 · L-4

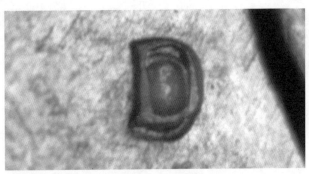

Description: A secondary D mintmark is evident south of the primary D.

	MS-63	MS-65	MS-66	MS-67
VARIETY:	$25	$50	$100	$350
NORMAL:	$4	$22	$38	

Comments: RPMs in the Kennedy series are highly collectible.

1964-D
FS-50-1964D-502

Variety: Repunched Mintmark
CONECA RPM 2
PUP: Mintmark
URS-6 · I-4 · L-4

Description: A secondary D mintmark is evident north of the primary D.

	MS-63	MS-65	MS-66	MS-67
VARIETY:	$25	$50	$100	$350
NORMAL:	$4	$22	$38	

Comments: This should be slightly more difficult to locate than the preceding.

1964-D
FS-50-1964D-503

Variety: Repunched Mintmark
CONECA RPM 3
PUP: Mintmark
URS-7 · I-4 · L-4

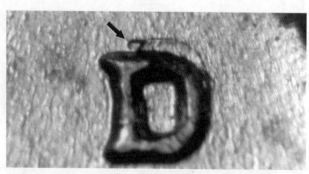

Description: A secondary D mintmark is evident northeast of the primary D.

	MS-63	MS-65	MS-66	MS-67
VARIETY:	$25	$50	$100	$350
NORMAL:	$4	$22	$38	

Comments: This may be the easiest of the three 1964-D RPMs listed to locate.

1965
FS-50-1965-801

Variety: Doubled Die Reverse
PUP: STATES, DOLLAR
URS-3 · I-3 · L-3

CONECA 1-R-II

Description: Doubling is evident on all outer lettering, all stars, and slightly on E PLURIBUS UNUM.

	MS-63	MS-65	MS-66	MS-67
VARIETY:	$15	$25	$300	$450
NORMAL:	$5	$15	$225	

Comments: Values for MS-66 and MS-67 indicate the true rarity of these high grades for a circulation-strike specimen.

1966
FS-50-1966-101

Variety: Doubled Die Obverse
PUP: IN GOD WE TRUST
URS-6 · I-4 · L-4

CONECA 5-O-III

Description: Very strong doubling is evident on IN GOD WE TRUST, the date, the designer's initials, and the entire profile.

	MS-63	MS-65	MS-66	MS-67
VARIETY:	$15	$25	$250	$400
NORMAL:	$5	$15	$190	

Comments: This is extremely rare above MS-65.

1966, SPECIAL MINT SET   FS-50-1966-102

Variety: Doubled Die Obverse
PUP: IN GOD WE TRUST
URS-4 · I-3 · L-3

CONECA 10-O-III

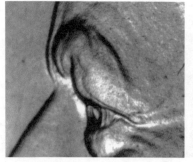 

Description: Very strong doubling is evident on IN GOD WE TRUST, the date, the designer's initials, and the entire profile.

	SMS-63	SMS-65	SMS-66	SMS-67
VARIETY:	$15	$35	$50	$75
NORMAL:	$5	$10	$25	$30

Comments: This variety is extremely rare above MS-65.

1966, SPECIAL MINT SET   FS-50-1966-103

Variety: Doubled Die Obverse
PUP: Profile (eye), WE TRUST
URS-8 · I-3 · L-3

CONECA 13-O-III

 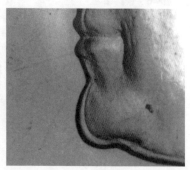

Description: Strong doubling is evident on the profile, IN GOD WE TRUST, the eye, the hair, and the designer's initials.

	SMS-63	SMS-65	SMS-66	SMS-67
VARIETY:	$35	$100	$150	$250
NORMAL:	$5	$10	$25	$30

Comments: This variety is very similar to the next.

1966, SPECIAL MINT SET — FS-50-1966-104

Variety: Doubled Die Obverse
CONECA 19-O-III
PUP: WE TRUST, date
URS-3 · I-4 · L-4

 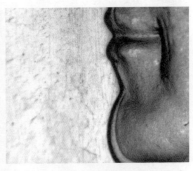

Description: Very strong doubling is evident on IN GOD WE TRUST, the profile, the eye, the hair, and the designer's initials. Additional doubling is evident on the TY of LIBERTY.

	SMS-63	SMS-65	SMS-66	SMS-67
VARIETY:	$35	$100	$150	$250
NORMAL:	$5	$10	$25	$30

Comments: This variety is very similar with the previous.

1966, SPECIAL MINT SET — FS-50-1966-901

Variety: Missing Designer's Initials
CONECA ADR-1-C
PUP: Reverse (between eagle's tail and leg)
URS-7 · I-4 · L-4

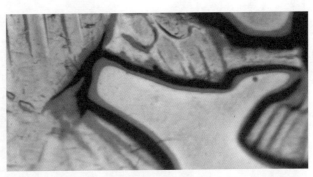

Description: The designer's initials on the reverse are totally missing.

	SMS-63	SMS-65	SMS-66	SMS-67
VARIETY:	$35	$100	$150	$250
NORMAL:	$5	$10	$25	$30

Comments: This variety is very rare and certain to become more popular!

1967, SPECIAL MINT SET — FS-50-1967-101

Variety: Quintupled Obverse Die
CONECA 6-O-II
PUP: RTY of LIBERTY
URS-5 · I-4 · L-4

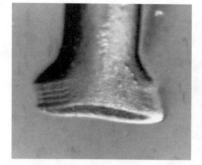 

Description: A prominent quintupled (at least) spread is evident on RTY of LIBERTY, with strong multiple images on all obverse lettering and portions of the hair.

	SMS-63	SMS-65	SMS-66	SMS-67
VARIETY:	$75	$125	$200	$300
NORMAL:	$7	$13	$22	$30

Comments: This is a very elusive variety!

1967 — FS-50-1967-102

Variety: Doubled Die Obverse
CONECA 7-O-II
PUP: WE TRUST
URS-2 · I-3 · L-2

Description: Doubling is visible on WE TRUST, on the date, and on portions of the hair under the R of LIBERTY.

	MS-63	MS-65	MS-66	MS-67
VARIETY:	$15	$25	$150	$250
NORMAL:	$3	$13	$121	

Comments: This is a circulation-strike coin.

1967 {FS-50-1967-801}

Variety: Doubled Die Reverse
PUP: UNITED STATES OF AMERICA, HALF DOLLAR
URS-5 · I-3 · L-2

CONECA 1-R-II

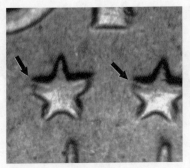 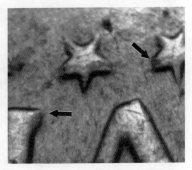

Description: The doubling is evident on all outer reverse lettering, all stars around the rim, and a few rays on the reverse.

	MS-63	MS-65	MS-66	MS-67
VARIETY:	$15	$25	$150	$250
NORMAL:	$3	$13	$121	

Comments: This is one of the stronger DDRs for this date. It is a circulation strike.

1968-D {FS-50-1968D-801}

Variety: Tripled Die Obverse
PUP: WE TRUST
URS-3 · I-3 · L-2

CONECA 2-O-II

Description: A tripled image is visible on IN GOD WE TRUST, the date, and the Y of LIBERTY.

	MS-63	MS-65	MS-66	MS-67
VARIETY:	$25	$50	$75	$150
NORMAL:	$4	$12	$32	

Comments: An early die state will command a premium over values shown.

1968-S, PROOF

FS-50-1968S-101

Variety: Doubled Die Obverse
CONECA 2-O-I
PUP: IN GOD WE TRUST
URS-7 · I-4 · L-3

Description: Very strong doubling is evident on all obverse lettering, on the date, and on the designer's initials.

	PF-65	PF-66	PF-67
VARIETY:	$150	$175	$225
NORMAL:	$8	$10	$12

Comments: This is a very popular variety!

1968-S, PROOF

FS-50-1968S-511

Variety: Inverted S Mintmark
CONECA—N/L
PUP: Mintmark
URS-6 · I-4 · L-3

Description: The S mintmark was punched into the die in an inverted orientation.

	PF-65	PF-66	PF-67
VARIETY:	$150	$175	$225
NORMAL:	$8	$10	$12

Comments: This is certain to become a highly sought after variety.

1968-S, PROOF — FS-50-1968S-801

CONECA 1-R-I

Variety: Doubled Die Reverse
PUP: UNITED STATES OF AMERICA
URS-4 · I-3 · L-3

Description: There is strong doubling evident on all lettering around the rim, and some tripled images on OF AMERICA.

	PF-65	PF-66	PF-67
VARIETY:	$50	$75	$100
NORMAL:	$8	$10	$12

Comments: This variety is somewhat underrated.

1970-S, PROOF — FS-50-1970S-101

CONECA 5-O-I

Variety: Doubled Die Obverse
PUP: WE TRUST
URS-5 · I-3 · L-3

Description: Strong doubling is evident on all obverse lettering, especially on WE TRUST.

	PF-65	PF-66	PF-67
VARIETY:	$75	$100	$150
NORMAL:	$11	$12	$14

Comments: Although known for some time, this variety is still very elusive.

1971-D

FS-50-1971D-101

Variety: Doubled Die Obverse

CONECA 4-O-V

PUP: GOD WE TRUST

URS-6 · I-3 · L-2

Description: Very strong doubling is evident on LIBERTY, the 71 of the date, and GOD WE TRUST.

	MS-63	MS-65	MS-66	MS-67
VARIETY:	$20	$35	$50	$100
NORMAL:	$2	$11	$22	$52

Comments: This variety can be found in Mint sets.

1971-D

FS-50-1971D-102

Variety: Doubled Die Obverse

CONECA 6-O-I

PUP: IN GOD WE TRUST

URS-7 · I-3 · L-2

Description: Doubling is very evident on IN GOD WE TRUST, the date, and LIBERTY. The lower portions of IN show at least a tripled die.

	MS-63	MS-65	MS-66	MS-67
VARIETY:	$20	$35	$50	$100
NORMAL:	$2	$11	$22	$52

Comments: As with the variety above, this can be found in Mint sets.

1971-S, PROOF

FS-50-1971S-101

Variety: Doubled Die Obverse
PUP: TRUST
URS-4 · I-3 · L-2

CONECA 4-O-V

Description: Doubling is most evident on WE TRUST and the last 1 in the date, with lesser doubling on IN GOD and ERTY (of LIBERTY).

	PF-65	PF-66	PF-67
VARIETY:	$75	$100	$150
NORMAL:	$11	$12	$14

Comments: This variety can still be found in Proof sets.

1971-S, PROOF

FS-50-1971S-102

Variety: Doubled Die Obverse
PUP: WE TRUST
URS-6 · I-3 · L-2

CONECA 6-O-I

YN

Description: Doubling is visible on WE TRUST, on the date, and on portions of the hair under the R of LIBERTY.

	PF-65	PF-66	PF-67
VARIETY:	$150	$200	$300
NORMAL:	$11	$12	$14

Comments: Premiums are considerable for this variety.

1971-S, PROOF — FS-50-1971S-801

Variety: Doubled Die Reverse
PUP: HALF DOLLAR
URS-4 · I-3 · L-2

CONECA 1-R-II

Description: Doubling is visible on HALF DOLLAR, OF AMERICA, the stars near those letters, the feathers, and the lower arrow shafts.

	PF-65	PF-66	PF-67
VARIETY:	$25	$75	$100
NORMAL:	$11	$12	$14

Comments: This may prove to be a very rare variety.

1972 — FS-50-1972-101

Variety: Doubled Die Obverse
PUP: IN GOD WE TRUST
URS-4 · I-3 · L-2

CONECA 1-O-II+V

Description: The doubling is very evident on IN GOD WE TRUST and the date.

	MS-63	MS-65	MS-66	MS-67
VARIETY:	$50	$75	$150	$250
NORMAL:	$2	$8	$45	

Comments: This variety is very rare above MS-65.

1972-D

Variety: Missing Designer's Initials
PUP: RTY of LIBERTY
URS-2 · I-4 · L-4

CONECA—N/L

PC

YN

Description: The designer's initials (FG) are totally missing from this die.

	MS-63	MS-65	MS-66	MS-67
VARIETY:	$50	$75	$150	$250
NORMAL:	$2	$7	$9	$10

Comments: This variety is not as well known as others.

1973-D

Variety: Doubled Die Obverse
PUP: WE TRUST
URS-6 · I-3 · L-2

CONECA 1-O-I

PC

Description: Doubling is evident on IN GOD WE TRUST, LIBERTY, and the date.

	MS-63	MS-65	MS-66	MS-67
VARIETY:	$25	$50	$75	$150
NORMAL:	$2	$10	$21	

Comments: This variety can be found with some searching.

1974-D

FS-50-1974D-101 (015)

Variety: Doubled Die Obverse

CONECA 1-O-I

PUP: WE TRUST

URS-10 · I-3 · L-2

Description: Strong doubling is evident on IN GOD WE TRUST, LIBERTY, and the date.

	MS-63	MS-65	MS-66	MS-67
VARIETY:	$50	$100	$200	$400
NORMAL:	$2	$13		

Comments: This variety can still be found in Mint sets. However, most have been searched.

1976-S, 40% UNC

FS-50-1976S-101 (016)

Variety: Doubled Die Obverse

CONECA 1-O-V

PUP: WE TRUST

URS-4 · I-3 · L-2

Description: Doubling is evident on WE TRUST.

	MS-63	MS-65	MS-66	MS-67
VARIETY:	$25	$50	$75	$100
NORMAL:	$3	$15	$15	$33

Comments: This is a 40% silver Uncirculated Mint set coin.

1979-S, PROOF 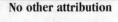 FS-50-1979S-501

Variety: Type II Mintmark **No other attribution**
PUP: Mintmark
URS-10 · I-5 · L-5

Type II Mintmark (Scarce)   *Type I Mintmark (common)*

Description: The mintmark style of 1979-S Proof coins was changed during production, creating two different types. Type II (with a well defined S) is rare, and is easily distinguished from the common Type I (with an indistinct blob).

	PF-63	PF-65	PF-66	PF-67
VARIETY:	$11	$13	$14	$15
NORMAL:		$10	$12	$22

Comments: Complete government-sealed Proof sets with all six coins of Type II command a substantial premium over the six individual coins. Of the six, the half dollar is likely the third most in demand.

1981-S, PROOF FS-50-1981S-501

Variety: Type II Mintmark **No other attribution**
PUP: Mintmark
URS-10 · I-5 · L-5

Type II Mintmark (Scarce)   *Type I Mintmark (common)*

Description: The mintmark style of 1981-S Proof coins was changed during production, creating two different types. Type II is rare, and is not easily distinguished from the common Type I. Type II is flat on the top curve of the S compared to Type I, which has a more rounded top. The surface of the Type II mintmark is frosted, and the openings in the loops are slightly larger.

	PF-63	PF-65	PF-66
VARIETY:	$4	$30	$50
NORMAL:	$4	$10	$11

Comments: Complete government-sealed Proof sets with all six coins of Type II command a substantial premium over the six individual coins.

1988-S, PROOF

FS-50-1988S-101

Variety: Doubled Die Obverse

CONECA 1-O-V

PUP: WE TRUST

URS-3 · I-3 · L-3

Description: Nice doubling is evident on IN GOD WE TRUST, the date, and the mintmark. Some doubling is also visible on LIBERTY.

	PF-65	PF-66	PF-67
VARIETY:	$100	$125	$150
NORMAL:	$7	$11	$12

Comments: This is one of the newer doubled dies, with the mintmark also doubled as a result of the doubled die.

1992-S, PROOF

FS-50-1992S-101

Variety: Doubled Die Obverse

CONECA 1-O-V

PUP: WE TRUST

URS-3 · I-3 · L-3

Description: Slight doubling is visible on WE TRUST and the mintmark.

	PF-65	PF-66	PF-67
VARIETY:	$100	$125	$150
NORMAL:	$13	$14	$16

Comments: This is one of the newer doubled dies, with the mintmark also doubled as a result of the die. This is a silver Proof coin.

Liberty Seated Dollars, 1840–1873

Liberty Seated dollars, like all Liberty Seated coinage, are widely collected. Despite the fact that most serious collectors are also astute variety collectors, there is not a definitive reference for varieties within the Liberty Seated dollar series. Nevertheless, long-time members of the Liberty Seated Collectors Club (LSCC) do have access to a tremendous amount of information. LSCC members often publish excellent articles about various Seated dollar varieties in the pages of the club's wonderful newsletter, the *Gobrecht Journal*.

Every few years, the *Gobrecht Journal—Collective Volume* is published by the club and contains all the articles printed in the newsletters since the last compilation. These collective volumes provide excellent reference material on Seated dollars, as well as on the other denominations in the Liberty Seated series. Each new book is offered to members before it is made available to the public. Unfortunately, the older volumes are now out of print and are obtainable only through dealers who specialize in used and out-of-print numismatic publications.

Clubs and Educational Information

We strongly recommend membership in the LLSC, which we believe to be one of the very best specialty clubs in numismatics. As of this writing, the annual dues are $15—a bargain, considering the amount of information available. If you join, you will be connecting with the most serious and knowledgeable collectors and dealers in the hobby. For more information, visit their outstanding web site at www.numismalink.com/lscc.html, or contact

Liberty Seated Collectors Club
Mark Sheldon, Secretary/Treasurer
P.O. Box 261
Wellington OH 44090

1865

FS-S1-1865-801

Variety: Doubled Die Reverse
PUP: U of UNITED
URS-8 · I-3 · L-3

No other attribution

Description: Doubling is evident only on the U of UNITED.

	F-12	VF-20	EF-40	AU-50
VARIETY:	$283	$383	$500	$1,075
NORMAL:	$283	$383	$500	$1,075

Comments: This is probably the most common variety for this date.

1868

FS-S1-1868-301

Variety: Misplaced Date
PUP: Denticles below date
URS-6 · I-3 · L-3

No other attribution

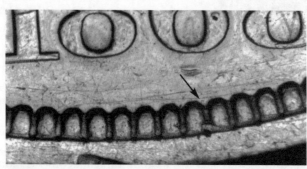

Description: The top portion of an 8 is evident within the denticles below the date.

	F-12	VF-20	EF-40	AU-50
VARIETY:	$300	$450	$550	$900
NORMAL:	$210	$345	$400	$725

Comments: This variety can still be located with some searching.

1869
FS-S1-1869-301

Variety: Repunched Date
PUP: 1 of date
URS-5 · I-3 · L-3

No other attribution

 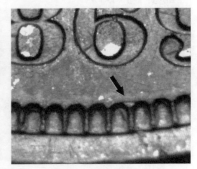

Description: The base of a secondary 1 is visible slightly south of the primary 1. The top of a date digit (likely a 6) is evident protruding from the dentils below the primary 6.

	F-12	VF-20	EF-40	AU-50
VARIETY:	$225	$300	$425	$700
NORMAL:	$160	$240	$329	$590

Comments: Other repunched dates for 1869 are also known.

1869
FS-S1-1869-302

Variety: Repunched Date
PUP: Between 1 and 8 of date
URS-5 · I-3 · L-3

No other attribution

Description: The top flag of a secondary 1 is evident midway between the primary 1 and the 8.

	F-12	VF-20	EF-40	AU-50
VARIETY:	$250	$400	$600	$800
NORMAL:	$160	$240	$329	$590

Comments: Other repunched dates for 1869 are also known.

1871

FS-S1-1871-301

Variety: Misplaced Date
PUP: Denticles below 8
URS-5 · I-3 · L-3

No other attribution

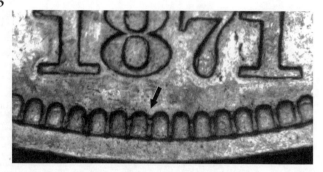

Description: The top of a digit (probably an 8) is evident protruding from the denticles below the 8 of the date.

	F-12	VF-20	EF-40	AU-50
VARIETY:	$200	$350	$450	$750
NORMAL:	$160	$240	$329	$590

Comments: Other misplaced dates between 1865 and 1873 may exist.

THE CHERRYPICKERS' GUIDE **HELPFUL HINTS**

Study and learn the Pick-Up-Points (PUPs) for each series so that you can focus your initial attention on these areas to find varieties. Don't forget the denticle area and the design above the date (especially on 19th-century coinage such as the Liberty Seated series) for misplaced numbers, etc. They hide, so use a good loupe and good light.

See appendix H for more Helpful Hints.

Trade Dollars, 1873–1885

Trade dollars are not widely collected by variety enthusiasts—at least not yet. The coins are relatively expensive for most dates; therefore, few enthusiasts can afford to collect all the varieties. Assembling a complete set can be a daunting task, even with unlimited funds. Nevertheless, significant varieties are known and can be found with some searching. Both minor and major doubled dies, and even over mintmarks, are available. There are also two different design types known for both the obverse and the reverse, as well as various pairings of these two types.

The varieties listed in this edition of the *Cherrypickers' Guide* illustrate most of the known varieties. Breen lists a few varieties, but the best overall reference for the series is *Silver Dollars and Trade Dollars of the United States: A Complete Encyclopedia*, by Q. David Bowers.

Trade dollars are a particular area of study for members of the Liberty Seated Collectors Club (LSCC), which issues its official publication, the *Gobrecht Journal*, three times each year. This 52-page newsletter is loaded with excellent educational articles and some of the best photography in the field. We strongly recommend membership in the LLSC, which we believe to be one of the very best specialty clubs in numismatics. As of this writing, the annual dues are $15—a bargain, considering the amount of information available. If you join, you will be connecting with the most serious and knowledgeable collectors and dealers in the hobby. For more information, visit their outstanding web site at www.numismalink.com/lscc.html, or contact

Liberty Seated Collectors Club
Mark Sheldon, Secretary/Treasurer
P.O. Box 261
Wellington OH 44090

Two Different Distinct Obverse and Reverse Hubs

There are two different hubs known for both the obverse and reverse of trade dollars. The differences, although somewhat subtle, are relatively easy to distinguish.

Variety	Identifying Characteristics
Type I Obv	LIBERTY ribbon tips point to the left. Hand holding olive branch has three fingers.
Type II Obv	LIBERTY ribbon tips point down. Hand holding olive branch has four fingers.
Type I Rev	Berry visible underneath eagle's sinister claw.
Type II Rev	No berry underneath eagle's sinister claw.

Varying Type I and Type II obverse and reverse marriages are known, with some combinations considerably rarer than others. Type I obverses were used on trade dollars from 1873 to 1876; Type II obverses were used on coins dated 1876 to 1885. Type I reverses were used on coins from 1873 to 1876; Type II reverses were used on coins dated 1875 to 1885. Several assessments of these are Type I and Type II combinations have been done and can be found in editions of the *Gobrecht Journal.*

1873-CC   FS-T1-1873CC-301

Variety: Misplaced Date
PUP: Denticles below date
URS-6 · I-3 · L-3

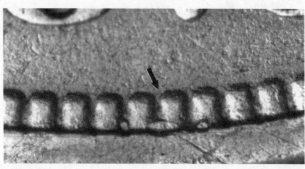

Description: The top portion of a 7 is evident protruding from the denticles below the date, centered between the 8 and 7.

	F-12	VF-20	EF-40	AU-50	MS-60
VARIETY:	$250	$450	$700	$1,100	$2,500
NORMAL:	$180	$326	$575	$900	$2,250

Comments: This variety is very prominent.

1875-S   FS-T1-1875S-501 (012.5)

Variety: Over Mintmark
PUP: Mintmark
URS-8 · I-3 · L-3

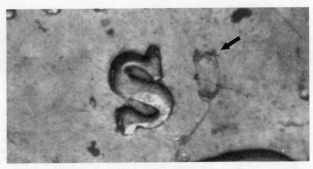

Description: The S mintmark is evident over a previously punched CC mintmark. The weak C from the underlying mintmark is evident right of the S.

	F-12	VF-20	EF-40	AU-50	MS-60
VARIETY:	$400	$600	$800	$1,000	$1,500
NORMAL:	$85	$105	$133	$200	$383

Comments: This is one of the more popular varieties in the series.

THE CHERRYPICKERS' GUIDE HELPFUL HINTS

If you can't discern a variety with a 7x loupe, it probably isn't significant.

See appendix H for more Helpful Hints.

1875-S

FS-T1-1875S-502

Variety: Over Mintmark
PUP: Mintmark
URS-5 · I-5 · L-4

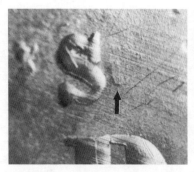 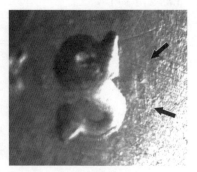

Description: The S mintmark is evident over a previously punched CC mintmark. The C is very weak, but visible, right of the S.

	F-12	VF-20	EF-40	AU-50	MS-60
VARIETY:	$400	$600	$800	$1,000	$1,500
NORMAL:	$85	$105	$133	$200	$383

Comments: This coin was in a Heritage Auction on April 25, 2002 (lot #4111). The variety is slight, but significantly different from the previous listing.

1876-CC

FS-T1-1876CC-801 (014)

Variety: Doubled Die Reverse
PUP: Right branch, E PLURIBUS UNUM
URS-7 · I-4 · L-4

Description: Doubling is evident on the branches on the right, the eagle's talons, the right wing tip, eagle's beak, and is very strong on E PLURIBUS UNUM. Weaker doubling can be detected on UNITED STATES OF AMERICA.

	F-12	VF-20	EF-40	AU-50	MS-60
VARIETY:	$200	$300	$500	$750	$3,000
NORMAL:	$115	$165	$250	$479	$2,500

Comments: Considered by most to be the strongest reverse doubled die in the series, this variety is one of the highlights of the trade dollar varieties and is thought to be extremely rare in grades above AU.

1876-S   FS-T1-1876S-101 (013)

Variety: Doubled Die Obverse
PUP: Liberty's hand and foot
URS-4 · I-4 · L-4

 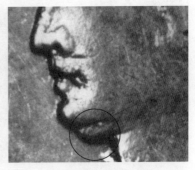

Description: Doubling is evident on Liberty's hand, chin, and left foot, and on the olive branch.

	F-12	VF-20	EF-40	AU-50	MS-60
VARIETY:	$600	$800	$1,200	$1,500	$2,000
NORMAL:	$83	$105	$142	$200	$392

Comments: This DDO is easily the rarest doubled die in the series, and is considered extremely rare in grades above AU. Most known examples are cleaned. The variety is known as the king of the trade dollar varieties.

1876-S   FS-T1-1876S-301

Variety: Repunched Date
PUP: 6 of date
URS-7 · I-2 · L-3

Description: The lower loop of a secondary 6 is evident within the loop of the primary 6.

	F-12	VF-20	EF-40	AU-50	MS-60
VARIETY:	$100	$150	$200	$250	$450
NORMAL:	$87	$105	$133	$200	$379

Comments: Surface doubling is also evident on the lower left of the 8 and the top of the 7.

1877 FS-T1-1877-101

Variety: Doubled Die Obverse
PUP: LIBERTY, wheat stalks
URS-5 · I-3 · L-3

Description: The doubling is visible on the wheat stalks, LIBERTY, IN GOD WE TRUST, and stars 11, 12, and 13.

	F-12	VF-20	EF-40	AU-50	MS-60
VARIETY:	$150	$200	$250	$350	$600
NORMAL:	$85	$105	$133	$225	$421

Comments: This is still considered a rare variety.

1877-S FS-T1-1877S-301

Variety: Repunched Date
PUP: 7 of date
URS-6 · I-3 · L-3

Description: A secondary 7 is evident protruding south from the last 7.

	F-12	VF-20	EF-40	AU-50	MS-60
VARIETY:	$150	$200	$250	$350	$600
NORMAL:	$83	$105	$142	$200	$367

Comments: This variety is probably the most prominent RPD in the series.

1877-S
FS-T1-1877S-801 (014.5)

Variety: Doubled Die Reverse
PUP: E PLURIBUS UNUM and UNITED STATES OF AMERICA
URS-5 · I-4 · L-4

Description: Doubling is evident on the E PLURIBUS UNUM, on UNITED STATES OF AMERICA, and on the ribbon.

	F-12	VF-20	EF-40	AU-50	MS-60
VARIETY:	$200	$300	$500	$750	$1,000
NORMAL:	$83	$105	$142	$200	$367

Comments: Considered a highlight of the trade dollar varieties, this is another very rare variety.

1877-S
FS-T1-1877S-802

Variety: Doubled Die Reverse
PUP: 420, TRADE
URS-8 · I-3 · L-3

Description: Minor doubling is evident on virtually all reverse lettering, especially on 420 GRAINS.

	F-12	VF-20	EF-40	AU-50	MS-60
VARIETY:	$150	$200	$250	$300	$600
NORMAL:	$83	$105	$142	$200	$367

Comments: This is one of the more common trade dollar varieties.

1878-S   FS-T1-1878S-801 (015)

Variety: Doubled Die Reverse
PUP: Arrows, 420
URS-7 · I-4 · L-3

Description: Strong doubling is evident on the entire lower left side, on the arrow points and shafts, on 420 GRAINS, and slightly on the motto.

	F-12	VF-20	EF-40	AU-50	MS-60
VARIETY:	$200	$300	$400	$500	$750
NORMAL:	$83	$110	$133	$200	$400

Comments: This variety is very difficult to find in AU and above.

1878-S   FS-T1-1878S-802

Variety: Doubled Die Reverse
PUP: UNITED, E PLURIBUS UNUM
URS-4 · I-3 · L-2

Description: Doubling with a close spread is evident on UNITED STATES, E PLURIBUS UNUM, and on the ribbon.

	F-12	VF-20	EF-40	AU-50	MS-60
VARIETY:	$150	$200	$300	$400	$600
NORMAL:	$83	$110	$133	$200	$400

Comments: The doubling is somewhat minor, but very interesting.

Sovereign Entities Grading Service

™   6402 EAST BRAINERD ROAD - SUITE "B"
WILLIAMSBURG PROFESSIONAL CENTER
P.O. BOX 8129
CHATTANOOGA, TENNESSEE 37421

™

EXPERIENCE THE MANY BENEFITS, SERVICES AND FEATURES *SEGS* OFFERS

- Superior Materials - Top Viewing Label
- "Heirloom" Patented Capsule - Will Not Contaminate Your Coin
- Fits Industry Standard Box - Counterfeit Proof
- Sealed Label Compartment - Stack-Lock System
- Inert Materials - No Abraded Capsules
- Customer Education - Customer Service
- Standard Service - Not Tier Pricing - No Body Bags
- Fingertip Classification and Retrieval
- SEGS Accepts Submissions From Individuals and/or Dealers
- No Minimum or Maximum Number of Coins Required
- Error and Variety Attribution Specialists
- No Net Grades - Problem Coins Encapsulated
- Pre-Screen - Cross Over - Sovereign Signature Series
  Authentication Service

NEED STANDARD SERVICE WITH STANDARD ATTRIBUTIONS?
ONLY $10.50 PER COIN PLUS S&H AND INSURANCE!

The only True "Heirloom" Capsule available on today's market!

Call Today Toll-Free and Request Your FREE Information, Submittal Package and Sample Holder!
On the Web: segscoins.com • Toll Free: 888-768-7261 • Fax: 1-423-510-8312

THE COLLECTOR'S CHOICE®

ANACS is "The Official Grading Service of CONECA,"
the world's largest organization of variety and error collectors.

ANACS presents the Clear View™ holder.
For a free ANACS submission form visit www.ANACS.com.

P.O. Box 200300, Austin, TX 78720-0300

800.888.1861

INTEGRITY
ACCURACY
RELIABILITY
SERVICE
TRUST

ANACS
America's Oldest Grading Service™

www.anacs.com

Morgan Dollars, 1878–1921

In the world of variety collecting, no other series will touch the popularity of Morgan silver dollars. Both the Morgan and Peace dollar varieties are known as VAMs, an acronym derived from the first letters of the last names of Leroy Van Allen and George Mallis, the two gentlemen who popularized collecting silver dollar die varieties.

VAMs are collected by thousands of enthusiasts. Often, a silver dollar valued at less than $20 could in fact be worth several thousand dollars because of some relatively minor, yet very rare, abnormality. A variation might be a die chip, an image from one side lightly visible on the other, a doubled or tripled die, a repunched mintmark or date, or even a slight die gouge. There are even some dramatic overdates.

We have expanded this section of the *Cherrypickers' Guide* to give collectors more information about this specialized category of variety collecting. We are grateful to Jeff Oxman, "Mr. VAM," for the dozens of new listings and their descriptions. Jeff is one of the true gentlemen of numismatics who are always willing to help promote the educational aspects of coin collecting.

In addition, in the Morgan dollar and Peace dollar sections we have included a condition census for each listing. These notations give the known grades of the top examples of the variety and help to emphasize its rarity. Having this information helps the collector find those examples that are true rarities.

Clubs and Educational Information

For those interested in learning more about the varieties of Morgan dollars, we highly recommend membership in the Society of Silver Dollar Collectors (SSDC). The club has a web site at www.vamlink.com, or you may write to

Jeff Oxman
P.O. Box 2123
North Hills CA 91393-0123
Email: ssdc@vamlink.com

1878, 8 TAIL FEATHERS

FS-S1-1878-005

Variety: Doubled Die Obverse

VAM 5

PUP: RIB of PLURIBUS

URS-5 · I-4 · L-4

Description: Doubling is visible on much of the obverse lettering, but is most evident on E PLURIBUS UNUM.

	VF-20	EF-40	AU-50	MS-60	MS-63	MS-65
VARIETY:	$50	$100	$200	$300	$900	$7,500
NORMAL:	$20	$23	$34	$86	$140	$1,075

Comments: The reverse, which is designated an "A¹c", is shared with eight other 8TF varieties. All but two are quite rare.

Census: 65, 64, 64, 64, 64, 64, 63

1878, 8 TAIL FEATHERS

FS-S1-1878-009

Variety: First Die Pair

VAM 9

PUP: Engraved left wing feather

URS-5 · I-4 · L-4

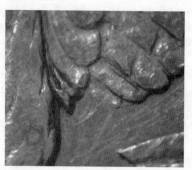

Description: An additional feather in the shape of a kidney bean is evident under the eagle's left wing (viewer's right).

	VF-20	EF-40	AU-50	MS-60	MS-63	MS-65
VARIETY:	$275	$400	$900	$2,500	$9,000	n/a
NORMAL:	$20	$23	$34	$86	$140	$1,075

Comments: The obverse and reverse dies of this variety are known to be the first pair of dies used to strike Morgan dollars on March 11, 1878. This is an important 8TF rarity!

Census: 64, 63, 63, 62, 60, 60, 58

1878, 8 TAIL FEATHERS

Variety: Obverse Die Gouge (Wild Eye)   **VAM 14-11**
PUP: Liberty's eye
URS-7 · I-5 · L-5

Description: Two spikes are visible protruding from the front of Liberty's eye.

	VF-20	EF-40	AU-50	MS-60	MS-63	MS-65
VARIETY:	$2,750	$4,000	$5,000	$6,500	$9,000	n/a
NORMAL:	$20	$23	$34	$86	$140	$1,075

Comments: Like the VAM 5, this major rarity has the "A1c" reverse. Fewer than a dozen specimens are known of this Top 100 variety and any sale is a landmark event.

Census: 67, 65, 65, 64, 63, 55, VF

1878, 8 TAIL FEATHERS

Variety: DDO/DDR   **VAM 15**
PUP: LIBERTY, eye, date
URS-6 · I-5 · L-4

Description: Strong doubling is evident on LIBERTY. A spike is visible in front of the eye and there is metal die fill in the loops of the first 8.

	VF-20	EF-40	AU-50	MS-60	MS-63	MS-65
VARIETY:	$125	$250	$600	$750	$1,000	n/a
NORMAL:	$20	$23	$34	$86	$140	$1,075

Comments: There are other doubled LIBERTY 8TF varieties, but only this one has this particular configuration of engraved feathers on the reverse under the eagle's wings.

Census: 64DM, 64DM, 64PL, 64PL, 64PL, 63DM, 63DM

1878, 7 OVER 8 TAIL FEATHERS | FS-S1-1878-032

Variety: 7 Over 3 Tail Feathers **VAM 32**
PUP: Tail feathers
URS-8 · I-5 · L-4

Description: Three extra tail feather tips protrude from under the seven tail feathers of the primary design. There is also a small die scratch in the field to the right of the cotton bolls and leaf on the obverse.

	VF-20	EF-40	AU-50	MS-60	MS-63	MS-65
VARIETY:	$125	$250	$400	$750	$1,500	n/a
NORMAL:	$15	$18	$28	$41	$92	$1,035

Comments: This is the second rarest of the 7 Over 8TF varieties and commands a significant premium.

Census: 64DM, 64DM, 64DM, 64PL, 64PL, 63DM, 63DM

1878, 7 OVER 8 TAIL FEATHERS | FS-S1-1878-044 (001)

Variety: TDO/DDR (King of VAMs) **VAM 44**
PUP: Tripled leaves, LIBERTY, cotton bolls, tail feathers
URS-7 · I-5 · L-5

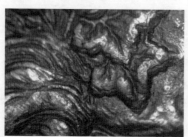 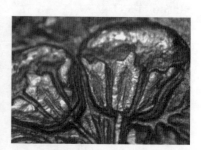

Description: This variety shows three to five weak tail feathers under the seven primary tail feathers. The obverse exhibits a tripled image on the cotton bolls and the leaves, and doubling on LIBERTY.

	VF-20	EF-40	AU-50	MS-60	MS-63	MS-65
VARIETY:	$1000	$2,000	$10,000	$15,000	$20,000	n/a
NORMAL:	$15	$18	$28	$41	$92	$1,035

Comments: Known as the King of VAMs, this variety is considered the top VAM and carries a premium commensurate with the title. There are fewer than a dozen Mint State specimens known. The same reverse die was used on VAM 33, which is the most common of the 7 Over 8 TF varieties. Our AU-50 VAM 44 recently sold for over $10,000.

Census: 63DM, 63, 62PL, 62PL, 62PL, 61PL, 61PL

1878, 7 TAIL FEATHERS — FS-S1-1878-115

Variety: TDO/DDR   **VAM 115**
PUP: Cotton bolls
URS-7 · I-4 · L-4

Description: Tripling is evident on the right edges of the cotton bolls in Liberty's bonnet.

	VF-20	EF-40	AU-50	MS-60	MS-63	MS-65
VARIETY:	$50	$75	$125	$750	n/a	n/a
NORMAL:	$15	$18	$28	$41	$92	$1,035

Comments: Note that there are two different reverses with this obverse: the VAM 115 and the VAM 198. Both are equally rare and valuable. The VAM 115 shows design detail where the eagle's right wing (viewer's left) joins the body, whereas the VAM 198 does not. VAMs 115 and 198 are both ultra-rare in all Mint State grades.

Census: 63, 62, 61, 61, 60, 58, 58

1878, 7 TAIL FEATHERS — FS-S1-1878-145

Variety: Broken Letters   **VAM 145**
PUP: UNUM, TRUST
URS-8 · I-4 · L-4

Description: The lower right serifs of N and M in UNUM are broken and the U and R of PLURIBUS are slightly doubled.

	VF-20	EF-40	AU-50	MS-60	MS-63	MS-65
VARIETY:	$35	$50	$100	$200	$400	n/a
NORMAL:	$15	$18	$28	$41	$92	$1,035

Comments: This is actually a doubled die obverse. The R of TRUST is *not* broken on the VAM 145, but is on VAM 166 (see next). VAMs 145 and 166 are very scarce in Mint State.

Census: 63, 63, 63, 62, 62, 62, 61

1878, 7 TAIL FEATHERS

FS-S1-1878-162

Variety: Broken Letters
VAM 162
PUP: M of UNUM
URS-7 · I-4 · L-4

Description: The bottom serifs of the N and M in UNUM are broken off.

	VF-20	EF-40	AU-50	MS-60	MS-63	MS-65
VARIETY:	$40	$75	$125	$250	$500	n/a
NORMAL:	$15	$18	$28	$41	$92	$1,035

Comments: This and the preceding listing have the same obverse, but a different reverse. Here the arm of the R in TRUST on the reverse motto is broken, whereas this is not the case with the VAM 145. The VAM 162 is very scarce in Mint State.

Census: 62, 62, 61, 61, 60, 58, 58

1878, 7 TAIL FEATHERS

FS-S1-1878-166

Variety: Triple Eye (Spikes)
VAM 166
PUP: Liberty's eye
URS-5 · I-4 · L-4

 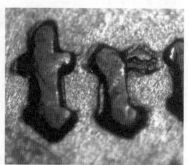

Description: The front of Liberty's eye shows two tiny spikes under the eyelid.

	VF-20	EF-40	AU-50	MS-60	MS-63	MS-65
VARIETY:	$250	$500	$1,000	n/a	n/a	n/a
NORMAL:	$15	$18	$28	$41	$92	$1,035

Comments: This VAM is one of the sleepers of the 1878 7TF set, and is missing from the collections of most VAM specialists. It is included here, not for its dramatic features, but for its rarity. This one is worth finding!

Census: 53, 50, 50, 45, 35 (population report attributions are less than reliable)

1878, 7 TAIL FEATHERS   FS-S1-1878-168

Variety: DDO/DDR   **VAM 168**
PUP: Liberty's eye
URS-4 · I-4 · L-3

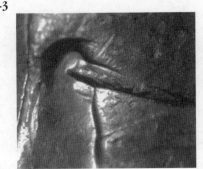 

Description: A doubled spike is evident in front of Liberty's eye, just below the eyelid. The P in PLURIBUS is doubled above the serifs on its base and at the top.

	VF-20	EF-40	AU-50	MS-60	MS-63	MS-65
VARIETY:	$75	$125	$250	n/a	n/a	n/a
NORMAL:	$15	$18	$28	$41	$92	$1,035

Comments: No Mint State specimens have been confirmed to date. This VAM is a desirable variety sought by many collectors.

Census: 53, 53, 50, 50, 45, 45, 45

1878, 7 TAIL FEATHERS   FS-S1-1878-188

Variety: Weak L in LIBERTY   **VAM 188**
PUP: L in LIBERTY
URS-4 · I-4 · L-4

 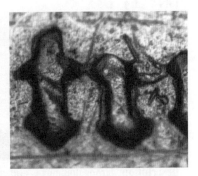

Description: Over-polished L in LIBERTY. The front leaf atop Liberty's headband is shortened. On the reverse, the arm of the R in TRUST is broken.

	VF-20	EF-40	AU-50	MS-60	MS-63	MS-65
VARIETY:	$75	$250	$750	n/a	n/a	n/a
NORMAL:	$15	$18	$28	$41	$92	$1,035

Comments: The L is so weak that it is almost missing entirely. The rarity of this VAM is under-appreciated. Now is the time to acquire one grading EF or above!

Census: 58, 53, 50, 45, 45, 45, 45

1878-CC

FS-S1-1878CC-006

Variety: DDO, Wide CC   **VAM 6**
PUP: Obverse leaves and widely spaced CC
URS-6 · I-4 · L-4

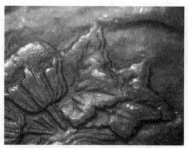 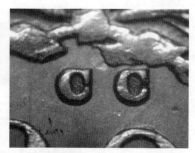

Description: Very strong doubling is evident on the leaves in Liberty's headdress and strong doubling on Liberty's ear. The date shows dramatic doubling to the right. The CC mintmark is level and widely spaced.

	VF-20	EF-40	AU-50	MS-60	MS-63	MS-65
VARIETY:	$100	$150	$175	$300	$600	n/a
NORMAL:	$81	$88	$96	$171	$321	$1,700

Comments: The VAM 6 mintmark is important, because the right C of the CC is widely spaced and actually touches the bottom of the wreath. There are only two such cases in the entire Morgan dollar series. Both are very scarce and desirable.

Census: 63PL, 63PL, 63, 62PL, 62, 62, 61

1878-CC

FS-S1-1878CC-018

Variety: DDO, Narrow CC   **VAM 18**
PUP: Obverse leaves and closely spaced CC
URS-7 · I-4 · L-5

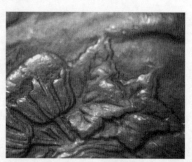 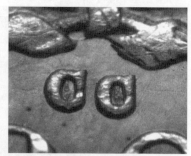

Description: Strong doubling is evident on the leaves, on Liberty's ear, and on the date. The reverse shows an uneven and closely spaced CC.

	VF-20	EF-40	AU-50	MS-60	MS-63	MS-65
VARIETY:	$100	$150	$200	$600	$1,500	n/a
NORMAL:	$81	$88	$96	$171	$321	$1,700

Comments: This variety has the same obverse as the VAM 6, but the reverse is different. Although both are highly prized, the VAM 18 is even rarer than the VAM 6. VAM 18 specimens often resemble Proofs.

Census: 64DM, 62DM, 62PL, 62PL, 62PL, 60PL, 60PL

1878-S

Variety: TDO (Tripled Eyelid)   **VAM 50**
PUP: Liberty's eye and junction of wing and body
URS-7 · I-3 · L-3

Description: Two spikes are evident in front of Liberty's eye, below the eyelid. The junction of the eagle's right wing (viewer's left) and the eagle's body shows areas suggesting that molten metal had been poured onto the struck coin.

	VF-20	EF-40	AU-50	MS-60	MS-63	MS-65
VARIETY:	$50	$75	$125	$175	$400	n/a
NORMAL:	$15	$16	$20	$32	$55	$208

Comments: This VAM is extremely interesting, but is not listed in either the Top 100 or Hot 50 books. Also interesting is that there was a second reverse die used with this same obverse.

Census: 63, 62, 60, 58, 55, 50, 45

1879-O

Variety: Repunched Mintmark   **VAM 4**
PUP: Mintmark, date
URS-7 · I-4 · L-3

Description: An O is evident far north, and another far south, of the primary O.

	VF-20	EF-40	AU-50	MS-60	MS-63	MS-65
VARIETY:	$25	$50	$100	$250	$500	n/a
NORMAL:	$12	$13	$15	$58	$146	$2,575

Comments: Long considered an O Over Horizontal O, we feel this VAM is actually an O/O/O. Two different obverses are known paired with this reverse. Both are desirable Top 100 varieties. (See VAM 28 listing for differences.)

Census: 63, 63, 63, 62, 62, 62, 61

1879-O

FS-S1-1879o-028

Variety: Repunched Mintmark
PUP: Mintmark
URS-7 · I-5 · L-4

VAM 28

Description: Doubling is visible on the 9 in the date.

	VF-20	EF-40	AU-50	MS-60	MS-63	MS-65
VARIETY:	$100	$250	$450	n/a	n/a	n/a
NORMAL:	$12	$13	$15	$58	$146	$2,575

Comments: The VAM 28 has the same reverse as the previously listed VAM 4 (O/O/O), but is paired with a different obverse die. On the VAM 4, the left side of the 9 is doubled and there is no doubling on the 7. On the VAM 28, however, the right side of the 7 is doubled and there is no doubling on the 9. Unlike the VAM 4, only a couple of Mint State VAM 28 specimens have been reported. These specimens are in great demand.

Census: 64, 62, 58, 55, 53, 50, 50

Rare Coin Investments (RCI)

· Buying
· Selling
· Consulting

*"Let me help you build
a World Class collection"*

Michael S. Fey, Ph.D., President

· Co-author, Top 100 Morgan Dollar Varieties: The VAM Keys
· Editor, Top 100 Insights & Value Guide Quarterly
· Specialist in Rare Die Varieties of U.S. & World Coins

Please visit: http://www.rcicoins.com

RCI, P.O. Box 9157, Morris Plains, NJ 07950
973-252-4000; 973-252-0481 (FAX)
E-mail: Feyms@aol.com

1879-S

FS-S1-1879S-901

Variety: B Reverse (Type of 1878)
PUP: Top arrow feather, eagle's breast
URS-10 · I-4 · L-4

VAM—Several

B Reverse - Flat Breast, Parallel Feather

C Reverse - Rounded Breast, Slanted Feather

Description: The Type B reverse shows the top arrow feather parallel to the arrow shaft, and the eagle's breast flat or concave. The C reverse exhibits slanted arrow feathers, and a more convex breast on the eagle.

	VF-20	EF-40	AU-50	MS-60	MS-63	MS-65
VARIETY:	$20	$25	$35	$90	$300	$6,500
NORMAL:	$12	$13	$15	$58	$146	$2,575

Comments: This variety is highly collectible, even by non-variety specialists. At present there are 17 different die pairs that together represent the 1879-S Flat Breast, or B-reverse varieties.

Census: 65, 65, 65, 65, 65, 65, 65, 65

1880
FS-S1-1880-006 (003)

Variety: Overdate   **(Spikes) VAM 6**
PUP: Second 8 of the date
URS-7 · I-4 · L-3

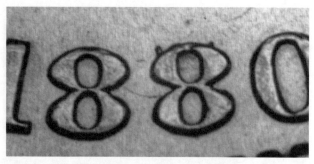

Description: Spikes can be seen above the second 8 in the date. The incomplete crossbar inside the 8 denotes the remains of the 7 in the underlying date.

	VF-20	EF-40	AU-50	MS-60	MS-63	MS-65
VARIETY:	$25	$50	$125	$400	$800	n/a
NORMAL:	$12	$13	$15	$24	$45	$650

Comments: This VAM 6 is one of the easiest 1880 overdates to detect. It is available in circulated grades, but is surprisingly difficult to find in Mint State condition.

Census: 64, 63, 63, 62, 62, 61, 60

1880
FS-S1-1880-007 (004)

Variety: Overdate   **Crossbar VAM 7**
PUP: Second 8 of date
URS-6 · I-5 · L-4

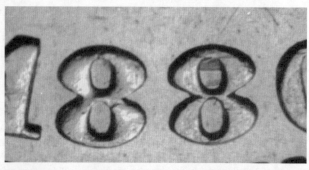

Description: The clear remains of an underlying 7 are visible as a recessed crossbar inside the second 8 at the top.

	VF-20	EF-40	AU-50	MS-60	MS-63	MS-65
VARIETY:	$250	$400	$750	n/a	n/a	n/a
NORMAL:	$12	$13	$15	$24	$45	$650

Comments: This VAM is very rare in AU and unknown in any Uncirculated grade.

Census: 58, 58, 58, 55, 55, 55, 55

1880 — FS-S1-1880-008 (005)

Variety: Overdate (Ears) VAM 8
PUP: Second 8 of date
URS-6 · I-5 · L-4

Description: The remains of an underlying date are visible as a small bump on the top right side of the second 8.

	VF-20	EF-40	AU-50	MS-60	MS-63	MS-65
VARIETY:	$250	$400	$850	n/a	n/a	n/a
NORMAL:	$12	$13	$15	$24	$45	$650

Comments: The VAM 8 may be going unnoticed because of its less than dramatic variety feature. Nevertheless, this variety is in tremendous demand as a key part of the 1880-(P) overdate set.

Census: 62, 58, 58, 55, 55, 53, 50

1880 — FS-S1-1880-023

Variety: Overdate VAM 23
PUP: Last 8 and 0 of the date
URS-7 · I-4 · L-4

Description: An underlying 79 is visible on the *surface* of the last 8 and 0. The 8 has a small ear of metal at the top left surface, and the 0 has metal remnants on the surface at K-8 and K-9.

	VF-20	EF-40	AU-50	MS-60	MS-63	MS-65
VARIETY:	$150	$400	$750	n/a	n/a	n/a
NORMAL:	$12	$13	$15	$24	$45	$650

Comments: Only one Mint State specimen has been reported to date, making high-grade AU examples highly desirable.

Census: 62, 58, 55, 55, 53, 50, 50

1880-CC

FS-S1-1880CC-004

Variety: Overdate

VAM 4

PUP: 80 of the date and flat breast reverse

URS-7 · I-5 · L-5

Description: The top crossbar and diagonal stem of an underlying 79 are clearly visible within the 8. Extensive polishing marks are evident within the 0.

	VF-20	EF-40	AU-50	MS-60	MS-63	MS-65
VARIETY:	$150	$200	$250	$450	$625	$2,000
NORMAL:	$125	$167	$225	$371	$404	$1,175

Comments: To add further excitement, the reverse is a B Reverse, Flat Breast leftover from 1878! The VAM 4 can be obtained in grades up through MS-66; nevertheless, it enjoys tremendous popularity at a time when all CC dollars remain the darlings of numismatics.

Census: 66, 66, 65, 65, 65, 65, 65 (population report attributions are less than reliable)

1880-CC

FS-S1-1880CC-005 (005.2)

Variety: Overdate

(High 7) VAM 5

PUP: Last 8 of the date

URS-7 · I-5 · L-5

 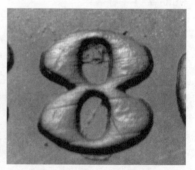

Description: An almost complete 7 can be seen inside the last 8 of the date. The top edge of the 7 touches the top inside of the 8.

	VF-20	EF-40	AU-50	MS-60	MS-63	MS-65
VARIETY:	$150	$225	$275	$475	$525	$2,000
NORMAL:	$125	$167	$225	$371	$404	$1,175

Comments: The clear overdate markings are icing on the cake in the current runaway bull market for Carson City dollars!

Census: 65, 65, 65, 65, 65, 65, 65 (population report attributions are less than reliable)

1880-CC

FS-S1-1880CC-006

Variety: Overdate (Low 7)
PUP: Last 8 of the date
URS-7 · I-5 · L-5

VAM 6

Description: A complete 7 is evident inside the last 8 of the date. The crossbar of the underlying 7 is visible in the top loop and the diagonal of the 7 is visible in the lower loop.

	VF-20	EF-40	AU-50	MS-60	MS-63	MS-65
VARIETY:	$150	$225	$275	$475	$525	$2,000
NORMAL:	$125	$167	$225	$371	$404	$1,175

Comments: The remnants of the underlying 7 on the VAM 5 are set higher than on the VAM 6. There is little or no controversy regarding claims that the VAM 6 is an overdate. If you are seeking a clear Morgan dollar overdate, this may be the one for you!

Census: 65, 65, 65, 65, 65, 65, 65 (population report attributions are less than reliable)

1880-CC

FS-S1-1880CC-007

Variety: Overdate
PUP: Dash under last 8; Reverse of 78
URS-7 · I-4 · L-5

VAM 7

 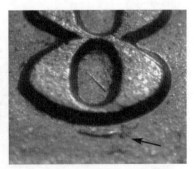

Description: This 1880-CC specimen has a Flat Breast reverse, no overdate markings, and a dash under the last 8.

	VF-20	EF-40	AU-50	MS-60	MS-63	MS-65
VARIETY:	$150	$200	$250	$450	$625	$2,250
NORMAL:	$125	$167	$225	$371	$404	$1,175

Comments: The VAM 7 is one of only two 1880-CC varieties that have a Flat Breast B Reverse. All the known 1880 dies used at the Carson City branch mint were overdates. Hence the VAM 7, which shows no decisive markings within the last 8, is still considered an overdate.

Census: 65, 65, 65, 65, 65, 65, 65 (population report attributions are less than reliable)

1880-O
FS-S1-1880o-004

Variety: Overdate
VAM 4
PUP: Ears above 8 and metal within upper loop of second 8
URS-8 · I-4 · L-4

Description: Excess metal representing the crossbar of an underlying 7 is evident within the upper loop. The 1 and the first 8 are slightly doubled to the right.

	VF-20	EF-40	AU-50	MS-60	MS-63	MS-65
VARIETY:	$25	$35	$60	$100	$550	n/a
NORMAL:	$12	$13	$16	$46	$300	$15,500

Comments: The micro O-Mint overdates are highly collectible.

Census: Mint State examples are available.

1880-O
FS-S1-1880o-005

Variety: Overdate
VAM 5
PUP: Ear above 8 and metal within upper loop of second 8
URS-8 · I-4 · L-4

 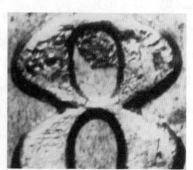

Description: There is excess metal inside the upper loop, simlar to VAM 4.

	VF-20	EF-40	AU-50	MS-60	MS-63	MS-65
VARIETY:	$25	$35	$65	$125	$600	n/a
NORMAL:	$12	$13	$16	$46	$300	$15,500

Comments: This VAM is different from the previous one in that it has an O Over O mintmark. The O-Mint overdates are highly collectible.

Census: Mint State examples are available.

1880-O
FS-S1-1880o-048

Variety: Hangnail/Overdate Variety
PUP: Eagle's right tail feather
URS-7 · I-4 · L-3

VAM 49

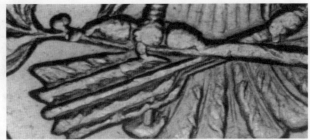

Description: On the reverse, a die gouge runs from the bottom of the arrow feather, across the feathers, and out the eagle's rightmost tail feather. On the obverse the top left of the second 8 has a spike.

	VF-20	EF-40	AU-50	MS-60	MS-63	MS-65
VARIETY:	$90	$175	$350	$450	n/a	n/a
NORMAL:	$12	$13	$16	$46	$300	$15,500

Comments: Formerly listed as VAM 6B. All specimens with this reverse should be carefully checked.

Census: 64, 64, 63, 63, 63, 63, 62

1881-O
FS-S1-1881o-005

Variety: Repunched Mintmark
PUP: Mintmark
URS-6 · I-3 · L-3

VAM 5

Description: A diagonal image, the remains of one or two additional O mintmark punches, are evident within the primary O.

	VF-20	EF-40	AU-50	MS-60	MS-63	MS-65
VARIETY:	$25	$35	$50	$100	$250	n/a
NORMAL:	$12	$13	$15	$25	$41	$1,125

Comments: Amazingly similar to the OMMs of the popular 1882-O Over S varieties, the VAM 5 is gaining in popularity with variety specialists.

Census: 64, 64, 63, 63, 63, 63, 62

1881-O
FS-S1-1881o-027

Variety: Doubled Die Obverse VAM 27
PUP: Ear
URS-7 · I-5 · L-4

Description: Clear doubling is visible on the back outside of Liberty's ear.

	VF-20	EF-40	AU-50	MS-60	MS-63	MS-65
VARIETY:	$25	$35	$50	$100	$250	n/a
NORMAL:	$12	$13	$15	$25	$41	$1,125

Comments: This Hot 50 variety is similar to the popular 1891-P VAM 2 and is at least as scarce. It can be difficult to locate on demand. Because it is a recent discovery, we do not yet know if it will become popular among VAM specialists.

Census: 63, 63, 63, 62, 62, 61, 61

1882-O
FS-S1-1882o-003 (005.25)

Variety: Over Mintmark VAM 3
PUP: Mintmark
URS-8 · I-5 · L-5

Description: The top surface of what is considered the S is level with the top surface of the O.

	VF-20	EF-40	AU-50	MS-60	MS-63	MS-65
VARIETY EDS:	n/a	$75	$250	$400	$950	n/a
VARIETY LDS:	$25	$40	$60	$200	$750	n/a
NORMAL:	$12	$13	$15	$25	$37	$585

Comments: This RPM is quite evident and has been nicknamed the O Over S Flush. Further study may determine this to be an O Over O, much like FS-S1-1880o-005.

Census EDS: 63, 63, 63, 62, 62, 61, 61, 61

Census LDS: 64, 64, 64, 64, 64, 64, 63, 63

1882-O   FS-S1-1882o-004

Variety: Over Mintmark   **VAM 4**
PUP: Mintmark
URS-8 · I-5 · L-5

Description: The top surface of what is probably the S is lower than the O.

	VF-20	EF-40	AU-50	MS-60	MS-63	MS-65
VARIETY EDS:	n/a	$2,500	$3,500	n/a	n/a	n/a
VARIETY LDS:	$25	$35	$50	$175	$800	n/a
NORMAL:	$12	$13	$15	$25	$37	$585

Comments: This RPM is known as the O Over S Recessed. While it is the most common of the 1882-O Over S varieties overall, this VAM is the rarest of them all in an early-die-state (EDS) example.

Census EDS: 58, 55, 55, 55, 45

Census LDS: 64, 64, 64, 64, 64, 64, 64, 64

1882-O   FS-S1-1882o-005

Variety: Over Mintmark   **VAM 5**
PUP: Mintmark
URS-8 · I-5 · L-5

Description: The top right portion on an underlying S mintmark is evident within the opening of the primary O mintmark.

	VF-20	EF-40	AU-50	MS-60	MS-63	MS-65
VARIETY EDS:	n/a	$75	$250	$350	n/a	n/a
VARIETY LDS:	$25	$35	$50	$175	$800	n/a
NORMAL:	$12	$13	$15	$25	$37	$585

Comments: This OMM had been nicknamed the Broken S. This is more common that the two listings above. The three OMMs for 1882-O are all nice finds.

Census EDS: 62, 62, 62, 62, 62, 61, 61, 61

Census LDS: 64, 64, 64, 64, 64, 64, 64, 64

1884 — FS-S1-1884-003

Variety: Large Dot
PUP: Designer's initial
URS-9 · I-5 · L-5

VAM 3

Description: A dot is visible after the designer's initial.

	VF-20	EF-40	AU-50	MS-60	MS-63	MS-65
VARIETY:	$20	$25	$30	$50	$125	n/a
NORMAL:	$12	$13	$14	$25	$38	$196

Comments: These dots varieties are thought to have been used as some type of identifier. This VAM is called the Large Dot variety, with the next listing, the VAM 4, known as the Small Dot variety.

Census: 65, 64, 64, 64, 64, 64, 64, 64 (combined VAM 3 and 4)

1884 — FS-S1-1884-004

Variety: Small Dot
PUP: Designer's initial
URS-7 · I-5 · L-5

VAM 4

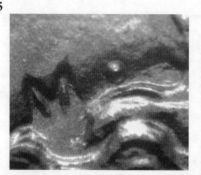 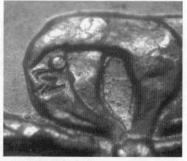

Description: A raised dot is evident after the designer's initial.

	VF-20	EF-40	AU-50	MS-60	MS-63	MS-65
VARIETY:	$20	$25	$30	$60	$150	n/a
NORMAL:	$12	$13	$14	$25	$38	$196

Comments: This VAM is considered the Small Dot variety, while the previous listing, VAM 3, is known as the Large Dot variety. The dots are reported to have been used as some type of identifier.

Census: 65, 64, 64, 64, 64, 64, 64, 64 (combined VAM 3 and 4)

1885 — FS-S1-1885-008

Variety: Dash Under Second 8
PUP: Date
URS-8 · I-5 · L-5

VAM 8

Description: There is a large, raised die chip below the second 8. The area above the "dash" below the second 8 has broken away on the die create this character effect. All specimen formal as far have a doubled arrowshaft on the reverse which indicates the VAM 22.

	VF-20	EF-40	AU-50	MS-60	MS-63	MS-65
VARIETY:	$15	$20	$30	$60	$125	n/a
NORMAL:	$12	$13	$14	$24	$37	$132

Comments: This is the most desirable of the several P-Mint dash varieties.

Census: 63, 62, 62,62, 62, 61, 61, 58

1885-CC — FS-S1-1885CC-004

Variety: Dash Under Second 8
PUP: Date
URS-8 · I-5 · L-5

VAM 4

Description: There is a large, raised die chip below the 8, as on the 1885-P, VAM 8/22.

	VF-20	EF-40	AU-50	MS-60	MS-63	MS-65
VARIETY:	$450	$500	$525	$550	$625	$1,500
NORMAL:	$450	$475	$480	$525	$530	$1,170

Comments: The space above the dash, as on the 1885-P VAM 22, has broken away on the die.

Census: 66, 65, 65, 65, 65, 64PL, 64, 64

1886

FS-S1-1886-001c

Variety: Clashed Die
PUP: Reverse, right field
URS-9 · I-5 · L-5

VAM 1C

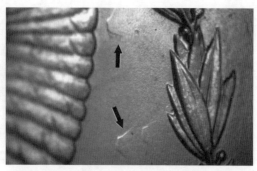

Description: Five heavy clash marks from the obverse die show on the right side of the reverse.

	VF-20	EF-40	AU-50	MS-60	MS-63	MS-65
VARIETY:	$15	$20	$30	$50	$75	$200
NORMAL:	$12	$13	$14	$24	$34	$124

Comments: This variety is available for modest premiums.

Census: 65, 65, 64, 64, 64, 64, 64, 64

1886

FS-S1-1886-020

Variety: Repunched Date
PUP: Date
URS-3 · I-5 · L-5

VAM 20

Description: The doubled date is evident in the loop of the lower 6. The other digits are also repunched, especially the lower base of the 1.

	VF-20	EF-40	AU-50	MS-60	MS-63	MS-65
VARIETY:	$75	$100	$200	$350	$650	n/a
NORMAL:	$12	$13	$14	$24	$34	$124

Comments: This is a newly reported and probably very rare variety!

Census: 63, 63, 61

1886-O

FS-S1-1886o-001a (005.27)

Variety: Clashed Die E Reverse
PUP: Reverse below eagle's tail feathers
URS-9 · I-5 · L-5

VAM 1A

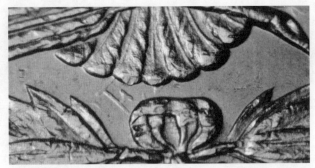

Description: A clashed die is evident on the E of LIBERTY, between the eagle's tail feathers and the bow on the wreath.

	VF-20	EF-40	AU-50	MS-60	MS-63	MS-65
VARIETY:	$50	$75	$200	$750	$4,000	n/a
NORMAL:	$12	$14	$62	$475	$3,000	$185,000

Comments: This popular VAM variety is always in demand.

Census: 63, 62, 62, 62, 62, 61, 61, 61

1887

FS-S1-1887-001b

Variety: Clashed Die E Reverse
PUP: Reverse below eagle's tail feathers
URS-4 · I-5 · L-5

VAM 1B

Description: The clashed die is evident on the E of LIBERTY and partially evident between the eagle's tail feathers and the bow.

	VF-20	EF-40	AU-50	MS-60	MS-63	MS-65
VARIETY:	$150	$300	$600	n/a	n/a	n/a
NORMAL:	$12	$13	$14	$24	$34	$124

Comments: This is a relatively new listing, and is very much in demand. Fewer than six are known at this time.

Census: 62, 50, 45, 40

1887, 7 OVER 6

FS-S1-1887-002 (005.3)

Variety: Overdate
PUP: Date
URS-7 · I-5 · L-5

VAM 2

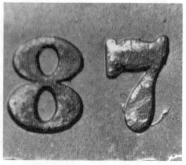

Description: The 7 of the date is punched over a 6. The lower loop of the 6 is clearly evident near the bottom of the 7.

	VF-20	EF-40	AU-50	MS-60	MS-63	MS-65
VARIETY:	$50	$75	$150	$350	$650	$4,000
NORMAL:	$12	$13	$14	$24	$34	$124

Comments: This is one of the most sought after varieties in the series, but it can still be cherrypicked!

Census: 65, 65, 64DM, 64DM, 64DM, 64DM, 64DM, 64PL

1887-O

FS-S1-1887o-002 (005.7)

Variety: Repunched Date
PUP: Date
URS-8 · I-5 · L-4

VAM 2

Description: The top flag of the secondary 1 is evident left of the primary 1. The lower foot of the secondary 7 is visible left of the primary 7. Tripling is evident on the top of the 7.

	VF-20	EF-40	AU-50	MS-60	MS-63	MS-65
VARIETY:	$50	$75	$100	$200	$350	n/a
NORMAL:	$12	$14	$20	$36	$92	$2,600

Comments: This variety is in the Top 100 VAM listings!

Census: No census data are currently available.

1887-O, 7 OVER 6
FS-S1-1887o-003 (005.5)

Variety: Overdate
VAM 3
PUP: Date
URS-7 · I-5 · L-5

Description: The 7 of the date punched over a 6. The lower loop of the 6 is clearly evident near the bottom of the 7.

	VF-20	EF-40	AU-50	MS-60	MS-63	MS-65
VARIETY:	$30	$50	$150	$350	$2,250	n/a
NORMAL:	$12	$14	$20	$36	$92	$2,600

Comments: This variety is very similar to the P-Mint variety. It is another of the more popular VAM varieties and is always in demand.

Census: 64, 64, 64, 64, 64, 64, 64, 64

1887-O
FS-S1-1887o-030

Variety: Clashed Die
VAM 30
PUP: Entire reverse
URS-4 · I-5 · L-5

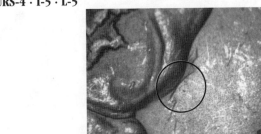

Description: Clashed details from the obverse die are clearly visible on the reverse.

	VF-20	EF-40	AU-50	MS-60	MS-63	MS-65
VARIETY:	$20	$40	$75	$150	$350	n/a
NORMAL:	$12	$14	$20	$36	$92	$2,600

Comments: A relatively new, yet highly sought after variety, this is a superb clashed die.

Census: 63, 63, 63, 62, 62, 62, 60, 60

1888-O

FS-S1-1888o-001a

Variety: Clashed Die E Reverse
VAM 1A
PUP: Reverse below eagle's tail feathers
URS-6 · I-5 · L-5

Description: On the reverse, the E of LIBERTY is faintly visible below the left side of the eagle's tail feathers. On the late die state, a strong die crack is evident on the obverse, from the rim through the R of PLURIBUS and down to the lower left of the L in LIBERTY.

	VF-20	EF-40	AU-50	MS-60	MS-63	MS-65
VARIETY:	$40	$60	$85	$140	$200	n/a
NORMAL:	$12	$13	$14	$24	$40	$360

Comments: This variety commands strong premiums over the normal coin.

Census: 64, 64, 64, 64, 63, 63, 63, 63

1888-O

FS-S1-1888o-002 (006)

Variety: Doubled Die Obverse
VAM 4
PUP: Lips
URS-8 · I-5 · L-5

Description: Doubling is evident on the lips, nose, eye, chin, entire profile, and part of the hair.

	VF-20	EF-40	AU-50	MS-60	MS-63	MS-65
VARIETY:	$75	$200	$1,000	$5,000	n/a	n/a
NORMAL:	$12	$13	$14	$24	$40	$360

Comments: There is still only one or two of this very dramatic doubled die known in Mint State. Find an MS-65 and name your price! This variety is affectionately known as "Hot Lips."

Census: 61, 58, 58, 58, 58, 58, 58, 58

1888-O

Variety: Die Break ("Scarface")
VAM 1b
PUP: Cheek
URS-5 · I-5 · L-5

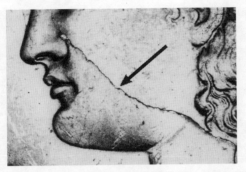

Description: There is a major die break on the obverse, running from the rim between the E and P, through the field, and all the way across Liberty's face and neck.

	VF-20	EF-40	AU-50	MS-60	MS-63
VARIETY:			$1,500	$2,500	$6,300
NORMAL:	$15	$16	$18	$25	$40

Comments: This is the largest die break reported in the Morgan dollar series, and is very rare in all grades.

Census: 63, 63, 63, 63, 63

1888-O

Variety: Oval O Mintmark
VAM—Various
PUP: Mintmark
URS-9 · I-5 · L-5

Description: Oval O mintmark

	VF-20	EF-40	AU-50	MS-60	MS-63	MS-65
VARIETY:	$25	$75	$150	$400	$600	n/a
NORMAL:	$12	$13	$14	$24	$40	$360

Comments: The following VAMs are included with this listing: 2, 5, 6, 17, 18, 21, and 24. All are very scarce in circulated grades, and extremely rare in Mint State.

Census: 63, 63, 62, 62, 62, 61, 58, 58

1889 FS-S1-1889-019a

Variety: Die Break (Bar Wing)   **VAM 19A**
PUP: Top of eagle's right wing (viewer's left)
URS-9 · I-5 · L-5

Description: The VAM 19a has this same reverse die as VAM 22 yet paired with a different obverse die. This VAM 19a has an obverse with a normal date, and VAM 22 has an obverse with the date set to the right of normal.

	VF-20	EF-40	AU-50	MS-60	MS-63	MS-65
VARIETY:	$25	$30	$40	$100	$150	$650
NORMAL:	$12	$13	$14	$24	$39	$276

Comments: The nicknames for many VAMs, a practice begun many years ago, are still used today. This die break variety is nicknamed the Bar Wing.

Census: 65, 65, 64, 64, 64, 64, 64, 64

1889 FS-S1-1889-022

Variety: Die Break (Bar Wing)   **VAM 22**
PUP: Top of eagle's right wing (viewer's left)
URS-9 · I-5 · L-5

Description: This VAM has this same reverse die as VAM 19a, yet paired with different obverse dies. The VAM 22 has an obverse with a far date, and the VAM 22 has an obverse with a normal date.

	VF-20	EF-40	AU-50	MS-60	MS-63	MS-65
VARIETY:	$25	$30	$40	$100	$150	$550
NORMAL:	$12	$13	$14	$24	$39	$276

Comments: Many of the older popular VAMs have become known by their nicknames. This die break variety is nicknamed the Bar Wing.

Census: 65, 65, 64, 64, 64, 64, 64, 64

1889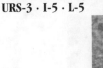

FS-S1-1889-023a

Variety: Obverse Clashed Die
VAM 23A
PUP: Field under jaw by neck
URS-3 · I-5 · L-5

Description: The IN of IN GOD WE TRUST shows clear evidence of a clashed die just beneath Liberty's jaw at her neck.

	VF-20	EF-40	AU-50	MS-60	MS-63	MS-65
VARIETY:	n/a	n/a	n/a	n/a	n/a	n/a
NORMAL:	$12	$13	$14	$24	$39	$276

Comments: The coin shown here is one of only four known examples of the full IN variety. Find an MS-65 and you can name your price!

Census: Only one BU and three circulated examples are known as of this date.

1889-O

FS-S1-1889o-001a (006.5)

Variety: Clashed Die E Reverse
VAM 1A
PUP: Reverse in field under tail feathers
URS-4 · I-5 · L-5

Description: The E of LIBERTY is evident in the field below the eagle's tail feathers and slightly left of the bow.

	VF-20	EF-40	AU-50	MS-60	MS-63	MS-65
VARIETY:	$200	$300	$750	$2,000	n/a	n/a
NORMAL:	$12	$14	$26	$96	$350	$4,225

Comments: Another of the famous and popular reverse clashed dies, this variety is extremely rare in Mint State, and unknown above MS-61.

Census: 61, 60, 58, 58, 58, 58, 58, 55

1890-CC

FS-S1-1890CC-004 (007)

Variety: Die Gouge Tailbar
PUP: Field between arrow feathers and wreath
URS-7 · I-5 · L-5

VAM 4

Description: A heavy die gouge extends from between the eagle's first tail feather and the lowest arrow feather to the leaves in the wreath below.

	VF-20	EF-40	AU-50	MS-60	MS-63	MS-65
VARIETY:	$200	$350	$750	$1,225	$3,000	n/a
NORMAL:	$82	$117	$146	$292	$795	$5,125

Comments: This is an extremely popular and highly marketable variety, especially in Mint State.

Census: This variety is unknown in MS-65.

1890-O

FS-S1-1890o-010

Variety: Die Gouges by Date
PUP: Area to the right of date
URS-9 · I-5 · L-5

VAM 10

Description: Die gouges are evident to the right of the date.

	VF-20	EF-40	AU-50	MS-60	MS-63	MS-65
VARIETY:	$20	$35	$50	$85	$200	n/a
NORMAL:	$12	$14	$19	$46	$89	$1,285

Comments: This so-called Comet Variety is an old variety that has been popular for 25 years. It is still unknown in MS-65.

Census: 64, 64, 64, 64, 64, 64, 64, 63

1891-O   FS-S1-1891o-001a

Variety: Clashed Die E Reverse   **VAM 1A**
PUP: Reverse in field under tail feathers
URS-5 · I-5 · L-5

Description: The evidence of a clashed die is seen below the eagle's tail feathers and slightly left of the bow, where the E in Liberty has been transformed from the obervse die.

	VF-20	EF-40	AU-50	MS-60	MS-63	MS-65
VARIETY:	$40	$90	$150	$400	$1,500	n/a
NORMAL:	$12	$14	$28	$80	$271	$6,000

Comments: The most evident and popular of the E reverse clashed dies, only one is known in MS-63 and none are known higher.

Census: 63, 62, 58, 58, 58, 58, 58, 55

1891-O   FS-S1-1891o-001b

Variety: Pitted Reverse Die   **VAM 1B**
PUP: Mintmark
URS-4 · I-5 · L-5

Description: The pitting on the reverse is visible around the ONE and on the bottom of the wreath above and between ONE and DOLLAR.

	VF-20	EF-40	AU-50	MS-60	MS-63	MS-65
VARIETY:	$50	$100	$300	n/a	n/a	n/a
NORMAL:	$12	$14	$28	$80	$271	$6,000

Comments: Discovered in 1997, this variety is rare in circulated grades, and unknown above AU.

Census: Census data are unknown at this time.

1895-S

FS-S1-1895S-003

Variety: RPM (S Over S)
PUP: Mintmark
URS-5 · I-5 · L-5

VAM 3

Description: A dramatic repunched mintmark is evident, with the secondary S northwest of the primary S. This secondary S only shows in the southwest quadrant of the upper loop outside of the primary S, with some elements of the secondary letter within the loops of the primary.

	VF-20	EF-40	AU-50	MS-60	MS-63	MS-65
VARIETY:	$400	$750	$1,500	$3,000	n/a	n/a
NORMAL:	$350	$690	$1,275	$2,750	$4,475	$15,000

Comments: This is a very dramatic RPM for this series. The variety is very expensive because of the rare date. The date also accounts for a relatively large percentage of the surviving coins likely being this RPM.

Census: 62, 62, 62, 62, 61, 61, 60, 58

1896

FS-S1-1896-020

Variety: Repunched Date
PUP: 6 of the date
URS-8 · I-5 · L-5

VAM 20

Description: The strong repunched date is evident only on the secondary 6. The left lower loop of the secondary 6 is evident within the lower loop of the primary 6.

	VF-20	EF-40	AU-50	MS-60	MS-63	MS-65
VARIETY:	$20	$25	$35	$60	$125	n/a
NORMAL:	$12	$13	$14	$24	$36	$144

Comments: This variety is one of the widest RPDs in the series.

Census: Census data are not available at this time.

1896-O

FS-S1-1896o-004 (008)

Variety: Micro O Mintmark
PUP: Mintmark
URS-8 · I-5 · L-5

VAM 4

Description: The O mintmark is smaller than the mintmark normally seen.

	VF-20	EF-40	AU-50	MS-60	MS-63	MS-65
VARIETY:	n/a	n/a	n/a	n/a	n/a	n/a
NORMAL:	$15	$17	$133	$775	$5,525	$115,000

Comments: This variety has been found to be made from counterfeit dies. Still, it is very popular and collectible among VAM enthusiasts.

Census: 50, 45, 45, 45, 40, 40, 40, 40

1896-O

FS-S1-1896o-019

Variety: Repunched Date
PUP: Date
URS-7 · I-5 · L-5

VAM 19

Description: A strong repunched date is evident with the secondary image north and east of the primary image. The secondary images are evident within the lower loops of the 8, the 9, and the 6.

	VF-20	EF-40	AU-50	MS-60	MS-63	MS-65
VARIETY:	$30	$100	$250	$900	n/a	n/a
NORMAL:	$15	$17	$133	$775	$5,525	$115,000

Comments: This variety was previously listed as VAM 1A. It is very rare in any grade.

Census: 61, 61, 60, 55, 55

1898-O

FS-S1-1898o-301 (008.5)

Variety: Repunched Date
PUP: Date
URS-1 · I-5 · L-5

VAM—N/L

Description: A secondary 8 is evident between the primary first 8 and the 9, and a secondary 9 evident between the primary 9 and the last 8.

	VF-20	EF-40	AU-50	MS-60	MS-63	MS-65
VARIETY:	n/a	n/a	n/a	n/a	n/a	n/a
NORMAL:	$12	$13	$14	$24	$37	$136

Comments: Discovered in 1995 by Jerry Sajbel, this is one of the strongest repunched dates of this series. To our knowledge, Jerry's is still the only specimen known. There are no sales reports to date.

Census: VF-35

1899-O

FS-S1-1899o-501 (008.7)

Variety: Micro O Mintmark
PUP: Mintmark
URS-8 · I-5 · L-5

VAM 4, 6, 31, and 32

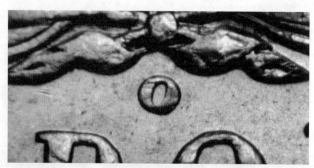

Description: The O mintmark is smaller than the mintmark normally seen.

	VF-20	EF-40	AU-50	MS-60	MS-63	MS-65
VARIETY:	$30	$45	$125	$250	$750	n/a
NORMAL:	$14	$15	$16	$24	$37	$128

Comments: The O mintmark punch used for this 1899-O die was probably from a punch intended for a Barber half dollar. There are five different dies known including the VAM 5, but all are very scarce—and very desirable. This and the 1880-O Micro O are the only two Micro O varieties considered genuine.

Census: 66, 65, 64, 64, 63, 63, 63, 63

1900   FS-S1-1900-016

Variety: DDR (C4 Over C3 Reverse)   **VAM 16**
PUP: Left olive on branch
URS-10 · I-4 · L-4

Description: Doubling is most evident as an extra olive to the right of the olive connected to the branch (illustrated). Doubling is also evident on the upper feathers of the eagle's left wing and on the inside of the OF in UNITED STATES OF AMERICA.

	VF-20	EF-40	AU-50	MS-60	MS-63	MS-65
VARIETY:	$20	$25	$35	$50	$75	$250
NORMAL:	$12	$13	$14	$24	$38	$164

Comments: Two different hubs used when producing the die. The first hub was the C3 reverse, and the second, and final, hub was the C4 reverse. VAM 18 is very similar. We suggest using the VAM book to determine the difference.

Census: 65, 65, 65, 64, 64, 64, 64, 64

1900-O   FS-S1-1900o-005 (009)

Variety: Micro O Mintmark   **VAM 5**
PUP: Mintmark
URS-6 · I-5 · L-5

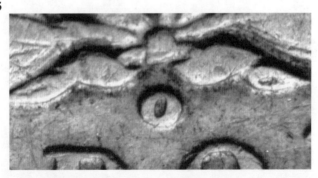

Description: The O mintmark is smaller than the mintmark normally seen.

	VF-20	EF-40	AU-50	MS-60	MS-63	MS-65
VARIETY:	n/a	n/a	n/a	n/a	n/a	n/a
NORMAL:	$12	$15	$16	$24	$37	$140

Comments: This variety has been found to be made from counterfeit dies. Still, it is very popular and collectible among VAM enthusiasts.

Census: 58, 50, 50, 45, 45, 40, 40, 40

1900-O

Variety: Obverse Die Break

PUP: Date area

URS-6 · I-5 · L-5

VAM 29A

Description: A die break is visible from the rim through the date to just below the lower point of the bust.

	VF-20	EF-40	AU-50	MS-60	MS-63	MS-65
VARIETY:	$100	$250	$500	n/a	n/a	n/a
NORMAL:	$12	$15	$16	$24	$37	$140

Comments: This variety, unknown in Mint State, is often confused with VAM 35. Look for any VAM 29A above AU-50.

Census: 58, 58, 58, 55, 55, 53, 53, 53

1900-O

Variety: Over Mintmark

PUP: Mintmark

URS-9 · I-5 · L-5

VAM—Various

Description: An O mintmark has been punched into the die over a previously punched CC mintmark.

	VF-20	EF-40	AU-50	MS-60	MS-63	MS-65
VARIETY:	$50	$80	$150	$275	$725	$2,750
NORMAL:	$12	$15	$16	$24	$37	$140

Comments: There are at least seven different dies, and therefore different VAMs, included in this listing. The VAM 9, shown on the right, is extremely rare.

Census: 65, 65, 65, 65, 65, 65, 65, 65

1901 — FS-S1-1901-003 (010)

Variety: DDR (Doubled Tail Feathers)   VAM 3

PUP: Tail feathers

URS-6 · I-5 · L-5

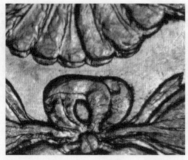

Description: Doubling is evident on IN GOD WE TRUST, as well as on the arrows, wreath, and bow, but it is the doubling on the eagle's tailfeathers that gives this variety the "Shifted Eagle" nickname.

	VF-20	EF-40	AU-50	MS-60	MS-63	MS-65
VARIETY:	$400	$800	$1,600	n/a	n/a	n/a
NORMAL:	$32	$75	$222	$1,350	$11,250	$225,000

Comments: Historically one of the more popular and important Morgan dollar varieties, only two Mint State coins are known, both low grades.

Census: 61, 60, 58, 58, 58, 58, 58, 58

1902-O — FS-S1-1902o-003

Variety: Micro O Mintmark   VAM 3

PUP: Mintmark

URS-5 · I-5 · L-5

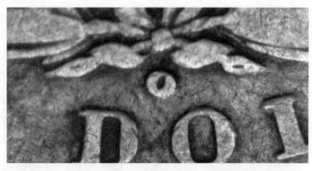

Description: The O mintmark is smaller than the mintmark normally seen.

	VF-20	EF-40	AU-50	MS-60	MS-63	MS-65
VARIETY:	n/a	n/a	n/a	n/a	n/a	n/a
NORMAL:	$12	$14	$15	$24	$37	$152

Comments: This variety has been found to be made from counterfeit dies. Still, it is very popular and collectible among VAM enthusiasts.

Census: 50, 50, 45, 45, 45, 45, 45, 40

1903-S
FS-S1-1903S-002 (011.5)

Variety: Small S Mintmark
VAM 3
PUP: Mintmark
URS-8 · I-5 · L-5

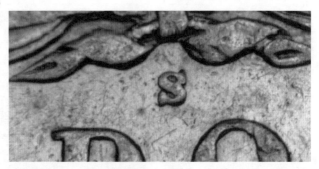

Description: The S mintmark is smaller than usual.

	VF-20	EF-40	AU-50	MS-60	MS-63	MS-65
VARIETY:	$500	$1,500	$4,000	n/a	n/a	n/a
NORMAL:	$90	$213	$1,000	$2,775	$4,750	$7,150

Comments: The S mintmark punched into this die may have been intended for the Barber half dollar series, but it is certainly not the normal mintmark for a Morgan dollar. This is the only known Morgan die with this small mintmark. It is unknown in Mint State. Find one and you can pay for a year of college!

Census: 55, 55, 53, 50, 50, 45, 45, 45

1921-D
FS-S1-1921D-001x

Variety: Double Cud
VAM 1x
PUP: Obverse at K-10
URS-1 · I-5 · L-5

Description: A double die break is evident above the E and P on E PLURIBUS UNUM. The breaks have progressed to the point where they have joined. In addition to the double die break, there is a pre-break die crack extending from the rim at K-7, through two stars, then back to the rim at K-6.

	VF-20	EF-40	AU-50	MS-60	MS-63	MS-65
VARIETY:	n/a	n/a	n/a	n/a	n/a	n/a
NORMAL:	$10	$11	$12	$29	$50	$240

Comments: A large die break of this magnitude, commonly referred to as a *cud*, is extremely rare on a Morgan dollar. To have a Morgan dollar with two die breaks is exponentially rarer. Only one specimen is known to date. The die crack may have progressed to a cud, with the die being removed from service afterward. No sales records exist for this coin.

Census: 45

Peace Dollars, 1921–1935

The Peace dollar series has been greatly overlooked until recently; however, there are many very interesting die varieties in this short and relatively inexpensive series. Both the Peace and Morgan dollar varieties are classified as VAMs, an acronym derived from the first letters of the last names of Leroy Van Allen and George Mallis, the two gentlemen who first popularized the varieties of the series.

VAMs are collected by thousands of enthusiasts. Often, a silver dollar valued

at less than $20 could in fact be worth several thousand dollars because of some minor, yet very rare, abnormality. A variation might be a die chip, an image from one side lightly visible on the other, a doubled or tripled die, a repunched mintmark or date, or even a slight die gouge. There are even some dramatic overdates.

In the *Cherrypickers' Guide*, third edition, there was only one listing for Peace dollars. We have expanded the listings in this volume to 20 varieties, all of which are very popular. We are grateful to Jeff Oxman, "Mr. VAM," for these new listings and their descriptions. Jeff is one of the true gentlemen of numismatics who is always willing to help promote the educational aspects of coin collecting.

In addition, in the Morgan dollar and Peace dollar sections we have included a condition census for each listing. These notations give the known grades of the top examples of the variety and help to emphasize its rarity. Having this information helps the collector find those examples that are true rarities.

Clubs and Educational Information

For those interested in learning more about the varieties of Peace dollars, we highly recommend membership in the Society of Silver Dollar Collectors (SSDC). The club has a web site at www.vamlink.com, or you may write to

SSDC
Jeff Oxman
P.O. Box 2123
North Hills CA 91393-0123
Email: ssdc@vamlink.com

1921
FS-S1-1921-1003

Variety: Line through L
PUP: Ray through DOLLAR
URS-7 · I-5 · L-5

VAM 3

Description: The ray that runs across the first L in DOLLAR cuts through the L, rather than appearing behind it.

	EF-40	AU-50	MS-60	MS-63	MS-65
VARIETY:	$150	$200	$300	$500	$2,750
NORMAL:	$97	$115	$179	$320	$1,875

Comments: Because of the unusual nature of the design change, this new discovery often attracts a lot of attention.

Census: 65, 65, 65, 65, 64, 63, 63, 63

1922
FS-S1-1922-001f

Variety: Die Break in Field
PUP: Field above DOLLAR
URS-5 · I-4 · L-4

VAM 1F

Description: A die break is evident in the field above DOLLAR

	EF-40	AU-50	MS-60	MS-63	MS-65
VARIETY:	$150	$350	$750	$1,500	n/a
NORMAL:	$10	$11	$15	$26	$120

Comments: This variety has turned out to be much rarer than previously thought, and is very scarce in grades above EF. Therefore, as soon as the occasional specimen enters the market, collectors rush to buy it. Prices have risen to reflect its popularity.

Census: 63, 62, 62, 58, 58, 55, 45

1922

FS-S1-1922-002a

Variety: Ear Ring

VAM 2A

PUP: Area at ear

URS-8 · I-5 · L-5

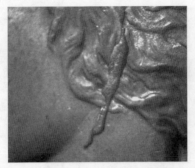 

Description: A major die break is located near Liberty's ear, dangling down to the neck.

	EF-40	AU-50	MS-60	MS-63	MS-65
VARIETY:	$100	$150	$350	$1,000	n/a
NORMAL:	$10	$11	$15	$26	$120

Comments: The whimsically named variety is listed in the *Official Guide to the Top 50 Peace Dollar Varieties*. It is one of the largest Peace dollar die breaks known and is highly sought after.

Census: 64, 64, 63, 63, 63, 63, 63, 63

1922

FS-S1-1922-002c

Variety: Extra Hair

VAM 2C

PUP: Die break at lower hair on obverse

URS-8 · I-5 · L-5

Description: An irregular line of raised metal runs along the back of Liberty's hair.

	EF-40	AU-50	MS-60	MS-63	MS-65
VARIETY:	$75	$125	$200	$350	n/a
NORMAL:	$10	$11	$15	$26	$120

Comments: As is true for other die breaks, several different die states are known and all are desirable. This VAM is also listed in the *Official Guide to the Top 50 Peace Dollar Varieties*.

Census: 65, 64, 64, 64, 64, 63, 63, 63

1922

FS-S1-1922-005a

Variety: Scar Cheek   VAM 5A
PUP: Die break at cheek level with mouth
URS-7 · I-5 · L-5

Description: Liberty's cheek shows a raised, almost triangular, chunk of metal along a vertical break in the die. The reverse is a lightly tripled.

	EF-40	AU-50	MS-60	MS-63	MS-65
VARIETY:	$75	$150	$300	$600	n/a
NORMAL:	$10	$11	$15	$26	$120

Comments: Originally listed as VAM 2G, this so-called Scar Cheek variety is popular and very scarce in Uncirculated grades.

Census: 64, 63, 63, 62, 61, 60, 58,·50

1922

FS-S1-1922-012a

Variety: Moustache   VAM 12A
PUP: Cheek
URS-8 · I-5 · L-5

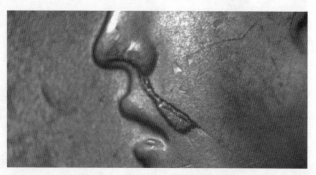

Description: A die break is evident on the cheek, level with the mouth.

	EF-40	AU-50	MS-60	MS-63	MS-65
VARIETY:	$100	$150	$300	$500	n/a
NORMAL:	$10	$11	$15	$26	$120

Comments: Originally listed as VAM 2B, this popular item is among the top five Peace dollar varieties and is listed in the *Official Guide to the Top 50 Peace Dollar Varieties.*

Census: 64, 64, 64, 63, 63, 63, 63, 63

1922

FS-S1-1922-401

Variety: High Relief – Design of 1921

VAM—N/A

PUP: Date

URS-1 · I-5 · L-5+

Description: The high relief on the date shows a 9 more closed than that of the regular 1922 specimens; the 2s of the date have curled bases. On the reverse, there is a distinct additional ray above the N in ONE.

	EF-40	AU-50	MS-60	MS-63	MS-65
VARIETY:	n/a	n/a	n/a	n/a	n/a
NORMAL:	$10	$11	$15	$26	$120

Comments: The existence of a 1922 Peace dollar with high relief design has long been the subject of journal articles and conversations among specialists. This is likely one of the rarer U.S. coins known to date. No sales records exist.

Census: Unique: NGC Photoproof AU-55, ID-1625701-001.

1923

FS-S1-1923-001a

Variety: Whisker Jaw

VAM 1A

PUP: Cheek and jaw

URS-9 · I-5 · L-5

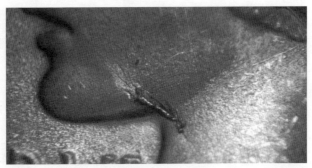

Description: A die break is evident bridging Liberty's cheek and jaw.

	EF-40	AU-50	MS-60	MS-63	MS-65
VARIETY:	$50	$75	$150	$250	$500
NORMAL:	$10	$11	$15	$26	$120

Comments: This is one of the more popular Peace dollar varieties, and is available in Mint State with little searching.

Census: 66, 65, 65, 65, 65, 65, 64, 64

1923
FS-S1-1923-001b

Variety: Extra Hair VAM 1B
PUP: Hair near nape of neck
URS-8 · I-5 · L-5

Description: A significant die break is visible in Liberty's hair running diagonally across the strands of hair. Die breaks may also be evident toward the back of Liberty's hair.

	EF-40	AU-50	MS-60	MS-63	MS-65
VARIETY:	$75	$125	$225	$350	n/a
NORMAL:	$10	$11	$15	$26	$120

Comments: This VAM is listed in the *Official Guide to the Top 50 Peace Dollar Varieties*.

Census: 64, 64, 64, 64, 63, 63, 63, 62

1923
FS-S1-1923-001c

Variety: Die Break (Tail on O of DOLLAR) VAM 1C
PUP: O of DOLLAR
URS-6 · I-5 · L-5

Description: A die break is evident trailing from the O of DOLLAR.

	EF-40	AU-50	MS-60	MS-63	MS-65
VARIETY:	$250	$500	$1,000	n/a	n/a
NORMAL:	$10	$11	$15	$26	$120

Comments: This variety is exceedingly rare in any grade!

Census: 62, 61, 60, 55, 45, 30, 30

1923

FS-S1-1923-001d

Variety: Whisker Cheek
PUP: Cheek by nose and mouth
URS-8 · I-5 · L-5

VAM 1D

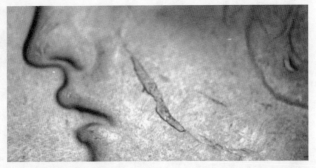

Description: The die break runs down Liberty's cheek toward the junction of the chin and necks.

	EF-40	AU-50	MS-60	MS-63	MS-65
VARIETY:	$75	$125	$300	$600	n/a
NORMAL:	$10	$11	$15	$26	$120

Comments: Bill Fivaz discovered this variety almost three decades ago. It is a favorite with specialists, and is listed in the *Official Guide to the Top 50 Peace Dollar Varieties*.

Census: 64, 63, 63, 63, 63, 62, 62

1923

FS-S1-1923-002

Variety: Doubled Die Obverse (Double Tiara)
PUP: Rays of tiara
URS-8 · I-5 · L-5

VAM 2VAM 1D

Description: The DDO is most evident in the wide spread on the rays of Liberty's tiara, especially those under the BER of LIBERTY.

	EF-40	AU-50	MS-60	MS-63	MS-65
VARIETY:	$20	$35	$45	$125	$300
NORMAL:	$10	$11	$15	$26	$120

Comments: This VAM is listed in the *Official Guide to the Top 50 Peace Dollar Varieties*.

Census: 66, 65, 64, 64, 63, 63, 63, 62

1923-S

Variety: Pitted Reverse
PUP: O of DOLLAR
URS-7 · I-5 · L-5

VAM 1C

Description: Pitting runs from the eagle's back tail-feathers, just to the right of the mintmark, upward to the N in ONE.

	EF-40	AU-50	MS-60	MS-63	MS-65
VARIETY:	$30	$50	$75	$150	n/a
NORMAL:	$10	$11	$22	$60	$4,325

Comments: This is the most important Pitted Reverse variety in the Peace dollar series and is listed in the *Official Guide to the Top 50 Peace Dollar Varieties*.

Census: 64, 64, 63, 63, 63, 63, 62, 60

1924

Variety: Broken Wing
PUP: Eagle's wing
URS-9 · I-5 · L-5

VAM 5A

Description: The die break runs down and across the entire width of the eagle's back.

	EF-40	AU-50	MS-60	MS-63	MS-65
VARIETY:	$75	$125	$225	$350	n/a
NORMAL:	$10	$11	$16	$30	$140

Comments: This die break is incredible to behold. Most would consider it one of the premier Peace dollar varieties. It is listed in the *Official Guide to the Top 50 Peace Dollar Varieties*.

Census: 65, 64, 64, 63, 63, 63, 62, 62

1925

FS-S1-1925-005

Variety: Missing Ray   VAM 5
PUP: Field between eagle's wing and talon
URS-8 · I-5 · L-4

Description: The partially effaced remains of bold clash marks are showing, but the topmost internal ray is missing.

	EF-40	AU-50	MS-60	MS-63	MS-65
VARIETY:	$25	$50	$80	$125	$300
NORMAL:	$10	$11	$15	$27	$128

Comments: This over-polished reverse is a unique variety type among Peace dollars. It fascinates collectors and is listed in the *Official Guide to the Top 50 Peace Dollar Varieties*.

Census: 66, 64, 64, 64, 64, 64, 63, 63

1926-S

FS-S1-1926S-004

Variety: Dot   VAM 4
PUP: Field below olive leaves
URS-8 · I-5 · L-5

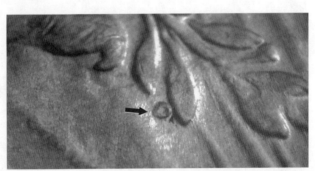

Description: A raised circular dot of metal appears just to the left of the bottom olive leaf.

	EF-40	AU-50	MS-60	MS-63	MS-65
VARIETY:	$20	$40	$65	$125	n/a
NORMAL:	$12	$15	$29	$71	$650

Comments: Listed in the *Official Guide to the Top 50 Peace Dollar Varieties*, this VAM is also known as the Extra Berry variety. There is nothing else like it in the series!

Census: 64, 64, 64, 64, 64, 63, 63, 63

1927-S

FS-S1-1927S-301

Variety: RPM S Over S North
VAM 4
PUP: Mintmark
URS-3 · I-5 · L-5

Description: The secondary S is slightly skewed counter-clockwise and overlaps the primary S. Doubling is most evident in the upper serif of the S.

	EF-40	AU-50	MS-60	MS-63	MS-65
VARIETY:	$45	$95	$150	$400	n/a
NORMAL:	$22	$58	$108	$300	$7,550

Comments: Until this S Over S mintmark was reported to us in December of 1997, we were unaware of the variety. The specimen examined was Mint State, but others have now been reported.

Census: 63

1928-S

S-S1-1928S-003

Variety: Doubled Die Obverse
VAM 3
PUP: WE TRUST
URS-8 · I-5 · L-5

Description: Strong doubling is evident on the OD of GOD, on WE, and on the TR of TRUST. Doubling is also evident on the right-most rays of the tiara, the designer's initials (AF), and some of the hair toward the right side of the coin.

	EF-40	AU-50	MS-60	MS-63	MS-65
VARIETY:	$50	$75	$175	$500	n/a
NORMAL:	$33	$49	$121	$440	$13,850

Comments: Although not rare, its "wow factor" makes this a popular variety. The VAM 3 should not be confused with the very similar VAM 4, on which the mintmark is higher than normal. The VAM 3 is listed in the *Official Guide to the Top 50 Peace Dollar Varieties*.

Census: 64, 63, 63, 63, 63, 63, 63, 63

1934-D
FS-S1-1934D-003

Variety: DDO, Medium D
PUP: WE TRUST, profile, mintmark
URS-11 · I-5 · L-5

VAM 3

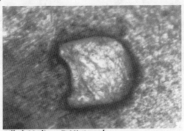 

Filled, Medium D Mintmark

Description: Doubling is evident on most letters of IN GOD WE TRUST, on Liberty's profile, and on some of the rays on the right side of the coin. The reverse exhibits a filled medium D mintmark.

	EF-40	AU-50	MS-60	MS-63	MS-65
VARIETY:	$25	$50	$100	$400	$1,750
NORMAL:	$17	$34	$85	$292	$1,400

Comments: This VAM 3 is somewhat common, but the wonderful doubled die adds some value. The same doubled die is paired with a small D mintmark in the next listing, which is considerably rarer.

Census: 66, 66, 66, 65, 65, 64, 64, 64

1934-D
FS-S1-1934D-004

Variety: DDO, Small D
PUP: WE TRUST of the motto, mintmark
URS-7 · I-5 · L-5

VAM 4

Clear, Small D Mintmark

Description: The obverse die exhibits strong doubling on most letters of IN GOD WE TRUST, the rays on the right, and especially on Liberty's profile. The mintmark on the reverse die is a small D, shaped much like that of the 1920s-era D punches.

	EF-40	AU-50	MS-60	MS-63	MS-65
VARIETY:	$125	$250	$750	$1,500	n/a
NORMAL:	$17	$34	$85	$292	$1,400

Comments: This VAM is quite rare and in very high demand by specialists.

Census: 64, 63, 63, 62, 62, 62, 60, 58

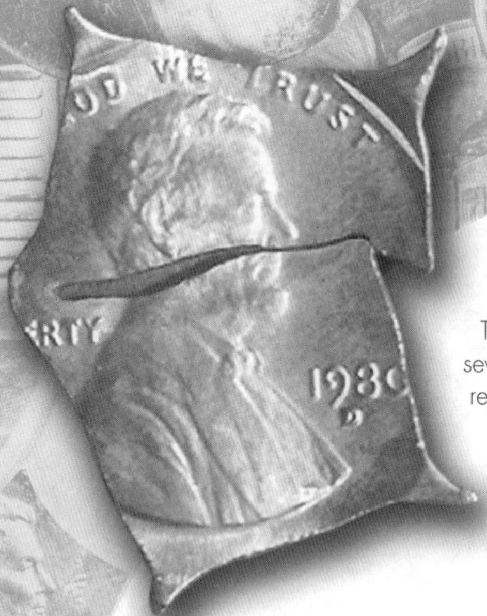

The error coin shown here sold
several years ago. I am looking to
replace it and other major errors.

Best Variety

Sportcards & Coins

My 52nd Year Dealing With Major Errors

- I have regular coins, too! And major error sports cards.
- Buyer and seller of multiple types of errors on the same coin.

Questions about coins or bills you have? Contact me!
My web site is under construction (soon to be: Bestvarietycoinerrors.com).
Snail mail is just fine (include a First Class stamp to receive a reply).
Be patient as I am a one-man store.

626-914-2273

Feel confident; I'm an expert in this field.
I am a Life Member of ANA (#2814), CONECA (#51), NASC, and CSNA.

*Visiting
Southern
California?
Stop in to my
custom-built
storefront.*

Best Variety, 358 W. Foothill Blvd, Glendora, CA 91741

(North of 210 Freeway. Exit Grand Ave. Go north past Route 66, up to Foothill Blvd.
Turn right and you're almost there.)

Modern Dollars

Eisenhower Dollars, 1971–1978
Susan B. Anthony Dollars, 1979–1981 and 1999
Sacagawea Dollars, 2000 to Date

Because of modern changes in the die making process in the United States Mint, very few significant varieties are known in these series, which began with the Eisenhower dollar in 1971. However, those that are known are generally in very high demand, especially those with a visually attractive difference. Many minor varieties are known, mostly in the Eisenhower series.

Eisenhower dollars are known with somewhat strong obverse and reverse doubled dies, and a couple repunched mintmarks. The Susan B. Anthony series contains a slight change in the obverse design (in 1979), changes in the mintmarks (in 1979 and 1981), and a repunched mintmark for the 1980-S Proof. Another variety for the Sacagawea dollar is known; it appears on the reverse, with lines of an unknown origin appearing to breach the breast of the eagle.

To date, only the Eisenhower dollar has been the topic of reference books. However, the Red Book (*A Guide Book of United States Coins*) offers additional information not contained elsewhere.

Clubs and Educational Information

As of this publication date, there are no clubs devoted strictly to the study of Eisenhower, Susan B. Anthony, and Sacagawea dollars, yet these series hold a number of nice varieties and are popular among collectors. For those interested primarily in the varieties within the series, we would suggest membership in CONECA, the national error and variety club. Each issue of their bi-monthly publication, the *Errorscope*, contains articles on errors and varieties of all type, and even from other countries. An application is available online at www.conecaonline.org/join, or by contacting Paul Funaiole at

CONECA
Paul Funaiole, Membership
35 Leavitt Lane
Glenburn ME 04401-1013

1971-S, PROOF — FS-S1-1971S-103 (015.8)

Variety: Doubled Die Obverse
CONECA 3-O-V
PUP: IN GOD WE TRUST
URS-4 · I-4 · L-3

Description: Strong doubling is evident on IN GOD WE TRUST, the date, and LIBER of LIBERTY.

	PF-63	PF-65	PF-66	PF-67
VARIETY:	$125	$250	$300	$450
NORMAL:	$8	$10	$11	$12

Comments: This obverse is also paired with a minor doubled die reverse.

1971-S, PROOF — FS-S1-1971S-106

Variety: Doubled Die Obverse
CONECA—Unknown
PUP: IN GOD WE TRUST
URS-4 · I-4 · L-3

Description: *Very* strong doubling is evident on IN GOD WE TRUST, the date, and LIBERTY.

	PF-63	PF-65	PF-66	PF-67
VARIETY:	$125	$250	$300	$450
NORMAL:	$8	$10	$11	$12

Comments: This listing is every bit as nice as the previous.

1971-S, MINT STATE, 40% SILVER   FS-S1-1971S-50

Variety: Repunched Mintmark   CONECA RPM 1
PUP: Mintmark
URS-6 · I-4 · L-4

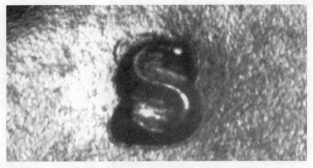

Description: A secondary S is evident protruding northwest of the primary S.

	MS-65	MS-66	MS-67
VARIETY:	$200	$350	$500
NORMAL:	$13	$30	$280

Comments: This is one of fewer than a half dozen RPMs known for the entire series.

1971-S, MINT STATE, 40% SILVER   FS-S1-1971S-401

Variety: Polished Die   CONECA—N/L
PUP: R of LIBERTY
URS-6 · I-4 · L-4

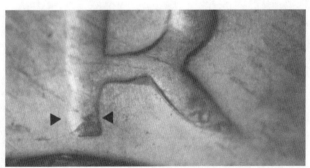

Description: The left leg on the R of LIBERTY has been over polished.

	MS-65	MS-66	MS-67
VARIETY:	$200	$350	$500
NORMAL:	$13	$30	$280

Comments: Affectionately referred to as the "pegleg" R.

1972-S, PROOF   FS-S1-1972S-101

Variety: Doubled Die Obverse   **CONECA—Unknown**
PUP: IN GOD WE TRUST
URS-5 · I-3 · L-3

Description: A medium spread can be detected on IN GOD WE TRUST, LIBERTY, and slightly on the date.

	PF-65	PF-66	PF-67
VARIETY:	$100	$150	$250
NORMAL:	$14	$18	$25

Comments: This is another exciting doubled die for which to search.

1973-S, PROOF, 40% SILVER   FS-S1-1973S-101

Variety: Doubled Die Obverse   **CONECA—Unknown**
PUP: IN GOD WE TRUST
URS-5 · I-3 · L-3

Description: A medium spread can be detected on IN GOD WE TRUST, LIBERTY, and slightly on the date.

	PF-65	PF-66	PF-67
VARIETY:	$150	$200	$300
NORMAL:	$14	$18	$25

Comments: This is another exciting doubled-die Eisenhower dollar for which to search.

1979-P FS-C1-1979P-301 (016)

Variety: Wide Rim (Near Date) CONECA—N/L
PUP: Date
URS-11 · I-4 · L-3

Wide Rim (Near Date) *Narrow Rim (Far Date)*

Description: The rim on some later 1979-P SBA dollars is wider than on original issues, making the date appear to be closer to the rim.

	MS-65	MS-66	MS-67
VARIETY:	$115	$320	$800
NORMAL:	$1	$20	$240

Comments: This variety, created in 1979 by a slight design alteration, carries the nickname "near date."

1979-S, PROOF FS-C1-1979S-501

Variety: Type II Mintmark CONECA—N/L
PUP: Mintmark
URS-9 · I-5 · L-5

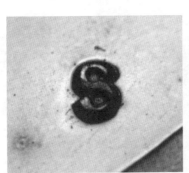

Rare "Type II" Mintmark *Common "Type I" Mintmark*

Description: The S mintmark punch was changed in 1979 to create a clearer S mintmark punch.

	PF-65	PF-66	PF-67	PF-68
VARIETY:	$82	$83	$85	$88
NORMAL:	$10	$11	$12	$14

Comments: The Type II mintmark is far rarer than the Type I. Any 1979-S Proof set in which all six coins bear the Type II mintmark is extremely rare and will command a higher value than six individual coins.

1980-S, PROOF

FS-C1-1980S-501

Variety: Repunched Mintmark
PUP: Mintmark
URS-3 · I-4 · L-4

CONECA—N/L

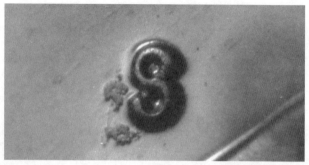

Description: The remnants of a previously punched S appear left of the primary S.

	PF-65	PF-66	PF-67	PF-68
VARIETY:	$300	$350	$400	$500
NORMAL:	$8	$9	$11	$13

Comments: Very few specimens of this variety have surfaced to date.

1981-S, PROOF

FS-C1-1981S-501

Variety: Type II Mintmark
PUP: Mintmark
URS-8 · I-5 · L-5

CONECA—N/L

Rare Type II Mintmark   Common Type I Mintmark

Description: The S-mintmark punch was changed in 1981 to create a clearer S-mintmark punch. The Type II mintmark for 1981 appears to have a flat spot on the top left of the upper loop, while the mintmark on the Type I is rounded.

	PF-65	PF-66	PF-67	PF-68
VARIETY:	$82	$83	$85	$88
NORMAL:	$10	$11	$12	$14

Comments: As with the 1979 Proof set, any 1981-S set with all six coins bearing the Type II mintmark is very rare and will command a higher value than six individual coins.

2000-P

FS-S1-2000P-901

Variety: Reverse Die Aberrations
PUP: Eagle's breast
URS-6 · I-4 · L-4

CONECA—N/L

Description: There are two spikes appearing through the breast of the eagle on the reverse.

	MS-65	MS-66	MS-67	MS-68
VARIETY:	n/a	n/a	n/a	n/a
NORMAL:	$10	$11	$12	$13

Comments: Some collectors have nicknamed this variety the "speared eagle."

2000-P

FS-C1-2000P-901

Variety: Enhanced Reverse Die
PUP: Tail Feathers
URS-14 · I-5 · L-5

Normal Feathers　　　　　*Enhanced Feathers*

Description: The feathers of the eagle are greatly enhanced, as evidenced in the photos.

	MS-65	MS-67
VARIETY:	n/a	n/a
NORMAL:	$3	$8

Comments: This variety is affectionately known as the "Cheerios" variety, as it was included as a promotion in boxes of Cheerios cereal. Values for these have not settled.

Your Rare Coins — ICG's Rare Talent
A Winning Combination!!

Keith Love
ICG's Senior Grader

Keith has been in the rare coin business for more than 20 years as a top wholesaler, PCGS grader, and finally ICG's founder and CEO. Keith co-created and has taught the ANA Advanced Coin Grading class for more than five years. The ANA calls Keith "A renowned expert."

J. P. Martin
ICG's Senior Numismatist

J.P. has been involved in the coin industry for more than 25 years. He worked at the ANA as a grader, authenticator and numismatist for almost 15 years. J.P. has written two ANA correspondence courses on grading and authenticating, starred in the ANA educational videos on grading and authenticating, and taught counterfeit detection to a number of Secret Service agents. J.P. is a rare coin genius.

Michael Fahey
ICG's Senior Numismatist

Michael has spent 25 years at ANACS and has been a grader at a third-party service longer than anyone in history. Michael is a columnist for *Coin World*, has written for The Numismatist, and has authored ANA Counterfeit Detection reports. Michael rejoins J.P. Martin as the two worked together for years at ANACS in Colorado Springs.

Walt Armitage
ICG's Senior Grader

Walt began his coin career more than 25 years ago. In addition to operating his own successful rare coin business, Walt has spent ten years grading at ICG and PCGS and set up the World Coin Grading program at both services. An ICG founder, Walt is one of the most respected numismatists in the world.

Larry Wilson
ICG Grader

Larry has more than 30 years experience in the rare coin industry. Working with Keith Love as a rare coin wholesaler, Larry has become one of the most educated numismatists in the country. Specializing in U.S. Type and Gold, Larry has served as a mentor to many of today's successful rare coin dealers.

James Davis
ICG Grader

Jim started collecting coins 35 years ago and soon figured out he had a true knack for the hobby and started buying and selling coins for profit. He is an ANA Life Member and took his first classes on grading and authenticating coins at the ANA in the early Eighties. He is the founder of the South Bay Coin Club and before joining ICG was the owner of four coin shops in Southern California. Davis enjoys error coins and is an expert in all U.S. coins.

Cameron Kiefer
ICG Grader

Cameron is a former Young Numismatist (YN) of the Year, the American Numismatic Association's (ANA) highest award, given annually to the most outstanding numismatist 21 years of age or younger. He is an active coin grading instructor at The ANA Summer Seminar and at many coin conventions. Cameron is certainly an up-in-coming star at ICG and in the numismatic world.

Sue Berg
ICG Grader

Sue has been in the rare coin business for seven years. Keith Love describes Sue as having "a discerning eye and great work ethic." Sue, a Colorado native, has been promoted more than anyone in ICG's history and is one of our most valued employees.

INDEPENDENT
COIN GRADING COMPANY
877-221-4424
customersatisfaction@icgcoin.com
www.icgcoin.com

COLLECTORS AND DEALERS REGISTER WITH ICG TO SUBMIT COINS!

Sign-up today and receive a certificate for 5 FREE coin grades (when submitting an additional 5 coins at ICG's regular 15-Day service) and a Submission Kit. All this for only $15 and you'll receive a $15 credit towards your first order. (So essentially it's FREE!)

☑ **YES** *Sign Me Up Now.* I'm a ❑ **Collector** ❑ **Dealer**   CV

Three Ways for You to Sign-Up:
1. E-mail this information to Paul at customersatisfaction@icgcoin.com
2. Fax this completed form to 303-221-5524
3. Mail this completed form to: ICG, 7901 E. Belleview, Suite 50 Englewood, CO 80111-6010

E-mail_____
Your email address allows ICG to alert you about sales & specials!
Name_____
Address_____
City_____ State_____ Zip+4_____
Phone (____)_____ Fax (____)_____
❑ VISA ❑ MasterCard ❑ AmEx ❑ Check
Card #_____ Exp. Date_____
Signature_____

Gold Coin Varieties

When considering gold varieties of any denomination, keep in mind one of our Helpful Hints: "A good point to remember and consider is that, generally speaking, as the numismatic value of a coin increases, the premium one might expect associated with that variety will go down."

If you will, compare these two coins: an 1888 Liberty Head $20 gold piece featuring a doubled reverse die, and a 1943-S Washington quarter exhibiting a doubled obverse die. Both show dramatic doubling of the images. Yet the 1888 Liberty Head $20 DDR will command little if any premium for a knowledgeable enthusiast, while the 1943-S quarter with the DDO will command a hefty premium.

The 1888 Liberty Head $20 coin is listed with a value of $605 in AU-50, a common grade for the coin. The listed price for the doubled reverse die is $625, virtually the same as the normal coin. The 1943-S Washington quarter is listed at $46 in MS-65. The same coin with a doubled obverse die is listed at $1,500 in MS-65. That represents a premium of $1,454, or a 3,161% premium for the doubled die.

The 1888 Liberty Head $20 piece has a total mintage of 226,161. Base upon average die-life estimates, there would have been about six to 10 reverse dies used for the entire mintage. Using those estimates, the 1888 Liberty Head $20 coin with the doubled reverse die would make up at least 10% of the total mintage.

The 1943-S Washington quarter has a total mintage of 21,700,000. Based upon average die-life estimates, there would have been about 434 obverse dies used for the entire mintage. Using those estimates, the 1943-S Washington quarter with the doubled obverse die would make up less than 4% of the total mintage.

There is also another consideration when comparing mintage estimates. During the time of gold coin production, the dies were not inspected very closely for abnormalities. Therefore, a doubled die in 1943 was more likely to be pulled from service than in 1888.

The important factor to consider is the percent of the total population having the die abnormality. The higher that percentage, the lower any premium percentage one might expect. This same analogy will hold true for commemorative coins, and any other coinage with a low regular-issue mintage.

One last comment: many of the gold varieties will bring a small premium in lower grades. However, as the value of the normal coin reaches higher, any premium will soon evaporate.

With a very few exceptions, a doubled die, repunched mintmark, or overdate on a gold coin is less likely to command any premium over the value of the normal coin.

1854, TYPE 2 — FS-G1-1854-1101

Variety: Doubled Die Obverse
PUP: UNITED STATES OF AMERICA
URS-9 · I-3 · L-2

CONECA—N/L

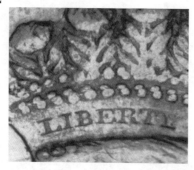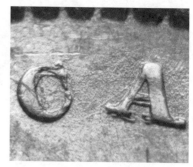

Description: Very strong doubling is evident on UNITED STATES OF AMERICA, the beads in the head-dress, the feathers, and portions of LIBERTY. Strong clash marks on the reverse are evident on the specimens we've seen.

	VF-20	EF-40	AU-50	MS-60	MS-63
VARIETY:	$300	$400	$550	$2,300	$9,150
NORMAL:	$260	$379	$492	$2,225	$9,150

Comments: A slight premium can be expected for the lower grades.

1854, TYPE 2 — FS-G1-1854-1301

Variety: Repunched Date
PUP: Date
URS-7 · I-3 · L-2

CONECA—N/L

Description: Secondary date digits are evident, with the secondary 1 slightly north of the primary, and the secondary 8, 5, and 4 slightly right of the primary.

	VF-20	EF-40	AU-50	MS-60	MS-63
VARIETY:	$300	$400	$550	$2,300	$9,150
NORMAL:	$260	$379	$492	$2,225	$9,150

Comments: The doubling visible on the word DOLLAR is the typical doubling known for Longacre's designs, such as Indian cents, Shield nickels, and others. This is not the result of a doubled die.

1856-S, TYPE 2 — FS-G1-1856S-501

CONECA—N/L

Variety: Repunched Mintmark
PUP: Mintmark
URS-10 · I-2 · L-2

Description: This bold repunched mintmark exhibits the secondary S wide to the northeast of the primary S.

	VF-20	EF-40	AU-50	MS-60	MS-63
VARIETY:	$750	$1,300	$1,975	$3,125	$6,375
NORMAL:	$750	$1,300	$1,975	$3,125	$6,375

Comments: Due to this being a better date and a more expensive coin, very little premium might be expected for this variety. Additionally, a larger percentage of the surviving coins of this date and mint would likely be this RPM.

1862, TYPE 3 — FS-G1-1862-101 (G-001)

CONECA—N/L

Variety: Doubled Die Obverse
PUP: UNITED STATES OF AMERICA
URS-7 · I-3 · L-2

Description: Doubling is evident on the entire obverse, including UNITED STATES OF AMERICA and the entire profile of Lady Liberty, most evident of which are the tops of the hair curls and the feathers.

	VF-20	EF-40	AU-50	MS-60	MS-63
VARIETY:	$175	$200	$225	$300	$850
NORMAL:	$130	$155	$170	$225	$800

Comments: Due to this being a better date and a more expensive coin, very little premium might be expected for this variety. Additionally, a larger percentage of the surviving coins of this date and mint would likely be this RPM.

1851

FS-G2.5-1851-301

Variety: Repunched Date
PUP: Date
URS-6 · I-3 · L-2

CONECA—N/L

Description: A secondary 1 is visible west of the primary first 1, and at the base slightly north on the second 1.

	VF-20	EF-40	AU-50	MS-60	MS-63
VARIETY:	$200	$250	$300	$350	$1,400
NORMAL:	$162	$190	$195	$300	$1,250

Comments: Being one of the more common dates, this variety may bring slight premiums, especially in the better "collector" grades below MS-63.

1853

FS-G2.5-1853-301

Variety: Repunched Date
PUP: Date
URS-7 · I-3 · L-2

CONECA—N/L

Description: A secondary 1 is evident slightly north on the primary 1, and the upper loop of a secondary 8 is barely visible within the upper loop of the primary 8.

	VF-20	EF-40	AU-50	MS-60	MS-63
VARIETY:	$200	$250	$300	$350	$1,400
NORMAL:	$162	$190	$195	$300	$1,125

Comments: Repunched dates are known throughout all gold coins of the 19th century.

1854-O

FS-G2.5-1854o-301 (G-002)

Variety: Misplaced Date
PUP: Date
URS-7 · I-3 · L-2

CONECA—N/L

Description: The 4 is repunched, with just an upright of a secondary 4 evident right of the primary 4. Additionally, the tip of the crosslet of a 4 is evident protruding from the bust, just below the lower hair curl.

	VF-20	EF-40	AU-50	MS-60
VARIETY:	$225	$250	$400	$1,500
NORMAL:	$190	$204	$350	$1,450

Comments: The values for this overdate represent an exception to the rule that gold varieties don't command much premium.

1862, 2 OVER 1

FS-G2.5-1862-301 (G-002)

Variety: Overdate 2 Over 1
PUP: Date
URS-5 · I-3 · L-2

CONECA—N/L

Description: This overdate exhibits a 2 over a 1. The 1 is evident between the ball of the 2 and the lower left leg.

	VF-20	EF-40	AU-50	MS-60	MS-63
VARIETY:	$1,000	$2,225	$3,250	$7,000	$29,250
NORMAL:	$205	$260	$492	$1,050	$3,125

Comments: The values for this overdate represent an exception to the rule that gold varieties don't command much premium.

1891
FS-G2.5-1891-801

Variety: Doubled Die Reverse
CONECA—N/L

PUP: AMERICA

URS-6 · I-3 · L-2

Description: Doubling is evident on most reverse elements, especially on the lower right side. The doubling is especially strong on AMERICA, the arrow tips, the eagle's claw, and the feathers.

	VF-20	EF-40	AU-50	MS-60	MS-63
VARIETY:	$250	$300	$350	$500	$1,400
NORMAL:	$175	$196	$233	$340	$1,125

Comments: This is a really dramatic doubled die! Possibly, most if not all of the 1891 quarter eagles exhibit this doubled die.

1882
FS-G3-1882-301

Variety: Repunched Date
CONECA—N/L

PUP: Date

URS-7 · I-3 · L-2

Description: A secondary 2 is evident north of the primary 2. This secondary 2 has obviously been polished, with only the right portion of the upper loop and the base visible.

	VF-20	EF-40	AU-50	MS-60	MS-63
VARIETY:	$660	$945	$1,400	$2,550	$10,500
NORMAL:	$660	$945	$1,400	$2,550	$10,500

Comments: Although this is a very appealing $3 gold variety, very little premium should be expected due to the high value of the "normal" coin.

1802, 2 OVER 1   FS-G5-1802/1-301

Variety: Repunched Date   CONECA—N/L
PUP: Date
URS-10 · I-4 · L-4

Description: The 2 is clearly punched over a 1.

	VF-20	EF-40	AU-50	MS-60	MS-63
VARIETY:	$3,250	$4,500	$6,150	$8,775	$18,850
NORMAL:	$3,250	$4,500	$6,150	$8,775	$18,850

Comments: There were no 1801-dated $5 gold pieces, and all known 1802-dated pieces are the overdate, 2 Over 1.

1819   FS-G5-1819-901

Variety: Repunched Letters   CONECA—N/L
PUP: 5D on reverse
URS-6 · I-3 · L-3

Description: The 5D (for "Five Dollars") on the reverse is listed in most references as 5D/50. The authors believe this is actually a 5D with the D over an inverted D.

	VF-20	EF-40	AU-50	MS-60	MS-63
VARIETY:	n/a	n/a	$36,500	n/a	$93,500
NORMAL:	n/a	$24,500	$36,500	n/a	$93,500

Comments: This reverse variety is actually more common than the 1819 without the repunching of the letter. "Normal" values shown are for the 1819 coin without the repunching.

1847 — FS-G5-1847-301 (G-003)

Variety: Misplaced Date
PUP: Denticles below date
URS-5 · I-3 · L-2

CONECA—N/L

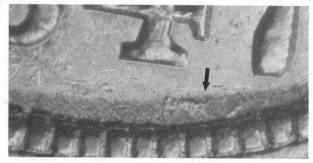

Description: The top of a 7 is clearly evident protruding from the denticles below the 4.

	VF-20	EF-40	AU-50	MS-60	MS-63
VARIETY:	$300	$400	$500	$1,200	$27,000
NORMAL:	$176	$196	$256	$1,200	$27,000

Comments: Remember, the premium will reduce as the normal coin's value increases.

1847 — FS-G5-1847-302 (G-004)

Variety: Misplaced Date
PUP: Front of neck
URS-4 · I-3 · L-2

CONECA—N/L

Description: A misplaced 1 is evident protruding from the front of the neck.

	VF-20	EF-40	AU-50	MS-60	MS-63
VARIETY:	$300	$400	$500	$1,200	$27,000
NORMAL:	$176	$196	$256	$1,200	$27,000

Comments: Remember, the premium will reduce as the normal coin's value increases.

1847 — FS-G5-1847-303

Variety: Repunched Date
PUP: Date
URS-5 · I-3 · L-2

CONECA—N/L

Description: The date is clearly repunched, with a secondary 1 south of the primary 1; the secondary 8 slightly south of the primary 8; and remnants of a secondary 7 far right of the primary 7.

	VF-20	EF-40	AU-50	MS-60	MS-63
VARIETY:	$300	$400	$500	$1,200	$27,000
NORMAL:	$176	$196	$256	$1,200	$27,000

Comments: Further study may prove this to be a triple punched date.

1847 — FS-G5-1847-304

Variety: Misplaced Date
PUP: Base of bust above 1
URS-4 · I-3 · L-2

CONECA—N/L

Description: The base of an errantly placed 1 is evident protruding from the very low, front portion of the bust, immediately above the primary 1.

	VF-20	EF-40	AU-50	MS-60	MS-63
VARIETY:	$300	$400	$500	$1,200	$27,000
NORMAL:	$176	$196	$256	$1,200	$27,000

Comments: This is a fairly new discovery.

1854 — FS-G5-1854-101 (004.5)

Variety: Repunched Date
PUP: Ear
URS-5 · I-3 · L-2

CONECA—N/L

Description: This is a fairly strong doubled die, with the doubling evident on the front hair curl above the ear, and the earlobe.

	VF-20	EF-40	AU-50	MS-60	MS-63
VARIETY:	$300	$400	$500	$1,600	$8,375
NORMAL:	$180	$252	$412	$1,575	$8,375

Comments: This is known as the "Earring" variety.

1881 — FS-G5-1881-301 (005)

Variety: Overdate
PUP: Date
URS-6 · I-3 · L-2

CONECA—N/L

Description: The 1881 date is clearly punched over an 1880 date. From the appearance of the repunching, each date was part of a four-digit logo punch.

	VF-20	EF-40	AU-50	MS-60	MS-63
VARIETY:	$290	$480	$535	$1,175	$2,645
NORMAL:	$163	$172	$188	$213	$820

Comments: This is a fairly well-known variety.

1881 FS-G5-1881-302

Variety: Repunched Date
CONECA—N/L
PUP: Date
URS-7 · I-3 · L-2

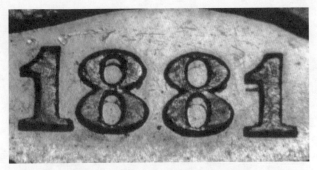

Description: Secondary digits are evident south on both 8's and the final 1.

	VF-20	EF-40	AU-50	MS-60	MS-63
VARIETY:	$200	$250	$300	$350	$900
NORMAL:	$163	$172	$188	$213	$820

Comments: This RPD is very easy to spot.

1881 FS-G5-1881-303

Variety: Repunched Date
CONECA—N/L
PUP: Date
URS-6 · I-3 · L-2

Description: All four secondary digits are evident north of the primary date.

	VF-20	EF-40	AU-50	MS-60	MS-63
VARIETY:	$200	$250	$300	$350	$900
NORMAL:	$163	$172	$188	$213	$820

Comments: This is a very eye-appealing variety.

1881   FS-G5-1881-304

Variety: Repunched Date
PUP: Date
URS-7 · I-3 · L-2

CONECA—N/L

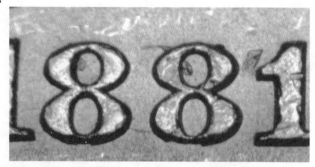

Description: The secondary digits are evident far left of the primary digits.

	VF-20	EF-40	AU-50	MS-60	MS-63
VARIETY:	$200	$250	$300	$350	$900
NORMAL:	$163	$172	$188	$213	$820

Comments: This is another very attractive repunched date.

1881   FS-G5-1881-305

Variety: Repunched Date
PUP: Date
URS-7 · I-3 · L-2

CONECA—N/L

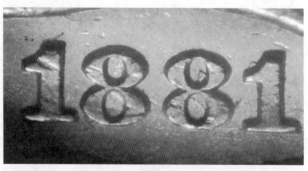

Description: The secondary digits are evident slightly left of the primary digits.

	VF-20	EF-40	AU-50	MS-60	MS-63
VARIETY:	$200	$250	$300	$350	$900
NORMAL:	$163	$172	$188	$213	$820

Comments: The weaker second 8 appears slanted slightly downward.

1899

FS-G5-1899-301

Variety: Repunched Date
CONECA—N/L
PUP: Date
URS-7 · I-3 · L-2

Description: The secondary digits are evident slightly northwest of the primary digits.

	VF-20	EF-40	AU-50	MS-60	MS-63
VARIETY:	$200	$225	$250	$300	$900
NORMAL:	$160	$168	$184	$204	$790

Comments: This is another very attractive repunched date.

1901-S

FS-G5-1901S-301

Variety: Overdate 1 Over 0
CONECA—N/L
PUP: Date
URS-7 · I-3 · L-2

Description: A secondary 0 is evident beneath the last 1 of the date.

	VF-20	EF-40	AU-50	MS-60	MS-63
VARIETY:	$205	$225	$235	$308	$850
NORMAL:	$160	$168	$184	$204	$790

Comments: This is a very eye-appealing overdate and a well-known variety.

1901-S

FS-G5-1901S-501

Variety: Large Over Small Mintmark
PUP: Mintmark
URS-7 · I-3 · L-2

CONECA—N/L

Description: The primary S mintmark is clearly punched over a smaller S.

	VF-20	EF-40	AU-50	MS-60	MS-63
VARIETY:	$200	$250	$300	$350	$900
NORMAL:	$160	$168	$184	$204	$790

Comments: This is a very interesting variety, and not well known.

1905-S

FS-G5-1905S-501

Variety: Misplaced Mintmark
PUP: Mintmark
URS-4 · I-3 · L-3

CONECA—N/L

Description: A secondary S mintmark is evident right of the primary S.

	VF-20	EF-40	AU-50	MS-60	MS-63
VARIETY:	$250	$300	$350	$500	$1,450
NORMAL:	$160	$168	$184	$372	$1,275

Comments: This is a very, very interesting variety.

1906 {FS-G5-1906-301}

Variety: Repunched Date
PUP: Date
URS-7 · I-3 · L-2

CONECA—N/L

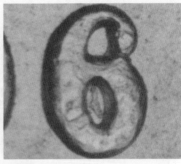

Description: A secondary 6 is evident within the lower loop of the primary 6.

	VF-20	EF-40	AU-50	MS-60	MS-63
VARIETY:	$200	$225	$250	$300	$900
NORMAL:	$160	$168	$184	$204	$790

Comments: An earlier die state specimen may show repunching of the 0 as well.

1911-S {FS-G5-1911S-501}

Variety: Repunched Mintmark
PUP: Mintmark
URS-7 · I-3 · L-2

CONECA—N/L

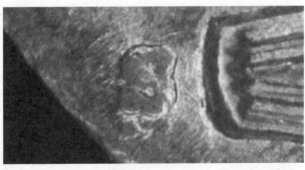

Description: A secondary S is evident south of the primary S.

	VF-20	EF-40	AU-50	MS-60	MS-63
VARIETY:	$300	$350	$400	$500	$2,825
NORMAL:	$254	$273	$284	$425	$2,825

Comments: This variety brings a small premium.

1846-O

FS-G10-1846o-301

Variety: Repunched Date, RPM
PUP: Date, Mintmark
URS-5 · I-3 · L-2

CONECA—N/L

 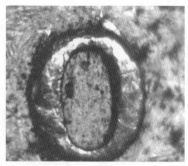

Description: The 6 is slightly repunched, with the secondary 6 visible slightly north of the primary 6. The mintmark is also slightly repunched, with the secondary O evident protruding from the top of the primary O.

	VF-20	EF-40	AU-50	MS-60
VARIETY:	$520	$1,350	$2,775	$13,500
NORMAL:	$520	$1,350	$2,775	$13,500

Comments: This variety is not very dramatic, but interesting.

1854-S

FS-G10-1854S-301

Variety: Misplaced Date
PUP: Area below date
URS-5 · I-3 · L-2

CONECA—N/L

Description: The base of a 1 is evident below the 1 and the 8.

	VF-20	EF-40	AU-50	MS-60
VARIETY:	$325	$400	$925	$8,000
NORMAL:	$308	$372	$925	$8,000

Comments: This MPD is very dramatic!

1883-S   FS-G10-1883S-301

Variety: Misplaced Date   CONECA—N/L
PUP: Denticles below date
URS-7 · I-6 · L-2

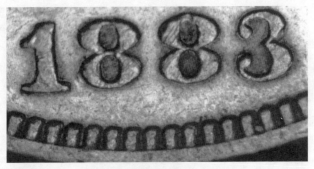

Description: A 3 is visible in the denticles below the date.

	VF-20	EF-40	AU-50	MS-60	MS-63
VARIETY:	$284	$290	$304	$650	$7,450
NORMAL:	$284	$290	$304	$650	$7,450

Comments: This is not a very dramatic MPD.

1889-S   FS-G10-1889S-501

Variety: RPM, DDR   CONECA—N/L
PUP: Mintmark, OF AMERICA
URS-6 · I-3 · L-2

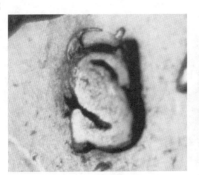 

Description: Doubling on the reverse is most evident on STATES OF AMERICA, WE TRUST, and portions of the ribbon. But the S/S north is the more dramatic of the two diagnostics, with the secondary S strong above the primary S.

	VF-20	EF-40	AU-50	MS-60	MS-63
VARIETY:	$325	$350	$400	$500	$1,500
NORMAL:	$284	$290	$294	$320	$1,200

Comments: The mintmark is the really interesting portion of this variety.

1891-CC

FS-G10-1891CC-501

Variety: Repunched Mintmark
PUP: Mintmark
URS-6 · I-3 · L-2

CONECA—N/L

Description: A secondary C is evident protruding from the right side of the second C of the primary CC mintmark.

	VF-20	EF-40	AU-50	MS-60	MS-63
VARIETY:	$400	$450	$525	$700	$4,675
NORMAL:	$392	$425	$492	$700	$4,675

Comments: Any CC mintmark variety is interesting.

1852

FS-G20-1852-301

Variety: Repunched Date
PUP: Date
URS-7 · I-3 · L-2

CONECA—N/L

Description: The weaker digits of the first date punch are all evident north of the primary digits.

	VF-20	EF-40	AU-50	MS-60	MS-63
VARIETY:	$600	$615	$775	$2,650	$14,550
NORMAL:	$600	$615	$775	$2,650	$14,550

Comments: This is a very evident repunched date.

1853, 3 OVER 2

FS-G20-1853-301 (G-008)

Variety: Overdate
PUP: Date
URS-7 · I-4 · L-4

CONECA—N/L

Description: The 3 of the primary date is punched over a clearly visible 2. There is a rust spot under the R of LIBERTY.

	VF-20	EF-40	AU-50	MS-60	MS-63
VARIETY:	$640	$2,200	$3,350	$33,650	n/a
NORMAL:	$600	$615	$690	$3,850	$36,500

Comments: This is a well-known variety.

1857

FS-G20-1857-301

Variety: Misplaced Date
PUP: Date
URS-6 · I-3 · L-2

CONECA—N/L

Description: What appers to be a 1 is evident protruding from the left side of the 5.

	VF-20	EF-40	AU-50	MS-60	MS-63
VARIETY:	$600	$615	$765	$2,775	$23,500
NORMAL:	$600	$615	$765	$2,775	$23,500

Comments: This is a very interesting variety, with a 1 so far misplaced.

1859-S
FS-G20-1859S-101 (G-011)

Variety: Doubled Die Obverse
CONECA—N/L
PUP: LIBERTY, profile
URS-5 · I-3 · L-3

Description: Doubling is evident on LIBERTY, the eye, hair curls, and profile.

	VF-20	EF-40	AU-50	MS-60
VARIETY:	$600	$735	$1,075	$4,400
NORMAL:	$600	$735	$1,075	$4,400

Comments: This variety will not command a premium.

1866
FS-G20-1866-801

Variety: Doubled Die Reverse
CONECA—N/L
PUP: IN GOD WE TRUST
URS-7 · I-3 · L-2

Description: This reverse die was created with a small-letter hub over a large-letter hub. The N of the IN on the motto is clearly doubled.

	VF-20	EF-40	AU-50	MS-60	MS-63
VARIETY:	$590	$610	$1,175	$5,600	$27,500
NORMAL:	$590	$610	$1,175	$5,600	$27,500

Comments: This variety is fairly well known among specialists.

1866-S WITH MOTTO — FS-G20-1866S-1301

Variety: Misplaced Date
PUP: Denticles just left of date
URS-5 · I-3 · L-2

CONECA—N/L

Description: The top of an 8 is evident protruding from the denticles left of the 1.

	VF-20	EF-40	AU-50	MS-60
VARIETY:	$590	$600	$2,000	$13,400
NORMAL:	$590	$600	$2,000	$13,400

Comments: This is a very evident variety.

1871-S — FS-G20-1871S-301

Variety: Misplaced Date
PUP: Denticles below date
URS-6 · I-3 · L-2

CONECA—N/L

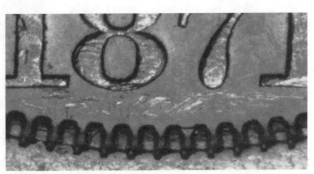

Description: The top of a digit, likely an 8, is evident protruding from the denticles below and between the 8 and 7.

	VF-20	EF-40	AU-50	MS-60	MS-63
VARIETY:	$590	$600	$615	$3,800	$16,500
NORMAL:	$590	$600	$615	$3,800	$16,500

Comments: This is another magical misplaced date.

1873   FS-G20-1873-101

Variety: Doubled Die Obverse   CONECA—N/L
PUP: LIBERTY
URS-6 · I-3 · L-2

Description: Doubling is evident on LIBERTY, the beads around the headband, and portions of the hair.

	VF-20	EF-40	AU-50	MS-60	MS-63
VARIETY:	$590	$600	$615	$870	$11,500
NORMAL:	$590	$600	$615	$870	$11,500

Comments: This is another very attractive doubled die.

1879   FS-G20-1879-801

Variety: Doubled Die Reverse   CONECA—N/L
PUP: LIBERTY
URS-6 · I-3 · L-2

Description: Strong doubling is evident on all reverse lettering, including E PLURIBUS UNUM, and the banner.

	VF-20	EF-40	AU-50	MS-60	MS-63
VARIETY:	$580	$590	$605	$775	$9,850
NORMAL:	$580	$590	$605	$775	$9,850

Comments: This is an extremely strong doubled-die reverse.

1883-S

FS-G20-1883S-501

Variety: Misplaced date
PUP: Denticles below date
URS-7 · I-3 · L-2

CONECA—N/L

Description: The top of an 8 is evident protruding from the denticles below the second 8.

	VF-20	EF-40	AU-50	MS-60	MS-63
VARIETY:	$580	$590	$605	$635	$9,750
NORMAL:	$580	$590	$605	$635	$9,750

Comments: Remember to look in the denticles for other misplaced dates.

1888

FS-G20-1888-801

Variety: Doubled Die Reverse
PUP: TWENTY DOLLARS
URS-6 · I-3 · L-2

CONECA—N/L

Description: Doubling is evident on most reverse lettering, but strongest on TWENTY DOLLARS, and the lower ribbon.

	VF-20	EF-40	AU-50	MS-60	MS-63
VARIETY:	$580	$590	$605	$635	$5,175
NORMAL:	$580	$590	$605	$635	$5,175

Comments: This is another very strong doubled die.

1896

FS-G20-1896-301

Variety: Repunched Date
CONECA—N/L
PUP: Date
URS-7 · I-3 · L-2

Description: Doubling is evident with all four digits, evident north of the primary date.

	VF-20	EF-40	AU-50	MS-60	MS-63
VARIETY:	$580	$590	$605	$635	$1,675
NORMAL:	$580	$590	$605	$635	$1,675

Comments: This is a very strong repunched date.

1909

FS-G20-1909-301

Variety: Overdate
CONECA—N/L
PUP: 9 of date
URS-8 · I-3 · L-2

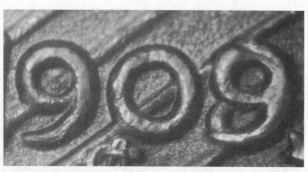

Description: The 9 in the date is punched over an 8.

	VF-20	EF-40	AU-50	MS-60	MS-63
VARIETY:	$600	$610	$645	$990	$4,625
NORMAL:	$600	$610	$615	$640	$2,525

Comments: This is a very well-known overdate, and relatively common.

1909-S
FS-G20-1909S-501

Variety: Repunched Mintmark
CONECA—N/L
PUP: Mintmark
URS-6 · I-3 · L-2

Description: The underlying S mintmark is evident below the primary S. There is a slight rotation to the underlying S compared with the primary S.

	VF-20	EF-40	AU-50	MS-60	MS-63
VARIETY:	$600	$610	$615	$640	$785
NORMAL:	$600	$610	$615	$640	$785

Comments: This is a very interesting RPM.

1911-D
FS-G20-1911D-501

Variety: Repunched Mintmark
CONECA—N/L
PUP: Mintmark
URS-6 · I-3 · L-2

Description: A secondary D mintmark is evident east of the primary D.

	VF-20	EF-40	AU-50	MS-60	MS-63
VARIETY:	$600	$610	$615	$640	$710
NORMAL:	$600	$610	$615	$640	$710

Comments: Although interesting, this RPM will not command a premium.

1922   FS-G20-1922-801

Variety: Doubled Die Reverse   CONECA—N/L
PUP: IN GOD WE TRUST
URS-6 · I-3 · L-2

Description: Doubling is evident on most reverse elements, but most visible on IN GOD WE TRUST, the rays, the eagle's talon, and DOLLARS.

	VF-20	EF-40	AU-50	MS-60	MS-63
VARIETY:	$600	$610	$615	$640	$710
NORMAL:	$600	$610	$615	$640	$710

Comments: This is a really super DDR! But as with most numismatically high-priced varieties, it is worth little or no premium.

1925   FS-G20-1925-801

Variety: Doubled Die Reverse   CONECA—N/L
PUP: Feathers, rays
URS-6 · I-3 · L-2

Description: Doubling is evident on the eagle's feathers, the rays, and IN GOD WE TRUST.

	VF-20	EF-40	AU-50	MS-60	MS-63
VARIETY:	$600	$610	$615	$640	$710
NORMAL:	$600	$610	$615	$640	$710

Comments: These doubled dies are generally well known. (See comments for FS-G20-1922-801.)

1926   FS-G20-1926-101

Variety: Tripled Die Obverse   CONECA—N/L
PUP: Rays, designer's initials
URS-7 · I-3 · L-2

Description: Tripling is evident on the date, rays, and designer's initials.

	VF-20	EF-40	AU-50	MS-60	MS-63
VARIETY:	$600	$610	$615	$640	$710
NORMAL:	$600	$610	$615	$640	$710

Comments: This is a well-known and common variety. (See comments for FS-G20-1922-801.)

Nashville Coin Gallery

~ Always Buying & Selling Quality Coins ~

*** Honesty *** Integrity *** Trust ***

Please Call **Pete Dodge** Today At

(615) 832-9904 (Cell)

See Our Prices & Order Coins Online At: **www.CoinBidders.com**

Authorized Dealer: PCGS (#548744) * NGC (#1945)
Life Member: American Numismatic Association (ANA LM #5839)
            Tennessee State Numismatic Society (TSNS LM #290)
Member: Industry Council for Tangible Assets (ICTA) * CCE/FACTS Network (CB9)

A GUIDE BOOK OF
—— DOUBLE EAGLE GOLD COINS——

In the field of United States gold, double eagles are without question the cream of the crop. With their grand size and hefty weight, these large coins are the most popular of America's gold pieces. However, there is more to like about double eagles than just their impressive physical substance. Quite simply, they are beautiful coins. The Saint-Gaudens series in particular, minted from 1907 to 1933, is widely regarded to feature the most attractive United States coinage design. Double eagles also bear testament to a rich and colorful history, from their popularity in the Old West to the relatively new status of certain Liberty Head double eagles as romanticized "treasure ship" coins.

A Guide Book of Double Eagle Gold Coins, written by Q. David Bowers—one of the legends of numismatics—is your complete history and price guide for these amazing pieces of America's past.

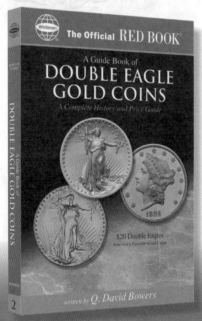

- 296 pages, including an eight-page color spread

- Year-by-year historical analysis of every double eagle, including varieties

- Comprehensive pricing for multiple grades

- Complete mintage figures

- Certified population reports

For a listing of available books visit www.whitmanbooks.com

Available at local hobby retailers, coin shops, and distributors.

For information, call toll free: **1-866-854-9763** email: customerservice@whitmanbooks.com

Classic Commemoratives, 1892–1954

Much *like the gold coin varieties, commemoratives will hold very little, if any, premium for die varieties.* Generally, fewer dies were used on the commemoratives than with gold coinage. If one die is doubled, you can expect a large percentage of the available coins to show that doubling. A very good example is the Stone Mountain Memorial half dollar with the doubled obverse die. Almost 1 in 10 specimens show evidence of the doubled die. Therefore, you can expect no premium associated with these.

Although the varieties may be common, they are interesting, nonetheless. If you are able to locate a very early-die-state specimen in very high grade, you might get a very small premium over the value of the regular coin. But, you might have to wait to find that one person who is willing to pay just a little more.

Clubs and Educational Information

If you're interested in commemorative coins, we highly recommend membership in the Society for U.S. Commemorative Coins. The SUSCC produces an educational newsletter, *Commemorative Trail*. This newsletter is jam-packed with great articles and features by some of the most knowledgeable numismatists of our time.

Additionally, the SUSCC has a web site where you can obtain more information, including membership details. As of this writing, dues are $20 annually. You might also want to join the club's online discussion group. Here you can ask questions of other members, and get accurate and quick answers to your questions. The discussion group's Web site is at http://groups.google.com/group/US-Commemorative-Coins.

For more information, visit www.suscconline.org, or you may contact the club secretary at

SUSCC
Gary Beedon, Secretary
P.O. Box 2335
Huntington Beach CA 92647
Email: beedon@earthlink.net

1892 WORLD'S COLUMBIAN EXPOSITION   FS-C50-1892-301

Variety: Repunched Date   CONECA—N/L
PUP: Date
URS-7 · I-3 · L-2

Description: This RPD shows secondary images evident protruding to the northeast from the 9 and 2. The secondary 2 is more evident than the 9.

	EF-40	AU-50	MS-60	MS-63	MS-65
VARIETY:	$15	$20	$35	$75	$565
NORMAL:	$10	$13	$29	$75	$565

Comments: Compare this variety with the next.

1892 WORLD'S COLUMBIAN EXPOSITION   FS-C50-1892-302

Variety: Repunched Date   CONECA—N/L
PUP: Date
URS-7 · I-3 · L-2

Description: This RPD shows secondary images evident protruding to the northeast from the 9 and 2, but slightly more eastward than the previous listing.

	EF-40	AU-50	MS-60	MS-63	MS-65
VARIETY:	$15	$20	$35	$75	$565
NORMAL:	$10	$13	$29	$75	$565

Comments: Compare this with the previous listing. They are slightly different.

1892 WORLD'S COLUMBIAN EXPOSITION · FS-C50-1892-303

Variety: Repunched Date
PUP: Date
URS-7 · I-3 · L-2

CONECA—N/L

Description: Unlike the previous two listings, this RPM is evident only on the 9, with the secondary image protruding to the east of the primary 9.

	EF-40	AU-50	MS-60	MS-63	MS-65
VARIETY:	$15	$20	$35	$75	$565
NORMAL:	$10	$13	$29	$75	$565

Comments: There seems to be no distinct difference in the rarity of these three listings.

1893 WORLD'S COLUMBIAN EXPOSITION · FS-C50-1893-301

Variety: Repunched Date
PUP: Date
URS-7 · I-3 · L-2

CONECA—N/L

Description: With this RPD, there are secondary images evident north on the 9 and 3.

	EF-40	AU-50	MS-60	MS-63	MS-65
VARIETY:	$15	$20	$35	$75	$600
NORMAL:	$10	$12	$23	$71	$600

Comments: The 3 especially on this RPD is fairly significant.

1915-S PANAMA-PACIFIC EXPOSITION FS-C50-1915S-501

Variety: Repunched Mintmark
PUP: Mintmark
URS-16 · I-3 · L-3

CONECA—N/L

Description: There is a secondary S protruding to the right of the primary S.

	EF-40	AU-50	MS-60	MS-63	MS-65
VARIETY:	$178	$365	$420	$625	$2,200
NORMAL:	$178	$365	$420	$625	$2,200

Comments: There is no premium to be expected from this variety. Another RPM, an S/S north, also exists.

1925 STONE MOUNTAIN MEMORIAL FS-C50-1925-101

Variety: Doubled Die Obverse
PUP: Date
URS-9 · I-3 · L-2

CONECA 2-O-III

Description: Doubling is strongly visible on STONE MOUNTAIN and 1925.

	EF-40	AU-50	MS-60	MS-63	MS-65
VARIETY:	$37	$52	$65	$77	$216
NORMAL:	$37	$52	$65	$77	$216

Comments: A significant percentage of all Stone Mountain Memorial half dollars have this doubled obverse die. There is also a doubled reverse die known, and is also common.

1925 FORT VANCOUVER CENTENNIAL   FS-C50-1925-102

Variety: Doubled Die Obverse   CONECA—N/L
PUP: Date, WE TRUST
URS-8 · I-3 · L-2

Description: The doubling is evident on the date and WE TRUST.

	EF-40	AU-50	MS-60	MS-63	MS-65
VARIETY:	$213	$261	$339	$358	$1,150
NORMAL:	$213	$261	$339	$358	$1,150

Comments: This is another commemorative variety that is very common and well-known.

1933-D OREGON TRAIL MEMORIAL   FS-C50-1933D-101

Variety: Tripled Die Obverse   CONECA—N/L
PUP: HALF DOLLAR, UNITED STATES OF AMERICA
URS-9 · I-3 · L-2

Description: A tripled image is evident on HALF DOLLAR, UNITED STATES OF AMERICA, and the lower portions of the map.

	EF-40	AU-50	MS-60	MS-63	MS-65
VARIETY:	$250	$295	$315	$330	$432
NORMAL:	$250	$295	$315	$330	$432

Comments: This is a very attractive, yet common, variety. Other Oregon halves also exhibit this characteristic.

1935 DANIEL BOONE BICENTENNIAL   FS-C50-1935-101

Variety: Doubled Die Obverse   CONECA—N/L
PUP: UNITED STATES OF AMERICA, HALF DOLLAR
URS-10 · I-3 · L-2

Description: Doubling is evident on UNITED STATES OF AMERICA, HALF DOLLAR, and the profile.

	EF-40	AU-50	MS-60	MS-63	MS-65
VARIETY:	$85	$88	$100	$115	$156
NORMAL:	$85	$88	$100	$115	$156

Comments: This exact same doubled die is also known on the 1937-D Boone half dollar. Most likely, this is a master die doubled die, and will be found on other Boone issues.

1936-D CALIFORNIA PACIFIC EXPO   FS-C50-1936D-501

Variety: Repunched Mintmark   CONECA—N/L
PUP: Mintmark
URS-9 · I-3 · L-2

 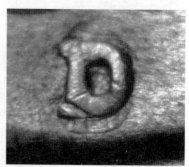

Description: A secondary D is evident south of the primary D.

	EF-40	AU-50	MS-60	MS-63	MS-65
VARIETY:	$62	$76	$120	$130	$148
NORMAL:	$62	$76	$120	$130	$148

Comments: This dramatic yet somewhat common repunched mintmark is sometimes seen on the California Pacific International Exposition (often called the San Diego) half dollar.

1951 CARVER/WASHINGTON — FS-C50-1951-801

Variety: Doubled Die Reverse
PUP: AMERICANISM
URS-9 · I-3 · L-2

CONECA—N/L

Description: The doubling is evident on all outer reverse lettering.

	EF-40	AU-50	MS-60	MS-63	MS-65
VARIETY:	$9	$10	$14	$25	$252
NORMAL:	$9	$10	$14	$25	$252

Comments: This is another doubled die that is likely a master die doubled die.

1953-S CARVER/WASHINGTON — FS-C50-1953S-801

Variety: Doubled Die Reverse
PUP: AMERICANISM
URS-9 · I-3 · L-2

CONECA—N/L

Description: As with the previous listing, the doubling is evident on all outer reverse lettering.

	EF-40	AU-50	MS-60	MS-63	MS-65
VARIETY:	$9	$13	$15	$19	$45
NORMAL:	$9	$13	$15	$19	$45

Comments: This is another doubled die that is likely a master die doubled die. No doubt this doubling is on other Carver/Washington issues.

Appendix A: Determining Die Doubling from Other Forms of Doubling

Explaining the difference between die doubling (doubled dies, repunched dates, and repunched mintmarks, among others) and the more confusing forms of doubling can be very challenging. Additionally, there are times when determining these differences can be frustrating for even a very experienced collector. This section will help you learn the differences. But reading alone will not do it all; you must examine numerous coins before you can expect to have a solid grasp of the differences between die doubling and other forms of doubling.

Die Doubling: Those Abnormalities We Love to Collect!
Die doubling is the type of doubling that exhibits a doubled image on the die itself, even before the coin is produced. Die doubling includes doubled dies, repunched dates, repunched mintmarks, overdates, over mintmarks, and repunched letters. Typically, die doubling will almost always exhibit splits in the serifs of the letters and/or numerals, with raised and rounded, secondary images.

Many 19th-century coins have letters and numerals that are flat on their top surfaces as compared with the rounded appearance of most 20th-century letters and numerals. Therefore, the key to identifying true die doubling on 19th-century coins will be the distinctive splits in the serifs.

On this Jefferson nickel, the distinctive splits in the serifs are evident, and the secondary images are "rounded" and can easily be detected.

This true 1969-S doubled die Lincoln cent exhibits the typical rounded secondary images. Notice also the "crease" between the images.

There is one class of doubled die that would not exhibit the normal characteristics mentioned for die doubling. Known as Class VI doubled dies, these doubled dies exhibit extra thickness on some letters and numbers. Most widely known on Lincoln cents, the doubling sometimes will exhibit letters that are slightly misshapened, such as the

The splits in the serifs on this 1887 Indian cent doubled die obverse are typical of what one would expect for most 19th-century coins with true die doubling.

lower bar of an E being curved. This curved shape will often be convex. Although some specialists may disagree, Class VI doubled dies generally command very small premiums—except in rare cases.

Strike Doubling

Strike doubling is the most often confused type of doubling and very often misidentified as a doubled die or repunched mintmark. Not only do novices con-

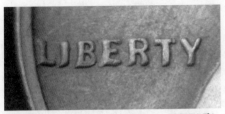

Notice the extra thickness of the letters in LIBERTY. This is typical of a Class VI doubled die, shown here on a Lincoln cent.

fuse this type of doubling with doubled dies, but specialists disagree as to what the correct terminology should be.

The term "strike doubling" is what we prefer and what we feel most accurately reflects the cause. Strike doubling is caused during the striking process. If one of the dies is loose as they come together to strike the coin, the loose die will twist slightly immediately as the hammer die starts to retract. This twisting die will actually cause some of the metal on the relief areas of the coin to "shear." Remember that the relief area on the coin is the recessed area on the die. This "shear" will almost always be flat and shelf-like, and will appear as if the metal has actually been moved or "sheared."

This LIBERTY on a Lincoln cent exhibits typical strike doubling. Notice the flat, shelf-like appearance of the secondary image.

Some will argue that the striking of the coin ends when the hammer die reaches the very end of its stroke. Thus, this should not be called strike doubling by their terms, but rather mechanical or machine doubling. In our opinion, this is like trying to split a hair. Additionally, we feel that machine or mechanical doubling can be even more confusing, as neither term indicates in which part of the minting process this happens. Either of those terms could refer to the coin counters at the end of the process! We feel strike doubling is best suited to describe the point of the minting process in which this doubling occurs.

Secondly, we all agree there are three basic areas of the minting process: planchet, die, and striking. This doubling occurs during the striking process, and not in the die-making or planchet-making process. We don't refer to incomplete planchets as a machine problem, although a machine causes them.

During our tours of the mints in Philadelphia and Denver, the personnel in both facilities confirmed the cause of strike doubling. Additionally, they stated that when they do encounter this doubling they tighten the dies into their holding collars and the doubling ceases. Whether you refer to this as strike doubling, machine doubling, mechanical doubling, or ejection doubling, the primary focus should be to understand the differences and educate others.

As a rule, strike doubling will exhibit a flat, shelf-like secondary image, contrary to the rounded secondary images of true die doubling. This secondary image will also usually be low to the field. There will be no splits in the serifs. On most Uncirculated and Proof coins, strike doubling will give the appearance that the metal has been "moved," much like that on hobo nickels or love tokens, and will have a very shiny appearance.

Strike doubling can affect all lettering on one or both sides, or could be detected on only one letter or a small portion of a device. Proof coins often exhibit strike doubling due to the excessive force employed. Strike doubling can also be evident on a coin with a true doubled die or true repunched mintmark.

There are several dates (and runs of dates) in several series that are well known for strike doubling. For instance, Mercury dimes from 1936 through 1942 often exhibit strike doubling, as do Lincoln cents from 1968 through 1972.

On this 1937 Buffalo nickel, the secondary images exhibit the flat, shelf-like doubling typical of strike doubling. The secondary image is low, close to the field.

Compare this 1969-S Lincoln cent doubled die with the strike doubling specimen to the right.

On this 1969-S cent, strike doubling is evident on the date and mintmark. Whenever the date and mintmark are both doubled, odds are that the doubling is strike doubling.

Although it may be difficult for a novice to understand, strike doubling can affect only the mintmark on a coin, creating what some may think is a repunched mintmark. In fact, this is fairly common, especially on Franklin halves and Washington quarters through 1964, and beyond. This is often because strike doubling first affects the deepest part of the die (the highest part of the coin), which in many cases is the deeply punched mintmark.

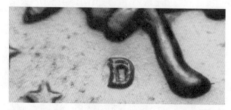

This is a genuine repunched mintmark on a Kennedy half dollar. Compare the doubling here with the next, which was caused by strike doubling.

This mintmark on a Franklin half dollar is the result of strike doubling. Notice the flat, shelf-like doubling, which is the primary characteristic of strike doubling.

Other Forms of Doubling

In addition to strike doubling, there are other forms of doubling that are often mistaken for die doubling. Among these is doubling caused by die fatigue, die polish, and doubling that is typical on coins designed by James B. Longacre.

Die Fatigue

Die fatigue is very often confused with a doubled die. In general, as a die deteriorates, the letters and/or numbers will develop wear, causing a secondary image on both sides of the letters or numbers (as though the edges of the letters or numbers have crumbled). This is caused due to stress in the metal of the die. This doubling will often, but not always, be in combination with an "orange-peel" effect on the fields of the coin, created by the stress in the metal on the dies.

Die fatigue is very evident and extreme on this Jefferson nickel. Notice the secondary images on both sides of the letters, and the "orange-peel" effect evident on the field.

Here is another example of die fatigue. Notice the edges of the I and T appearing to merge into the field. Also, the letters have less definition than one would expect.

Die fatigue is very common on Washington quarters from the 1980s and 1990s, Jefferson nickels from 1955 to date, and Roosevelt dimes from 1965 to date.

Die Polish

Excessive polishing of the dies can also cause a doubled image on the struck coin. As dies are being polished, excessive force is sometimes used in certain areas. When this occurs, the result of the polishing can be the appearance of a doubled image due to "spreading" the edges of the letters or numbers.

"Longacre" Doubling

This unofficial term was coined by J.T. Stanton as an easy way to describe the doubling that is typical on many coins designed by James B. Longacre. These include Indian Head cents, nickel three-cent pieces, Shield nickels, and many gold issues. We're certain many readers have seen this doubling before; almost all of the letters are doubled, with the secondary image appearing on both sides of the letters. Some specialists believe this is caused by the shoulder of the punch penetrating the die, causing the secondary step. Others feel this is intentional, designed to help with the metal flow into the tight crevices of the die. Although this doubling is evident on many of the coins that Longacre designed, it is not seen on all of his coins. This would likely remove the theory that the secondary or "stepped" image was planned to help with metal flow. Longacre doubling will not add premium to a coin's value.

Excessive die polishing is the cause of the doubled image on the 3 of the date.

On this Indian Head cent, the doubling that is typical on many of Longacre's designs is evident. Notice that the secondary image is visible on both sides of the letters.

Die Doubling I.Q. Test

The 10 photographs hear exhibit some examples of die doubling, strike doubling, and even some other forms of doubling. Take a few minutes to see for yourself whether you can accurately identify the various forms of doubling.

Note: Although most variety collectors do not feel coins exhibiting other forms of doubling should command any premium, some collectors believe they are collectable and actively pursue specimens exhibiting this type of doubling. We feel there is absolutely nothing wrong with this and encourage those who decide to take this course. The question is and should be "Are you having fun in your collecting pursuits?"

Test photo 1

Test photo 2

Test photo 3

Test photo 4

Test photo 5

Test photo 6

Test photo 7

Test photo 8

Test photo 9

Test photo 10

Answers to the test photographs:

1. strike doubling; 2. strike doubling; 3. doubled die; 4. strike doubling; 5. doubled die; 6. die fatigue; 7. strike doubling; 8. repunched mintmark; 9. doubled die; 10. strike doubling.

In test photo 10, notice that the date and the mintmark both exhibit similar doubling. This should be a red flag. There are very few examples on which a doubled die and RPM both are evident on the same side of the same coin. Keep in mind that until very recently, the mintmark was punched into the die after the die was made. Therefore, if the die is doubled, the mintmark is not necessarily doubled.

Additional copies of this section are available free of charge to ANA member clubs for educational purposes, and single copies for individual members. Postage is always appreciated, but not required. Write to J.T. Stanton, P.O. Box 15487, Savannah, GA S31416-2187.

Subscribe Today

Only One Place Can You Get...

- **Accurate Fair Market Values**
- **Current Fair Market Values**
- **The Fair Market Value Price Guide**

The NumisMedia Monthly Price Guide is a 40+ page publication with concise listings of the most recent **Fair Market Value** prices for coins offered by dealers in the numismatic community. The Fair Market Value prices listed represent accurately graded, sight-seen coins that are accepted by a majority of the dealers across the country.

The NumisMedia Online FMV Price Guide offers current, real world prices for U.S. coins. We also offer online auctions, and online advisory by the most respected dealers in the hobby.

www.numismedia.com

Appendix B: Which Magnifier Is the Best to Use?

What magnification should I use when searching for varieties? Which magnifier is the best to use? Do I need a microscope? These are three of the more common questions ever broached concerning this subject. All too often a collector will believe more magnification is better, but most often less is actually best. However, with varieties in particular and coin collecting in general, the strength of the magnification is not as important as the *quality*.

Virtually every variety of any significance can be detected with a 7x glass, if it's of good quality. Additionally, a good 7x magnifier is the recommended loupe for the most accurate coin grading. A lesser quality magnifier will only distort the image, making proper identification even more difficult. On the other hand, a good-quality glass with too much magnification is almost always overkill, as it can cause one to overlook key identification points.

Magnifier (Loupe)
An H.E. Harris magnifier (or loupe, pronounced "loop") is a common sight at coin shows. You will see dealers and collectors slip them out of their pocket to examine interesting coins. (Some wear them on a chain or string around their neck, for constant easy access.) These magnifiers fold into their chrome cases to protect the lens, which is usually 4x to 8x or greater strength.

Most serious collectors and almost all dealers will use a Hastings triplet magnifier; usually a 7x or 10x power is preferable. The "Hastings" magnifier is not a brand but a method of manufacture. The Hastings triplet has a three-glass (or plastic) optic, which ensures clarity throughout the entire lens and produces virtually no distortion.

Some manufacturers use 10x or 17x designations. However, without quality optics, the 10x or 17x will mean nothing. We've seen some magnifiers marked with a 17x, yet a 10x Hastings triplet will provide more detail, better clarity, and a wider field of view. And remember, if you can't see a variety with a 7x glass, it's likely not worth searching for.

A good, 7x Bausch & Lomb Hastings triplet will normally run about $45. However, with some searching on the Internet, you can find a good, 7x Hastings triplet for under $25. A good glass is vital in the study of varieties.

Stereoscopes (microscopes) are handy, fun, and very educational, but these are not absolutely necessary for the study of varieties. Should you have the desire to add one to your array of collecting tools, a good stereoscope can be obtained for as little as $250 (though most will run around $500 or more). Be sure to get a stereoscope—one that has two eyepieces. This will allow the very best in clarity and use. A stereoscope is great for taking photographs, and for studying the minute differences evident on every coin.

Check with your local supplier or favorite online dealers. See what they recommend. We strongly advise spending a little more for a good-quality product. You'll reap the rewards soon afterward.

Appendix C: Proof and Mint Set Varieties

Several people have suggested that we publicize which Proof sets and Mint sets contain significant varieties. Therefore, this list should be helpful to all collectors. Beginning with those modern Mint sets from 1947, and Proof sets from 1950, there are many years of one or the other that are absent of a significant variety. Not all of the known varieties are significant. Should anyone encounter a significant variety that is not listed, please contact coauthor J.T. Stanton so the list can be updated.

Again, this list is just to be used as a guide. Those Proof listings in bold type are considered the most desirable.

Mint Sets

Year	Denom	Variety
1949	5¢	D/S—over mintmark (although known, most have already been removed)
1954, Small Date	25¢	doubled die reverse
1960, Small Date	5¢	(P)—doubled die obverse (found in sets labeled as Small Date)
1960, Small Date	10¢	(P)—doubled die obverse (found in sets labeled as Small Date)
1960, Small Date	25¢	(P)—doubled die obverse (found in sets labeled as Small Date)
1961	50¢	D/D—repunched mintmark
1963	10¢	(P)—doubled die obverse
1963	25¢	(P)—doubled die obverse (P)—doubled die reverse
1963	50¢	(P)—doubled die obverse (P)—doubled die reverse
1968	10¢	(P)—doubled die obverse
1968	25¢	D—doubled die reverse
1969	5¢	D/D—repunched mintmark
1969	10¢	D/D—repunched mintmark
1969	25¢	D/D—repunched mintmark
1969	50¢	D—doubled die reverse
1970	1¢	D/D—repunched mintmark D—doubled die obverse
1970	10¢	D—doubled die reverse
1970	25¢	D—doubled die reverse
1970, Small Date	50¢	D—doubled die reverse
1971	5¢	D/D—repunched mintmark
1971	10¢	D/D—repunched mintmark D—doubled die reverse
1971	50¢	D—doubled die obverse D—doubled die reverse
1972	1¢	(P)—doubled die obverse
1972	5¢	D—doubled die reverse
1972	50¢	D—doubled die reverse
1973	50¢	(P)—doubled die obverse D—doubled die obverse
1974	50¢	D—doubled die obverse D—doubled die reverse
1981	5¢	D—doubled die reverse
1984	50¢	D/D—repunched mintmark
1987	5¢	D/D—repunched mintmark
1987	10¢	D/D—repunched mintmark
1989	5¢	D—doubled die reverse
1989	10¢	P—doubled die reverse
1989	50¢	D/D—repunched mintmark
1991	5¢	D—doubled die obverse

Proof Sets

1950	10¢	doubled die reverse
1950	50¢	doubled die obverse
1951	1¢	doubled die obverse
1951	**5¢**	**doubled die obverse**
1952	**25¢**	**"Superbird"**
1953	1¢	doubled die obverse
1953	**5¢**	**doubled die obverse**
1953	25¢	doubled die obverse
		recut tail feathers
1954	1¢	doubled die obverse
1954	10¢	doubled die obverse
1954	50¢	doubled die obverse
1955	1¢	doubled die obverse doubled die reverse
1955	**5¢**	**tripled die reverse**
1956	1¢	doubled die reverse
1956	10¢	doubled die reverse
1956	50¢	doubled die obverse
		doubled die reverse
1957	**5¢**	**quadrupled die obverse**
1957	50¢	doubled die reverse
1959	25¢	doubled die obverse
1960, Small Date	**1¢**	**doubled die obverse** (Large/Small) **doubled die obverse** (Small/Large)
1960	5¢	doubled die reverse
1960	10¢	doubled die obverse
1960	**10¢**	**doubled die reverse**
1960	**25¢**	**doubled die reverse**
1960	50¢	doubled die obverse
1961	5¢	doubled die reverse
1961	25¢	doubled die obverse
1961	**50¢**	**doubled die reverse**
1962	25¢	doubled die obverse
1962	50¢	doubled die obverse
1963	**10¢**	**doubled die reverse**
1963	25¢	doubled die reverse
1964	10¢	doubled die obverse
1964	50¢	doubled die obverse
1968-S	1¢	doubled die obverse
1968-S	5¢	repunched mintmark
1968-S	10¢	doubled die obverse
1968-S	**10¢**	**doubled die reverse** **doubled die obverse**
1968-S	**10¢**	**No S**
1968-S	25¢	repunched mintmark
1968-S	**25¢**	**doubled die reverse**
1968-S	**50¢**	**doubled die obverse**
1969-S	25¢	doubled die obverse
1969-S	**25¢**	**repunched mintmark**
1970-S	**10¢**	**No S**
1970-S	50¢	doubled die obverse
1971-S	1¢	doubled die obverse
1971-S	**5¢**	**No S**
1971-S	50¢	doubled die obverse
1975-S	10¢	doubled die reverse
1975-S	**10¢**	**No S**
1979-S	1¢	Type II mintmark
1979-S	5¢	Type II mintmark
1979-S	10¢	Type II mintmark
1979-S	25¢	Type II mintmark
1979-S	50¢	Type II mintmark
1979-S	$1	Type II mintmark
1981-S	1¢	Type II mintmark
1981-S	5¢	Type II mintmark
1981-S	10¢	Type II mintmark
1981-S	25¢	Type II mintmark
1981-S	50¢	Type II mintmark
1981-S	$1	Type II mintmark
1982-S	25¢	doubled die obverse
1983-S	**10¢**	**No S**
1990-S	**1¢**	**No S**
1990-S	25¢	doubled die obverse
1995-S	25¢	doubled die obverse

411

Appendix D: When Cherrypickin', Use Courtesy and Respect!

Many years ago, a dealer friend of ours indicated he would never allow anyone, other than a few select people, to cherrypick his stock. Fortunately, we were among that select group, but he had legitimate complaints regarding most of those who try to cherrypick varieties.

His experiences are not unlike those of many other dealers. All too often those who typically are most interested in cherrypickin' varieties totally disregard the dealer's other and potentially more profitable customers. Many cherrypickers will take up space and time, and then often walk away without a single purchase. Is that right? Is that fair to the dealer?

Before we get directly into the courtesy aspect of this article, we would like to remind you that there is nothing wrong with cherrypickin'. We use our knowledge just as another dealer or collector would use their knowledge to buy the best deal. A dealer who is trying to buy an 1892-S Barber quarter in Fine condition for a client will usually cherrypick to get the best possible coin for their money. Dealers with excellent grading skills will often cherrypick coins that may be undergraded, thereby making a nice profit on the purchase. That has been occurring for decades in our hobby.

But when the term cherrypick is used today, most hobbyists naturally think of those who search for varieties among a stock of normal coins. Those of us involved with varieties have studied long and hard for the knowledge that we have. However, to make the most of this knowledge, we must use some common sense, and we must *always* respect a dealer's main objective—to make a profit. They are at shows and in the coin business to make money to support their families. This is their livelihood, and we must respect their time and space at all times. If you don't feel you can afford them this courtesy, don't consider cherrypickin' for varieties. Those of us who do respect a dealer's time and space do not want a few inconsiderate people to ruin the pickings for the rest of us.

There are a few "courtesy" pointers that we'd like you to keep in mind. Remember that you are very likely a small customer for them. They can almost certainly make more money from another customer in a tenth of the time they might spend with you. Remember that *you need the dealers* for cherrypickin'—they could live quite well, thank you, without you!

If you're at a show and you've spotted a dealer whose stock you would like to search, and that dealer is busy, simply go to another dealer for a while. If you are seated at a dealer's table looking over their stock, and they start to get busy, let them know that you realize you're taking up their space and time, in a respectful way, and that you will come back when they aren't as busy. I promise the dealer will remember your courtesy and respect, and you're more likely to be welcomed back when time permits.

I've often had a dealer ask what I'm looking for. I'll generally tell them that I'm looking for various varieties, and that will usually suffice. Don't lie. Never lie! But you don't have to tell everything. If the dealer persists, I'll usually tell them about a few of the more scarce varieties, and explain that there is a market for those varieties. Remember most dealers couldn't care less about the varieties that aren't listed in the Red Book. They will usually say "fine," and you can continue looking.

However, the best-case scenario is that you can teach this dealer something about varieties. As you and the dealer become better known to each other, he or she may start to look for some of the varieties, and save them for you. Sure, you'll likely pay a little more than the price of the normal coin for them, but far less than the actual value of the variety. In short, you've added a pair of eyes to your cherrypickin'. You'll get a new supply for varieties and at prices that will enable you to realize a very nice profit. I even have dealers tell me to name the price, and I've had dealers ask for only the value of the normal coin.

I have a habit that I think is extremely important. If I'm at a dealer's table, and if for some reason I need to reach into my pocket or lap, I'll plainly open my hands above the table, turn them over and rub them together, then do what I need to do. I rarely say anything, and I won't make a big deal of it, but I make sure it's obvious. Why? The dealer will know for sure that you are not "palming" a coin. I do this with dealers I know well and dealers I don't know. It's now a habit. One dealer I know well actually told me one time I didn't need to do that, he trusted me completely; I simply explained it was a habit. He did respect that, and I'm sure he understood. The main point here is to *never* give any dealer any opportunity to even think you are doing something wrong. I've seen people who hold a want list or magnifier in their laps, then take the coin below the table's surface, out of view of the dealer. That is very wrong, whether cherrypickin' or not, and will often cause a dealer not to welcome you back. Always think of how you would want a customer to act if you were the dealer, and *always be respectful*. And be respectful even if the dealer may seem rude.

There are some other points to cover as well. Never let a dealer feel cheated when you buy a coin, or you'll never be welcomed back. Never brag about what you've purchased from a dealer if there is any possible way that can get back to the dealer. Always be polite and courteous, and being friendly never hurts either. Try to put yourself into their shoes once in a while. Usually, their main objective is to sell coins they have and know best, for a profit. Many dealers specialize in certain areas.

One last tip: as a rule if I find a super variety for the price of a regular coin, and for some reason I don't want the dealer to key in on that one coin, I will buy a few other coins at the same time to draw less attention to the coin that I really want. These coins will be coins I know I can get back a large percentage of my money quickly. Who cares? You'll make a bundle on that nice cherry! Buy a couple of coins with firm markets, such as an MS-63 Morgan dollar, or a couple of Proof sets.

Above all, always use *courtesy and respect* in all your dealings, act in a professional manner. You'll make some friends along the way, and I will guarantee you'll come out ahead in the long run!

Appendix E: 1979-S and 1981-S Proof Mintmark Varieties

The Type I and Type II mintmark varieties for the 1979-S and 1981-S Proof sets are very well known, yet many people become confused when trying to identify one from the other. This appendix illustrates the four mintmark styles for each denomination.

Compare these descriptions to the photos, and you'll be able to identify the correct types.

The 1979-S Type I mintmark has a squared, filled S, very indistinct.

The 1979-S Type II mintmark is clear and well formed.

The 1981-S Type I is a worn version of the 1979-S Type II.

The 1981-S Type II, although somewhat similar to the Type I, is distinguishable by the flattened top surface of the S. Some specialists will argue that the S must be clear in both loops. Most agree the S can show some slight filling, but the mintmark punch must show that flattened top surface. This is usually the most difficult for anyone to comprehend. But the key is really very simple—that flatness on the top surface.

Cents

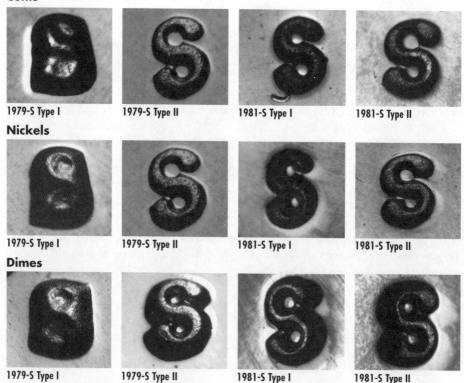

| 1979-S Type I | 1979-S Type II | 1981-S Type I | 1981-S Type II |

Nickels

| 1979-S Type I | 1979-S Type II | 1981-S Type I | 1981-S Type II |

Dimes

| 1979-S Type I | 1979-S Type II | 1981-S Type I | 1981-S Type II |

Quarter Dollars

1979-S Type I   1979-S Type II   1981-S Type I   1981-S Type II

Half Dollars

  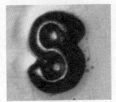 

1979-S Type I   1979-S Type II   1981-S Type I   1981-S Type II

Dollars

1979-S Type I   1979-S Type II   1981-S Type I   1981-S Type II

THE CHERRYPICKERS' GUIDE HELPFUL HINTS

Don't get discouraged if you haven't found any significant varieties for a while—they're out there, and eventually you'll uncover some. Remember, knowledge is power, but it's only relevant when you use it!

See appendix H for more Helpful Hints.

Appendix F: Recommended Reading: Mint Errors and Varieties

The following is a list of recommended readings for the error/variety collector. This list can by no means stay complete, as new books are available regularly, but it will give you an excellent foundation and a wealth of knowledge. The old axiom "Buy the book before the coin" should apply even more strongly to the error/variety collector than to the regular segment of the hobby. Most of these books are available through any coin dealer.

General

The following books not only cover errors and varieties, but regular coins as well. Naturally, these books should be included in any numismatist's library.

A Guide Book of United States Coins by R.S. Yeoman and edited by Ken Bressett, commonly known as the Red Book, is the book with which any numismatic library should begin.

Walter Breen's Complete Encyclopedia of U.S. and Colonial Coins. This is undoubtedly the best book anyone interested in die varieties can add to their library. It's not cheap, but much of the information contained cannot be found anywhere else and will certainly be the bible for variety collectors for years to come.

Series Topics

The following books highlight a specific series or subject. These books are a tremendous asset to anyone seriously interested in the noted topic.

A Guide Book of Flying Eagle and Indian Head Cents by Richard Snow.

Flying Eagle and Indian Cent Die Varieties by Larry R. Steve and Kevin Flynn. (OOP)

Flying Eagle, Indian Cent, Two Cent & Three Cent Doubled Dies by Kevin Flynn (OOP)

The Complete Guide to Lincoln Cents by David Lange.

The Lincoln Cent Doubled Die by John Wexler. (OOP)

The RPM Book—Second Edition: Lincoln Cents by James Wiles.

The Complete Price Guide and Cross Reference to Lincoln Cent Mint Mark Varieties by Brian Allen and John A. Wexler. (OOP)

The Authoritative Reference on Lincoln Cents by John Wexler and Kevin Flynn. (OOP)

Looking Through Lincoln Cents by Charles Daughtrey.

The Authoritative Reference of Three Cent Nickels by Kevin Flynn.

A Guidebook of Shield and Liberty Head Nickels by Q. David Bowers.

The Shield Five Cent Series by Ed Fletcher. (OOP)

The Complete Guide to Shield and Liberty Nickels by Gloria Peters and Cynthia Mohon. (OOP)

Treasure Hunting Liberty Head Nickels by Kevin Flynn and Bill Van Note. (OOP)

The Complete Guide to Buffalo Nickels, Second Edition by David W. Lange.

Treasure Hunting Buffalo Nickels by John Wexler, Ron Pope, and Kevin Flynn. (OOP)

The Best of the Jefferson Nickel Doubled Dies by John Wexler and Brian Ribar.

The Jefferson Nickel RPM Book by James Wiles, Ph.D.

The Complete Guide to Liberty Seated Half Dimes by Al Blythe. (OOP)

The Complete Guide to Liberty Seated Dimes by Brian Greer. (OOP)

The Complete Guide to Barber Dimes by David Lawrence. (OOP)

The Authoritative Reference on Barber Dimes by Kevin Flynn.

The Complete Guide to Mercury Dimes (2nd ed.) by David W. Lange.

Treasure Hunting Mercury Dimes by Kevin Flynn. (OOP)

The Authoritative Reference on Roosevelt Dimes by John Wexler and Kevin Flynn.

The Comprehensive Encyclopedia of United States Liberty Seated Quarters by Larry Briggs. (OOP)

The Complete Guide to Barber Quarters by David Lawrence. (OOP)

The Authoritative Reference on Barber Quarters by Kevin Flynn

The Washington Quarter Dollar Book—Volume One, 1932–1941 by James Wiles.

A Guide Book of Washington and State Quarters by Q. David Bowers.

The Washington Quarter Dollar Book—Volume Two, 1942–1944 by James Wiles.

The Washington Quarter Dollar Book—Volume One, 1945–1949 by James Wiles.

The Best of the Washington Quarter Doubled Dies by John Wexler and Kevin Flynn. (OOP)

The Ultimate Guide to Attributing Bust Half Dollars by Glenn R. Peterson.

Early Half Dollar Varieties, by Al C. Overton.

The Complete Guide to Liberty Seated Half Dollars by Randy Wiley and Bill Bugert. (OOP)

The Complete Guide to Barber Halves by David Lawrence. (OOP)

Treasure Hunting Walking Liberty Half Dollars by Kevin Flynn and Brian Raines.

The Complete Guide to Walking Liberty Half Dollars by Bruce Fox. (OOP)

Treasure Hunting Franklin and Kennedy Half Dollar Doubled Dies by Kevin Flynn and John Wexler.

The Kennedy Half Dollar by James Wiles.

Commemorative Coins of the United States—A Complete Encyclopedia, by Q. David Bowers. (OOP)

A Guide Book of Morgan Silver Dollars by Q. David Bowers.

Comprehensive Catalog and Encyclopedia of Morgan and Peace Dollars (4th ed.) by Van Allen and Mallis.

Top 100 Morgan Dollar Die Varieties: The VAM Keys by Michael Fey and Jeff Oxman.

The Authoritative Reference on Eisenhower Dollars by John Wexler, Bill Crawford, and Kevin Flynn.

The RPM Book by John Wexler and Tom Miller. (OOP)

The Error Coin Encyclopedia by Arnold Margolis.

The Encyclopedia of Doubled Dies, volumes 1 and 2, by John Wexler.

Periodicals

These magazines regularly feature varieties and errors.

Errorscope The bi-monthly magazine of CONECA, the national error/variety club. Membership information is available from the CONECA Web site at www.conecaonline.org

Error Trends Coin Magazine This is a highly educational monthly magazine devoted to the error/variety hobby, weighted toward errors. Subscription information is available from Arnold Margolis, P.O. Box 158, Oceanside NY 11572-0158.

Appendix G: Coin Clubs and Groups

An important part of hobby fulfillment is membership in coin clubs. The advantages are many, most important of which would be the camaraderie and accumulation of knowledge. We all need both.

Even if you can't travel to meeting locations and shows, many of the clubs (most, in fact) produce newsletters that are highly educational and encourage participation. One of the best ways to learn about any specific numismatic subject is to participate. Writing articles is another way. It seems that with every article I write the research necessary to ensure accurate information adds to my own numismatic knowledge. It never fails.

Many specialized coin clubs have been born in the virtual environment of the relatively new medium called the Internet. These are often interactive clubs, and offer all members a great opportunity to ask questions of specialists, share knowledge, and meet others with similar interests.

This appendix lists a group of numismatic organizations dedicated to subjects that should interest most of our readers. The information noted, including membership fees, addresses, etc., is as accurate as possible at the time of publication. A visit to a group's web site can offer the latest information.

Nationwide Clubs and Group

The American Numismatic Association. This is the largest coin-collecting group in the world. The monthly magazine, *Numismatist*, contains articles submitted by members on a wide array of topics. Additionally, the ANA's library is second to none and is available to all members. Other great benefits are also included as a part of your membership.

American Numismatic
Association
818 N. Cascade Ave.
Colorado Springs CO 80903-3279
Phone: 719-632-2646
Fax: 719-634-4085
Email: ana@money.org
Web site: www.money.org

CONECA (Combined Organizations of Numismatic Error Collectors of America). CONECA is a worldwide organization that specializes in the study of errors and varieties. Their bi-monthly newsletter *Errorscope* is filled with educational topics. Additionally, CONECA's web site has a huge listing with descriptions of several thousand repunched mintmarks and doubled dies. And access to that is free to all!

CONECA
c/o Paul Funaiole
35 Leavitt Lane
Glenburn ME 04401-1013
Email: pfunny1@adelphia.net
Web site: www.conecaonline.org

NCADD (National Collectors Association of Die Doubling). NCADD is a group devoted to collecting coins with die doubling, repunched mintmarks, over mintmarks, doubled dies, overdates, etc. The *Hub*, NCADD's bimonthly newsletter, is loaded with features and general educational articles.

NCADD
c/o Brian Ribar
2053 Edith Place
Merrick NY 11566-3306
Web site: www.geocities.com/ResearchTriangle/Facility/4968/NCADD.html

Online Clubs and Groups

Variety Coins. This is a great online group with a very active discussion board. Most variety specialists belong and are active on the boards. Ask a question, get several answers, all of which will prove useful. Membership is free.

Web site: groups.msn.com/VarietyCoins/message-board

Coin Varieties. Much like the above, this is a discussion group for those with an interest in coin varieties. Many variety specialists and enthusiasts hold membership (free) and are active in the discussions.

Web site: groups.yahoo.com/group/coinvarieties

Error World. This online group specializes in coin errors and varieties. Most consider Error World one of the first online groups for this segment of the hobby. Like the majority of others, membership is free.

Web site: www.surok.addr.com/index.html

Shield Nickels. Another excellent online group for enthusiasts of Shield nickels. Like many of the others, the discussion groups are filled with excellent information. There is no better discussion group available for the variety enthusiast. And best of all, you can join free!

Web site:
groups.yahoo.com/group/Shield_Nickels/

Specialized Clubs and Groups

John Reich Collectors Society. "The purpose of the John Reich Collectors Society is to encourage the study of numismatics, particularly United States gold and silver coins minted before the introduction of the Liberty Seated design, and to provide technical and educational information concerning such coins." JRCS has a great newsletter, and conducts meetings at various times of the year.

John Reich Collectors Society
P.O. Box 135
Harrison OH 45030-0135
Email: jrcs19@adelphia.net
Web site: www.jrcs.org

Liberty Seated Collectors Club. LSCC is one of the stronger groups dedicated to any design or series. LSCC members receive the *Gobrecht Journal* quarterly, which is filled with some of the most educational articles available anywhere.

LSCC
Mark Sheldon, Secretary-Treasurer
P.O. Box 261
Wellington OH 44090
Email: John.McCloskey@notes.udayton.edu
Web site: www.numismalink.com/lscc.html

Appendix H: Helpful Hints

These hints (also sprinkled throughout the main text) will help make your search for those elusive varieties more pleasant and more productive.

Helpful Hint #1
Please read the information in the front of this book. It sets the tone for the material that follows and makes it easier to interpret the information for each listing.

Helpful Hint #2
Strike doubling can often be confused with the more valuable die doubling, such as a doubled die or repunched mintmark. To help ensure you know the difference, take time to read, read, and re-read appendix A.

Helpful Hint #3
Remember, if you can't see the characteristics of a coin clearly, you'll likely miss the important one. Don't take a chance. Always use a good, Hastings triplet magnifier (7x or 10x). The added expense will be more than offset by just one nice find. There are additional magnifying suggestions in appendix B.

Helpful Hint #4
Check all the coins in your 1960 and 1968 Proof sets. These are known to have nice doubled dies for each denomination, some on the obverse and some on the reverse. For a complete list of known Mint set and Proof set varieties, refer to appendix C.

Helpful Hint #5
Generally speaking, varieties known in Mint and Proof sets are more difficult to sell or auction than other varieties. Obviously, exceptions are known. Many enthusiasts would prefer to locate their own varieties, thereby enjoying the hunt.

Helpful Hint #6
Check the coins already in your collection. In many cases, collectors will find a variety they had no idea they had. In some cases, these unfound varieties can be quite valuable. This first happened to J.T. Stanton back in 1982, and it can happen to you!

Helpful Hint #7
Always check coins produced between 1941 and 1945. Most of the dramatic varieties from the 20th century were produced during WWII, when the U.S. government was trying to conserve metals, energy, and time. There are still significant discoveries to be made.

Helpful Hint #8
Keep in mind that as the numismatic value of a coin increases, the premiums attached to its varieties tend to decrease. A doubled die on a 1901-S Barber quar-

ter would add no significant value to the coin because of the already high numismatic value, and very few dies were used to produce that date. Another so-called white elephant would be an RPM on a Mint State 1936-D Washington quarter.

Helpful Hint #9
The varieties listed in this book are only the tip of the iceberg. Even more are yet to be discovered. Always examine closely any coin you obtain. You may soon discover that one great variety wanted by every collector in the hobby! And let us know when you do.

Helpful Hint #10
Don't forget to inspect the denticles of a coin, especially those near and beneath the date, for variety characteristics. Dozens of significant varieties exhibit portions of numbers within or protruding from the denticles. Most of these are prized additions to a collection.

Helpful Hint #11
If you can't discern a variety with a 7x loupe, it probably isn't significant.

Helpful Hint #12
Don't get hung up on just the varieties listed in this book. There are many nice, yet-to-be-discovered "cherries" out there waiting for you to pick!

Helpful Hint #13
Read and re-read the appendix on die doubling.

Helpful Hint #14
Study and learn the Pick-Up-Points (PUPs) for each series so that you can focus your initial attention on these areas to find varieties. Don't forget the denticle area and the design above the date (especially on 19th-century coinage such as the Liberty Seated series) for misplaced numbers, etc. They hide, so use a good loupe and good light.

Helpful Hint #15
Don't get discouraged if you haven't found any significant varieties for a while—they're out there, and eventually you'll uncover some. Remember, knowledge is power, but it's only relevant when you use it!

Helpful Hint #16
Rooting for the Atlanta Braves and Atlanta Falcons has always brought us good luck in cherrypickin'. We suggest you try it!

Appendix I: Tips on Mailing Coins

Sooner or later, most of us will be sending coins through the mail. These coins may be worth anywhere from only a dollar or two up to several thousand. Whatever their value, you'll want to protect and insure those coins in the best way possible and ensure they arrive at their destination safely and in good condition. The following information will help guide you as you choose the best way to package and mail your coins.

Packaging and Mailing: Envelopes

Many valuable coins are lost in the mail as a result of improper packaging. In most such cases, the packages are flimsy, too small, or improperly addressed; or they exhibit no return address, or use materials too thin to withstand the stress of our mail system. A package that is smaller than normal can easily fall off a conveyor, and may not be spotted for several days or even weeks. Always assume that your package will encounter harsh handling, will slip off conveyors, get caught in machinery, fall off a truck, or worse (always expect the worst). Yes, your package *should* be handled perfectly, and in 99.9% of cases it *is* handled properly. However, even with the most modern, exacting machinery and qualified staff, packages still have a significant chance of being damaged or lost. And you can't discount fate when mailing a package.

The question comes down to this—are you willing to risk that your irreplaceable coins will be handled perfectly on their journey through our mail system? We don't, nor should you. Please don't think we're picking on the United States Postal Service, as we are not. They do a great job at a very reasonable price. But even they will tell you that perfection is unknown—with them, and with any other business.

If you're sending just a few coins, they can safely be housed in a Safe-T-Mailer or similar package, which is a sticky, corrugated cardboard self-sealing enclosure. You can even place the coins carefully between two pieces of heavy cardboard (material from a cardboard box works well), and tape it securely closed. Tape is far preferable over staples, as staples can ruin an important coin. The continued use of staples sooner or later will result in damage. The Safe-T-Mailer (or similar brand) package can be placed in a regular business-size envelope (the heavier the paper quality, the better) for safe mailing provided the coins are not too heavy or bulky. In cases where the coins are too heavy or bulky for use of an envelope, a box should be used (provided the coins are well protected). You should make sure your coins do not rattle or even move in the box. There should be no noise or shifting coming from a package. Not only are coins *lost* because of improper packaging, but even more are *damaged* because someone didn't properly protect them before shipping. Incidentally, the Safe-T-Mailers (or similar brand) are available at any local coin supply house or an online supplier.

If you mail coins frequently, consider the purchase of some 28-lb., #11 brown kraft policy envelopes. The policy envelopes open and close on the short end, which offers better security—they are easier to seal, plus they are less likely to come open during transit. And if by chance they do come open, the opening is smaller, further decreasing the chances of something coming out. Additionally, the 28-lb. brown kraft envelopes are heavier, offering yet again better security. The slightly larger size enables you to include as many as two corrugated mailers plus additional papers. Also, this size envelope will easily handle several 4" x 6 " photos, with no folding and without infringing on the margins of the envelope.

The #11 kraft policy envelopes can be purchased from almost any local printer or most stationery stores—brick and mortar, or virtual. Do not settle for a #11 "regular" envelope, which has the normal v flap on the long side. You want the sealing flap on the short end, which will add additional security and which makes this a "policy" envelope. A policy envelope is much easier to seal and will offer better security. Once you use them, you will appreciate how easy they are to seal securely. The primary cause of damage to an envelope in transit is the flap catching on equipment. The policy envelope, due to the small flap, dramatically reduces damage.

You should consider having these envelopes pre-printed with your name and address, and the words "PHOTOS—PLEASE DO NOT BEND" about two thirds of the way down on the left side. Those five simple words further disguise the contents—just another small step in providing as much security as possible while the package travels through the system. You should never write the word "COINS" or indicate the contents of the package in any way, as advertising such valuable items may jeopardize their delivery. Don't worry about the PHOTOS statement on the outside; there is nothing wrong about using these for other mailings.

The envelopes will likely cost about $60 to $75 per 500 without printing, or about $110 to $135 with printing. Although these are more expensive than the cheap #10 envelopes, consider that the cost per piece is only about 15¢, which is not much considering the total package cost including postage and insurance. And that 15¢ is negligible when you consider the value and added security.

Packaging and Mailing: Boxes

When you use a box to package and mail coins, make sure it is sturdy enough to withstand the rough trip through our postal system. It's a good idea to protect the coins using bubble pack, Styrofoam packing peanuts, wadded-up paper, or some other fill. It's also advisable to use a box somewhat larger than needed, adding fill as necessary. Ideally, coins should be placed at least a half inch from any side of the box. This larger box, along with the fill, will reduce the chances of damage to the coins when the box is opened. We've often received very small boxes, sealed so securely we had no idea where the box seams were. Therefore, we were forced to cut into the carton with a box cutter to open it. When we do that, there is always a chance of the knife blade contacting a coin, damaging it. Obviously when doing so we would keep the blade of the cutter near an edge—but we have known people to place coins in contact with the edge of a box. Again, use a box larger than necessary, and protect the coins inside with wrapping. You should always assume the worst and prepare for it.

Consider how the recipient might try to open the package! Tape the box securely with heavy-duty tape prior to wrapping with outer wrap. We've found that a large kraft paper grocery bag does a very adequate job for wrapping, and you should use brown kraft tape (the kind you moisten) on the outside. The proper tape is also available in white and with reinforced threads. The reinforced tape adds still another level of added security. We have even drawn a dotted line on the outside, with a notation of "Cut here to open," which indicates for the recipient the best place to cut open the box safely.

When considering your tape choices, remember to use only a tape that will clearly retain and not smear the ink from the rubber stamps the Post Office uses. This is usually the kind of tape that requires moisture to activate the adhesive. Never use Scotch or cellophane tape, or any tape with a shiny surface. Never! Scotch tape will often tear, or cause ink to smear when it is fresh (and at times even when dry), and it can often be removed without evidence of such removal. The ability to remove tape undetected is a critical one, as the postal stamp is a vital part of security when using Registered Mail (or any mail for that matter). When the Post Office receives a Registered Mail package, the clerk is charged with affixing their cancellation stamp along each and every seam or tape edge. The purpose of this is so that anyone can easily determine if the package has been opened, or if tape has been added or removed. This is the basis for the requirement of the specified tapes. Many post offices have a brown tape available for use in sealing packages, but all those we have seen do not meet the standards for Registered Mail. Plastic tape or duct tape is also not acceptable for Registered Mail.

You can usually find the proper tape at your local stationery store, at superstores, and even online. Don't skimp on the tape—it's inexpensive and using too much is better than too little. Even if your Post Office is lax and will accept a tape that will allow the rubber stamp to smear, don't give in. These are your coins, or you are responsible for them. The guidelines mentioned are for security. If you insure your coins or send a package via Registered Mail, don't take a chance with inferior or inappropriate tape or packaging. If the coins are important enough to use Registered Mail, then they are important enough to use proper supplies.

Packaging and Mailing: Procedures

Here are some final thoughts on mailing materials and procedures. The advantage of having envelopes printed with your return address reduces the chances of a thief placing their own return address in that position, especially if the return address is printed with large type. This has been done! If a bogus return address label is placed on your package, and if the package cannot be delivered, it will be returned to that bogus address. Place your Registered Mail label (the red label with control numbers) very close to the top of the addressee line. Thieves have been known to place an addressee label over the mailing address on the package so the merchandise will be mailed and delivered to a location where the culprits can obtain it. By placing that Registered Mail label very close to the addressee block, you are adding just another level of security. That makes it more difficult to place a bogus address label over the address you intended. Let me stress this important point: when using a box to ship, use a larger box than needed. In this way you'll reduce the chances of a coin being damaged when the package is opened. Plus it's much easier on the recipient, and often on the mailer.

Address all packages carefully, and make sure your return address is properly displayed, and as large as feasible on the package. It's a very good habit of including the addressee and sender information inside the package. We have actually had packages returned after being destroyed in transit. Fortunately, we had an invoice in the package, plus another piece of paper, with a name and address on both, which enabled the USPS to return the package and its contents.

The above instructions and recommendations apply to both Insured and Registered/Insured letters and packages. It's also a good idea to place your postage and/or Registered or Insured number stickers so near the addressee block that it would be unlikely an address label can cover your addressee block.

The best option now available to reduce odds of an address being changed is to use the new USPS online mailing system. We are now using this service completely, and have found that it saves a lot of time, and also money! After you enter the package data, you actually print a label that contains your return address, the recipient's name and address, Registration or Insured numbers, and the postage! Oh yes, we almost forgot—when using the online shipping for Priority Mail and other services, Delivery Confirmation is free. You can also have the USPS send an email to the recipient acknowledging the package is coming (this includes any tracking information).

Signing up for this web service is free and simple. The USPS bills your credit card for the postage. You need only enter your address once. (From that time forward, the system will have your name and address for label data.) Next you enter the recipient's name and address; you can save this to your own personal address file on the USPS web site. If you mail to that person again, their information is readily available, and you don't have to enter it again. (No, this is not a paid advertisement.)

Insured / First Class Mail

While the maximum coverage on Insured Mail is now $5,000, compare the costs of Registered Mail with Insured / First Class. Consider that Registered Mail is many times more secure than simple Insured / First Class Mail. To give you an idea, banks and the Bureau of Engraving and Printing use Registered Mail to transport extremely large sums of currency. That is due to the security the USPS places on Registered Mail. Visit their website a www.usps.com for the most current shipping and insurance rates.

Insured / First Class parcels are signed for by the recipient (or his/her agent) upon delivery, and the Post Office retains the signature slip. When mailing the package, the sender retains a portion of the insured form for their records, with an adhesive portion of the label affixed to the package. This small label on the package includes the insurance item number of the package, and the Postal Service can obtain any information they might need from that number. You will complete the reverse of the primary insurance form yourself for your own records.

Also with insured mail (and this is where the risk comes in), there is no paper trail other than the shipping documents and the receiving documents. If the package is accidentally delivered to the wrong address, there will be no record of the person who received the package other than a signature. And if you think a person can be tracked solely by a signature, then think again. Identification is rarely required for Insured / First Class Mail, and in some instances insured mail is left in a mailbox (or P.O. Box) without the requirement of a signature.

Claims may be filed on lost Insured Mail packages after a prescribed period subsequent to mailing (usually 30 days), and the total insured amount can be recovered by the sender if the parcel is not located. However, the sender must jump through a lot of hoops to get the insured amount, including the submission of actual receipts. As a rule, the USPS will only reimburse the cost of the item(s) and not the owner's stated value. Be advised that this process takes time, often up to three months or more, to process, and it's been known to take over six months to recover a loss!

The Most Secure Way of Mailing Merchandise

Registered Mail is by far the safest way to send merchandise, coins, currency, or even large sums of cash through the postal system, although it is more expensive than Insured / First Class. When taking into consideration coins or currency that are costly, difficult, or impossible to replace, the cost of Registered Mail is incredibly affordable and worth the money. The importance of sending your packages by Registered Mail cannot be over emphasized. Certified Mail never offers any insurance if a package is lost. *Coins should never be sent via Certified Mail. Never!*

With Registered Mail, each postal employee along the delivery path who handles the package must sign for it. This is maximum accountability. In this way, if a Registered Mail package is lost the last employee who signed for the package is responsible. No exception. United States Postal Service employees realize this accountability. In fact, some employees have been discharged and/or harshly investigated and reprimanded for losing control of a Registered Mail package. (Discharge is the usual result.)

In most post offices, only one or two employees have access to Registered Mail. Registered Mail awaiting claim is stored in a locked cabinet. Postal employees are required to obtain positive ID before delivery. If the employee is very familiar with the recipient, they will often release the package after obtaining a signature without requiring ID. The requirements for release of a Registered Mail package are so stringent, employees are not to release a Registered Mail package even to a spouse, unless the addressee has previously signed an authorization form.

Registered Mail packages are only insured if insurance has been purchased at the time of mailing. With Registered Mail, there is a fee for postage, a fee for the Registered Mail service, and if insurance is desired, the cost of that insurance. A package can be mailed via Registered Mail without insurance, but the minimum insurance is only a few cents more. Consult your local Post Office or www.usps.com for fees, including insurance. (Please note that currently the maximum coverage for Registered Mail is $25,000 per package.)

The major difference between Insured / First Class and Registered Mail is that Registered Mail is recorded, accounted for, and signed for by every postal employee who takes charge of the package along the way until the recipient acknowledges possession. Any lost article can be traced to the point where the receipt signature ceased.

Again the recipient signs a slip upon receipt and the Post Office retains the form. The receipt the sender keeps at the time he/she mails the package is much more complete than that for Insured Mail, as it lists full addresses of both the sender and the recipient, the Registry number of the parcel, the total cost break-down including the amount it is registered for, and as on the Insured / First Class, the round Post Office date stamp. Those who use a lot of Registered Mail can use a book to track these packages, designed especially for this purpose. This book has a place for all the necessary information. The two key advantages of this book are that the sender's name and address is entered only once for as many as eight packages, and the sender can maintain a copy of the page in their Firm Mailing Book (USPS Form 3877). Some postal centers will allow the sender to use only two or three entries, but some will require all eight entries to be completed. Talk to your local postal service representative.

Be Wary of Certified Mail!

Never send coins or anything of value by Certified Mail! Never! Certified Mail offers no monetary protection whatsoever, and if your package is lost you cannot recover any part of the value. It is strictly a method to ensure a certain letter or parcel is delivered—nothing more. This service is provided primarily for legal documents that do not require any insurance. There is not even assurance the package is received by the actual addressee. It is allowable for anyone to receive the package. With Certified Mail you have no recourse if the package is lost, and the Post Office declines responsibility. If a Certified Mail package is lost, it will be up to you to prove the addressee was the actual recipient, which is next to impossible, and then up to your civil resources to obtain the value.

Return Receipt

For a small additional fee, you may include a (green card) Return Receipt Request on the letter or package that you are mailing. When this card is returned to you, it will be a confirmation that your package was received. The person who accepted it at the other end must sign and date the card, which verifies delivery. However, this can only be secured at the time your package is presented for mailing.

This information should be of great value to collectors, especially those who don't often mail merchandise that needs value protection. A little extra time spent on packaging and ensuring that the item is sent in the proper manner will save you a lot of headaches down the road.

USPS.com

The U.S. Postal Service has produced something they can be proud of. The web site maintained by the Postal Service is excellent! There are hundreds of pages of informative data that will help you determine what best suits your shipping needs. Plus (and this is the best part) postage and official forms can be obtained online, most directly from the site. However, those that are not available on the site can be ordered online, along with boxes, envelopes, and supplies—all of which can be delivered to your door. In many cases this will enable you to skip some of those long lines at the Post Office.

Hopefully, this information will help you understand the mailing options that are best for you. If all else fails, call your local Postal Service office and speak to a customer service representative. They are there to help you.

Appendix J: Coin Submission Guidelines

Readers, collectors, dealers, and enthusiasts submit most of the varieties that you see listed in the *Cherrypickers' Guide*. If you have a variety you would like to have examined by author J.T. Stanton, please follow these guidelines for submitting coins for consideration. In all cases please **write first** to ensure the timing will be appropriate. You can write via email or snail mail, though email is preferred.

1. All coins should arrive in flips, coin envelopes, or slabs. Please, don't send a coin in a 2×2 holder with staples. Coins received in a package with staples *will be returned* without consideration. Please be sure that your name is on each individual package. Write your name on the flip insert, envelope, or on a piece of paper taped to the slab.

2. Please be very specific in describing the area of each coin that exhibits the area of interest. It is best to include a separate sheet with a description of each coin. If more than a couple of coins are included, it helps to sequentially number each coin.

3. You must clearly state in your letter the value of the total package. This is the amount of insurance that will be purchased for the return of the coins.

4. Adequate return postage and handling (plus any examination and/or photography fees) *must* be included for the return of your coins. Coins will be returned only via Registered Mail with insurance. Registered Mail is the safest form of mail. Please don't ask to have your coins sent back to you either uninsured or via First Class insured mail.

5. Again, please write first to ensure an appropriate arrival time for your package.

Examination Fees and Photography Costs
The cost for examination is $5 per coin. If you want photographs of any of your coins, the cost is $5 per photo. The photos will be provided as 4x6 prints. A digital copy of the photo will be available via email. Other photo options (different size prints, slides, etc.) are available upon request. There is no charge for photos if you don't want copies.

Return Postage, Insurance, and Handling
Again, this is for *Registered Mail only*—the only way your coins will be returned. Re-turn postage and insurance is $10.00 per package plus $1 for each $1,000 of insurance or partial thereof. Minimum cost is $11.00. Please see the table on the following page for a breakdown of Postal Insurance and Handling fees current as of this publication.

Postal Insurance Fee Structure

Abbreviation	Postage, Insurance, Handling
$1,000.00 or less	$11.00
Up to $2,000.00	$12.00
Up to $3,000.00	$13.00
Up to $4,000.00	$14.00
Up to $5,000.00	$15.00
Up to $6,000.00	$16.00
Up to $7,000.00	$17.00
Up to $8,000.00	$18.00
Up to $9,000.00	$19.00
Up to $10,000.00	$20.00

Never use Certified Mail to send coins. There is no insurance available for Certified Mail. Therefore, if a Certified Mail package is lost, there is no insurance benefit. You can send a Registered Mail package with a Delivery Confirmation at extra cost, but there is always a delivery record available for all Registered Mail. Please be sure to package your coins safely, securely, and without any indication of the contents.

These photo and postage rates are effective as of publication, and are subject to change. Please confirm prices when you write. For coin submissions, contact

J.T. Stanton
P.O. Box 15487
Savannah GA 31416-2187
Email: jtstanton@aol.com

Note: Whitman Publishing, LLC, is not involved in receiving, examining, or returning coins. No guarantee is made that a coin will be used in future editions of the book. Write to J.T. Stanton before mailing coins.

Appendix K: Fivaz/Stanton Number Cross-Reference Chart

The Fivaz/Stanton numbering system has changed! The previous numbering system was very confined, and drastically limited the number of new listings that could added. Our new system is rational and, best of all, infinite. The new system is clearly illustrated and described in the "How to Use This Book" section.

With this cross-reference chart, you'll be able to see the new numbers assigned to all previous listings. The first column indicates the *new* FS number, followed by the old FS number (if there was a listing), the date and mint of the coin, and finally a brief description. Abbreviations listed in the date and mint section, include L for Longacre's intial, LL for large letters, br for bronze, and NC for no cents. Due to space limitations, the description is very brief and should not be used in an attempt to identify a variety.

These new numbers can easily be used in an abbreviated format, by using only the final three or four digits in the full number. A variety is always described with the denomination and date, so duplicating that number in a description is not really necessary. The final three or four digits will describe the variety's FS number when the denomination and date is identified.

This new numbering system will enable us to continue to add new listings for as many new varieties as necessary.

New FS#	Old FS#	Date/Mint	Brief Description
Half Cents			
HC-1804-301	001	1804	Cohen 2
HC-1804-302	002	1804	Cohen 4
HC-1805-301	003	1805	Cohen 2
HC-1806-301	004	1806	Cohen 3
HC-1808-301	005	1808/7	Cohen 1
HC-1809-301	006	1809 L	Cohen 1
Large Cents			
LC-1843-301	001	1843	Newcomb #17
LC-1846-301	002	1846	Newcomb #23
LC-1846-302	002.5	1846	Newcomb #25
LC-1847-301	003	1847	Newcomb #36
LC-1847-302	004	1847	Newcomb #43
LC-1849-301	005	1849	Newcomb #25
LC-1850-301	005.5	1850	Newcomb #24
LC-1851-301	006	1851	Newcomb #42
LC-1851-302	006.5	1851	Newcomb #44
LC-1856-301	007	1856	Newcomb #22
Flying Eagle Cents			
01-1857-101	002	1857	DDO 2-O-I; UNITED STATES OF AMERICA, beak, eye, tail
01-1857-102	002.3	1857	DDO 3-O-I; UNITED STATES OF AMERICA, beak, eye, tail; not as strong as 101
01-1857-103	002.7	1857	DDO 6-O-I and RPD; doubling on UNITED STATES OF

New FS#	Old FS#	Date/Mint	Brief Description
			AMERICA, beak, eye, and tail
01-1857-104	002.8	1857	DDO 5-O-II; doubling evident on UNITED STATES OF AMERICA, beak, and wing
01-1857-301	001.5	1857	RPD very strong south on all four digits
01-1857-401	001	1857	Obv of '56; rectangular opening of O, long center serifs of F
01-1857-402	003	1857	Obverse clashed with Liberty Seated half dollar obverse
01-1857-403	004	1857	Obverse clashed with Liberty Head $20 gold obverse
01-1857-901	005	1857	Reverse clashed with Liberty Seated quarter reverse
01-1858-101	005.5	1858LL	Snow 2, DDO
01-1858-301	006	1858LL	Snow 1, Overdate 8/7 Die1
01-1858-302	006.1	1858LL	Snow 7, Overdate 8/7 Die 2
Indian Head Cents			
01-1859-301	006.3	1859	Snow 1, RPD
01-1859-302	006.2	1859	Snow 2, RPD
01-1859-303	006.35	1859	Snow 3, RPD
01-1860-401	006.4	1860	Transitional design; Pointed Bust of 1860
01-1861-301	006.45	1861	Snow 1, RPD
01-1863-801	006.46	1863	Snow 10, DDR
01-1864-1101	006.47	1864 br	Snow 4, DDO

APPENDIX K: FIVAZ/STANTON NUMBER CROSS-REFERENCE CHART

New FS#	Old FS#	Date/Mint	Brief Description
01-1864-1301	006.48	1864 br	Snow 2, RPD
01-1864-2301	006.7	1864 L	Snow 1, RPD
01-1864-2302	006.71	1864 L	Snow 3, RPD
01-1864-2303	006.72	1864 L	Snow 4, RPD
01-1864-2304	006.5	1864 L	Snow 5, RPD
01-1864-2305	006.55	1864 L	RPD
01-1864-2306	006.73	1864 L	Snow 13, RPD
01-1865-301	007.4	1865	Snow 1, Plain 5 — RPD
01-1865-302	007.45	1865	Plain 5 — RPD
01-1865-303	007.5	1865	Snow 3, Plain 5 — RPD
01-1865-304	007.56	1865	Snow 2, Plain 5 — MPD
01-1865-1101	007	1865	Snow 2, Fancy 5 — DDO
01-1865-1301	007.3	1865	Snow 1, Fancy 5 — RPD
01-1865-1302	007.55	1865	Snow 4, Fancy 5 — RPD
01-1865-1401	007.2	1865	Snow 14, Fancy 5 — Obverse Die Gouge
01-1866-101	007.6	1866	Snow 1, DDO, Multiple MPD
01-1866-301	007.7	1866	Snow 2, RPD
01-1866-302	007.9	1866	Snow 3, RPD
01-1866-303	007.8	1866	Snow 11, RPD
01-1867-301	008	1867	Snow 1, RPD
01-1867-302	008.1	1867	Snow 4, RPD
01-1868-101	008.2	1868	Snow 1, DDO
01-1868-102	008.26	1868	Snow 4, DDO, RPD
01-1868-103	008.25	1868	Snow 5, DDO. RPD, MPD
01-1868-301	008.23	1868	Snow 8, MPD
01-1869-301	008.3	1869	Snow 3, RPD (formerly believed to be 1869/8)
01-1869-302	008.5	1869	Snow 1, RPD
01-1870-101	008.6	1870	Snow 1, 2, DDO Snow 1,2,13,22,28
01-1870-102	008.82	1870	Snow 5, DDO, RPD, MPD
01-1870-301	008.81	1870	Snow 4, RPD
01-1870-302	008.8	1870	Snow 8, MPD, DDR
01-1870-801	008.7	1870	Snow 2, 3, DDR
01-1872-301	008.9	1872	Snow 1, RPD
Note: 1873 "Close 3" varieties are numbered 101-999.			
01-1873-101	009	1873	Snow 1, Closed 3 DDO
01-1873-102	009.1	1873	Snow 2, Closed 3 DDO
Note: 1873 "open 3" varieties are numbered 1101-1999.			
01-1873-1301	009.3	1873	Snow 1, Open 3 RPD
01-1874-101	009.33	1874	Snow 1, DDO
01-1878-301	009.4	1878	Snow 2, MPD
01-1880-101	009.41	1880	Snow 1, DDO, MAD Reverse
01-1882-301	009.43	1882	Snow 6, MPD
01-1883-301	009.45	1883	Snow 2, MPD
01-1883-801	009.46	1883	Snow 6, DDR
01-1884-301	009.48	1884	Snow 1, MPD
01-1887-101	009.5	1887	Snow 1, DDO
01-1888-301	010	1888/7	Snow 1, Overdate #1
	010.5	1888	No variety — delisted
01-1888-302	010.7	1888/7	Snow 2, Overdate #2
01-1888-303	010.73	1888	MPD; base of 1 in ribbon
01-1888-304	010.74	1888	MPD; 8 in hair curl
01-1888-305	010.75	1888	MPD; two 8's in hair curl
01-1889-301	010.8	1889	Snow 3, RPD
01-1889-801	010.81	1889	Snow 1, DDR

New FS#	Old FS#	Date/Mint	Brief Description
01-1890-101	010.85	1890	Snow 1, TDO
01-1890-301	010.82	1890	Snow 3, MPD
01-1890-302	010.84	1890	Snow 6, MPD
01-1891-101	010.88	1891	Snow 1, DDO
01-1891-301	010.87	1891	Snow 3, RPD
01-1892-301	010.89	1892	Snow 8, RPD
01-1892-302	010.9	1892	Snow 1, RPD
01-1892-401	010.91	1892	Heavy die scratches
01-1893-301	010.95	1893	Snow 2, RPD
01-1894-301	011	1894	Snow 1, RPD
01-1894-302	011.2	1894	Snow 2, MPD
01-1895-301	011.3	1895	Snow 1, RPD
01-1895-302	011.31	1895	Snow 9, RPD
01-1896-301	011.4	1896	Snow 1, RPD
01-1897-301	011.6	1897	Snow 8, RPD
01-1897-302	011.5	1897	Snow 1, MPD
01-1898-301	011.65	1898	MPD; 8 in denticles
01-1898-302	011.66	1898	Snow 5, MPD
01-1899-301	011.7	1899	Snow 1, RPD
01-1899-302	011.75	1899	Snow 13, RPD
01-1900-301	011.751	1900	Snow 1, RPD
01-1903-301	011.76	1903	Snow 10, MPD
01-1903-302	011.765	1903	Snow 6, MPD
01-1908-301	011.77	1908	MPD; 8 slightly left and below primary 8 in denticles
01-1908-302	011.79	1908	Snow 9, MPD
01-1909-101	011.9	1909	Snow 1, Doubled L

Lincoln Cents

New FS#	Old FS#	Date/Mint	Brief Description
01-1909-1101	012	1909 V.D.B.	DDO, 1-O-IV
01-1909-1102	012.1	1909 V.D.B.	DDO, 2-O-VI
01-1909S-1501	012.2	1909-S	S/S RPM #1
01-1909S-1502	012.3	1909-S	S/S, Horizontal S; RPM #2
01-1910S-501	012.7	1910-S	S/S, RPM #2
01-1911D-501	012.8	1911-D	D/D, RPM #1
01-1911D-502	012.81	1911-D	D/D, RPM #2
01-1911D-503	012.82	1911-D	D/D, RPM #3
01-1911D-504	012.83	1911-D	D/D, RPM #4
01-1911S-501	012.85	1911-S	S/S, RPM #1
01-1917-101	013	1917	DDO, 1-O-V
01-1922-401	013.2	1922	"No D" Variety; Die Pair #2 only
01-1925S-101	013.3	1925-S	DDO, 1-O-VI
01-1925S-501	013.31	1925-S	S/S RPM #1
01-1927-101	013.5	1927	DDO, 1-O-I
01-1927D-501	013.51	1927-D	D/D, RPM #1
01-1928S-501	013.6	1928-S	Large S mintmark variety
01-1929S-501	013.65	1929-S	S/S, RPM #1
01-1930D-501	013.7	1930-D	D/D, RPM #2
01-1930S-501	013.73	1930-S	S/S, RPM #1
01-1934-101	013.79	1934	DDO
01-1934D-501	013.81	1934-D	D/D/D/D, RPM #3
01-1934D-502	013.8	1934-D	D/D, RPM #4
01-1935-101	013.9	1935	DDO, 1-O-V
01-1936-101	014	1936	DDO, 1-O-IV
01-1936-102	015	1936	DDO, 2-O-V
01-1936-103	016	1936	DDO, 3-O-V
01-1938D-501	016.4	1938-D	D/D, RPM #1

New FS#	Old FS#	Date/Mint	Brief Description
01-1938S-501	016.51	1938-S	S/S, RPM #1
01-1938S-502	016.5	1938-S	S/S/S, RPM #2
01-1939-101	017	1939	DDO, 1-O-I
01-1941-101	018	1941	DDO, 1-O-I
01-1941-102	018.1	1941	DDO, 2-O-I
01-1941-103	018.3	1941	DDO, 5-O-IV
01-1941S-501		1941-S	Large S variety
01-1942-102	018.7	1942	DDO, 4-O-V
01-1942-103	018.9	1942	DDO, 6-O-IV
01-1942D-501	018.91	1942-D	D/D, RPM #2
01-1942D-502	018.92	1942-D	D/D, RPM #4
01-1942S-101	018.94	1942-S	DDO, 1-O-IV and S/S RPM #1
01-1942S-501	018.93	1942-S	S/S/S, RPM #12; very strong north and west
01-1943-101	018.97	1943	DDO, 1-O-VI; very strong class VI
01-1943D-501	019	1943-D	D/D, RPM #1; very strong D/D southwest
01-1943D-502	019.1	1943-D	D/D, RPM #13
01-1943S-101	019.5	1943-S	DDO, 1-O-IV
01-1944D-501	020	1944-D	D/S, OMM #1; very wide north
01-1944D-502	021	1944-D	D/S, OMM #2; centered under D
01-1944D-503	021.1	1944-D	D/D, RPM #2
01-1944D-504	021.11	1944-D	D/D, RPM #7
01-1946S-501	021.2	1944-S	S/D, OMM #1; D well centered under S
01-1947-101	021.3	1947	DDO, 1-O-I
01-1947S-501	021.31	1947-S	S/S, RPM #4
01-1949D-501	021.33	1949-D	D/D/D, RPM #1
01-1950S-501	021.34	1950-S	S/S, RPM #4 S/S north
01-1951-101	021.35	1951 PF	PF DDO, 1-O-II
01-1951D-101	021.4	1951-D	DDO, 1-O-V
01-1951D-501	021.5	1951-D	D/S, OMM #1; S well centered under D
01-1951D-502	021.52	1951-D	D/S, OMM #2; S slightly south of being centered under D
01-1951D-503	021.51	1951-D	Misplaced D mintmark in date
01-1952D-501	021.6	1952-D	D/S, OMM #1; very likely over S mintmark
01-1953-101	021.7	1953 PF	PF DDO, 1-O-II
01-1953D-501	021.73	1953-D	D/D, RPM #1
01-1954D-501	021.76	1954-D	D/D/D, RPM #1; very strong north and south of primary D
01-1955-101A	021.8	1955	DDO, 1-O-I (raw — uncertified)
01-1955-101B	021.8	1955	DDO, 1-O-I (certified)
01-1955-102	021.9	1955	2-O-II+V
01-1955D-101	021.93	1955-D	DDO, 1-O-IV+VII
01-1955D-501	021.94	1955-D	D/D/D, RPM #3; secondary D centered and wide east
01-1955D-502	012.95	1955-D	D/Horizontal D (presently unique)
01-1955S-501	021.97	1955-S	S/S/S, RPM #1; both secondary stepped northwest
01-1956D-501	022	1956-D	D/D, RPM #8; separated south
01-1956D-502	022.1	1956-D	D/D, RPM #1

New FS#	Old FS#	Date/Mint	Brief Description
01-1956D-511	1956-D	OMM #1, D and S, separated northwes between 1 and 9 of date
01-1958-101	022.15	1958	DDO, 1-O-I
01-1959-101	022.2	1959	DDO, 1-O-II
01-1959-102	022.3	1959	DDO, 4-O-II
01-1959-501	022.5	1959-D	D/D/D, RPM #1
01-1960-101	025	1960 PF	DDO, Large/Small Date 1-O-III
01-1960-102	024	1960 PF	DDO, Small/Large Date 2-O-III
01-1960-103	023	1960 PF	TDO, Large/Small Date 3-O-III
01-1960D-101	025.5	1960-D	DDO and RPM Small/Large Date, RPM #1
01-1961D-501		1961-D	RPM #1, D/Horizontal D
01-1963D-101	025.8	1963-D	DDO, 3/3
01-1964-801	026	1964	DDR, 1-R-I
01-1964-802	027	1964	DDR, 58-R-II
01-1968D-501	027.3	1968-D	RPM #1
01-1968D-801	027.4	1968-D	DDR, 1-R-V
01-1968S-101	027.5	1968-S PF	DDO, 12-O-II
01-1969S-101	028	1969-S	DDO, 1-O-I
01-1970S-101	029	1970-S	DDO, 1-O-I
01-1970S-102	030	1970-S PF	DDO, 3-O-III, Large/Small Date
01-1970S-103	030.1	1970-S	DDO, 5-O-VII
01-1970S-104	030.4	1970-S PF	DDO, 7-O-I
01-1970S-105	030.6	1970-S PF	DDO, 13-O-I
01-1970S-1401	N/L	1970-S	Small Date; circulation strike
01-1970S-1402	030.2	1970-S PF	Small Date; Proof
01-1971-101	031	1971	DDO, 1-O-II
01-1971-102	030.7	1971	DDO,
01-1971S-101	032	1971-S PF	Proof DDO, 1-O-II
01-1971S-102	033	1971-S PF	Proof DDO, 2-O-II+V
01-1971S-103	033.1	1971-S PF	DDO, 4-O-V
01-1972-101	033.3	1972	DDO, 1-O-I
01-1972-102	033.52	1972	DDO, 2-O-I
01-1972-103	033.53	1972	DDO, 3-O-I
01-1972-104	033.54	1972	DDO, 4-O-I
01-1972-105	033.55	1972	DDO, 5-O-I
01-1972-106	033.56	1972	DDO, 6-O-I
01-1972-107	033.57	1972	DDO, 7-O-I
01-1972-108	033.58	1972	DDO, 8-O-I
01-1972-109	033.59	1972	DDO, 9-O-VII
01-1972S-101	033.7	1972-S PF	Proof DDO, 1-O-I 3
01-1980-101	034	1980	DDO, 1-O-V
01-1980D-501	034.1	1980-D	D and S mintmark variety; S in field between D and 8 of date
01-1982-101	034.5	1982	CLD, DDO, 2-O-V
01-1983-101	035	1983	DDO, 1-O-V
01-1983-102	035.1	1983	DDO, 2-O-V
01-1983-103	035.2	1983	DDO, 3-O-V
01-1983-401	035.3	1983	Obverse die damage with reverse cud (possible unusual DDO)
01-1983-801	036	1983	DDR, 1-R-IV
01-1984-101	037	1984	DDO, 1-O-IV
01-1984-102	038	1984	DDO, 2-O-II

Chart continued on next page.

New FS#	Old FS#	Date/Mint	Brief Description
01-1984D-101	039	1984-D	DDO, 1-O-II+VI
01-1992D-901		1992-D	Type 1 reverse; touching AM of AMERICA
01-1994-801	039.9	1994	DDR, 1-R-IV
01-1995-101	040	1995	DDO, 1-O-V
01-1995D-101	041	1995-D	DDO, 3-O-V
01-1997-101	043	1997	DDO (?); Doubled Ear
01-1998-901		1998	Type 2 reverse; wide AM of AMERICA
01-1999-901		1999	Type 2 reverse; wide AM of AMERICA
01-2000-901		2000	Type 2 reverse; wide AM of AMERICA
01-2004-801		2004	DDO (minor) and DDR (significant) — all reverse lettering
01-2004D-101		2004-D	Doubled Die Obverse

Two-Cent Pieces

02-1864-401	000.5	1864	Small Motto
02-1864-102	001	1864	DDO, 1-O-II (Leone-64Lg-06G)
02-1864-301	001.5	1864	RPD (Leone 64Lg-100E)
02-1864-302	001.7	1864	RPD (Leone 64-Lg-24H)
02-1864-901	001.8	1864	Reverse die clashed with obverse of Indian Head cent

Note: 1865 "Plain 5" varieties are numbered 101-999.

02-1865-101	002	1865	Plain 5; DDO 2-O-III (Leone 65P-1o1r)
02-1865-301	002.3	1865	Plain 5; RPD (Leone 65P-5o1r)

Note: 1865 "Fancy 5" varieties are numbered 1101-1999.

02-1865-1301	002.5	1865	Fancy 5; RPD (Leone 65F-1o1r)
02-1865-1302	002.7	1865	Fancy 5; RPD (Leone 65F-2o1r)
02-1865-1303	002.8	1865	Fancy 5; RPD (Leone ??)
02-1865-1304	002.9	1865	Fancy 5; MPD (6 or 8 in digits below primary 8)
02-1867-101	003	1867	DDO, 1-O-V (Leone 1o1r)
02-1868-301	003.5	1868	MPD (6 in digits below primary 6)
02-1869-101	004.2	1869	DDO
02-1869-301	003.9	1869	RPD and MPD (6 in digits below primary 6)
02-1869-302	004	1869	RPD
02-1870-101	004.3	1870	DDO
02-1871-101	005	1871	DDO; circulation strike (struck from the Proof die)
02-1871-102		1871 PF	DDO; all 1871 Proof two-cent pieces are from this die; common
02-1872-101	006	1872	DDO

Three-Cent Silver Pieces

3S-1851-301	001	1851	RPD
3S-1851-302	001.5	1851	RPD
3S-1852-301	002	1852	1852/inverted date
3S-1852-302	002.3	1852	RPD
3S-1852-801	002.5	1852	Doubled Die Reverse
3S-1853-301	003	1853	RPD

New FS#	Old FS#	Date/Mint	Brief Description
3S-1854-301	004	1854	RPD — wide west
3S-1862-301	007	1862/1	2/1 overdate

Nickel Three-Cent Piece

3N-1865-101	003.5	1865	DDO
3N-1865-301	001	1865	MPD; flag of 5 in denticles
3N-1865-302	001.5	1865	RPD; wide west
3N-1865-303	002	1865	MPD; flag of 5 deep in denticles
3N-1865-304	002.5	1865	RPD; strong south (blunt tip 5)
3N-1866-101	004	1866	DDO, 1-O-IV
3N-1869-301	004.3	1869	RPD
3N-1869-302	004.5	1869	RPD
3N-1869-801	004.7	1869	DDR, 1-R-III
3N-1870-101	005	1870	DDO, RPD
3N-1870-301	005.5	1870	MPD
3N-1870-302	005.6	1870	MPD, DDR
3N-1871-101	006	1871	TDO, 1-O-I
3N-1875-301	006.5	1875	MPD; 1 in neck; very common (~1 in 3)
3N-1881-301	006.8	1881	RPD
3N-1887-301	007	1887	Overdate 7/6; circulation-strike version only
3N-1887-302	007	1887 PF	Overdate 7/6; Proof version

Shield Nickels

05-1866-101	001.7	1866	DDO, F-22
05-1866-102	001.5	1866	DDO, F-214
05-1866-301	001	1866	RPD, F-08
05-1866-302	001.1	1866	RPD, F-10
05-1866-303	001.2	1866	RPD, F-20
05-1866-304	001.3	1866	RPD, F-16
05-1866-305	001.4	1866	RPD, F-13

Note: 1867 "With Rays" varieties are numbered 101-999.

05-1867-301	002.1	1867	With Rays; RPD, F-8; likely a small/large date, larger logotype under
05-1867-302	002.4	1867	With Rays; RPD, F-9
05-1867-303	002.7	1867	With Rays; RPD, F-2
05-1867-304	002.6	1867	With Rays; MPD, F-01
05-1867-305	002.75	1867	With Rays; F — N/L; 1 punched in shield
05-1867-501	NEW	1867	With Rays; rev die clashed with obv; date showing very strong; super!

Note: 1867 "No Rays" varieties are numbered 1101-1999.

05-1867-1101	NEW	1867	No Rays; prototype rev die. PF only. Star points to first A of AMERICA
05-1867-1102	001.8	1867	No Rays; DDO, 3-O-III F-59
05-1867-1103	002	1867	NR; DDO, 1-O-IV and RPD
05-1867-1301	001.9	1867	No Rays; RPD, F-23
05-1867-1302	002.15	1867	No Rays; RPD, F-25
05-1867-1303	002.2	1867	No Rays; RPD, F-21
05-1867-1304	002.25	1867	No Rays; RPD, F-20
05-1867-1305	002.3	1867	No Rays; RPD, F-22
05-1867-1306	002.35	1867	No Rays; RPD north, F — N/L
05-1867-1307	002.5	1867	No Rays; RPD, F-38
05-1867-1308	002.9	1867	No Rays; RPD, F-42

New FS#	Old FS#	Date/Mint	Brief Description
05-1867-1309	002.45	1867	No Rays; MPD, F—N/L
05-1868-101	003	1868	DDO, 1-O-IV
05-1868-102	003.65	1868	TDO, 10-O-III+IV; Reverse of '68; will be moved
05-1868-103	003.8	1868	DDO, 6-O-III
05-1868-104	003.9	1868	DDO, 9-O-IV
05-1868-105	003.95	1868	DDO, DDR
05-1868-106	003.96	1868	DDO, 3-O-IV; Reverse of '68???; will be moved
05-1868-107	003.97	1868	DDO, 11-O-IV and RPD
05-1868-301	003.2	1868	RPD, F-19
05-1868-302	003.3	1868	RPD, F—N/L; Reverse of '68???; will be moved
05-1868-303	003.35	1868	RPD, south, F—N/L
05-1868-304	003.4	1868	RPD, east, F—N/L
05-1868-305	003.45	1868	RPD, multiple, F—N/L
05-1868-306	003.5	1868	RPD, date touching ball, F—N/L
05-1868-307	003.7	1868	RPD
05-1868-308	003.75	1868	RPD, wide southeast
05-1868-309	003.85	1868	RPD, Reverse of '68???; will be moved
05-1868-310	003.98	1868	RPD, F-20
05-1868-311	003.985	1868	RPD and missing leaf
05-1868-312	003.1	1868	MPD; 1 in ball of shield; Reverse of '68???; will be moved
	003.55	1868	MPD; photo was an Indian Head cent; will be removed
05-1868-314	003.6	1868	MPD; 6 or 8 in denticles; F-2
05-1868-401	003.99	1868	Missing leaf and circular scribe mark

Reverse varieties of 1868: these are *only* 1868 nickels with the reverse of 1868!

New FS#	Old FS#	Date/Mint	Brief Description
05-1868-901	002.98	1868	Variety 5 has no broken letters; earliest die state
05-1868-902	002.99	1868	Variety 5.5 has a partially broken C of CENTS
05-1868-903	002.94	1868	Variety 1 has a fully broken C of CENTS
05-1868-904	002.95	1868	Variety 2 has a broken C and S of CENTS
05-1868-905	002.96	1868	Variety 3 has a broken C and S of CENTS, plus the S of STATES
05-1868-906	002.97	1868	Variety 4 is same as #905 plus a broken D of UNITED

Note: 1869 "Narrow Date" varieties are numbered 101-999.

New FS#	Old FS#	Date/Mint	Brief Description
05-1869-301	005	1869	Narrow Date

Note: 1969 "Wide Date" varieties are numbered 1101-1999.

New FS#	Old FS#	Date/Mint	Brief Description
05-1869-1101	004	1869	DDO 1-O-III
05-1869-1102	004.5	1869	DDO 2-O-V and RPD (tripled)
05-1869-1103	005.67	1869	DDO 3-O-IV+V and RPD
05-1869-1301		1869	Normal or "wide" date as opposed to the narrow date FS 301
05-1869-1302	005.3	1869	RPD, F-104
05-1869-1303	005.4	1869	RPD, F-202
05-1869-1304	005.5	1869	RPD, F-408
05-1869-1305	005.6	1869	RPD, F-409
05-1869-1306	005.68	1869	RPD, F-105

New FS#	Old FS#	Date/Mint	Brief Description
05-1869-1307	005.2	1869	MPD; 1 in ball above date
05-1869-1401		1869	Missing Leaf variety (Fletcher #116-119)
05-1870-101	005.7	1870	DDO, 1-O-III and RPD south F-03
05-1870-102	005.74	1870	DDO, F-12
05-1870-103	005.75	1870	DDO and RPD, very wide east
05-1870-301	005.77	1870	RPD, MPD, RPD wide southwest, and RPD with 1 in denticle
05-1870-302	005.76	1870	MPD with 0 in denticles southwest of primary 0
05-1870-801	005.9	1870	DDR 2-R-III rev of '70 (lic) over rev of '67 (lia)
05-1870-802	005.93	1870	DDR; Reverse of '67; ~3 known; discovered by Brad Meadows
05-1871-101	006	1871	DDO
05-1871-301	006.5	1871	RPD, F-02
05-1872-101	007	1872	DDO, F-121
05-1872-102	007.1	1872	DDO, F-123
05-1872-103	007.2	1872	DDO, 1-O-III, F-124
05-1872-104	007.3	1872	DDO, 4-O-III, F-109
05-1872-105	007.4	1872	TDO, F-05
05-1872-106	007.5	1872	DDO, F-116
05-1872-107		1872 PF	DDO plus a rotated die F-06
05-1872-108	1872		DDO, RPD
05-1872-301	007.6	1872	RPD, F-104; moderate north
05-1872-302	007.65	1872	RPD, F—N/L; very strong with 7 south 3x
05-1872-303	007.7	1872	RPD, F-103
05-1872-304	007.76	1872	RPD, 72 repunched north
05-1872-305	007.77	1872	RPD, MPD; very nice variety
05-1872-306	007.9	1872	RPD, F-02
05-1872-307	007.75	1872	MPD; 2 north right of ball; very, very nice
05-1872-308	007.8	1872	Small over large date
05-1872-309		1872	

Note: 1873 "Close 3" varieties are numbered 101-999.

New FS#	Old FS#	Date/Mint	Brief Description
05-1873-101	008	1873	Close 3; DDO, 2-O-IV, F-04
05-1873-102	008.7	1873	Close 3; DDO, 3-O-IV, F-05
05-1873-103	008.8	1873	Close 3; DDO, F-06
05-1873-104	008.85	1873	Close 3; DDO, F-04
05-1873-1101	008.3	1873	Open 3; DDO, F-113
05-1873-1102	008.5	1873	Open 3; DDO, MPD, F-102
05-1873-1301	009	1873	Open 3; RPD, Large Date over Small Date
05-1873-1302	009.3	1873	Open 3; RPD, F-103
05-1873-1303	009.5	1873	O3; RPD, F-110 (Open 3/2)
05-1873-1304	009.7	1873	Open 3; RPD
05-1874-101	010	1874	DDO, F-05
05-1874-102	010.4	1874	DDO, F-12; very strong on shield and motto
05-1874-103	010.5	1874	DDO, 4-O-V, F-08
05-1874-104	010.6	1874	DDO; very strong south; full annulet separation
05-1874-301	010.7	1874	RPD, F-02
05-1874-302	010.8	1874	RPD, F-01
05-1875-101	011	1875	DDO, 1-O-III, F-04

Chart continued on next page.

New FS#	Old FS#	Date/Mint	Brief Description
05-1875-102	011.3	1875	DDO, 2-0-V, F-05
05-1875-103	011.5	1875	DDO, RPD, F-03
05-1876-101	012	1876	TDO, 1-0-II+III, F-04
05-1876-102	012.1	1876	DDO, 2-0-III
05-1876-103		1876	DDO, RPD, polish lines, F-08
05-1882-301	012.5	1882	RPD

Note: 1883 Shield nickels are numbered 101-999.

05-1883-301	013	1883/2	Overdate Die #1, F-08
05-1883-302	013.1	1883/2	Overdate Die #2, F-09
05-1883-303	013.2	1883/2	Overdate Die #3, F-10
05-1883-304	013.3	1883/2	Overdate Die #4,
05-1883-305		1883/2	Overdate Die #5
05-1883-306	012.8	1883	RPD F-04
05-1883-307	012.9	1883	RPD, F-02

Liberty Head Nickels

Note: 1883 Liberty Head nickels are numbered 1101-1999.

05-1883-1301	013.7	1883 NC	RPD; base of 1 low and left from first 8
05-1884-301	013.8	1884	RPD
05-1886-301	013.9	1886	RPD
05-1887-801	013.9	1887	DDR, 1-R-III
05-1888-101		1888	DDO; most evident on Liberty's ear
05-1890-301	014.3	1890	RPD
05-1897-301	014.48	1897	RPD
05-1898-301	014.49	1898	RPD
05-1898-302	014.495	1898	RPD; very strong east of primary date
05-1899-301	014.5	1899	RPD; some believe to be a 9/8
05-1900-801	014.7	1900	DDR; moderate on all reverse elements

Note: Any 1883 "With CENTS" varieties would be in a range from 2101 through 2999.

Buffalo Nickels

Note: 1913 Type 1 nickels are numbered 101-999.

05-1913-401		1913	Two Feather Variety
05-1913-801		1913	DDR; most evident on E PLURIBUS UNUM and buffalo's hind leg
05-1913-901	014.85	1913	Type 1; 3-1/2 leg reverse
05-1913D-401	014.861	1913-D	Two Feather Variety
05-1913S-401		1913-S	No initials (Fred Moore)
05-1913S-402		1913-S	Two Feather Variety

Note: 1913 Type 2 nickels are numbered 1101-1999.

05-1913-1101	014.8	1913	Type II; DDO, 1-0-VI (listed in CPG 4-1 as Type I)
05-1913-1801	014.86	1913	Type II; DDR, 1-R-II+VI
05-1914-101	014.87	1914	DDO; Overdate 4/3
05-1914D-101	014.88	1914-D	DDO; Overdate 4/3
05-1914S-101	014.89	1914-S	DDO; Overdate 4/3
05-1915-101	014.9	1915	DDO, 1-0-IV
05-1915-401	014.91	1915	Two Feather Variety
05-1915-402		1915	Missing initial
05-1915D-401		1915-D	Two Feather Variety
05-1915D-501	015	1915-D	RPM #1, D/D north
05-1915S-501	015.5	1915-S	RPM #1

New FS#	Old FS#	Date/Mint	Brief Description
05-1915S-502	015.6	1915-S	RPM #2
05-1916-101	016	1916	DDO #1, 1916/1916
05-1916-401	016.3	1916	No F; missing designer's initial
05-1916-402		1916	Two Feather Variety
05-1916-403		1916	No F; Two Feather Variety
05-1916S-401		1916-S	Missing initial
05-1917-401	016.411	1917	Two Feather Variety
05-1917-402		1917	Missing initial
05-1917-801	016.4	1917	DDR, 1-R-III
05-1917-802	016.41	1917	DDR, 2-R-IV
05-1917D-401	016.43	1917-D	Two Feather Variety
05-1917D-901	016.42	1917-D	3-1/2 leg reverse
05-1917S-401	016.44	1917-S	Two Feather Variety
05-1917S-402		1917-S	Missing initial
05-1918-401	016.46	1918	Two Feather Variety
05-1918-801	016.45	1918	DDR, 1-R-II
05-1918D-101	016.5	1918-D	DDO, 1918/17
05-1918S-401	016.6	1918-S	Two Feather Variety
05-1919-101		1919	DDO; evident on profile, upper hair braid
05-1919-401	016.61	1919	Two Feather Variety
05-1919-402		1919	Missing initial
05-1919D-401		1919-D	Two Feather Variety
05-1919D-801		1919-D	Doubled Die Reverse (NGC)
05-1920-401		1920	Two Feather Variety
05-1920-402		1920	Missing initial
05-1920D-501	016.63	1920-D	RPM #1
05-1920S-401	016.631	1920-S	Two Feather Variety
05-1920S-901		1920-S	3-1/2 legged variety
05-1921-401	016.633	1921	Two Feather Variety
05-1921S-401	016.635	1921-S	Two Feather Variety
05-1924-401		1924	Missing initial
05-1925D-401	016.638	1925-D	Two Feather Variety
05-1925S-401	016.641	1925-S	Two Feather Variety
05-1925S-501	016.64	1925-S	RPM #1
05-1926D-401		1926-D	Two Feather Variety
05-1926D-402		1926-D	Missing initial
05-1926D-901		1926-D	3-1/2 leg reverse
05-1927D-401		1927-D	Two Feather Variety
05-1927D-501	016.7	1927-D	RPM #1
05-1927D-901	016.65	1927-D	3-1/2 leg reverse
05-1927S-101	016.75	1927-D	DDO
05-1927S-401		1927-S	Two Feather Variety
05-1929-101	016.8	1929	DDO (Fivaz)
05-1929S-401		1929-S	Two Feather Variety
05-1930-101	017	1930	DDO, 1-0-IV
05-1930-801	017.5	1930	DDR, 1-R-IV
05-1930-802	017.3	1930	DDR, 2-R-IV
05-1930-803	017.4	1930	DDR, 3-R-IV
05-1930S-101		1930-S	DDO, 1-0-VI; extra thickness on the letters and date
05-1930S-401	017.711	1930-S	Two Feather Variety
05-1930S-501	017.71	1930-S	S/S, RPM #2
05-1935-801	018	1935	DDR, 1-R-V
05-1935-802		1935	DDR, 2-R-VI
05-1935-803	018.1	1935	DDR, 3-R-V

New FS#	Old FS#	Date/Mint	Brief Description
05-1935D-401		1935-D	Missing initial
05-1935D-502	018.5	1935-D	D/D/D/D, RPM #2
05-1935S-801	018.6	1935-S	DDR, 1-R-IV
05-1936-101	018.7	1936	DDO, 1-O-VI
05-1936-401		1936	Missing initial
05-1936-801	018.8	1936	DDR, 1-R-II+VI-(4)
05-1936D-501		1036-D	D/D, RPM #1
05-1936D-502	019.5	1936-D	D/D/D, RPM #2
05-1936D-511	019.8	1936-D	D/D/S, OMM; actually D/D/D/S
05-1936D-901	019	1936-D	3-1/2 leg reverse
05-1936S-501	020	1936-S	S/S south; CONECA RPM #1
05-1937D-901	020.2	1937-D	3-legged variety
05-1937D-902		1937-D	3-1/2 leg variety; top of back leg polished and missing
05-1937S-501		1937-S	S/S west, CONECA RPM #1
05-1937S-502		1937-S	S/S/S, CONECA RPM #2
05-1938D-501		1938-D	D/D south, CONECA RPM #1
05-1938D-502		1938-D	D/D west, CONECA RPM #2
05-1938D-503		1938-D	D/D west, CONECA RPM #3
05-1938D-504		1938-D	D/D west, CONECA RPM #4
05-1938D-511	020.5	1938-D/S	D/D/D/S, CONECA OMM #1
05-1938D-512		1938-D/S	D/S, CONECA OMM #2
05-1938D-513		1938-D/S	D/S, CONECA OMM #3
05-1938D-514		1938-D/S	D/S, CONECA OMM #4
05-1938D-515		1938-D/S	D/S, CONECA OMM #5

Jefferson Nickels

Note: 1938 P, D, S Jefferson varieties will be numbered 1101-1999, as varieties are listed.

New FS#	Old FS#	Date/Mint	Brief Description
05-1938-1101	021	1938	DDO, 1-O-III
05-1938-1105	021.5	1938	DDO, 5-O-II-(4)
05-1939-801	022	1939	DDR, 1-R-IV
05-1939-802	022.5	1939	DDR, 2-R-II+VI
05-1939-901	023	1939 PF	Reverse of 1940; Type II Steps
05-1940-901	024	1940 PF	Reverse of 1938; Type I Steps
05-1941D-501	024.3	1941-D	RPM; D/D southeast
05-1941S-501	024.5	1941-S	Large S mintmark
05-1941S-502		1941-S	Large S; RPM #2, S/S overlapping
05-1941S-503	024.6	1941-S	Inverted mintmark
05-1942-101	025	1942	DDO, 2-O-IV
05-1942-102	026	1942	DDO, 3-O-IV
05-1942D-501	027	1942-D	RPM, D/Horizontal D, RPM #1
05-1943P-101	028	1943-P	DDO, 1943/2-P
05-1943P-106	029	1943-P	DDO, 6-O-I ; Doubled Eye variety
05-1945P-801	030	1945-P	DDR, 1-R-III
05-1945P-803	030.3	1945-P	DDR, 3-R-II+VI
05-1945P-804	030.5	1945-P	DDR, 4-R-II-(6) + RPM #1
05-1946D-501	031	1946-D	D/Inverted D, RPM #2
05-1946S-101	031.5	1946-S	DDO, 1-O-V
05-1949D-501	032	1949-D	D/S, OMM #1
05-1951-101	032.5	1951 PF	DDO, 1-O-V
05-1953-101	032.7	1953 PF	DDO, 1-O-I
05-1954D-501	032.9	1954-D	RPM; some believe this to be an OMM, D/S
05-1954S-501	033	1954-S	OMM #1 D/S

New FS#	Old FS#	Date/Mint	Brief Description
05-1954S-502	033.1	1954-S	S/S, RPM #1
05-1955-801	035	1955 PF	DDR, 1-R-II-(3)
05-1956-801	035.2	1956	QDR, 18-R-II-(4)
05-1957-101	035.8	1957 PF	QDO
05-1958D-501		1958-D	D/D; D over Horizontal D
05-1960-801	036	1960 PF	DDR, 1-R-II
05-1961-801	037	1961 PF	DDR, 13-R-II
05-1963-801	037.3	1963	TDR
05-1964D-501	037.5	1964-D	RPM #5
05-1968S-501	038	1968-S PF	S/S east; RPM #2

Note: Any 2004-P "Peace Medal" varieties will be numbered 101-999, as varieties are listed.

Note: Any "Keelboat" varieties will be numbered 1101-1999, as varieties are listed.

New FS#	Old FS#	Date/Mint	Brief Description
05-2004P-101		2004-P	DDO-001; evident on LIBERTY, IGWT, star, and date; Peace reverse
05-2005D-901		2005-D	Die gouge on reverse through buffalo ("Speared Buffalo")

Bust Half Dimes

New FS#	Old FS#	Date/Mint	Brief Description
H10-1829-301	000.1	1829	1829/8; 8 on top surface of 9
H10-1834-301	000.3	1834	3 Over Inverted 3 in date

Liberty Seated Half Dimes

New FS#	Old FS#	Date/Mint	Brief Description
H10-1838-901		1838	Rusted die reverse; rusting evident at about K-3 and K-4
H10-1840o-901	000.5	1840-O	Transitional reverse; Large Letter reverse with open buds
H10-1842o-301		1842-O	Repunched Date; evident on 8 and 2
H10-1843-301	000.6	1843	RPD; 1 and 8 evident south of primary, 4 visible light south
H10-1844-301	000.63	1844	RPD; 1, 8, and 4 south of primary, also 1 north of primary
H10-1845-301	000.65	1845	RPD; 84 protruding south from base of rock
H10-1845-302	000.66	1845	RPD; all 4 digits doubled WNW of the primary date
H10-1848-301	001	1848	Large Date
H10-1848-302	001.3	1848	Overdate; 1848/7/6
H10-1849-301	001.5	1849	Overdate; 1849/8
	001.55	1849	Overdate; 1849/6 (?)
H10-1853-301	001.8	1853	MPD; date protruding from rock; Blythe says 1853/2
H10-1856-301	001.9	1856	MPD; 8 in rock above primary 8
H10-1858-301	002	1858	RPD; Breen 3090
H10-1858-302	003	1858	RPD; date over inverted date
H10-1861-301	003.6	1861	1861/0 overdate
H10-1865-301	003.8	1865	RPD; circulation strike of V-1
H10-1871-301	003.9	1871	MPD; portion of a digit in rock
H10-1872-101	004	1872	DDO
H10-1872S-301	005	1872-S	MPD; 1 in skirt right of ribbon end

Bust Dimes

New FS#	Old FS#	Date/Mint	Brief Description
10-1824-901		1824	Broken wing reverse; relatively common

Chart continued on next page.

New FS#	Old FS#	Date/Mint	Brief Description
10-1829-301	001	1829	Curl Base 2
10-1829-901	002	1829	Small/Large 10c
10-1830-301	003	1830	Overdate 30/29

Liberty Seated Dimes—No Stars (1838 only)

10-1838o-501		1838-O	Normal mintmark
10-1838o-502		1838-O	RPM south

Liberty Seated Dimes—Small Stars Obverse, No Drapery, Closed Bud Reverse—1838–1840

10-1838-801	003.27	1838	DDR; all of this type are the DDR

Liberty Seated Dimes—Large Stars Obverse, No Drapery, Closed Bud Reverse—1838–1840

10-1838-401		1838	Cracked obverse die #1
10-1838-402		1838	Cracked obverse die #2
10-1838-403		1838	Cracked obverse die #3
10-1838-802	003.27	1838	Doubled Die Reverse; same reverse die as 1838-801
10-1838-901		1838	Die flaw rev; large chip between N and M of ONE DIME
10-1840-401		1838	Whiskers at chin; "Whiskers" variety

Liberty Seated Dimes—Large Stars Obverse, Partial Drapery, Closed Bud Reverse—1838–1839

10-1839o-501	003.28	1839-O	RPM; O/O southeast
10-1839o-502		1839-O	Huge O mintmark

Liberty Seated Dimes—Large Stars Obverse, With Drapery, Open Bud Reverse—1840–1853, 1856–1860-S

10-1841-301		1841	Repunched Date; repunched 184
10-1841-302		1841	Repunched Date; repunched 841
10-1841o-301		1841-O	Small O mintmark
10-1841o-302		1841-O	Large O mintmark
10-1841o-901	003.3	1841-O	Transitional reverse; closed bud; Small O mintmark
10-1841o-902		1841-O	Transitional reverse; closed bud; Large O mintmark
10-1843-301		1843	Repunched Date

Liberty Seated Dimes—Arrows Added

10-1853-1301		1853	Repunched Date
10-1854o-501		1854-O	Incomplete mintmark punch, "U" shaped; Breen 3286
10-1856-1101		1856 SD	Small date; Doubled Die Obverse
10-1856-301		1856	Repunched Date
10-1856o-2301		1856-O	Large O; Repunched Date
10-1872-101	003.4	1872	Doubled Die Obverse
10-1872-301	003.45	1872	Repunched Date
10-1872-801		1872	New DDR; entire reverse rotated about 175 degrees

Liberty Seated Dimes—No Arrows, Close 3

10-1873-301		1873	Repunched Date; secondary images west of primary images

Liberty Seated Dimes—With Arrows

10-1873-2101	003.5	1873	Doubled Die Obverse
10-1875-301		1875	MPD; strong 1 in denticles
10-1876CC-101	004	1876-CC	Doubled Die Obverse; level CC mintmark

New FS#	Old FS#	Date/Mint	Brief Description
10-1876CC-102	004	1876-CC	Doubled Die Obverse; right C high
10-1876CC-103	004	1876-CC	Doubled Die Obverse; right C low
10-1876CC-301	003.7	1876-CC	MPD; digits in skirt by shield (#301 listed in CPG #3 as P-Mint coin, actually CC-Mint coin)
10-1876CC-901	005	1876-CC	Type II Reverse
10-1887S-501		1887-S	Repunched mintmark; S/S slightly north
10-1888S-501		1888-S	Repunched mintmark; S/S Greer 101
10-1889-801	005.3	1889	DDR
10-1890-301	005.5	1890	MPD
10-1890-302	005.6	1890	MPD; multiple digits in drapery
10-1890S-501		1890-S	Repunched mintmark; Greer 105
10-1890S-502	006	1890-S	Repunched mintmark #2; wrong photo in CPG #3
10-1891-301	1891		MPD; multiple digits in denticles
10-1891O-501	008	1891-O	Repunched mintmark #2; O/Horizontal O
10-1891S-501	007	1891-S	Repunched mintmark #1; Greer 101

Barber Dimes

10-1892-301	008.3	1892	RPD
10-1892-302	008.4	1892	RPD
10-1892O-301	008.5	1892-O	RPD
10-1893S-501	009	1893-S	RPM #1
10-1895S-301	009.2	1895-S	RPD; secondary image north of primary on 9 and 5
10-1896-301	009.3	1896	RPD; secondary image south on 8, 9, and 6
10-1897-301		1897	RPD
10-1897-302		1897	RPD
10-1899O-301		1899-O	RPD (south)
10-1899O-501		1899-O	RPM
10-1900O-501		1900-O	RPM
10-1901O-501	010	1901-O	RPM
10-1903-301		1903	RPD
10-1903O-301		1903-O	RPD; some think 3/2—we doubt it
10-1904S-501		1904-S	Slanted S mintmark
10-1906-301		1906	RPD
10-1906D-301		1906-D	RPD, RPM
10-1906D-302		1906-D	RPD, RPM; different from above
10-1906D-303		1906-D	RPD, MPD
10-1906O-301		1906-O	RPD, MPD
10-1906S-301		1906-S	RPD, RPM; Breen 3552
10-1907-301		1907	RPD
10-1907D-301		1907-D	RPD
10-1907O-501		1907-O	RPM
10-1908-301		1908	RPD
10-1908-302		1908	Possible overdate 08/07 low
10-1908-303		1908	RPD; multiple punches
10-1908D-301	010.220	1908-D	RPD; possible overdate
10-1908D-302	010.210	1908-D	RPD
10-1908D-303	010.200	1908-D	Overdate

New FS#	Old FS#	Date/Mint	Brief Description
10-1908D-304	010.225	1908-D	RPD
10-1908D-305	010.230	1908-D	RPD
10-1908D-306	010.235	1908-D	RPD
10-1908D-307	010.240	1908-D	RPD
10-1908O-301	010.250	1908-O	RPD; wide right
10-1908O-302	010.260	1908-O	RPD
10-1912S-101		1912-S	DDO; obverse letters, date, and ribbon ends
Mercury Dimes			
10-1928S-501		1928-S	Large S mintmark
10-1929S-101	010.3	1929-S	Doubled Die Obverse
10-1931D-101		1931-D	DDO/DDR
10-1931S-101		1931-S	Doubled Die Obverse
10-1935S-501		1935-S	RPM south (strike doubling on N side of mintmark)
10-1936-101	010.5	1936	Doubled Die Obverse
10-1936S-110		1936-S	Very likely 1936/192
10-1937-101		1937	Doubled Die Obverse
10-1937S-101		1937-S	Doubled Die Obverse
10-1939-101		1939	Doubled Die Obverse
10-1939D-501		1939-D	D/D south
10-1940S-501		1940-S	RPM west and serifs— S/S/S/S
10-1941-101		1941	Doubled Die Obverse
10-1941D-101	010.58	1941-D	DDO/DDR, 1-O-V+1-R-II
10-1941S-501	010.6	1941-S	RPM #1
10-1941S-502		1941-S	Unknown RPM; CPN #13
10-1941S-511	010.65	1941-S	Large S mintmark
10-1941S-801		1941-S	Doubled Die Reverse; minor
10-1942-101	010.7	1942/1	1942/1 Doubled Die Obverse
10-1942D-101	010.8	1942/1-D	1942/1-D Doubled Die Obverse, RPM 4
10-1942D-501		1942-D	1942-D/D RPM 5
10-1943S-501		1943-S	S/S RPM #1
10-1943S-511		1943-S	Large S, Trumpet Tail S
10-1944D-501		1944-D	RPM #3
10-1945D-501		1945-D	RPM #1 D/D northeast
10-1945D-506	010.95	1945-D	D/Horizontal D
10-1945S-503	011	1945-S	S/Horizontal S
10-1945S-511		1945-S	Possible S/D
10-1945S-512		1945-S	Micro S variety
Roosevelt Dimes			
10-1946-101	011.4	1946	Doubled Die Obverse and Doubled Die Reverse (4-O-V + 3-R-II)
10-1946-102		1946	Doubled Die Obverse; same obverse die as above, but no DDR
10-1946-103	011.5	1946	Doubled Die Obverse
10-1946-104		1946	Doubled Die Obverse
10-1946-801		1946	Doubled Die Reverse
10-1946-802		1946	DDR; very unusual, strong at only a couple of positions
10-1946D-501		1946-D	D/D south; unlisted
10-1946D-502		1946-D	D/D south
10-1946D-503		1946-D	D/D south
10-1946S-501	011.7	1946-S	RPM #1 and DDR 1-R-II+V; illustrated in CPN 11
10-1946S-502	011.6	1946-S	RPM #2 and DDR 2-R-IV

New FS#	Old FS#	Date/Mint	Brief Description
10-1946S-503		1946-S	Possibly CONECA RPM 13; actually tripled, S/S/S
10-1946S-504		1946-S	Sans serif S; very rare
10-1947-101	011.9	1947	Doubled Die Obverse; illustrated in CPN 13
10-1947S-501	013	1947-S	S mintmark over D mintmark
10-1947S-502	012	1947-S	S mintmark over D mintmark
10-1947S-503		1947-S	Repunched mintmark; S over S north
10-1947S-504		1947-S	Repunched mintmark; S over S rotated clockwise
10-1947S-801	013.5	1947-S	Doubled Die Reverse
10-1948-801		1948	Doubled Die Reverse
10-1950-801		1950 PF	Proof; Doubled Die Reverse
10-1950D-501		1950-D	New D/S OMM
10-1950D-801	014	1950-D	Doubled Die Reverse; very strong
10-1950S-501	014.5	1950-S	Originally listed as a S/D, now S over inverted S, by CONECA
10-1953D-501		1953-D	D/Horizontal D MM RPM #3
10-1954-101		1954 PF	Doubled Die Obverse
10-1954-801		1954	Unusual doubled die reverse; base of torch and oak stem
10-1954S-501		1954-S	Repunched mintmark
10-1956-101		1956 PF	Proof; Doubled Die Obverse
10-1959D-501	014.8	1959-D	D/Inverted D mintmark
10-1959D-502		1959-D	Repunched mintmark; D/D west
10-1959D-503		1959-D	Repunched mintmark; D/D northwest
10-1960-101		1960 PF	Doubled Die Obverse
10-1960-102A	015	1960 PF	Doubled Die Obverse; early die state
10-1960-102B	015	1960 PF	Doubled Die Obverse; late die state
10-1960-801	015.5	1960 PF	Doubled Die Reverse
10-1960D-501		1960-D	Repunched mintmark; D/D/D east
10-1961D-801	015.8	1961-D	Doubled Die Reverse
10-1962D-505		1962-D	D/Horizontal D
10-1963-101	016	1963	Doubled Die Obverse
10-1963-801	017	1963 PF	Doubled Die Reverse (listed incorrectly in CPG #3 as 5-R-II+V)
10-1963-802	017.5	1963 PF	Doubled Die Reverse
10-1963-803	018	1963 PF	Doubled Die Reverse
10-1963-804		1963 PF	Doubled Die Reverse
10-1963-805		1963	Doubled Die Reverse
10-1963D-801	018.2	1963-D	Doubled Die Reverse
10-1964-101	018.4	1964 PF	DDO; Doubled Die Obverse
10-1964-801		1964	Doubled Die Reverse
10-1964-802	018.3	1964	Doubled Die Reverse
10-1964D-101	018.45	1964-D	Doubled Die Reverse
10-1964D-501		1964-D	Repunched mintmark; D/D northeast
10-1964D-502	018.7	1964-D	Misplaced mintmark; D protruding from torch
10-1964D-503		1964-D	Repunched mintmark; D/D south
10-1964D-504		1964-D	Repunched mintmark; D/D south

Chart continued on next page.

439

New FS#	Old FS#	Date/Mint	Brief Description
10-1964D-505		1964-D	Repunched mintmark; D/D south
10-1964D-506		1964-D	Repunched mintmark; D/D south
10-1964D-801	018.5	1964-D	DDR
10-1964D-802		1964-D	DDR
10-1964D-803		1964-D	DDR
10-1967-101	019	1967	DDO
10-1968-101	019.5	1968	DDO
10-1968S-101	020	1968-S PF	DDO
10-1968S-102	020.2	1968-S PF	DDO
10-1968S-501		1968-S PF	No S mintmark
10-1968S-502		1968-S PF	Repunched Mintmark; also a very minor doubled die obverse
10-1968S-801	020.3	1968-S PF	DDR
10-1968S-802		1968-S PF	DDR
10-1969D-501	020.4	1969-D	Repunched mintmark; D/D wide northeast
10-1970-801	020.6	1970	DDR
10-1970D-801		1970-D	DDR
10-1970D-802		1970-D	DDR
10-1975S-501		1975-S PF	Repunched mintmark; S/S north
10-1982-501	021	1982	No "P" mintmark; circulation strike; strong obverse
10-1982-501		1982	No "P" mintmark; circulation strike; weak obverse
10-1983D-501		1983-D	Repunched mintmark; D/D north
10-1985P-501		1985-P	Ghost in neck; similar to a P
10-1986P-501		1986-P	Ghost in field; similar to a P
10-1987P-501		1987-P	Ghost in field; similar to a P
10-2004D-101		2004-D	DDO; doubled ear, rotated

Twenty-Cent Pieces

New FS#	Old FS#	Date/Mint	Brief Description
20-1875S-301		1875-S	MPD; 8 in denticles
20-1875S-302		1875-S	Possible MPD in denticles below 7, RPM #1

Bust Quarters

New FS#	Old FS#	Date/Mint	Brief Description
25-1831-301		1831	RPD; 1 and 8 south
25-1833-801		1833	DDR
25-1834-901		1834	Recut "OF A" in UNITED STATES OF AMERICA

Liberty Seated Quarters

New FS#	Old FS#	Date/Mint	Brief Description
25-18400-501		1840-O	WD; Large O mintmark
25-18410-101	001	1841-O	Doubled Die Obverse, CONECA 1-O-III
25-18430-301		1843-O	Repunched Date; 1 and 8 north
25-18430-501	001.5	1843-O	Large O mintmark
25-1845-301		1845	Repunched Date; Large 5/Small 5
25-1847-301	002.3	1847	MPD; 8 protruding from base of rock
25-1847-801	002	1847	RPD, Doubled Die Reverse, 1-R-II
25-1850-301		1850	RPD; 1 in denticles
25-1853-301		1853	RPD; 5 and 3 evident slightly below the primary digits, slanted

Liberty Seated Quarters—Arrows and Rays

New FS#	Old FS#	Date/Mint	Brief Description
25-1853-1301	003	1853	1853/4 Overdate
25-18530-501		1853-O	O Over Horizontal O
25-18540-501	004	1854-O	Huge O mintmark
25-1856-301		1856	MPD; 1 and 6 punched in gown
25-1856S-501	005	1856-S	Large S / Small S mintmark
25-1857-901	006	1857	Reverse clashed die; clashed with reverse of Flying Eagle cent
25-18570-301	006.2	1857-O	MPD; 1 and 8 in denticles
25-1872-301		1872	RPD; 1 and 8 repunched south of the primary digits
25-1875-301	006.75	1875	MPD; 1 and 7 in denticles
25-1876-301		1876	MPD; top of a 6 in denticles below 6
25-1876-302	006.8	1876	MPD; 1 evident south and west of primary 1 and S and W of primary 8

Liberty Seated Quarters

New FS#	Old FS#	Date/Mint	Brief Description
25-1876-303	06.85	1876	MPD; 6 in rock
25-1876-304		1876	RPD; triple 6
25-1876-305		1876	MPD; top of 1 and 8 in denticles
25-1876CC-301		1876-CC	RPD; 1, 8, and 7 close south
25-1876S-301	006.88	1876-S	MPD; 7 and 6 in denticles
25-1876S-302		1876-S	MPD; digit in denticles under 8
25-1877CC-301		1877-CC	RPD; 1, 8, and 7 close south
25-1877S-501	007	1877-S	RPM #1, S/Horizontal S
25-1891-301	007.5	1891	MPD

Barber Quarters

New FS#	Old FS#	Date/Mint	Brief Description
25-1892-101	007.7	1892	Doubled Die Obverse; IN GOD WE TRUST
25-1892-301		1892	Tripled Die Obverse, RPD; very minor TDO, very nice RPD
25-1892-801		1892	Tripled Die Reverse
25-18920-101	007.8	1892-O	Doubled Die Obverse; IN GOD WE TRUST
25-18920-301	007.9	1892-O	RPD; very strong south
25-1892S-501		1892-S	RPM; S/S northwest
25-19020-301		1902-O	MPD; digit evident in denticles below O of date
25-1907D-301		1907-D	Doubled Die Obverse, RPD
25-1907S-501		1907-S	RPM; S/S southeast
25-1908D-301		1908-D	MPD; 8 in denticles between 0 and 8 (likely an 0)
25-1914D-101	007.99	1914-D	Doubled Die Obverse
25-1916D-501	008	1916-D	D/D, RPM #2

Standing Liberty Quarters

New FS#	Old FS#	Date/Mint	Brief Description
25-1918S-101	008.5	1918-S	Overdate doubled die obverse; 1918/7-S
25-1928S-501		1928-S	Inverted S mintmark
25-1928S-502		1928-S	Repunched mintmark
25-1929S-401		1929-S	Very interesting and bold die clash
25-1930S-501		1930-S	Interesting mintmark; likely a small S over large S

New FS#	Old FS#	Date/Mint	Brief Description
Washington Quarters			
25-1932-101		1932	DDO; doubled earlobe
25-1934-101	009	1934	DDO, 1-O-I
25-1934-401		1934	Light Motto
25-1934-402		1934	Medium Motto (common)
25-1934-403		1934	Large Motto (common)
25-1934D-501	009.5	1934-D	Small D; D of 1932
25-1935-101	010	1935	DDO, 1-O-II+V
25-1936-101	011	1936	DDO, 1-O-I
25-1937-101	012	1937	DDO, 1-O-IV
25-1939D-501	012.3	1939-D	D/S (D over S mintmark)
25-1939S-101		1939-S	DDO
25-1940D-101	012.5	1940-D	DDO, 1-O-III
25-1940D-501	012.4	1940-D	RPM #2; D wide left of primary D
25-1941-101	012.7	1941	Doubled Die Obverse
25-1941-102	012.9	1941	Doubled Die Obverse
25-1941-801	013	1941	TDR, 4-R-III+V
25-1941D-801		1941-D	1-R-V; strong on OF AMERICA, weak QUARTER DOLLAR
25-1941S-501		1941-S	Large mintmark; Trumpet Tail style
25-1941S-502		1941-S	S/S, far north; small style mintmark
25-1942-101		1942	Doubled Die Obverse
25-1942-801	014	1942	Doubled Die Reverse
25-1942-802	014.3	1942	Doubled Die Reverse
25-1942-803		1942	Doubled Die Reverse
25-1942D-101	015	1942-D	Doubled Die Obverse
25-1942D-801	016	1942-D	Doubled Die Reverse
25-1943-101	016.5	1943	DDO; strong on motto, weaker on LIB and date
25-1943-102		1943	DDO; strong on LIBERTY, weaker on motto and date
25-1943-103	016.7	1943	DDO; strong on motto, weaker on LIB and date
25-1943D-101		1943-D	DDO; eye, hair curls, initials, lip, chin
25-1943S-101	017	1943-S	Doubled Die Obverse
25-1943S-501	017.3	1943-S	Trumpet Tail S
25-1943S-502		1943-S	Slightly smaller and slightly different S (Large S is common)
25-1943S-503		1943-S	South, with filled upper loop of primary mintmark
25-1943S-504		1943-S	Knob evident south of primary mintmark
25-1944-101		1944	DDO; light spread on IGWT and minor on date and LIB
25-1944D-101		1944-D	Doubled Die Obverse — most evident on LIBERTY
25-1944S-101	017.5	1944-S	Doubled Die Obverse
25-1945-101	018	1945	Doubled Die Obverse
25-1945S-101		1945-S	Doubled Die Obverse; IGWT, date, and TY of LIBERTY
25-1945S-102		1945-S	Doubled Die Obverse; thick on IGWT, Liberty
25-1946-101		1946	Doubled Die Obverse; IGWT, date, and slightly on LIBERTY
25-1946-801		1946	DDR and DDO; UNITED STATES OF AMERICA, EPU, slightly on QD

Chart continued on next page.

New FS#	Old FS#	Date/Mint	Brief Description
25-1946D-501		1946-D	Secondary mintmark weak but evident north of the primary
25-1946S-501		1946-S	S/S north, RPM #2
25-1947-101		1947	Doubled Die Obverse; LIBERTY only
25-1947S-501		1947-S	S/S west, RPM #1
25-1947S-502		1947-S	S/S south
25-1948S-501	018.4	1948-S	S/S/S/S, N and N and very wide northeast
25-1949D-501		1949-D	D/D/D — One D north, another horizontal west
25-1949D-601		1949-D	Possible D/S; several dies reported; only this appears to be D/S
25-1950-801	019	1950	Doubled Die Reverse; eagle's beak, wings, etc.
25-1950D-801	020	1950-D	Doubled Die Reverse; talons, feathers, and arrow tips
25-1950D-802		1950-D	DDR; extra thickness on all lettering, especially QUARTER DOLLAR
25-1950D-502		1950-D	D/D, RPM #2
25-1950D-601	021	1950-D	D/S, OMM #1
25-1950S-501		1950-S	S/S, north, RPM #1
25-1950S-601	022	1950-S	S/D, OMM #1
25-1950S-801		1950-S	Joe Miller
25-1951D-101		1951-D	DDO; nice on LIBERTY, okay on IGWT, weak on date
25-1952-901		1952 PF	"Superbird"; unusual S evident on breast of eagle
25-1952-902		1952 PF	"Superbird," plus recut tail feathers and DDO
25-1952D-101		1952-D	DDO, Class I; nice on all obverse lettering
25-1952D-501		1952-D	Huge D mintmark
25-1952S-501		1952-S	S/S/S, serifs and far north
25-1952S-502		1952-S	S/S, north
25-1953-101		1953 PF	All obverse lettering and date
25-1953-901		1953 PF	Recut tail feathers
25-1953D-801	022.2	1953-D	All reverse lettering, strong-est USA and E PLURIBUS UNUM
25-1953D-501		1953-D	Inverted D over D
25-1953D-601		1953-D	OMM #1, D/S (actually D/D/D/S/S)
25-1956-701		1956 PF	Unusual reverse die gouges
25-1956-701		1956	Reverse die gouge
25-1956-901		1956	Type B reverse on circ strike; intended for Proofs; *rare*
25-1956D-501		1956-D	D over inverted D mintmark
25-1957-901		1957	Type B reverse on circ strike; intended for Proofs; *rare*
25-1957D-901		1957-D	Recut tail feathers
25-1958-901		1958	Type B reverse on circ strike; intended for Proofs; *rare*
25-1959-101	022.45	1959 PF	DDO Strong on IGWT, weaker on other elements
25-1959-901		1959	Type B reverse on circ strike; intended for Proofs; *rare*
25-1959D-501		1959-D	D/D mintmark, interesting as secondary mintmark tilted slightly
25-1960-801	022.5	1960 PF	DDR all reverse elements; small/large design
25-1960-901		1960	Type B reverse on circ strike;

New FS#	Old FS#	Date/Mint	Brief Description
			intended for Proofs; *rare*
25-1961-101		1961 PF	IGWT, LIBERTY, date, queue; PUP is IGWT
25-1961-901		1961	Type B reverse on circ strike; intended for Proofs; *rare*
25-1961D-501		1961-D	RPM, D/D northeast; secondary is wide northeast
25-1961D-502		1961-D	D/D north
25-1962-101		1962 PF	Strong on all obverse lettering, similar to class VI
25-1962-901		1962	Type B reverse on circ strike; intended for Proofs; *rare*
25-1962D-501		1962-D	Unl RPM D/D strong north, 1/2 letter height (Rizdy)
25-1963-101	023	1963	Date, motto, and LIBERTY
25-1963-102		1963	Obverse like 101; reverse on all rim lettering
25-1963-103		1963	Only on 63 of date; strongest on 6
25-1963-801		1963	Doubling evident on C and M of AMERICA, first T of STATES
25-1963-802		1963 PF	Doubling on all reverse lettering, strong spread on AMERICA
25-1963-901		1963	Type B reverse on circ strike; intended for Proofs; *rare*
25-1963D-101		1963-D	DDO 4-O-II+V; all lettering and date, weakest on IGWT
25-1964-101		1964	DDO evident on IN GOD WE TRUST; similar to 63 die 1
25-1964-801		1964	DDR all reverse lettering
25-1964-802	024.5	1964	Evident on QUARTER DOLLAR
25-1964-803 OF AMERICA		1964	Doubling strongest on STATES
25-1964-804		1964	DDR evident on UNITED with light doubling
25-1964-901		1964	Type B reverse on circ strike; intended for Proofs; *rare*
25-1964-902		1964	Type C reverse
25-1964D-101 GOD WE TRUST		1964-D	Doubling most evident on IN
25-1964D-501		1964-D	D/D east; 1/2 letter width
25-1964D-502		1964-D	D and second D far north protruding from branch
25-1964D-801	025	1964-D	Evident on STATES OF AMERICA, QUARTER DOLLAR
25-1964D-901		1964-D	Type B reverse on circ strike; intended for Proofs; *rare*
25-1964D-902		1964-D	Type C reverse; intended for production beginning in 1965
25-1965-101	026	1965	DDO, very strong, evident on all obverse lettering
25-1965-102		1965	Doubled Die Obverse; very strong on LIBERTY
25-1965-801		1965	Doubled Die Reverse; primarily on QUARTER DOLLAR
25-1966-801	026.3	1966	DDR; very rare and very strong on all lettering
25-1967-101	026.5	1967 SMS	Doubled Die Obverse; evident on all obverse lettering
25-1967-801		1967 SMS	DDR; light on lower branches, leaves, QUARTER DOLLAR
25-1968D-801		1968-D	Doubled Die Reverse; very strong on all reverse lettering

New FS#	Old FS#	Date/Mint	Brief Description
25-1968S-101		1968-S PF	DDO; evident on all lettering, 1/2 letter width
25-1968S-501		1968-S PF	S/S, north
25-1968S-801	027	1968-S PF	Doubled Die Reverse; very strong on all lettering
25-1969D-501	027.06	1969-D	D/D slanted west; found in Mint Sets
25-1969D-502		1969-D	D/D slightly west
25-1969S-101	027.08	1969-S PF	Doubled Die Obverse; very strong on all lettering and date
25-1969S-501	027.1	1969-S PF	Repunched mintmark; S/S/S north and south
25-1970D-101	027.3	1970-D	DDO; evident on all lettering, weaker on LIBERTY
25-1970D-102		1970-D	DDO; evident most on LIBERTY, slightly on date and IGWT
25-1970D-801		1970-D	DDR; evident on all reverse lettering; *strong*
25-1970D-802		1970-D	Doubled Die Reverse; evident on all reverse lettering
25-1971-801	027.7	1971	Doubled Die Reverse; very strong on all reverse lettering
25-1971D-801	027.8	1971-D	DDR; very strong on UNITED STATES OF AMERICA
25-1976D-101	028	1976-D	DDO; most on LIBERTY, and in EDS on motto and date
25-1976D-102		1976-D	DDO, 2-O-V CCW; evident on LIBERTY only
25-1979S-501		1979-S PF	Type II mintmark
25-1981S-501		1981-S PF	Type II mintmark
25-1982S-101		1982-S PF	DDO; IGWT, date, and slightly on LIBERTY
25-1989D-501		1989-D	D/D, west
25-1990S-101		1990-S PF	Slight doubling on date and mintmark
25-1995S-101		1995-S PF	DDO on date, mintmark, ribbon, hair, west on LIBERTY and IGWT
25-1996P-701		1996-P	Strange; die abraded through bust (must see photos)
25-2004D-5901		2004-D	Wisconsin quarter, Extra Leaf High (lines pointing up)
25-2004D-5902		2004-D	Wisconsin quarter, Extra Leaf Low (lines pointing down)

Bust Half Dollars

50-1806-301		1806	6 punched over an inverted 6
50-1806-901		1806	STATES/STATAS; an A is evident under the E of STATES
50-1808-301		1808	1808/7 repunched date
50-1812-101		1812	Doubled LIBERTY
50-1812-901		1812	Reverse die clashed; BER of LIBERTY evident
50-1829-301		1829	Curled base 2 of date over a flat based 2

Liberty Seated Half Dollars

50-1840-301		1840	Repunched Date; 4 and 0 of date repunched south; Reverse of '39
50-1840-302		1840	1 and 8 repunched west, 4 and 0 repunched north; small letters
50-1842-301		1842 SD	Repunched Date; 842 repunched south

New FS#	Old FS#	Date/Mint	Brief Description
50-1842-801	000.5	1842 SD	UNITED STATES OF AMERICA and eagle doubled
50-18430-301		1843-O	1, 8, and 4 repunched south; 3 repunched north
50-18440-301	001	1844-O	RPD; secondary digits repunched north into rock
50-18450-301	001.5	1845-O	Very strong RPD east; lower secondary 5 very evident
50-18450-302	002	1845-O	Strong RPD; tripled digits, secondary images south
50-18450-303		1845-O	Nice RPD; secondary images west
50-18450-501	002.5	1845-O	RPM O punched over a previously punched horizontal O
50-1846-301	003	1846	6 of date punched correctly over a horizontal 6
50-1847-101		1847	DDO; evident on the shield and LIBERTY
50-1847-301	004	1847	1847/6 overdate
50-1849-301	004.5	1849	RPD; secondary image of lower part of four digits evident west
50-1853-401		1853	Very strong clashed obv die; rays of reverse evident at rock
50-1853-801	004.7	1853	DDR; very strong on UNITED, lighter on HALF
50-1853-802		1853	DDR; best on HALF DOL, AMERICA, and arrows
50-1853-803		1853	DDR; STATES
50-1855-301	005	1855	1855/4 overdate
50-18550-501	006	1855-O	O Over Horizontal O mintmark
50-18560-301		1856-O	RPD; 1 secondary south, 5 and 6 secondary north
50-1858-101		1858	DDO; evident on drapery, skirt, foot, and rock
50-1858-301		1858	RPD; very unusual RPD, right of first 8 and 5
50-1858-302		1858	Misplaced date; 8 protruding from skirt above first 8
50-18580-301		1858-O	MPD; 8 protruding from rock above second 8
50-18580-901		1858-O	Unusual die clash of reverse; leg of eagle
50-18590-301		1859-O	RPD; 1 secondary image south, and 9 secondary image north
50-19610-401	007	1861-O	Die crack on obverse; Confederate obverse die
50-1865-301		1865	RPD; 1 has secondary image north, 5 has secondary image south
50-1866-301		1866	MPD; 6 (possibly two 6's) in rock above last 6
50-1866-302	007.01	1866	MPD; 6 in denticles after last 6
50-1867-801		1867	DDR; evident on motto, beak, eye, and wings

Liberty Seated Half Dollars — Arrows at Date

New FS#	Old FS#	Date/Mint	Brief Description
50-1873-1101	007.1	1873	DDO; evident on shield, gown, foot, scroll, and lower stars
50-1873-1301		1873	MPD; digit is evident in denticles below arrows
50-1876-301	007.4	1876	RPD; Large/Small Date; small date is likely that of a 20c

Chart continued on next page.

New FS#	Old FS#	Date/Mint	Brief Description
			punch
50-1876-302		1876	RPD; two secondary digits (likely 6) evident west of 7 and 6
50-1876-303	007.3	1876	MPD; a digit is evident in denticles below 7; not WB 103
50-1876-304		1876	Two digits evident in denticles below 8
50-1876-401		1876 PF	Very unusual variety; top of letter C (matching mintmark style) evident punched in Liberty's neck
50-1877-301	007.5	1877	1877/6; 6 is evident on high surface of 7

Barber Half Dollars

New FS#	Old FS#	Date/Mint	Brief Description
50-1892-301	007.7	1892	RPD; very strong with secondary date south
50-1892-801	007.8	1892	DDR; all lettering, arrows, EPU, ribbon, leaves, stars
50-18920-501	007.9	1892	Micro O mintmark; believed to have been a quarter dollar punch
50-1909S-501		1909-S	Inverted S mintmark
50-1911S-501		1911-S	RPM; very strong with secondary image west of primary

Liberty Walking Half Dollars

New FS#	Old FS#	Date/Mint	Brief Description
50-1916D-501	008	1916-D	RPM; D/D strong southwest, C — RPM #1
50-1936-101	008.4	1936	DDO; very strong at date; tail of 9 and 3 totally separated
50-1936-102		1936	DDO; evident at date, IGWT, shoe, skirt, rays; C-1-O-II
50-1936D-101		1936-D	DDO; evident on date, shoe, skirt, ground; C-1-O-II
50-1936S-101		1936-S	DDO; evident on date, shoe, skirt, ground; C-1-O-II
50-1939D-101	008.45	1939-D	DDO; evident on date, IGWT, shoe, skirt
50-1939D-501		1939-D	RPM; D/D north; CONECA RPM 1
50-1941D-501		1941-D	RPM; D/D northwest; CONECA RPM 1
50-1941S-501		1941-S	RPM; S/S southwest; listed by Fox as S/Horizontal S
50-1942-101	009	1942	DDO; evident on breast (master die DDO)
50-1942-801	008.5	1942	DDR; evident on AMERICA, HALF DOLLAR, feathers
50-1942D-101		1942-D	DDO; evident on breast (master die DDO)
50-1942D-501	010	1942-D	Formerly believed to be D/S OMM; it is not!
50-1942S-101		1942-S	DDO; evident on breast (master die DDO)
50-1943-101	010.5	1943	DDO; date, IGWT, LIBERTY, skirt, etc.
50-1943D-101	010.5	1943-D	DDO; date, IGWT, LIBERTY, skirt, etc.
50-1943D-501		1943-D	Reported as a D/S; same die as for the 1942-D; not D/S!
50-1943S-101	010.5	1943-S	DDO; date, IGWT, LIBERTY, skirt, etc.
50-1944D-901		1944-D	Hand-engraved designer's

New FS#	Old FS#	Date/Mint	Brief Description
			initials
50-1944S-501	010.6	1944-S	RPM #4; S/S north
50-1944S-502	010.7	1944-S	RPM #2; S/S southwest
50-1944S-511		1944-S	Inverted S mintmark
50-1945-901		1945	No designer's initials
50-1946-101		1946	DDO; evident on breast, robe, IGWT
50-1946-801	011.1	1946	DDR; evident on E PLURIBUS UNUM, branches, feathers; C-1-R-III
Franklin Half Dollars			
50-1948-801		1948	DDR; EPU, HALF DOLLAR, AMERICA, clapper
50-1948D-801		1948-D	DDR; EPU, HALF DOLLAR, AMERICA, clapper
50-1949S-501	011.3	1949-S	S/S south;C-RPM #2 (incorrectly listed in CPG #3 as 001.3)
50-1950-101		1950 PF	DDO; date, LIBERTY, IN GOD WE TRUST
50-1951S-801	011.5	1951-S	DDR; primarily evident on E PLURIBUS UNUM
50-1953S-501		1953-S	S/S, northwest
50-1954-101		1954 PF	DDO; evident on date, IN GOD WE TRUST, LIBERTY
50-1955-401		1955	Clashed obverse die; "Bugs Bunny"
50-1956-101		1956 PF	DDO; most evident on date, IN GOD WE TRUST
50-1956-801		1956 PF	DDR; evident extra thickness all lettering, spread on EPU
50-1956-802		1956 PF	TY II/TY I DDR; doubled eagle (note: we need photos!)
50-1957-801		1957 PF	DDR; US of A, H D (all), EPU, eagle, right of bell; class II and VI
50-1957D-501		1957-D	D/D; rotated counter-clockwise
50-1959-801		1959	DDR; evident on EPU west (nice separation) and on eagle
50-1960-101	012	1960 PF	DDO; evident on date, TRUST, and LIBERTY
50-1961-801	013	1961 PF	DDR; very strong on EPU, UNITED, and HALF
50-1961-802		1961 PF	DDR; evident on all outer lettering, EPU, eagle's tail feathers
50-1961-803		1961 PF	DDR; evident on all outer lettering, eagle, EPU
50-1962-101		1962 PF	DDO; evident on 2 of date and lightly on lettering
Kennedy Half Dollars			
50-1964-101	013.2	1964 PF	DDO; evident on WE TRUST, RTY, date
50-1964-102		1964	DDO; strong on WE TRUST, LIBERTY and date
50-1964-103		1964 PF	DDO; medium on IGWT, LIBERTY, date, and hair
50-1964-401		1964 PF	Accented Hair variety
50-1964-402		1964 PF	Normal Hair variety (normal type; very common)
50-1964-801		1964	DDR; evident on UNITED STATES OF AMERICA, stars, ribbon, EPU

New FS#	Old FS#	Date/Mint	Brief Description
50-1964D-101	013.4	1964-D	DDO; evident on IGWT, LIBERTY, initials, hair
50-1964D-102			Reserved for future listing
50-1964D-103	013.5	1964-D	TDO; evident on IGWT, RTY, and date, tripled on WE TRUST
50-1964D-104		1964-D	DDO; evident on IN GOD, LI, and 19
50-1964D-105	013.6	1964-D	TDO; evident on IGWT, TY and hair, tripled on WE TRUST
50-1964D-106		1964-D	DDO; evident on WE TRUST, TY and hair
50-1964D-107			Reserved for future listing
50-1964D-108		1964-D	TDO; evident on IGWT, date, initials, RTY
50-1964D-501		1964-D	RPM #1; D/D south
50-1964D-502		1964-D	RPM #2; D/D north
50-1964D-503		1964-D	RPM #3; D/D northeast
50-1965-801		1965 (BS)	DDR; moderate doubling on all outer lettering, stars
50-1966-101	013.8	1966 (BS)	DDO; evident on IN GOD WE TRUST, profile, date
50-1966-102		1966 SMS	DDO; evident on IN GOD WE TRUST, profile, eye
50-1966-103		1966 SMS	DDO, on IGWT, LIBERTY, profile, tripling on WE TRUST
50-1966-104		1966 SMS	DDO; on IN GOD WE TRUST, LIBERTY, date, profile
50-1966-901		1966 SMS	No designer's initials
50-1967-101		1967 SMS	DDO; actually quintupled; evident IGWT, LIBERTY, date
50-1967-102		1967	DDO; evident on IN GOD WE TRUST, LIBERTY, date
50-1967-801		1967	DDR; all reverse lettering, stars, rays; minor DDO
50-1968D-101		1968-D	Tripled Die Obverse; evident on IGWT, date, and LIBERTY
50-1968S-101	014	1968-S PF	DDO; evident on IN GOD WE TRUST, LIBERTY, date
50-1968S-511		1968-S PF	Inverted S mintmark
50-1968S-801		1968-S PF	Doubled Die Reverse; all reverse lettering and element
50-1970S-101		1970-S PF	Doubled Die Obverse; all obverse lettering
50-1971D-101	014.3	1971-D	DDO; evident on IBERTY, 71, GOD WE TRUST
50-1971D-102		1971-D	DDO; all obverse lettering, best on IGWT; very evident on hair
50-1971S-101		1971-S PF	Doubled Die Obverse; WE TRUST and date
50-1971S-102	014.5	1971-S PF	DDO; all lettering, date, and upper hair
50-1971S-801		1971-S PF	Doubled Die Reverse; all reverse lettering, stars
50-1972-101		1972	DDO; IN GOD WE TRUST, Y of LIBERTY, and date
50-1972D-901		1972-D	Missing designer's initials
50-1973D-101	014.8	1973-D	Doubled Die Obverse; all lettering, date, and hair
50-1974D-101	015	1974-D	DDO; all letters and date, but mostly on WE TRUST
50-1976S-101	016	1976-S	DDO; light spread on WE TRUST; Unc 40% silver

New FS#	Old FS#	Date/Mint	Brief Description
50-1977D-101		1977-D	Doubled Die Obverse; primarily evident on WE TRUST
50-1979S-501		1979-S PF	Type II mintmark
50-1981S-501		1981-S PF	Type II mintmark
50-1988S-101		1988-S PF	Silver Proof; most lettering, best on WE TRUST, date, and mintmark
50-1992S-101		1992-S PF	Silver Proof; most lettering, best on WE TRUST, date, and mintmark

Liberty Seated Dollars

New FS#	Old FS#	Date/Mint	Brief Description
S1-1865-801		1865	DDR; relatively minor; doubled U of UNITED
S1-1868-301		1868	MPD; top of 6 or 8 evident in denticles below 6
S1-1869-301		1869	RPD; 1 is doubled south of primary 1
S1-1869-302		1869	RPD; base of second 1 is midway up between the 1 and 8
S1-1869-303		1869	MPD; top of a 6 or 9 evident in denticles below 6
S1-1871-301		1871	MPD; top of an 8 evident in denticles below the primary 8

Trade Dollars

New FS#	Old FS#	Date/Mint	Brief Description
T1-1873CC-301	012.3	1873-CC	MPD; top of digit in denticles below between 8 and 7
T1-1873CC-302		1873-CC	MPD; top of digits (an 8 and 7) in denticles below 8 and 7
T1-1875S-501	012.5	1875-S	OMM S/CC; CC mintmark weak, but visible
T1-1875S-502		1875-S	Similar to above; from NGC, Heritage auction 4-25-02
T1-1876-301		1876	RPD; secondary 6 evident within loop of 6
T1-1876CC-801	014	1876-CC	DDR; all reverse elements, especially branch, talons, wing
T1-1876S-101	013	1876-S	DDO; evident on all obverse elements
T1-1877-101		1877	DDO; evident on LIBERTY and wheat fons
T1-1877S-301		1877-S	RPD; final 7 is repunched w/2nd number south of primary
T1-1877S-801	014.5	1877-S	DDR; E PLURIBUS UNUM, ribbon, US of A and top of eagle
T1-1877S-802		1877-S	DDR; lower reverse elements, TRADE DOLLAR, 420 GRAINS
T1-1878S-801	015	1878-S	DDR; evident on all reverse elements; very strong
T1-1878S-802		1878-S	DDR; evident on UNITED STATES and EPU; not dramatic

Morgan Dollars

New FS#	Old FS#	Date/Mint	Brief Description
S1-1878-005		1878 8TF	VAM 5; DDO
S1-1878-009		1878 8TF	VAM 9; first die pairing
S1-1878-014		1878 8TF	VAM 14.11; ???
S1-1878-015		1878 8TF	VAM 15; DDO; doubled LIBERTY
S1-1878-032		1878 7/8	VAM 32; DDR; doubled tail feathers
S1-1878-044	001	1878 7/8	VAM 44; TDO/DDR
S1-1878-115		1878 7TF	VAM 115/199.1; tripled leaves

New FS#	Old FS#	Date/Mint	Brief Description
S1-1878-145		1878 7TF	VAM 145/162; broken M ??
S1-1878-162		1878 7TF	VAM 162; bottom serifs on N and M of UNUM broken, R of TRUST
S1-1878-166		1878 7TF	VAM 166; spiked P
S1-1878-168		1878 7TF	VAM 168; broken R of TRUST
S1-1878-188		1878 7TF	VAM 188; over-polished L
S1-1878-220		1878 7TF	VAM 220; tripled R of PLURIBUS
S1-1878-901		1878 7TF	Various; Reverse of 1878, flat breast, parallel arrow feathers
S1-1878-902		1878 7TF	Various; Reverse of 1879, round breast, slanted feathers
S1-1878CC-006		1878-CC	DDO; headress and ear; reverse wide, level CC
S1-1878CC-018		1878-CC	DDO; headress and ear; reverse close, uneven CC
S1-1878S-050		1878-S	Tripled Die Obverse; tripled eyelid
S1-18790-004		1879-O	RPM; O/O/O (formerly O Over Horizontal O)
S1-18790-028		1879-O	RPM; O/O/O (formerly O Over Horizontal O)
S1-1879S-301		1879-S	Reverse of '78; several VAM listings
S1-1880-006		1880	80/79 overdate; "spikes"
S1-1880-007		1880	80/79 overdate; "crossbar"
S1-1880-008		1880	80/79 overdate; "ears"
S1-1880-023		1880	80/79 overdate
S1-1880CC-004		1880-CC	Overdate
S1-1880CC-005		1880-CC	Overdate
S1-1880CC-006		1880-CC	Overdate
S1-1880CC-007		1880-CC	Overdate; Reverse of '78
S1-18800-004		1880-O	Overdate
S1-18800-005		1880-O	Overdate
S1-18800-048		1880-O	"Hangnail" (was VAM 1a)
S1-18800-016		1880-O	Checkmark
S1-18800-017		1880-O	Checkmark
S1-18800-021		1880-O	Checkmark
S1-18810-005		1881-O	O/O; RPM
S1-18810-027		1881-O	DDO
S1-18820-003		1882-O	OMM; O/S; early die state
S1-18820-003		1882-O	OMM; O/S; late die state
S1-18820-004		1882-O	OMM; O/S; recused; early die state
		1882-O	OMM; O/S; recused; late die state
		1882-O	OMM; O/S; broken S; early die state
S1-18820-005		1882-O	OMM; O/S; broken S; late die state
S1-1883-010		1883	DDO
S1-1884-003		1884	Dot
S1-1884-004		1884	Dot
S1-1884-005		1884	DDO
S1-1885-008		1885	Dash variety
S1-1885CC-004		1885-CC	Dash variety
S1-1886-001C		1886	Clashed die
S1-1886-020		1886	RPD
S1-18860-001A		1886-O	Clashed E reverse; clashed die

Chart continued on next page.

New FS#	Old FS#	Date/Mint	Brief Description
S1-1887-001B	1887		Clashed E reverse
S1-1887-002	1887		Overdate 7/6
S1-18870-002	1887-O		RPD
S1-18870-003	1887-O		Overdate 7/6
S1-18870-030	1887-O		Clashed dies
S1-18880-001A	1888-O		Clashed E reverse
S1-18880-001B	1888-O		Die break
S1-18880-004	1888-O		DDO; "Hot Lips"
S1-18880-015	1888-O		DDR/RPM
S1-18880-301	1888-O		Oval O
S1-1889-019	1889		Die break
S1-1889-022a	1889		Die break
S1-1889-023a	1889		Clashed die
S1-18890-001a	1889-O		Clashed E reverse
S1-18890-002	1889-O		VAM 2 (?); oval O; various VAMs
S1-18890-017	1889-O		Oval O; included above?
S1-1890CC-004	1890-CC		Tailbar
S1-18900-010	1890-O		Die gouges
S1-18900-020	1890-O		DDO
S1-18910-001a	1891-O		Clashed E reverse
S1-18910-001b	1891-O		Pitted Die
S1-1895S-003	1895-S		RPM; S/S
S1-1895S-004	1895-S		RPM; S/S
S1-1896-020	1896		RPD; formerly listed as VAM 1a
S1-18960-004	1896-O		Micro O
S1-18960-019	1896-O		RPD
S1-18960	1896-O		Formerly listed as VAM 1A
S1-18980-501	1898-O		RPD
S1-18990-004	1899-O		Small O
S1-1900-011	1900		DDR
S1-1900-016	1900		C4/C3 reverse
S1-19000-005	1900-O		Small O
S1-19000-301	1900-O		O/CC
S1-19000-029a	1900-O		Die break
S1-1901-003	1901		DDR
S1-1902-004	1902		DDO
S1-19020-003	1902-O		Small O
S1-1903S-002	1903-S		Small S

Note: 1921 Morgan dollar varieties will be numbered using three digits, 0 or 00 plus the VAM number.

S1-1921-301	1921		Wide reeding
S1-1921D-001a	1921-D		Over-polished
S1-1921D-001x	1921-D		Double cud
S1-1921S-001a	1921-S		Die scratch
S1-1921S-001b	1921-S		Die gouges

Peace Dollars

Note: 1921 Peace dollar varieties will be numbered using 4 digits, 10 or 100 plus the VAM number.

S1-1921-1003	1921		DDR; line through R
S1-1922-001f	1922		Field break
S1-1922-002a	1922		Earring
S1-1922-002c	1922		Extra hair
S1-1922-005a	1922		Scarcheek
S1-1922-012a	1922		Moustache
S1-1922-401	1922		High Relief; design type of 1921

New FS#	Old FS#	Date/Mint	Brief Description
S1-1923-001a	1923		Whisker Jaw
S1-1923-001b1	1923		Extra Hair
S1-1923-001b2	1923		Extra Hair
S1-1923-001c	1923		Tail on O
S1-1923-001d	1923		Whisker Cheek
S1-1923-002	1923		Double Tiara
S1-1923S-001c	1923-S		Pitted reverse
S1-1924-005a	1924		Broken Wing
S1-1925-005	1925		Missing Ray
S1-1926S-004	1926-S		Dot Variety
S1-1927S-101	1927-S		RPM; S/S rotated CCW
S1-1928S-003	1928-S		DDO
S1-1934D-003	1934-D		DDO; Medium D
S1-1934D-004	1934-D		DDO; Small D

Eisenhower Dollars

C1-1971S-103	015.8	1971-S PF	Dramatic DDO on all obverse characters; clad Proof
C1-1971S-106		1971-S PF	DDO, 6-0-I; all obverse |letters and date
C1-1971S-501		1971-S PF	RPM; S/S northwest; 40% silver, Uncirc. "Blue Pack"
C1-1972S-101		1972-S PF	Medium tripling on |IN GOD WE TRUST, LIBERTY, date
C1-1973S-101		1973-S PF	DDO; most evident on IN GOD WE TRUST; 40% silver, Proof

Susan B. Anthony and Sacagawea Dollars

C1-1979P-301	016	1979-P	Near Date variety
C1-1979S-501		1979-S PF	Type II mintmark
C1-1980S-501		1980-S PF	RPM; mintmark repunched northeast of primary S
C1-1981S-501		1981-S PF	Type II mintmark
C1-2000P-901		2000-P	Spikes through breast of eagle

Gold Dollars

G1-1854-1101		1854 Ty 2	DDO/Clashed reverse; strong on obverse lettering, clash
G1-1854-1301		1854 Ty 2	RPD on all four digits
G1-1856S-501		1856-S	RPM, S/S; wide northeast; very strong
G1-1862-101	G-001	1862	DDO; evident on UNITED STATES OF AMERICA, top of crown, beads, hair

Quarter Eagles

G2-1851-301		1851	RPD; evident on 1, 5, and 1
G2-1853-301		1853	RPD; evident on 1 and 8
G2-18540-301		1854-O	MPD; crosslet of 4 in hair curl above 4
G2-1862-301	G-002	1862/1	Overdate, 1862/1
G2-1891-801		1891	DDR; most evident on AMERICA, arrow tips, D of 2-1/2 D

$3 Gold

G3-1882-301		1882	RPD; 1882/2

Half Eagles

G5-1802-301		1802	1802/1; strong overdate; fairly common
G5-1819-901		1819	On reverse, 5D over 50, possibly 5D/inverted D

New FS#	Old FS#	Date/Mint	Brief Description
G5-1847-301	003	1847	MPD; top of 7 evident in denticles below 4
G5-1847-302	004	1847	MPD; 1 evident in neck of Liberty
G5-1847-303		1847	RPD; 1 and 8 evident south of primary; evident right of 7
G5-1847-304		1847	MPD; base of 1 evident in bust
G5-1854-101	004.5	1854	DDO; evident on hair and ear; known as "Earring" variety
G5-1881-301	005	1881	1881/0; overdate 1881/1880
G5-1881-302		1881	Repunched date; 1881/881
G5-1881-303		1881	RPD; 1881/1881; secondary date north of primary
G5-1881-304		1881	RPD; 1881/1881; secondary date west of primary
G5-1881-305		1881	RPD; 1881/1881; secondary slightly north and west
G5-1899-301		1899	RPD; evident on 899
G5-1901S-301		1901-S	Overdate; 1901/0-S
G5-1901S-501		1901-S	Large S over small S mintmark
G5-1905S-501	006.5	1905-S	S and S; wide east
G5-1906-301		1906	RPD; 6/6
G5-1911S-501		1911-S	Repunched mintmark; S/S, south

Eagles

New FS#	Old FS#	Date/Mint	Brief Description
G10-18460-301		1846-O	RPD and RPM; 1846/6 and O/O north
G10-1853-301	007	1853	1853/2 Overdate; evident within opening of 3
G10-1854S-301		1854-S	MPD; base of 1 evident below and between 1 and 8
G10-1883S-301		1883-S	MPD; 3 evident in denticles below primary 3
G10-1889S-501		1889-S	DDR on STATES OF AMERICA, arrows; strong RPM, S/S
G10-1891CC-501		1891-CC	RPM; secondary second C evident far right of primary

Double Eagles

New FS#	Old FS#	Date/Mint	Brief Description
G20-1852-301		1852	RPD; all digits repunched north
G20-1853-301	G-008	1853	Overdate, 1853/2; evident with 2 inside opening of 3
G20-1857-301		1857	MPD; a digit (likely 1) evident at center right of 5
G20-1859S-101		1859-S	DDO; evident on LIBERTY, hair curl, eye, neck, and profile
G20-1865-301		1865	MPD; digits in denticles; nice
G20-1866-801		1866	DDR; dual hub; small IN over large IN of motto
G20-1866S-1301		1866-S	MPD; digit evident left of primary 1 in denticles
G20-1871S-301		1871-S	MPD; digit in denticles (likely a 7); RPD (1 only)
G20-1873-1101		1873	Open 3; DDO, LIBERTY
G20-1879-801		1879	DDR; most reverse lettering
G20-1883S-301		1883-S	MPD; digit evident in denticles below second 8
G20-1888-801		1888	DDR; strongest on TWENTY DOLLARS and lower ribbon
G20-1896-301		1896	RPD; all digits doubled with secondary images north

New FS#	Old FS#	Date/Mint	Brief Description
G20-1908-801		1908	DDR; evident on eagle's beak, upper lettering
G20-1909-301		1909/8	Overdate; 1909 over a 1908 date
G20-1909S-501		1909-S	RPM; S/S, southeast
G20-1911D-501		1911-D	RPM; D/D, east (photo from Camire)
G20-1922-801		1922	DDR; evident on motto, lettering, rays, talons
G20-1925-801		1925	DDR; eagle's feathers, rays, IN GOD WE TRUST (NGC)
G20-1926-101		1926	TDO; evident on rays, date, stars, and other elements

Classic Commemoratives

New FS#	Old FS#	Date/Mint	Brief Description
C50-1892-301	C-000.5	1892	Columbian Expo half dollar; RPD, 2/2, north
C50-1892-302		1892	Columbian Expo half dollar; RPD, 2/2, northeast
C50-1892-303		1892	Columbian Expo half dollar; RPD, 89/89, east
C50-1893-301		1893	Columbian Expo half dollar; RPD, 3/3, north
C50-1915S-501		1915-S	Pan-Pac half dollar; RPM, S/S, east; very strong
C50-1925-101	C-001	1925	Stone Mountain half dollar; DDO, 1-O-III
C50-1925-102		1925	Vancouver half dollar; DDO
C50-1933D-101		1933-D	Oregon Trail half dollar; TDO
C50-1935-101		1935	Boone half dollar; DDO (possibly a master die DDO)
C50-1936D-501		1936-D	San Diego half dollar; RPM, D/D, south
C50-1951-801		1951	Carver/Washington half dollar; DDR (possibly a master die DDR)
C50-1953S-801		1953-S	Carver/Washington; DDR (possibly a master die DDR)

About the Authors

J.T. Stanton

J.T. Stanton began collecting coins in 1959 and began to specialize in the error/variety segment of the hobby in 1982. He has received numerous hobby recognitions and awards including the American Numismatic Association's Medal of Merit. Other ANA recognition includes the Glenn Smedley Memorial Award, the Outstanding Adult Advisor Award, and two ANA Presidential Awards. He was an ANA Summer Seminar instructor for 11 years and initiated the annual "Errors and Varieties and Modern Minting Process" class.

J.T. has served on the board of governors of the ANA (1995 to 1997), on the board of directors of CONECA (Combined Organizations of Numismatic Error Collectors of America), and as president of CONECA from 1987 to 1990.

Other awards J.T. has received include CONECA's Dr. Lyndon M. King Jr. Award, Krause Publications' Numismatic Ambassador Award, and the A.J. Vinci Memorial Excellence in Numismatic Education Award (#6) of Florida United Numismatists (FUN). J.T. has also been elected to CONECA's Hall of Fame.

He lives with his wife Susan in Savannah, has two sons, Jamie and Jeffery, and two grandsons, Thomas (JT III) and Henry.

Bill Fivaz

Bill Fivaz has been collecting coins since 1950, and along with J.T. Stanton is one of the country's most respected authorities on numismatic errors and varieties. His numerous awards include the most prestigious recognition of the American Numismatic Association—the Farran Zerbe Award, presented in 1995. Bill is also a recipient of the ANA Medal of Merit (1984, 1989). He was named a Krause Publications Numismatic Ambassador in 1982, and was recognized with the ANA Adult Advisor Award (for Young Numismatists) in 1991. He was selected as the ANA Numismatist of the Year in 2001 and elected to the ANA Hall of Fame in 2002.

Bill has been an Educational Forum speaker at FUN conventions since 1979, and an instructor for the ANA's Summer Seminar for more than 25 years. He has written hundreds of articles on a wide array of topics, and is a consultant to ANACS, SEGS, and several other authentication services. Bill's contributions are noted in many of today's most popular and respected hobby books, including the *Guide Book of United States Coins* (the "Red Book"). He is the author of the *United States Gold Counterfeit Detection Guide*.

Bill is a former member of the board of governors of the ANA, and a former member of the board of directors of CONECA.

He has been married to his wife Marilyn for 50 years, and has a son, Bill, a daughter, Diane, two grandchildren, Erin and Jake, and a great-granddaughter, Ella.

CONECA
New Member Application / Renewal Form

Today's Date: _____/_____/_____

Membership Type: _____ Regular/Annual Member - $25.00
_____ Young Numismatist (under 18) - $7.50

Mailing Options: _____ U.S. bulk rate - No extra charge
_____ First Class or Outside the U.S.A. - $12.50 additional

Total: _____ Amount Due

Name: _____

Address: _____

City: _____State: _____

Zip +4 Code: _____

Phone: _____ Email: _____

Recommended by: *The Cherrypickers' Guide*

Comments/Interests:
_____

_____

Send application and check/money order (payable to CONECA) to:

CONECA
Paul Funaiole, Membership
35 Leavitt Lane
Glenburn ME 04401-1013

*Your membership is subject to approval by the Membership Committee and
subject to the rules and regulations set forth in the CONECA Constitution and By-Laws.*

GENUINE U.S. MINT MISTAKES

*You're one of a kind — no two alike,
just like these coins.
A penny for your thoughts!*

We may not have the exact date /type
you want. Please give second choices!

Custom Paperweights

Paperweights with coins start at $31.95,
with white lettering and undated, and for
$36.95 you can get black-lettering with
one of the incased coins dated either
1981, 1982, or 1983. White lettering
works best on a dark-wood desktop, while
the black lettering looks best on a light
colored desktop. Pens are included and
prices stated include delivery.

5 Choices of expressions to choose from. Either the one shown, or "These coins are one in a million
- just like you," or "Money Problems? Most everyone have them, even the U.S. Mint," or "Just another Government mis-calculation," or "The Goverment never makes mistakes."

Best Variety
Sportcards & Coins

My 52nd Year Dealing With Major Errors

- I have regular coins, too! And major error sports cards.
- Buyer and seller of multiple types of errors on the same coin.

Questions about coins or bills you have? Contact me!
My web site is under construction (soon to be: Bestvarietycoinerrors.com).
Snail mail is just fine (include a First Class stamp to receive a reply).
Be patient as I am a one-man store.

626-914-2273

For Mail Orders, Paypal or Checks OK for payment. In my store ALL credit cards accepted.

Feel confident; I'm an expert in this field.
I am a Life Member of ANA (#2814), CONECA (#51), NASC, and CSNA.

*Visiting
Southern
California?
Stop in to my
custom-built
storefront.*

Best Variety, 358 W. Foothill Blvd, Glendora, CA 91741
(North of 210 Freeway. Exit Grand Ave. Go north past Route 66, up to Foothill Blvd.
Turn right and you're almost there.)

AMERICAN
NUMISMATIC
ASSOCIATION

Membership has its perks.

Have **12** issues of *Numismatist* magazine — packed with feature stories, hobby news, collecting tips and ANA updates — delivered to your doorstep.

Learn from the **experts** and join a 33,000-member community.

Borrow books from the
largest numismatic lending library in the world.

Get **consumer awareness** information.

Receive **discounts**
on numismatic books and supplies, collection insurance and car rentals.

Submit your coins directly to NGC and

NCS for **grading** and **conservation**.

JOIN TODAY!

DISCOVER THE WORLD OF MONEY AND HOW MEMBERSHIP WORKS FOR YOU.

800.514.2646
membership@money.org | www.money.org

CP

Stack's

For 71 years we have been treating our clients and their collections with

Dignity and Respect

When the time comes to auction your coins ... coins that you and your loved ones have spent a lifetime carefully acquiring, *think Stack's!*

Here at Stack's we have helped clients build some of the world's most famous collections over the course of generations. Regardless of its size, we understand the hard work and planning that went into the formation of your collection and we show that same level of dedication and personal attention in the cataloguing and auctioning of your coins.

Year after year our award winning catalogues and record breaking prices realized are the envy of the industry. Stack's has conducted more top-quality numismatic auctions than any American rare coin firm in history. You owe it to yourself to deal with the experts that care. Contact Lawrence R. Stack or Harvey G. Stack for a consultation.

123 W 57th St. • New York, NY 10019 • (212) 582-2580
FAX: (212) 245-5018 • *www.stacks.com* email: info@stacks.com
Auctions • Appraisals • Retail • Since 1935

The most respected name in numismatics

Reader Comments

What People are Saying About the Cherrypickers' Guide

The *Cherrypickers' Guide* is a standard reference in the hobby, a popular book that has been used and enjoyed by countless thousands of readers. Here are some sample comments from our mailbag:

"Bill Fivaz and J.T. Stanton have produced the **ultimate reference for variety collectors**: the *Cherrypickers' Guide*. The title suggests that it's all about money, but that misses the point. Variety collecting has become increasingly popular over the last several years, with new discoveries constantly turning up. Without the latest information, such as that presented by Bill and J.T., the collector cannot possibly know if a new variety has been found. As a cataloger, I keep a copy of the *Cherrypickers' Guide* on my desk, and refer to it constantly. When I travel to conventions, I never leave home without it."

Mark Borckardt
Numismatic researcher

"Every ANACS grader has a copy of the *Cherrypickers' Guide* on his or her desk. It is **one of my all-time Top 10** favorite numismatic books. . . ."

Randy Campbell
Silver dollar specialist
ANACS grader and authenticator

"I purchased a copy of the third edition of the *Cherrypickers' Guide* from my local dealer. I immediately starting looking through my collection and found a few of the lesser varieties listed. However, the biggest surprise was finding a 1971-S Proof Lincoln cent, doubled die obverse in my own collection! The value was listed at $1,000, but **I never expected to get that kind of money for my $1.50 investment**. Several coin shows later, a dealer actually offered me $1,200 for my 1971-S doubled die obverse. **I was elated**! The money from the sale of that coin enabled me to purchase a nice, high grade 1922 'Plain' Lincoln to finally complete my collection."

Jamie Giello
Collector

"Fivaz and Stanton—they're the ones who **almost singlehandedly brought *fun* back to coin collecting**, along with, incidentally, a horde of new and enthusiastic collectors."

James Taylor
President, ANACS

"Treasure hunting **makes this hobby fun**. The *Cherrypickers' Guide* is your map."
Bob Grellman
Copper coin specialist

"The *Cherrypickers' Guide* illustrates vividly, with sharp photos and descriptive text, the importance of die varieties. . . . This book is for both the novice and experienced collector, and **definitely belongs in your numismatic library**."
Remy Bourne
Numismatic literature specialist and dealer

"It just gets **better and better and better**. . . ."
Ed Hesse
Owner, The Reeded Edge

"The *Cherrypickers' Guide* is **one of those great ideas** that seem to revive the hobby every generation or so. Its impact on the collecting of varieties has already been profound, and this newest edition is filled with fascinating varieties that until now have been known only to a handful of specialists. The team of Fivaz and Stanton have produced **a handy and fun book** that will always be within arm's reach of my desk."
David W. Lange
Research director, NGC

"There are always special moments that stand out in a columnist's memory. I recall the first time I mentioned the *Cherrypickers' Guide* in my weekly coin column distributed by the Los Angeles Times Syndicate. I made note of a few listings and offered a free list to any reader submitting a self-addressed stamped envelope. Anticipating no more than a few requests, local editors were inundated with letters. I can well imagine the collector response to volume one (half cents through nickels), comprising some 450 pages. It should be **a hobby best seller**."
Ed Rochette
Numismatic author

"With all the current interest in errors and varieties, this new edition has to be your first purchase—it will answer all your questions about 'what's different' on that coin you found. For the advanced specialist, the long wait for the updated edition is now over. This is **the most anticipated numismatic book of the year!**"
Fred Weinberg
Specialist and dealer in errors and varieties